Introduction to

LEISURE SERVICES

Seventh Edition

Introduction to

LEISURE SERVICES

Seventh Edition

H. Douglas Sessoms

Karla A. Henderson

VENTURE PUBLISHING, INC.
STATE COLLEGE, PA

Production: Richard Yocum
Photographs courtesy of D. James Brademas
Cover Design: Sandra Sikorski
Manuscript Editing: Michele L. Barbin

Library of Congress Catalogue Card Number 94-60935
ISBN 0-910251-66-5

To our students: Our future

TABLE OF CONTENTS

Chapter Two—
A Living History   33

CHAPTER THREE—
THE CONCEPTUAL BASE OF LEISURE AND RECREATION 65

Chapter Four—
Economic Considerations and
the Commercial Recreation Sector   99

Chapter Five—
Public Recreation and Parks Services   137

Chapter Six —
Membership and Private Not-for-profit
(Quasi-Public) Recreation Services   177

CHAPTER SEVEN—
SPECIAL RECREATION SERVICES   215

CHAPTER NINE—
THE PROFESSIONALIZATION
OF THE RECREATION AND PARK SYSTEM   281

FOREWORD

The seventh edition of *Introduction to Leisure Services* continues the long history of describing professional parks and recreation begun by Harold D. Meyer and Charles K. Brightbill in 1948 with their *Community Recreation: A Guide to its Organization and Administration.* As one might expect, the profession, as reported in that pioneering text, is quite different from that which has evolved. Yet, the need to chronicle the events which have shaped it and the theories which undergird it remain. That has been true with all of the editions.

To Meyer and Brightbill, recreation and parks were separate but related professions. They viewed the provision of recreation services as a community responsibility that involved the private, public and commercial sectors; parks were the concern of foresters and natural resources specialists. In the second and third editions of their work, they began to view the two as one field of service—parks and recreation. The profession was taking form and in their tradition Meyer and Brightbill not only discussed the changes taking place, they were also giving the profession leadership with their advocacy and philosophical positions. Through their texts and other writings, thousands of students were influenced, including me.

In 1969, I joined Harold Meyer in revising the fourth edition of *Community Recreation.* Five years later I assumed major responsibility for its revision and was the sole author for number six, entitled *Leisure Services.* It was in this edition that a differentiation was made between parks and recreation and leisure services, a broader concept which has parks and recreation as one of its elements. That work was a descriptive analysis of the leisure service delivery system and those agencies which are at its forefront. Although some attention was given to the mass cultural aspects of society and the theories which underlie service delivery, the book continued to focus on the organizational components and issues confronting the system and the profession which gives it structure.

In this edition of *Leisure Services,* the seventh, Karla A. Henderson joins me as the second author. Together we have attempted to update the changes which have occurred in the field during the past decade and set a realistic framework for what we believe will occur as we approach the 21st Century.

Although this edition does not differ significantly in format from the previous work, its content is contemporary with particular attention being given to current trends in leisure services. We now have a much greater body of research from which to draw as well as an awareness of the need for parks and recreation to provide programs which reflect the diversity of society. We have tried to use the history of the profession as a backdrop for examining current situations as well as a basis for explaining emerging social issues and their influence on the provision of services.

The current social setting of the United States does suggest that a wide range of settings and a wide variety of roles are now being performed by park and recreation professionals which will shape the professional preparation of future practitioners. We have also tried to describe for you the function, philosophy and structure of our major leisure service agencies, the issues confronting leisure service providers, and the directions which we feel the parks and recreation profession is moving. We acknowledge that many perspectives could have been taken in accomplishing this task, but we offer one which we feel appropriate to introduce you to the field of leisure services.

We are deeply indebted to many colleagues in the preparation of this work. They have been good sources of information, good critics, and understanding friends. Among them are our cohorts at the University of North Carolina—Lee Meyer, Charles Bullock, Deborah Bialeschki, Neta Lord and Jeanette Rozier. We are especially grateful to Richard Gitelson at the Pennsylvania State University, to Mark Havitz at the University of Waterloo, and to Leandra Bedini at the University of North Carolina at Greensboro who, along with Deb Bialeschki, provided materials for several of the chapters. We are appreciative to the American Academy for Park and Recreation Administration and James Brademas of the University of Illinois for providing us with all the photos used in this text. We also want to express our thanks to Ching-Chang Hsaio who assisted with the library research and Anne Sessoms who aided in the typing and editing of the manuscript. Most of all, we are indebted to the professionals such as Brightbill and Meyer who have paved the way for us and to those who continue to be our mentors in moving this profession forward with their thought and deed.

H.D.S., 1994

CHAPTER ONE

The Overview

In 1992, against a backdrop of a nagging worldwide recession and a sluggish United States economy, Americans spent over 400 billion dollars in their pursuit of pleasure. Expenditures for vacation trips, ocean cruises, tennis and golf matches, weekend outings, and other forms of recreation behavior were several billion dollars greater than were expenditures for national defense (according to the Academy of Leisure Sciences, 1993). Leisure and recreation continue to be a major force in the economic and social life of twentieth century America.

Work and leisure are interrelated activities. The exact nature of their relationship has long been the subject of speculation among economists, sociologists, and other social and behavioral scientists. Formerly it was believed that we would work no longer than it took us to maintain the lifestyle to which we had become accustomed, and that most workers would be content with subsistence and would stop working when their incomes rose beyond that level (U.S. Department of Labor [USDL], 1980). That theory did not hold for long for workers seemed to enjoy the acquisition of goods made possible by higher wages.

Consequently a new theory was developed. Economists hypothesized that any increase in work time induced by a higher wage would also heighten worker fatigue and increase the value of leisure time, "that the financial discretion gained by larger incomes, coupled with the increased fatigue accompanying long hours would ultimately limit the amount of time a person would work at a given wage" (USDL, p. 9). They assumed there would be a trade-off between work and leisure. What they failed to realize were the effects of the computer and telecommunication revolution which have altered work patterns, the growth of temporary jobs, the increasing number of families with both adults working outside the home, and an expanding service economy with its accompanying low wage base. In other words, they failed to understand the impact of postindustrialism. Rather than increasing leisure, Americans, today, perceive they have less leisure. But in its scarcity is hope. Leisure and recreation have become more valued as a desirable alternative for expression and satisfaction. Americans want both a livable income and more free time, still preferring the former to the latter, but the margin of preference for more income over free time is shrinking.

Park and recreation services are a product of industrialization and the leisure-work trade-off. With increased industrialism workers sought leisure, and a system of services and activities evolved to meet their needs, expectations, and desires. This system began as a social movement during the early 1900s and by the latter half of the twentieth century it had reached full maturity. It has involved both the private and public sectors and has been the subject of many governmental studies and reports. According to the National Recreation and Park Association, nearly every city and town in the United States has an organized recreation and parks service. Billions of tax dollars are spent each year for the acquisition, construction, and operation of parks and recreation programs and facilities.

Concurrent with the expansion of recreation and park services has been the growth of the leisure service industry. Few industries have expanded more rapidly in the last two decades than those that cater to people's recreation behavior. The demand for camping facilities, vacation areas, and other recreation settings has exceeded our supply of areas and opportunities. Theme parks, jogging trails, and lighted tennis courts dot the landscape. Denim, the cloth traditionally associated with workers' clothing, has become the fabric of the recreation participant. Designer jeans, ski sweaters, nylon sweat suits, and running shoes are standard wearing apparel for millions of recreating youth and adults.

Whether the desire for more free-time activity will replace work as our dominant activity is a matter of speculation. Some economists, as reported in one worktime preference study (Best, Bosserman & Stern, 1979), felt that "on the one hand, low economic growth inflation, and the mid-life financial squeeze of the maturing baby boom generation could stultify or lessen current interest in exchanging income for time. On the other hand, the continued growth of women workers and dual-income families, increasing portions of longer-living older workers, trends toward recurrent education in mid-life, and the possibility that values may be shifting away from materialism could push American society toward an increasing desire for work-time reduction" (Best et al., p. 143). They conclude that a large minority (possibly even the majority) of today's workers would be willing to forego some increase in income for additional free time. If their estimates are correct, the demand for recreation services will continue to increase, especially for males. For females, it may be a different story since their conclusion did not take into account the findings of a more recent study. According to Desaulniers and Theberge (1992) women are more likely to want to continue to work for pay than take their gains in free time as the latter would probably have to be spent doing nonpaid work at home. Changes in work preferences and schedules, therefore, need to consider gender differences and gender related divisions of labor.

Parks and Recreation: A Growing Concern

At every level of government, recreation and park concerns are present. In the United States, over 70 federal agencies are charged with developing programs and policies that affect recreation and leisure behaviors, or they are actively involved in the supervision and maintenance of recreation resources. These extend from the regulatory agencies such as the Fish and Wildlife Service with its restrictions on hunting and fishing, to the direct service agencies such as the National Park Service and the Department of Defense with their multiprogram thrusts. At the state level, recreation resource management and the offering of technical assistance to local communities are major responsibilities of state recreation agencies. All 50 states have designated recreation and park services involved in the overall planning and development of their outdoor recreation facilities. Many have recreation divisions offering consulting services to local communities and private groups. Tourism is a major industry of several states, while all states have one or more departments promoting their tourism potential and attractions.

The expansion of the interstate highway system and the growing travel industry has forced state and local governments to plan and develop their out-door recreation resource areas to serve both visitors and local citizens. Nearly every form of outdoor recreation activity has experienced a dramatic increase in participation during the past three decades. According to the National Sporting Goods Association (1991), walking, swimming and bicycle riding were the top three outdoor recreation pursuits of adults in 1990.

The demand for all types of activities also has been felt at the local level. No longer are local public park and recreation departments content merely to offer the traditional athletic leagues and playground programs. They have responded by developing services for the elderly, childcare and latchkey programs for the young, and self-supporting aquatic and fitness centers. In addition to their traditional role of operating playgrounds, parks, and community buildings, some communities have assumed responsibility for the management of sports arenas, cultural centers, and nature museums. In 1990, over eight billion dollars were spent by local governments on their community recreation and park systems (*Statistical Abstract...*, 1992).

Americans are not the only ones benefiting from the new leisure and recreation opportunities. In Japan, multitiered golf driving ranges have been constructed. Each weekend millions of people crowd into trains to leave the city for the tranquillity of the countryside. In Europe, growing recreation concerns have given rise to a variety of leisure movements. Factories close for weeks so their employees may take holidays. The countryside (i.e., rural recreation) and sports arena programs are well-supported in England and Germany. Even the emerging third world countries, with their limited technology, are aware of the importance of recreation and parks and are taking steps to make sure their citizens and visitors have ample opportunities for enjoyment, and that their unique wildlife and resources are protected. The world movement has matured to the point that in 1991 an international school (World Leisure and Recreation Association International Center for Excellence—WICE) was established in the Netherlands to prepare or update professionals from all over the world for park and recreation responsibilities.

The Private Sector

Getting together for a good time is "as American as apple pie." The provision of recreation opportunities has been a long-standing concern of various private groups, both membership and not-for-profit organizations, as well as commercial establishments. The playground movement began as a philanthropic activity. Private, not-for-profit organizations such as the Young Men's and Young Women's Christian Associations and the Boy and Girl Scouts have provided free-time activities for millions of youth and adults since their inception at the turn of the century. They have been joined by a new form of private recreation expression, the membership associations. These organizations tend to emphasize participation in a favorite activity such as tennis, rather than in a set of general services for a specific age group, such as teenagers. Although they often employ professionals to direct their programs, they are controlled by their members. Swim clubs, tennis clubs, private recreation associations, and hobbyist groups are typical of this group. They typically have no national or state affiliation and tend to restrict their memberships to local residents. In some ways, these groups are similar to the more conventional country clubs but differ in their limited activity focus and social purpose. This private recreation phenomenon,

The Pee Wee Tennis Program, purchased from Wilson and offered here by the Champaign [IL] Park District, introduces children between the age of five and eight to tennis in a fun and exciting manner.

for example, along with an increasing number of specialized magazines devoted to hobbies and individualized recreation pursuits, supports the observation that work may no longer be a central focus for many Americans. An integrated and holistic lifestyle with leisure as a critical element seems to be evolving.

Amusement, diversion, and technology have contributed to the growth of mass leisure. Advances in the production and the distribution of goods, coupled with an increasing level of affluence, have resulted in new forms of entertainment and amusement. Nine out of every ten Americans, for example, own one or more television sets; ticket sales for college and professional football games continue to increase each year. The development of electronic technologies has given us a variety of new ways to play and socialize—video games, VCRs, CDs, and cellular telephones. Tourism has become a year-round activity; in many areas, resort motels no longer offer an off-season price. "Off-season" simply no longer exists. Theme parks such as Walt Disney World and Busch Gardens have had an enormous impact upon local economies; they have expanded the range of recreation opportunities available to those seeking the commercial recreation experience. Central to this growth of the private recreation sector is the desire for diversion, the need to escape, and a growing interest in controlling one's personal life.

The Pursuit of Pleasure

Accompanying the growth of the amusement industry has been the acceleration of opportunities for the more personalized participant expression. Americans no longer have to be entertained; they have the equipment and ability to participate and "just do it" in whatever "turns them on." The only limiting factors are knowledge of the resources available and attitudes toward their free-time expressions. Boats, motors cameras, trailers, computers, space-age fabrics, and freeze-dried foods are readily available. Often the problem among affluent Americans is not having something to do, but having so much available that they do not know where to begin. For those with disabilities or those who suffer from various forms of discrimination or economic difficulty, the situation is quite different. Accessibility and opportunity are still major concerns.

Although amusement and having a good time are American traditions, the notion of leisure as an end in itself is still somewhat foreign to many. For them, recreation illiteracy is still a problem. Few nations have exhibited more respect for the work ethic than has the United States. Work has been treated as sacred and all other activities have been the servants to economic productivity and consumption. Because of this, some philosophers and social scientists have viewed leisure as a threat, as something for which we are not prepared.

> The leisure problem is fundamental. Having to decide what we shall do with our leisure is inevitably forcing us to reexamine the purpose of human existence, and to ask what fulfillment really means.
>
> Julian Huxley

> ...a perpetual holiday is a good working definition of hell.
>
> George Bernard Shaw

> If we say that the twentieth is leisure's century, and if we want to be that, we should know what is involved. Yet once you know what leisure is, you still may not want it. Leisure requires a sacrifice.
>
> Sebastian De Grazia

> The danger of increasing leisure time voluntarily is that it could replace one inequity with another—as inequality of income creates inequality of time. The poorest third would work just as many hours as ever—or more, as more work became available—while the top two-thirds would gradually become a leisured class. The people who would gain free time would be those who already had the financial resources that make it possible—education, homes, and a bank account. They would be mainly white and mainly upper and middle class.
>
> Juliet B. Schor

The leisure society has been predicted for many years. Charles Brightbill (1966) wrote that America was moving toward a leisure-centered society. Twenty years later in the middle of the Reagan Revolution, there was little evidence to support Brightbill's claims. The opposite appeared true. More people were working longer hours even though the rate of the unemployed remained high at seven percent. Although Congress enacted legislation in 1968 designating that certain holidays (e.g., Memorial Day, Veterans Day, Martin Luther King's Birthday) were to be celebrated on Mondays, thereby giving federal employees several long weekends each year, America still ranked below most industrial nations in the average number of vacation days granted workers. Whereas the U.S. average is twenty per year, that is half the number taken by Germans and sixteen less than enjoyed by citizens of Sweden.

Shifts In Work Patterns

A variety of shifts in work patterns has occurred. The workday has been shortened. The 40-hour workweek has been accepted as the standard, although some writers such as Sebastian De Grazia (1962) and Juliet Schor (1991) question whether the workweek is really 40 hours since people now spend more time traveling to and from the job than they did in former years. And, with 60 percent of U.S. females in the work force, more hours are spent in the "second shift" doing housework after spending the day at work (Hoschild & Machung, 1990). Some scholars (Schor, 1991) have even described "the overworked American(s)." In addition, the number of temporary or part-time workers who may hold two or more jobs has risen. Scheduling of one's leisure has become increasingly difficult for the American family with two adults working, children in year-round schools, and multigenerational family responsibilities. Central to these shifts have been a variety of technological developments, fluctuations in the demographics, urbanization, and changing values and attitudes.

Western Technology

Western technology has resulted in superabundance. Each year the rate of technological change seems to accelerate with an endless number of improved items and gadgets on the market. Breakthroughs in electronics and chemistry have provided new construction materials, methods, and manufacturing processes. The leisure industries, particularly those related to outdoor recreation pursuits, have benefited from these advances. Lightweight, durable, attractive equipment is available for recreation enthusiasts. The contemporary system of "buy now and pay later" enables more people to acquire and utilize these goods. The electronics industry has provided families with home entertainment centers, high-tech equipment, and portable sound systems. The clothing industries provides apparel for every occasion and activity.

In past centuries, advances in material production have required increased amounts of labor and capital as well as technological achievements. Society has held that for more materials to be produced, more workers, natural resources, and markets were needed. Today, the situation has changed. Although the need for workers remains, the new industrial methods and processes often require fewer laborers to produce increased quantities of goods. America is facing the prospect that it may no longer need everyone to work. The alternative to high rates of unemployment seems to be modifications in patterns of work and leisure.

Population Shifts

As with technology, America has undergone several major population shifts (Figure 1-1). Rapid growth was evidenced with three baby booms in the 1920s, 1950s and 1980s. Conversely, declining birth rates occurred the decades of the 1930s, 1960s, and 1970s. Throughout the century, the percentage of older persons, those over 65 years of age, has increased dramatically from two and a half percent of the population in 1900 to twelve percent in 1990. The United States has changed from being primarily a rural nation to a society of urban dwellers. In 1900, 50 percent of the population resided in farming areas; today, less than one quarter live there. It was also experiencing a rapid growth in new immigrants, especially those of Hispanic and Asian heritage. Moreover, the population has shifted from one region of the nation to another. States such as California, Florida, Texas, and Arizona (i.e., the Sunbelt) have experienced tremendous rates of growth, while the farming states of the Midwest and the urban centers of the Northeast and Midwest have lost population. Consequently, shifts in political power have occurred; the governmental rule of one person, one vote has affected the balance of political power in many regions. All of these shifts—changing residential patterns, changing population ratios, and changing political power bases—have had an effect on the parks and recreation system, particularly the demand for open space, the need for more specialized services, the location of recreation facilities and opportunities, and the need to be more sensitive to diversity in the population.

In some instances, it has taken riots and environmental crises to focus the attention of public officials on the fact that their program offerings have not changed, even though the clients they serve are different and their resources are overworked. While the population of many of our cities' central core has declined, the number of teenagers, young adults, and older adults residing there has increased. Inasmuch as these are the least employed elements of the population, our metropolitan areas continue to experience various financial crises. On the other hand, the rapid growth areas of the Sunbelt have a different problem: trying to respond to the recreation demands of their growing population which frequently exceeds their resources and thereby threatens to destroy many of the features that had attracted their new residents to the region in the first place.

Figure 1-1
U.S. Population, Size, and Age Structure: 1970, 1980, and 1990

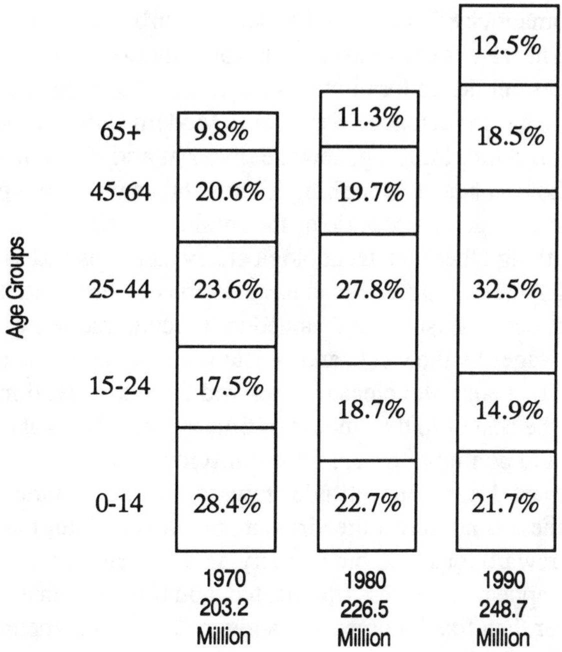

Age Groups	1970	1980	1990
65+	9.8%	11.3%	12.5%
			18.5%
45-64	20.6%	19.7%	
25-44	23.6%	27.8%	32.5%
15-24	17.5%		14.9%
		18.7%	
0-14	28.4%	22.7%	21.7%
	1970	1980	1990
	203.2 Million	226.5 Million	248.7 Million

Source: *1993 Statistical Abstract*, p. 15.

Urban Values

According to Bergier (1981), it is important to understand the role social values play in determining our recreation patterns and changing recreation interests. When sociologists refer to social values, they are speaking about those beliefs and behaviors that a society holds important to its welfare. A person's value system gives direction for choosing between alternative forms of behavior and is used to judge the relative importance of any experience. Every society develops a social value system and young people are taught to honor those things that are considered essential. As societies change, different interest groups develop and the value system is altered. Because each person has a different perception of what life ought to be, and these perceptions are a product of unique experiences, different behaviors emerge. It is not surprising, therefore, to find social drinking acceptable in some groups but not in others, or that some groups place a premium on family activity while others stress individual pursuits and interests. In a heterogeneous society, a multitude of value structures exist, yet all of them are somewhat similar in that they reflect the dominant values of urban America. Core to that system are the values that have formed the successful economic and industrial order.

Although the pastoral existence of the small town and farm community way of life is often romanticized, the United States is an urban society with an urban value system. The values of "conspicuous consumption" and "conspicuous display" as well as our desire for immediate action and convenience packaging have had their effects on recreation behaviors. Modern campsites are expected to have electricity, indoor plumbing, sewage disposal and concrete slabs for the campers. For the less hearty "roughing it" now takes place in a plush motel or in a comfortable cottage at a seaside or mountain resort.

Probably nothing other than technological advances has had as much impact on the changing American lifestyle as have notions of time and its use. Traditionally, time has been measured and valued in its economic sense. Labor is paid for by the hour, wages by the week, and pensions according to the number of years worked. For many, the pleasures derived from a recreation outing is directly related to the cost or to the amount of time required for that experience. We have been, and continue to be, a time conscious society.

Within the past decade our attitudes toward time have undergone some change. Promptness is no longer the virtue it once was and, for many, play is no longer simply a reward for work, but a satisfying experience in its own right (see Table 1-1). Life appears to be less fragmented, and time is seen as a series of related events rather than fixed moments in a given day. It is sometimes viewed as biological time, in which a person can follow his or her own impulses, rather than mechanical time with predetermined actions and expectations to occur at a specified moment. This notion of biological time has rapidly gained acceptance among the young and may emerge as a dominant time concept during the 1990s. Probably no contemporary recreation scholar has devoted more attention to various concepts and perceptions of time and its relationship to leisure expressions and values than has James F. Murphy (1981). He attempts to resolve the dilemma inherent in the acceptance of biological time as the dictator of life's rhythms in an industrial world by writing that "the basis of leisure in postindustrial society clearly gains significance when its meaning is attached to the industrial rhythms of life, but its attributes and character emerge only when interpreted by the individual who makes of it what is pertinent and valuable to his or her personal life regimen" (Murphy, p. 88). Time and its use are highly valued.

From the very beginning, the promoters and supporters of organized park and recreation systems have held that recreation and play experiences are of value. They have said that recreation programs should be provided because they build character, add to the good life, instill feelings of democracy and self-reliance, and help individuals to become disciplined and productive persons. Furthermore, recreation activities have been seen as a form of education and as a means to refresh the industrial worker. Consequently, most of the early recreation programs were designed for children, were highly active, and were generally promoted to prevent delinquency. Though little scientific evidence supports the claim, conventional wisdom suggests that if a person knows how to play fairly, he or she will be a good worker and citizen.

Table 1-1
Participation in Sports Activities by Selected Characteristics: 1990
(rounded to nearest million*)

Activity	All Persons		Sex		Age					
	Number	Rank	Male	Female	7-17	18-24	25-34	35-44	45-64	65+
Total	**225**	**(X)**	**109**	**116**	**38**	**26**	**44**	**38**	**47**	**32**
Aerobic exercising	23	10	4	20	3	5	8	4	3	1
Backpacking /wilderness camping	11	24	7	4	2	2	3	2	1	0
Baseball	16	17	13	3	9	2	2	1	0	0
Basketball	26	8	19	7	13	4	6	2	1	0
Bicycle riding	55	3	28	27	21	6	11	8	7	2
Bowling	40	6	21	19	9	7	10	7	5	2
Calisthenics	13	19	6	7	3	2	4	2	2	1
Camping (vacation/ overnight)	46	4	24	22	12	5	11	9	7	2
Exercise walking	71	1	25	46	6	7	15	14	19	11
Exercising with equipment	35	7	19	17	4	7	10	7	6	2
Fishing–fresh water	41	5	28	14	9	5	10	7	7	3
Fishing–salt water	12	21	9	3	2	2	3	2	3	1
Football	14	18	12	2	8	3	2	1	0	0
Golf	23	12	17	6	2	3	6	5	5	2
Hiking	22	13	11	11	4	2	6	5	4	1
Hunting with firearms	19	15	16	2	3	3	5	3	3	1
Racquetball	8	25	6	2	1	2	3	1	1	0
Running/jogging	24	9	13	11	7	4	6	4	2	0
Skiing–alpine/downhill	11	22	7	5	3	3	3	2	1	0
Skiing–cross country	5	26	3	2	1	1	1	1	1	0
Soccer	11	23	7	4	8	1	1	0	0	0
Softball	20	14	12	9	7	4	6	3	1	0
Swimming	67	2	32	36	22	10	14	10	9	3
Target shooting	13	20	10	3	2	3	4	2	2	0
Tennis	18	16	10	8	5	4	5	2	2	0
Volleyball	23	11	11	12	8	5	7	3	1	0

* zeros represent less than one million participants, not zero participants.

Source: *1992 Statistical Abstract*, p. 241

Even with a greater appreciation of leisure as a right to be enjoyed, the work ethic remains at the heart of the Western value system. Most Americans believe that one should earn leisure, be self-supporting, and take pride in achievements. Although the hobo and drifter are often portrayed by novelists as living a leisurely life, society continues to disdain people who are homeless or on welfare because they are not a part of the employment system. Success is valued and people believe that those who use their skills wisely and for the advancement of business and industry should be highly rewarded. It should come as no surprise that our industrial and economic leaders are the highest paid occupational group.

Our value system both shapes the direction of our recreation interests and dictates the procedures to be used in providing recreation opportunities. To a large extent, America has approached the provision of recreation services in much the same way that it has handled its educational and welfare programs. It has blended private and commercial resources with those of government. Initially the private recreation associations, primarily those supported by private philanthropy and meant to benefit youth, were the backbone of the organized recreation movement. Government restricted its role largely to the acquisition and development of park lands and open space. Commercial leisure businesses addressed the growing demand for spectator sports and mass entertainment including places to go and services to make visits enjoyable. The national emergencies of the Depression and World War II increased government's responsibility and participation in the provision of recreation opportunities. Today, all levels of government are actively involved in the promotion and development of recreation and park services and have formed a "partnership" with private and commercial interests. In the 1990s, this partnership may be even more critical to the mission of the parks and recreation movement than before.

The Leisure Service Delivery System

When there is a social need (i.e., a societal expression for the exhibiting of some form of behavior necessary for the maintenance of that society, such as national defense), people organize themselves for action. Less complex societies have handled their educational, religious, and recreation behaviors through the activities and structures of the family and other immediate peer group units. Complex societies develop delivery systems to meet these needs. Specific responsibilities are assumed by each element of these systems so that the demands of the society are met. The leisure service delivery system is comprised of governmental, private (not-for-profit and membership organizations), and commercial interests. The park and recreation element (which the authors use synonomously with professional practice) is the primary concern of this text, although attention is given to all the elements which comprise the larger leisure service delivery system.

Parks and recreation is in an evolutionary state (see Table 1-2). Various distinct periods of development have contributed to its current programs and services and various authors have described each of its stages. Among the first to do so was Clarence Rainwater (1922), who analyzed the parks and recreation system using community organizational theories. He saw it evolving as a neighborhood/community organizational phenomenon. More recent writers such as Richard Knapp and Charles Hartsoe (1979) and Michael and Holly Chubb (1981) have viewed the system differently. Knapp and Hartsoe have concentrated largely upon the history of the National Recreation Association from 1906 to 1965. They viewed the history of that organization as parallel to the recreation movement. The Chubbs, on the other hand, have placed the development of leisure services in the context of the various stages that society has gone through since 1700. All of these writers agree that there have been discernible stages in the history of leisure services.

Table 1-2
Stages of Development of the Organized Recreation and Park Service

	Stage One 1890-1916*	Stage Two 1917-1955*	Stage Three 1956-1976*	Stage Four 1977-*
Program focus	Conservationist and youth services	Parks and diversionary activity	Outdoor recreation and environmental concerns	Entrepreneurial approach to local services; public policy issues
Leadership	Volunteers	Volunteers and professionals	Professionals	Professionals and volunteers
Major provider of services	Private interests	Federal and local governments	Federal and state governments	Local and federal governments; private interests

*approximations

Source: *1992 Statistical Abstract,* p. 241

Each stage of development has given form to the public, private, and commercial elements comprising the leisure service delivery system. Some interesting dichotomies and philosophical conflicts have resulted and continue to affect the definition of leisure and the role that park and recreation professionals are expected to play in providing those services. Four concerns have been dominant forces in one or more of its stages or eras of development: youth, diversionary activity, conservation and outdoor recreation, and public policy and entrepreneurialism.

Stage One: Services to Youth

The desire to serve the "underprivileged" child characterized the earliest stage of recreation services. Voluntary youth organizations, such as the Boy and Girl Scouts, the Playground Association of America (later the National Recreation Association), and the YMCA and YWCA, dominated the movement and provided the basic programs. They relied heavily upon private and voluntary financial support and utilized the methods and techniques most frequently associated with today's social group work programs. Recreation experiences were seen as a means to an end: the building of character and the development of better communities.

Stage Two: Diversionary Activity

The second stage of development emerged during the Great Depression and reached its zenith in the late 1940s. Recreation services became a governmental responsibility; recreation was seen as an activity needed to break the monotony of poverty and relieve the tensions of war. It was during this period that local communities developed park and recreation commissions and charged them with the responsibility of providing diversionary recreation opportunities. The number of community recreation buildings, athletic fields, and other sports facilities increased. Organized recreation took a mass approach, and for many, sports became synonymous with recreation. Commercial enterprises were largely concerned with pleasing the spectator through entertainment.

Stage Three: Outdoor Recreation and the Environment

The third period began with the expansion of outdoor recreation interests in the late 1950s. Private investments coupled with expanding federal and state programs had an impact on leisure behaviors. Camping, water and winter sports, and vacation travel grew significantly. The nurturing and development of natural resources to accommodate these interests, and the need for recreation and park professionals with managerial and planning skills to manage these efforts, characterize this era of development. During this stage, federal and state governments assumed greater responsibility in providing opportunities for individual recreation pursuits. Commercial interests offered the equipment and attire necessary to make these experiences pleasurable. It was during this era when a host of public policy issues began to emerge.

Stage Four: Entrepreneurism and Public Policy

Initially, public policy concerns were largely restricted to the role of government as a regulatory agency in the protection of the environment. The affluence of the 1960s and 1970s placed great demands upon natural resource agencies. They were pushed to their limit to accommodate the growing outdoor recreation interests while also trying to protect the environment from overuse. Partially in response to both the demand for accommodations and a growing service economy, private entrepreneurs recognized the potentials of leisure as a market. Entrepreneurship was furthered by the tax revolt of the late 1970s that reduced considerably the ability of the public sector to provide programs without seeking some recovery costs from the participants. Recovery costs mean the park and recreation agency only partially pays for the programs with the remaining costs paid by the users. Public park and recreation agencies also had to become more entrepreneurial, offering more programs that were either self-sustaining or recovered costs. They also began to contract some of their operations such as maintenance to private contractors. Political actions and debate have characterized the public policy/entrepreneurial era.

With the election of Ronald Reagan in 1980, the United States moved fully into this fourth stage. The issue became one of who—private interest or government—was responsible for providing basic recreation services. With cutbacks in federal appropriations for the acquisition of land, the burden of providing capital for recreation developments shifted from the federal to state and local governments. Rather than be a direct supplier of opportunity, some governmental agencies assumed a facilitator role; that is, they provided the facility and technical assistance but let others do the programming; commercial and private providers were expected to become more active as suppliers. This shift has influenced programs of professional preparation of recreation and parks personnel as courses in marketing strategies, economic theory, and management are now included in many undergraduate curricula in recreation and parks administration. Activity courses and the social sciences have taken a back seat. Some park and recreation educators say that recreation has moved away from its humanistic approach to services to a more businesslike or entrepreneurial approach. In the process some segments of the populations, especially people outside the dominant white middle class structure, have been left out.

These distinct periods in the history of parks and recreation and leisure services are reflected in the programs and organizational structures of the many groups providing activities for free-time expression. Programs tend to be either diversionary, management-oriented, or directed toward personal development and social change. Diversion is most often observed in industrial recreation settings or programs for the military; personal development is characteristic of hospitals and youth-serving agencies. The management orientation is increasingly common in public recreation and park agencies, especially in administering park systems, although the importance of parks and recreation and its contribution to community life are being justified in health and fitness terms (Godbey, 1991). All three areas of programs have been present in each stage, but the emphasis varies from era to era. A more extensive history of the organized recreation and park movement is presented in Chapter Two.

Basic Elements of the Leisure Service Delivery System

The leisure service delivery system is comprised of three basic sectors or elements: public services; private, not-for-profit and membership agencies; and the business or commercial element. Each sector has its own unique features and mission; each has had its eras in which it appeared to be the basic provider of recreation activities. Together, however, they provide society's system for accommodating leisure interests. They embrace many subsystems and are highly interactive and complementary. A comparison of different aspects of each element is presented in Table 1-3.

Table 1-3
Comparison Among Elements of the Leisure Service Delivery System

Philosophy of Service

PUBLIC
Enrichment of the life of the total community by providing opportunities for the meaningful use of leisure. Nonprofit in nature.

PRIVATE
Enrichment of the life of participating members by offering opportunities for meaningful use of leisure, frequently with emphasis on the group and individual. Nonprofit in nature.

COMMERCIAL
Attempt to satisfy public demands for recreation experiences and services in an effort to produce profit.

Objectives of Service

PUBLIC
To provide leisure opportunities that contribute to the social, physical, educational, cultural, and general well-being of the community and its people.

PRIVATE
Similar to public, but limited to the membership it serves. It seeks to provide opportunities for close group association with an emphasis on citizenship, behavior, and life philosophy value; provide activities that appeal to members.

COMMERCIAL
To provide activities or programs which will appeal to customers. Seeks to meet competition; net a profit while serving the public.

Type of Agencies

PUBLIC
Governmental units (federal, state, county, and local) such as park and recreation departments, recreation and park districts, state park departments.

PRIVATE
Boy Scouts, Girl Scouts, Camp Fire Girls, "Y" organizations, tennis clubs, swim clubs, neighborhood recreation associations.

COMMERCIAL
Corporations, syndicates, partnerships, private ownership. Examples: motion picture, television, and radio companies; resorts; theme parks; professional sports.

Table 1-3 (continued)
Comparison Among Elements of the Leisure Service Delivery System

Finance

PUBLIC   Primarily by taxes. Also by gifts, grants, trust funds, fees, and charges.
PRIVATE   By gifts, grants, endowments, donations, drives, and membership fees.
COMMERCIAL   By investment of the owner or promoters. By the users: admission and charges.

Facilities

PUBLIC   Community buildings, parks (national, state, local), athletic fields, play-grounds, playfields, stadiums, camps, beaches, museums, zoos, golf courses.
PRIVATE   Settlement houses, youth centers, athletic facilities, play areas, clubs, camps, and aquatic areas.
COMMERCIAL   Theaters, clubs, taverns, night clubs, lounges, race tracks, bowling lanes, amusement parks, and stadiums.

Leadership

PUBLIC   Professionally prepared to provide and manage comprehensive recreation programs; frequently subject to Civil Service regulations. Uses volunteers as well as professionals.
PRIVATE   Professionally prepared to provide programs, frequently on a social group-work basis; volunteers as well as professionals.
COMMERCIAL   Professionally prepared to design and manage services which will produce a profit, in compliance with state and local laws; no volunteers. Business and sales oriented personnel.

Membership

PUBLIC   Unlimited—open to all.
PRIVATE   Limited by organizational restrictions, such as age, sex, or religion.
COMMERCIAL   Limited by law (local, state, and federal); traditions and customs; and economics (those who have the price to pay).

Swimming pools can be found in public, private and commercial sectors of the leisure service delivery system.

Basic Definitions

As in most fields of study, certain basic terms and concepts need interpretation. Following is a brief discussion of some of these terms and concepts; a more comprehensive discussion is presented in Chapter Three. Other key definitions are included in the Glossary (page 333).

Recreation and Park Service

The role of the leisure services profession may be viewed in two divergent and valid ways. One view holds that park and recreation professionals should be primarily concerned with the management of selected natural resources for individualistic recreation pursuits. The agency provides the opportunity; the participant plans and directs his or her activities. The second view acknowledges the responsibility of recreation and parks as the developer and administrator of recreation opportunities. The agency is the direct provider of the service and, to a large degree, directs or schedules the activities of its participants. The first view is more often associated with the commercial element or with the natural resource segment of the public system. The second approach is more commonly associated with the private element and the recreation segment of the public system.

These two segments, natural resources and recreation programs, of the public sector were brought together in the 1960s through the merger of several park and recreation organizations. Until then they were separate but related social movements: the park movement and the recreation movement. Those most closely allied with the development of parks had their historic roots in the conservation reform movement of the 1890s. The primary responsibilities of the park professionals were to manage resources and to interpret those resources to the public. Those preparing for employment in this segment typically came from schools of forestry and natural resources. Their training was founded in the biological and natural sciences; to them, the provision of the recreation experience was not a primary responsibility, but recreation occurred through the individual's understanding and use of the resource.

The second group of specialists, the recreation professionals, was more activity and people-oriented. They had strong ties with the educational and social welfare reform movements of the early 1900s. They typically came from undergraduate programs in physical education or sociology and were interested in recreation as either a diversionary or character-building experience. Those professionals who viewed recreation as a means to an end tended to be employed by social service or treatment-oriented agencies. They viewed recreation as activity, as an end in itself, and were generally employed to administer or direct sports programs. Both viewed the natural resource as secondary to the recreation experience.

With this insight into the origins of the parks and recreation movement, it is easy to understand why people frequently respond to the recreation and parks major as "Oh, you're in P.E.," or "Oh, you're going to be a forest ranger."

In the past twenty years great strides have been made to establish parks and recreation as a distinct field with unique characteristics and social roles. Park and recreation professionals are not physical educators, forest rangers, or social workers. They are specialists in parks and recreation. What they are expected to do still depends upon three things: (1) the public's perception of parks and recreation; (2) the past experience of the managing agency that employs park and recreation specialists; and (3) the educational biases of the teachers who prepare park and recreation professionals.

The merger of the park movement and the recreation movement into a single force has been accomplished at the professional level by the formation of the National Recreation and Park Association (NRPA); however, the differences in the background, training, and perceptions of those who administer recreation and park systems have made it difficult to standardize basic concepts and definitions. Various writers have attempted to unravel the problem of definitions, but few agreements have been reached. The accreditation of parks and recreation curricula and the enactment of certification and registration programs may ultimately define the field and the role professionals are expected to assume (Henkel, 1987).

Leisure and Leisure Time

The study of leisure has two basic approaches. One group of writers conceives leisure as an attitude toward existence; the other sees leisure as free time or a set of free-time activities (see Figure 1-2). The former view is philosophical in nature, whereas the latter is highly operational and has its base in scientific theory and practice. Free or nonobligated time and activity participation can be measured, but it is difficult to know when one is at leisure; only those experiencing leisure know that it is happening. Leisure, as a philosophical notion, is a preindustrial concept. The ancient Greeks and Romans discussed leisure as freedom from obligation: the state of mind in which a person was truly free from all encumbrances. In that context work was viewed as drudgery and obligation, not as an activity to be done during a specific time period for pay. The concept of time as clock or mechanical time is an industrial world view. The definition of leisure as free time is a result of technological thinking.

When one accepts leisure as a state of mind, the time and type of activity engaged in has little to do with where the activity occurs or what type of rewards will be achieved. According to John Neulinger (1976), it is possible for one to be at leisure when "at work" (i.e., engaged in some activity for which one is paid a fee or salary). Satisfactions may come from any experience; one's

Figure 1-2
The Uses of Our Leisure
by percent of workers who feel that work influences selected leisure activities
(at least some of the time) by sex

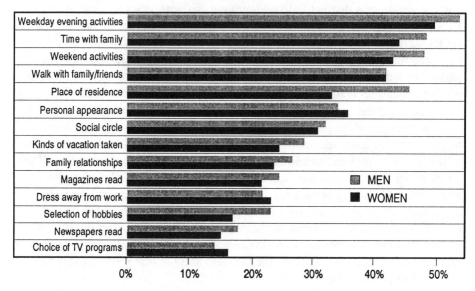

Source: *The Roper Organization*, 1991; reported in *American Demographics*, August 1992, p. 13.

motives are of prime importance, not the time in which the activity is pursued. In this context, a person is at leisure when in harmony with his or her own rhythms and when intrinsically motivated.

Students of leisure services who view leisure as free time hold that leisure, by definition, is time free from work. Therefore, one cannot be at leisure, regardless of the satisfactions derived, while being paid to perform an activity. In this context, leisure is earned; it is time freed by and from work and therefore cannot occur when one is at work.

The issue of definition has not been decided, although the movement is toward a middle ground of thinking. These positions are acknowledged as separate and distinct but interrelated concepts. We accept leisure as a state of being and leisure time as nonwork time; leisure experience is more likely to occur during one's free time but is not limited to it or to any specific activity.

Leisure and Recreation

Leisure and recreation are frequently used interchangeably, especially when the two are defined as free-time experiences or something done for pleasure in one's free time. Ask people what they do in their leisure and they will frequently give you the same response as when you ask what they do for recreation. Yet *leisure* and *recreation* are not synonymous. Generally, recreation is thought of as an activity engaged in during one's free or discretionary time. As David Gray (1980) wrote, it may also be viewed as any pleasurable experience that is intrinsically motivated.

The "pleasurable activity" aspect is more frequently mentioned when one is defining recreation than when one is defining leisure. Both are seen as experiences which are ends in their own right; however, recreation is also viewed as a means to an end especially among those professionals who use the recreation experience as a treatment modality or therapy.

The issues of definition are more critical to the profession than they are to the public. For most people, leisure is viewed as free time, something which occurs after work is done. Recreation is held to be those activities engaged in during leisure time. This is an industrial world view of leisure and recreation that may not be totally satisfactory to the recreation theorists or which may not apply to all groups of people. Furthermore, the public has accepted that park and recreation departments are responsible for providing opportunities for selected recreation experiences. These departments are not expected to provide all of the public's recreation expressions, nor are they necessarily viewed as leisure service agencies. Leisure is generally viewed in a broader context than is recreation and may include "doing nothing" as well as "doing something."

Leisure Services and Recreation and Parks

As stated previously, the leisure service delivery system is comprised of public, private, and commercial sectors or elements, each offering opportunities for activity participation during one's free time. Recreation and parks tends to cut across the delivery system but is most closely allied with the public (governmental) sector. Problems arise when recreation professionals assume the two—parks and recreation, and leisure services—are the same and believe their responsibility is to monitor and plan for the public's general leisure expressions. The public has never mandated parks and recreation to be its leisure guardian, only to provide it with opportunities for certain kinds of recreation expressions. Included in that mandate is the development and maintenance of certain resources, the provision of certain types of programs and services, and the promotion and care of certain cultural and historic activities and sites. It expects the private not-for-profit membership and commercial recreation elements to take care of the rest.

One of the problems confronting parks and recreation is the many meanings assigned to the word "recreation." It is most frequently used to describe those activities done during free time for the satisfaction derived from those experiences. However, recreation is also used to describe the service delivery system providing those experiences we call "recreation" and that field of work employing those who earn their living by providing those experiences. To resolve the problem of definition, it is suggested that "recreation" be used as a noun only when describing the recreation experience. At all other times, it should be used as a modifier such as recreation profession, recreation facility, or recreation activity.

No activity is inherently recreational. All activities have recreation potential, but some more than others. This is due to the public's acceptance of certain activities as recreation, especially those that are normally pursued during one's free time and tend not to be engaged in for economic gain. More often than not, the basic skills were learned during childhood and are now enjoyed on the weekend, after work, or on a holiday. Sports such as tennis, golf, racquetball, and social occasions such as picnics and beach trips are typically described as recreation. It is understandable in this context that so many recreation activity lists frequently contain the same group of choices and that recreation and park agencies tend to offer the same type of programs. The public has come to expect and define recreation in terms of these activities.

When you ask people what they do for recreation, they typically answer with some activity. They do not see recreation as an attitude but as a specific activity. Consequently, communities have organized their services to make available opportunities for these activities. This action is the basis of our parks and recreation service, and when professionals say they are "in recreation," they are talking about their field of work, not the recreation experience. It would be helpful to remember this as one approaches the study of parks and recreation. *Recreation*, then, is an activity or experience; *parks and recreation* is one of the structures (professions) that provides some of those experiences. *Leisure time* is that time available for the pursuit of any free-time expression of which recreation may be a part. *Leisure* refers to the personal experience associated with what an individual does. The *leisure service delivery system*, also known as *leisure services*, accommodates the free-time interests of the public, which may include its voluntary activities, its family and social activities, as well as a wide range of so-called recreation activities.

The Provider and the Recipient

In the attempt to professionalize the recreation and parks movement, specific terms have been developed to distinguish those who provide the recreation service from those who participate in it. Those individuals who provide recreation, parks, and leisure services are generally referred to as recreation professionals but are sometimes called recreation specialists. Those professionals who become certified by the National Recreation and Park Association are called "Certified Leisure Professionals (CLP)." Therapeutic recreation professionals are certified as "Certified Therapeutic Recreation Specialists (C.T.R.S.)." In this textbook, recreation professional is used to describe a professionally prepared individual who is employed, generally by a parks and recreation organization, to further the goals of the leisure service delivery system. Those individuals participating in the recreation experience are called "participants" regardless of whether the public, private, or commercial sectors are being addressed.

Summary

Several issues have been introduced in this chapter. All have implications for understanding the development of the remainder of the book and for addressing the future of leisure services. Through the following chapters, a number of issues and concerns will be addressed in depth. By the end, you should be able to think about possible answers to a number of questions. Will a national policy on work and leisure differ from that of the past? Will the availability of more free time and changing attitudes toward time and its use move Americans away from the work ethic? Will a static or sluggish economy retard the public's interest in a shorter workweek, or will workers elect the trade-off of free time rather than more income? If so, what effects will this trade-off have on future economics and on the distribution of our resources and labor? Will people be wise in their use and development of fragile natural resources as they seek new forms of energy or new areas to play? Can American citizens maintain the same high standard of living and reduce levels of consumption? All social institutions, not just the leisure service delivery system, will be effected by response to these questions.

Professional roles and responsibility are the primary concerns of the leisure service delivery system. What should be the focus of the parks and recreation system? Should more attention be given to the development and nurturing of the natural resources, or should parks and recreation agencies devote more attention to the supervising of people at play? Who are the primary constituents of parks and recreation: those who come to the facilities and ask only for the opportunity to use their equipment and free time as they wish, or people who need outreach programs and services for their personal development? What should be the basic strategy of leisure service agencies: to market their services to specific target populations, or should they provide a smorgasbord of activities and services and let the public choose which it prefers or wants? Will the adult and older adult segments of the population who are more numerous in an aging society, become the basic groups serviced by parks and recreation, or will parks and recreation continue to emphasize programs for children and teenagers? Is the public parks and recreation service the basic unit of service, or is its role that of supplementing and complementing the services offered by private and commercial interests?

Finally, who are the professionals and what distinguishes them from the technicians and support staff who also work in parks and recreation? What type of education is needed to prepare professionals? At what level, undergraduate and graduate, should this professionalization occur? Is the professional basically a manager of services, or are his or her responsibilities those of a technician? Is the role of the professional the same in every setting, or does the specific character of the managing agency such as a municipality, hospital, or military installation determine the role of the professional? The answer to these questions will determine the future of the parks and recreation movement. Some possible keys to their resolution may be found by studying the past, the way the system came into being, and the way it currently works.

The Overview 25

Suggestions and Study Guides

1. Recreation behaviors and patterns of activity are a barometer of a society's behaviors and attitudes. Trends in recreation behaviors are constantly changing as the world changes. In light of that, you are encouraged to read such weekly news magazines as *U.S. News and World Report, Time,* and *Newsweek,* especially those issues that have major articles on leisure. Also, it is suggested that an occasional perusal of *The Wall Street Journal* or *Forbes Magazine* will help keep you in touch with the changing markets and patterns of recreation expenditure.

2. Interview a dozen or so people randomly in supermarkets, bars, or theaters to learn their definition of leisure, recreation, and work. These are settings where people tend to be sociable or willing to be interviewed. Compare their definition of these terms with those offered in the text.

3. Develop an argument in support of recreation and park services in times of economic scarcity; in times of economic abundance. How do these arguments differ in terms of your justification or support of the recreation and parks system?

4. Do a simple content analysis of a Sunday newspaper. See how many times the terms *recreation, amusement, entertainment, leisure,* and *parks* appear in boldface print or as a headline. Also, estimate the percentage of space given to recreation and leisure concerns, such as articles and advertisements of a recreational nature, pictures involving leisure themes, calendars of events, or conservation issues.

A Chronology of Recreation and Park Events

1821-25 Beginnings of physical education, Salem and Northampton, MA.

1826-28 College gymnasia built at Harvard, Yale, and other New England colleges.

1832 Congress gives land to Arkansas for a public spa; later became the Hot Springs National Park.

1853 Central Park, New York City created; designed by Olmstead and Vaux.

1854 Young Men's Christian Association (YMCA) established.

1864 Congress grants Yosemite Valley to California to be operated as a state park; later became Yosemite National Park.

1867 U.S. Office of Education established. Fairmount Park established, Philadelphia.

1872 Purchase of playground land, Brookline, MA. First national park created at Yellowstone, WY.

1875 American Forestry Association established.

1880 First church camp organized; prominent citizens in Canada and United States signed petition calling for the preservation of Niagara Falls.

1885 Association for the Advancement of Physical Education founded; later known as the American Alliance for Health, Physical Education, Recreation and Dance (AAHPERD).

1886 Boston playground with leadership established; Ontario, Canada created a provincial park at Niagara Falls.

1887 Settlement House movement started, New York City; two years later (1889) Jane Addams opened Hull House in Chicago, IL.

1888 Amateur Athletic Union of United States established. New York puts Playground Law into effect. Public evening lectures given in New York Schools.

1892 Sierra Club founded by John Muir.

1893 Illinois creates legislation permitting the establishment of local park districts.

1894 Metropolitan Life Insurance Company in New York City forms first employee association.

1895　First state legislation passed for the establishment of a county park system in Essex County, NJ.

1898　School buildings opened as evening recreation centers, New York City. American Institute of Park Executives established.

1903　Southside Park Commission (Chicago, IL) votes $5,000,000 for development of neighborhood parks and playgrounds.

1904　Playground Board established in Los Angeles, CA.

1905　National Audubon Society founded. U.S. Forest Service established.

1906　Playground Association of America (later known as the National Recreation Association) organized. Both the Boys' Clubs of America and the National Young Women's Christian Association are established. U.S. Congress passes Antiquities Act to establish national monuments, historic and prehistoric landmarks and structures.

1909　*Normal Course in Play* first published by Playground Association of America.

1910　Boy Scouts of America, American Camping Association, and Camp Fire Girls established.

1911　National Education Association proclaims leisure an educational concern and suggests school grounds be used for recreation purposes.

1912　Girl Scouts of America established. Milwaukee, WI passes a referendum of 0.2 mill tax levy for public recreation administered by the Board of Education.

1914　U.S. Agricultural Extension Service and National Association of College Unions established.

1916　National Park Service established. Agreement between United States and Great Britain signed for protection of migratory birds.

1917　War Camp Community Service and other national private agency programs for military established. National Committee on Women's Athletics organized.

1921　National Conference on State Parks established.

1924　White House Conference on Outdoor Recreation is held.

1926　National Recreation School organized by the National Recreation Association.

1932 First International Recreation Congress, Los Angeles, CA.

1933 National Park Service, National Parks and Monuments, National Military Parks, National Battlefield Parks and Sites, National Memorials, and National Capital Parks consolidated into National Park Service. Tennessee Valley Authority created.

1933-36 Establishment of Emergency Services of Federal Government during the Depression and provision for recreation services and facilities (Works Progress Administration, Public Works Administration, National Youth Administration, Civilian Conservation Corps, and the like).

1935 Wilderness Society founded.

1936 Blue Ridge Parkway created (first national parkway). Parks, Parkway, and Recreational Study Act passed by U.S. Congress. Lake Mead, NV becomes first national recreation area.

1937 College Conference for Training Recreation Workers, University of Minnesota. Congress establishes the Cape Hatteras National Seashore, NC.

1938 Society of Recreation Workers of America (later known as the American Recreation Society) formed.

1940-41 Federal Aid Highway Act authorizes expenditure of funds for roadside parks. Federal recreation services established to meet needs of military and defense workers in World War II (Recreation Division, Federal Security Agency; Special Services, War Department; Recreation and Welfare, Navy Department). Establishment of Recreation and Club Services for Military Personnel and the United Service Organizations. National Industrial Recreation Association formed.

1944 Flood Control Act passes authorizing the Corps of Engineers to provide recreation areas at Corps impoundments

1945 Girls' Clubs of America is created. National Recreation Policies Committee established. North Carolina establishes first state recreation commission.

1946 Federal Interagency Committee on Recreation is created. U.S. Congress holds first hearings on bill to establish Federal Recreation Service but no action taken.

1954 National Association of Recreation Therapists and Council for the Advancement of Hospital Recreation organized.

1955 Disneyland, CA opened by Walt Disney Productions.

1956 International Recreation Association (later the World Leisure and Recreation Association) and President's Committee on Physical Fitness established. National Park Service embarks on Mission "66" program of protecting, improving, and developing national parks. National Recreation Month observed for first time.

1957 "Operation Outdoors" of the U.S. Forest Service, a program to improve recreation facilities in the national forests, started.

1958 Outdoor Recreation Resources Review Commission (ORRRC) established. National Cultural Center Act passed by Congress; construction begins on the Kennedy Center, DC.

1960 Alaska establishes plan to acquire, develop, and administer a system of state parks and recreation facilities. National Committee on the Encroachment of Park and Recreation Lands and Waters established.

1961 Open Space and Urban Development Act passed. U.S. Travel Service established in the Department of Commerce.

1962 Bureau of Outdoor Recreation (later the Heritage Conservation and Recreation Service) established in the U.S. Department of the Interior to coordinate and stimulate outdoor recreation development.

1963 Civil Rights Act passed; discrimination at public and commercial sites is prohibited. Vocational Rehabilitation Administration establishes training grant program to develop therapeutic recreation specialists.

1965 Five professional organizations merge to create the National Recreation and Park Association (NRPA). Fifty-one conservation bills passed by U.S. Congress, including the Highway Beautification Act.

1965-68 Johnson Administration establishes War on Poverty with several programs impacting on urban recreation and park concerns.

1968 Wild and Scenic Rivers and Architectural Barriers Acts passed by U.S. Congress. National Trail Systems established. Bureau for Education of the Handicapped begins training and research grant program.

1971 "Legacy of Parks" program established.

1972 Title IX, Education Act, requires equal opportunity for both males and females in college and high school sports. Gateway East, NY/ NJ, and Gateway West, CA, recreation areas established.

1974 Public Law 92-144 passed; requires education in the least restrictive environment and cites need for recreation for the handicapped.

1977 First university recreation and parks curricula accredited by the National Council on Accreditation.

1978 National Parks and Recreation Act authorizes $1.2 billion for improvements of urban and national parks (UPARRS). Proposition 13, restricting local property taxes, passed in California. President places 56 million acres of land in Alaska under control of the National Park Service.

1980 The Alaska National Interest Lands Conservation Act enacted.

1981 Secretary of Interior abolishes the Heritage Conservation and Recreation Service and reduces the Land and Water Conservation Fund and Urban Parks and Recreation Recovery grants. Public issues become the focus of concern.

1982 EPCOT opens as a part of Walt Disney World, FL.

1986 The Commissions on Post-Secondary Accreditation grants recognition to the NRPA/AALR Council on Accreditation to accredit parks and recreation curricula.

1987 Report of the President's Commission on Americans Outdoors calling for more involvement of the private sector in providing outdoor recreation opportunities.

1990 Congress passes the Americans With Disabilities Act thereby opening even greater opportunities, including leisure services, for those with disabilities.

1991 The administering of the first National Certification examination for Certified Leisure Professionals and for Certified Therapeutic Recreation Specialists.

References

Academy of Leisure Sciences. (1993). *Leisure—The new center of the economy?* Unpublished papers of the Academy of Leisure Sciences.

Bergier, M. (1981). A conceptual model of leisure-time choice behavior. *Journal of Leisure Research, 13*(2), pp. 139-158.

Best, F., Bosserman, P., & Stern, B. (1979). Income-free time trade-off preferences of U.S. workers: A review of literature and indicators. *Leisure Sciences, 2*(2), pp. 119-141.

Brightbill, C. (1966). *Education for a leisure-centered living.* Harrisburg, PA: Stackpole Books.

Chubb, M., & Chubb, H. (1981). *One third of our time?* pp. 21-44. New York, NY: John Wiley and Sons.

De Grazia, S. (1962). *Of time, work and leisure.* New York, NY: The Twentieth Century Fund.

Desaulniers, S., & Theberge, N. (1992). Gender differences in the likelihood that work reduction will lead to an increase in leisure. *Loisir & Societe, 15*(1), pp. 135-154.

Godbey, G. (1991). Redefining public parks and recreation. *Parks and Recreation, 26*(10), pp. 56-61, 74.

Gray, D. (1980). What is this thing called recreation? *Parks and Recreation, 15*(3), pp. 62-64, 94.

Henkel, D. (1987). Professionalism—The saga continues. *Parks and Recreation, 20*(8), pp. 50-54, 69.

Hoschild, A., & Machung, A. (1990). *The second shift.* New York, NY: Viking Press.

Knapp, R. and Hartsoe, C. (1979). *Play for America.* Arlington, VA: National Recreation and Park Association.

Murphy, J. (1981). *Concepts of leisure (2nd ed.).* Englewood Cliffs, NJ: Prentice-Hall.

National Sporting Goods Association. (1991). *Sports participation in 1990: Series 1.* Mt. Prospect, IL: National Sporting Goods Association.

Neulinger, J. (1976). The need for and the implications of a psychological conception of leisure. *The Ontario Psychologist*, (6), pp. 16-17.

Rainwater, C. (1922). *The play movement in the United States*. Chicago, IL: The University of Chicago Press.

Schor, J. (1991). *The overworked American: The unexpected decline of leisure*. New York, NY: Basic Books.

Statistical abstract of the United States: 1992 (112th ed.). Washington, DC: U.S. Government Printing Office.

Statistical abstract of the United States: 1993 (113th ed.). Washington, DC: U.S. Government Printing Office.

U.S. Department of Labor. (1980). *Exchanging earnings for leisure: Findings of an exploratory national survey on work time preferences*, pp. 7-9. Washington, DC: U.S. Government Printing Office.

CHAPTER TWO

A Living History

The history of recreation, parks, and leisure is fascinating. A wide variety of leisure behaviors and attitudes have been recorded throughout time. Sebastian De Grazia (1964), Adriano Tilgher (1958), Gary Cross (1990) and Thomas Goodale and Geoffrey Godbey (1988) are among those who have developed scholarly analyses of the evolution of work and leisure concepts and have described the recreation and play behaviors of earlier civilizations. Foster Rhea Dulles' *Recreation in America* (1965) is a classic study of those behaviors in the United States. Richard F. Knapp and Charles E. Hartsoe (1979) offer a definitive study of the emergence and professionalization of the organized parks and recreation system.

The history of the parks and recreation movement is important; the past serves as a backdrop for today's explanations and actions. Human beings are adaptive creatures and have shaped recreation expressions and organizations to meet their needs throughout the ages. Each generation has developed the attitudes necessary to support the structures which accommodate and sustain leisure actions. Change is inevitable, however, and in some instances patterns and attitudes have served as a deterrent to new approaches. Consequently conflicts and misunderstandings have sometimes resulted. A study of the past helps to understand the basis of conflicts and provides a framework for understanding what may lie ahead in the future.

Leisure and Recreation in Earlier Times

Assuming that leisure is defined as moments of freedom from responsibility and the struggle to survive, people have experienced leisure in some form or another since the dawn of history. The initial struggle, of course, was to survive. People had to find and grow food, provide shelter and clothing, and protect themselves from enemies. As they progressed through the various stages of tool making, both the nature of leisure expressions and the amount of time available to pursue leisure interests changed. As Josef Pieper (1963) suggested in the title of his study on the growth of Western civilization, "Leisure is the basis of culture." Meyer and Brightbill (1964) agreed, and added, "There is no better marked trail of the development of leisure, and the desire of man for self-expression, than the rise of the arts" (p. 5).

From the cave drawings of the Cro-Magnon in Lascaux, France, to the most contemporary exhibit at the New York Metropolitan Museum of Art, human beings have artistically portrayed and recorded their feelings and history. Paleolithic people had their toys, diversions, and artistic expressions, conditioned by the technology and resources available to them. The arts first found importance in Western culture in the ancient civilizations of Egypt, Babylonia, and Crete. Utilitarian objects, such as vessels to carry water and clothing to protect the body, were embellished and became objects of beauty. The decorative refinement of artifacts verifies the desire to express and create, to go beyond the utilitarian function of the object, to make things of beauty. Language in spoken, written, and lyrical forms as well as control of the body through athletics and dance also went beyond simple utilitarian function. Early civilizations contributed greatly to an understanding of the history of recreation, leisure, and play.

Egypt

The art contained in the tombs of the Egyptian pharaohs that depicted daily life among the earlier people of the Nile has given information about their leisure and free-time activities. Egypt enjoyed a civilization that lasted for thousands of years, from approximately 5000 BC into the Roman Era. The Egyptians developed a highly complex and structured civilization with a variety of social classes, each with its own patterns of leisure behavior. Dancing was a favorite interest of the lower classes and was performed widely in exhibition groups. Entertainment and spectator activities were generally known to the more affluent, while the working classes enjoyed their drinking houses. The children of both classes had toys and played chess and backgammon. Holidays and public festivals abounded. Choral and orchestral musical works, drama, bullfighting, and gymnastics were popular activities. The therapeutic recreation field traces its history to these times when, as treatment for mental depression, afflicted Egyptians were sent to resort areas as part of their therapy. The nobility enjoyed a great deal of free time and the Egyptian influence was felt throughout the Mediterranean region.

Little is known about the attitudes of the Egyptians toward leisure and work, although it is assumed that leisure expressions were highly sanctioned and encouraged by the people living in this area of the world. The hunting preserves of the Egyptians and the hanging gardens of Babylon might be considered early signs of interest in setting aside outdoor areas for personal enjoyment, one of the purposes of our modern parks. The Assyrians created animal parks, the forerunner of our modern zoos (Ceram, 1971). A sense of pleasure seeking and a commitment by the ruling groups to create opportunities and environments for the pursuit of pleasure was evident in this early society.

Greece

Greece was a civilization of city-states, each with individual leisure expressions and favored forms of activity. For example, the Spartans with their national fixation on warfare, enjoyed sports, music, and artistic expressions that reinforced nationalism and prepared them for battle. The Athenians, on the other hand, stressed education in their free-time activities. To the Athenians sports were important, but so were theatrical and choral performances, debates, and religious and civil rituals. Throughout the Greek Islands, holidays were numerous. It is estimated that the ancient Greeks enjoyed 50 to 60 holidays annually.

The arts and sports flourished during the Golden Age of Greece, which spanned from 1200 to 500 BC. Plato wrote in his *Laws* that a man is not educated unless he is able to sing and dance at the same time. A balanced education for males was considered to be one that stressed physical activity for the body, music and poetry for the soul, and mathematics and philosophy for the mind. The ideal state was achieved when the mind and body were in harmony *(arete)* and when one was in control and able to translate thought into meaningful action. Composing music and writing poetry were favorite pastimes of the free men of Athens. Troupes of acrobatic dancers and thespians traveled the countryside. The great playwrights produced both tragedies and comedies which are still performed today. Scores of citizens went to the theater to be inspired and entertained. Probably no other civilization has so strongly supported the arts and athletics.

The Olympic Games were established in 732 BC in honor of the god Zeus. They were Panhellenic, being open only to freeborn male Greeks with a focus on the amateur ideal. They continued until the fifth century AD, when commercialism, athletic specialization, and gambling so totally corrupted the original concept of the games that they were rejected by the people. By that time, the Olympics had become an international affair with Rome being the dominating influence on both Olympic form and purpose. To encourage and facilitate athletic performances, public parks, hunting preserves, gymnasiums, and related athletic facilities were constructed. In the latter days of the ancient Greek civilization, a tendency existed for spectatorism to replace individual participation, particularly in sports and the performing arts.

Possibly the most significant contribution of the ancient Greeks to an understanding of work and leisure was not the specific form of activities they pursued, but the attitude they held toward activity in general. To the Greeks, work was a curse and an obligation from which free men should escape. It should be remembered that less than twenty percent of the Athenian population were free men; the civilization of ancient Greece was built upon the efforts of slaves, and little is known about their attitudes or leisure expression. Further, little is known about the values of women as related to free time activities. It may be assumed that they, too, shared the dominant values and interests of the Greek culture although not all of its opportunities.

The Greeks approached life in a holistic manner. The need to fulfill social and personal obligations was accepted, but no division of life's activities (work and leisure) according to time in which they occurred. Leisure was conceived as a state of being in which activity was performed for its own gratification; it was an end in itself and seen as an opportunity to discover truth and know beauty. Aristotle wrote that one must learn to be idle. It was generally held that leisure was synonymous with freedom and the preferred state of life.

According to De Grazia (1964), our concept of leisure comes from the notion of *schole,* as does our word "school" (p. 16). Originally *schole* meant to have peace and quiet: later it meant to have time for oneself. Contemplation was considered one of the best ways to find truth and happiness. Labor, therefore, like all activity that detracted from a person's understanding of self was seen as an enemy of freedom and was to be performed by women and slaves. Politics, the arts, and learning were the occupations of free men.

Ancient Rome

In many ways, the Roman and Greek civilizations were similar. The Romans adopted activities of ancient Greece and built upon their interest in sports and theater. But Rome was not Greece. Whereas Greece was a nation of agrarian city-states, Rome was an urban society. Its civilization lasted some 700 years (from 300 BC to AD 400) and, at its height, its population exceeded a million people. Roman engineers and architects were among the finest of the ancient world, and its roads and aquatic systems were unparalleled for centuries.

Rome was given to entertainment and spectator events. The Roman holiday is not a myth. It is estimated that Rome celebrated over 100 holidays a year.

Festivals and games characterized most of these occasions; massive arenas were constructed to accommodate huge crowds. It is believed that the Circus Maximus could accommodate 385,000 onlookers. For many, the Colosseum, constructed in AD 80, is synonymous with the life of ancient Rome. They associate Rome with sports and entertainment.

While education and learning were the essential ideals of Greece, politics and government were the dominant institutions of Rome. Free men were expected to contribute to the political and social life of the state. Physical activity was seen both as an end in itself and as a means to keep physically fit. Many historians hold that the ancient Romans had a body fixation somewhat like their modern American counterparts. By the fourth century, over 800 public baths were available which could accommodate crowds of 60,000 persons on any given day. Romans also enjoyed parks and the outdoors. They were the first to establish greenhouses, using mica for window panes (Jensen, 1977). Parks and recreation were a part of their life experience.

The Latin word for leisure was *otium*. *Negotium* was the opposite; it meant obligation or work. Work was a negation of leisure. Because all free men were expected to contribute to the life of the state, they were advised to alternate their work with play. Both were seen as necessary expressions. Leisure never took on the contemporary connotation of free time nor the Greeks' sense of time for contemplation but was viewed as opportunity for diversion, entertainment, and pleasure.

With the growth of affluence (Romans also used slaves to do the manual labor necessary for the maintenance of their civilization), free Romans delighted more and more in personal pleasures. Writers such as Seneca and Juvenal urged their fellow citizens to turn away from self-indulgences, to take time for philosophy and learn to live, but few listened. Hedonism, a philosophy of immediate gratification, eventually replaced Epicureanism, a philosophy of the rational uses of the senses, developed by the Greeks.

In the latter days of Rome, commercialism and professionalism of sports and entertainment dominated the leisure movements of the society. Gambling and prostitution were sanctioned by the state. By the time of Tiberius (AD 14-37) debauchery had become a way of life for Rome. In analyzing the reasons for Rome's decline, some writers suggest that its misuse of leisure contributed significantly to its demise:

> When faced by the challenge of excess wealth, luxury, and time,
> they [Romans] responded as a nation by yielding to corruption
> and losing the simple virtues that had made them strong as a nation (Kraus, 1978, p. 137).

The East

If space permitted, a review of ancient history in Asia, particularly China, would also reveal a strong relationship between play and the creative efforts of a people. The history of Chinese literature starts early and has no Dark Age. Poetry and philosophy have been a part of the Chinese culture for thousands of years. The simple lines of Chinese paintings have been a highly respected form of art since the days of ancient Rome. Oriental dancing is even older, and the stringed instruments and cymbals of Asian music came from its early civilization. The teachings of Buddhism stressed the value of leisure, of self-control through reflection and study, of freedom from vanities. These concepts were not too different from the ancient Greeks.

For hundreds of years, the world has admired the skills of the Japanese craftspeople as they worked their metal, stone, ivory, and paper into objects of art and beauty. Almost any events such as births, weddings, or harvest times were occasions for a celebration by the ancient Chinese. These customs still persist throughout the Eastern world. Probably no people have contributed more significantly to puppetry as an art form than have the Japanese, but neither Japan nor China has approached the organizing of recreation and leisure systems as did those civilizations influenced more by the European and Mideastern traditions. Therefore, the history of the park and recreation movement evolved primarily from Western history.

The Near East

The industrial world's work ethic is deeply rooted in the Hebraic-Greco traditions. Like the ancient Greeks, the ancient Hebrews considered work a painful duty as well as an obligation for all people to atone for the original sin, "the fall from the Garden of Eden." Thus, work had a sacred meaning, became a part of God's plan; leisure was a time for meditation and self-expression. In the Old Testament, the reader is reminded to have leisure and to use it to know God (Psalm 65:11), to celebrate the Sabbath as a day of "gratitude and thanksgiving," as "a gift of grace...rather than a reward for work" (Goodale and Godbey, p. 62).

The early Christians extended this tradition. They were warned by their teachers to "take no heed of tomorrow" and not to be concerned with the gaining of wealth and material things. Duties were to be performed, but making a profit was not the ultimate goal. Early Christians held that work was meant to sustain oneself; beyond that, it had little value. The same was true for other worldly activities, including play. Seeking truth through prayer and contemplation was the preferred use of free time, since the preparation for Christ's return was the central concern of the early Christians.

The Middle Ages

The leisure and recreation aspect of culture cannot be clearly separated from the economic and political characteristics of an era. They are influenced by each other and reflect the larger events shaping the social order. This lesson is demonstrated in that period of history known as the Middle or Dark Ages.

The Middle Ages, which began with the fall of the Roman Empire, lasted for approximately one thousand years (AD 500-1400). Largely agricultural and feudal, these times gave rise to a well-defined class system in Europe. There were primarily four dominant groups: the clergy, the lords, the artisans or craftsmen, and the serfs (farm hands).

The church had a powerful influence on the people during this period with its rules and rigidity. To some degree the monasteries, which had been originally established for the protection and support of those given to religious study, fostered a division of labor. Manual labor was done by the lay brothers who could not do the spiritual work. Those given to the intellectual and conceptual were viewed as engaged in an important activity, something not everyone could do.

A well-integrated social structure with each class performing a vital role for the maintenance of the system existed. The artisans produced the utilitarian objects such as pots and shoes, while the serfs grew and harvested the grain. The lords protected the walled cities and governed the land. The clergy provided the overall religious direction and value system. The relationship between church and state was an interesting one: the church developed the rules; the state enforced them. These rules, combined with the daily toil of the serfs, left little opportunity for the working people to enjoy any kind of pleasure beyond the telling of stories, the singing of songs, and, occasionally, taking part in folk games and dances. Literature, drama, and dancing were reserved for the leisure class.

There was great sport in fighting among different manors. The lord of each would employ horsemen and knights to serve as both soldiers and athletes. This was the period of chivalry; contests and tournaments with the combative sports of fencing and jousting were favored. Some authorities believe that sports such as bowling and bait casting were also practiced as early as the thirteenth century.

Riding, falconry, and hunting were equally popular pursuits. Although hunting was a serious study as early as the second century when Julius Pollux wrote *Onomasticon,* it was not until the Middle Ages, when the Celtic tribes of Northern Europe developed greyhounds to chase the game, when hunting became a true sport with the chase being as important as the capture (Carls, n.d.). Hunting preserves were established for the wealthy and protected by them. Poaching was a crime. One of the earliest hunting preserves in England, the New Forest, was established by William the Conqueror in 1087.

The majority of people in the Middle Ages, however, had few opportunities for personal enjoyment. Life was difficult with continual threats from the plague, warring tribes, and harsh weather. Even so, within the walled towns of medieval Europe, the children played, holidays were celebrated, and artisans gathered in their guild halls for social activity. Knowledge of the outside world came primarily from tales of battle described by knights and squires and the songs and poems of wandering singers and troubadours.

Possibly the most significant events of the Middle Ages which directly relate to an understanding of leisure were the writings of such philosophers as St. Augustine, St. Benedict, and St. Thomas Aquinas. Their works reflect the emerging attitudes of Western civilization toward concepts of work and leisure. According to them, work changed from being an obligation or a duty to be performed until Christ returned, to an activity of dignity and purpose. St. Thomas Aquinas even developed a hierarchy of professions and trades in which he ranked agriculture first and commerce last. He divided society into guilds and corporations according to the relationship of each to God's plan. The doctrine of the just price, which held that laborers should be paid only enough to support their family, was established. If profits were achieved, they should be used for charity and the good of the church. All men were considered to have the right to work and earn the just wage. If they were unable to do so, it was the responsibility of society to care for them. A man fortunate enough to enjoy affluence was under no obligation to work, but was expected to spend his time in the political, civic, and religious activities of the community or state. The role of women during this time was primarily to care for the family and assist in maintaining the social system. Equality of the sexes was only in the "eyes of God;" men were expected to protect and control the secular order. Aquinas' views provide a transition from a world dominated primarily by a central church to one in which governments (known as the State) would actively promote activities for the common good of the people. He wrote that it should be a system "that conforms to the diversity and capacities of its citizens; [that] when such conformity is present, harmony will be achieved—as common good and individual good reinforce each other" (Dare, Welton & Coe, 1987, p. 78). In time, recreation was to become a community responsibility to reinforce social and individual good.

The Emerging Era

The world changed greatly after the Middle Ages. Science and technology were on the rise. The Church of Rome became under siege by those who wanted other explanations, another type of governance and a reform of church doctrine and behaviors. The Industrial Revolution was imminent. Science, religion, and politics were on a collision course. Historians called this the Age of

Enlightenment, or the Renaissance, which was closely followed by the Reformation, and the rise of capitalism.

The Renaissance and Reformation

The Renaissance was characterized by a revival of the more artistic and sensitive forms of recreation expression. Sports and games became less brutal, even though many remained as forms of combat in a more highly civilized guise. New interests and styles developed in the arts, particularly in painting, sculpture, and architecture. Formal ballroom dancing and ballet became popular art forms; opera houses and courtly activity were encouraged. Patrons supported the arts and employed their own musicians. Much of our classical church music comes from this era. This period was one of slow but certain enlightenment. Increasingly, the formal private gardens were opened to the public on a limited basis as fashion and architecture grew in importance. People began to understand the world and use its resources to make a better life for all. The opening of trade to the East gave Europeans a taste of luxury goods along with new views of life and leisure. This era included Shakespeare, Cervantes, Rabelais, and El Greco.

Scientific discovery and explanations also began. Scientists such as Copernicus, Galileo and Leonardo da Vinci wrote of their discoveries. Unlike the ancient Greeks who tried to explain the nature of things through natural law, the Renaissance scientists were interested in using laws to control nature. Nature was viewed as an enemy to be subdued and controlled. To some degree, the origins of the conflict between the mastery of the environment and the protection of it (the issues of utilization verses conservation) are founded here.

The Reformation was a period of reaction against the stifling influences of a corrupt church. The balance of power and wealth shifted from the church to the princely states and monarchies. During the sixteenth and seventeenth centuries, feudalism came to an end, modern science began, trade became worldwide, and the parochial school approach to education was replaced by the neoclassical approach, which gave greater emphasis to science and math. Humanism became the guiding philosophy of the era, a philosophy emphasizing the dignity of people and their achievements.

Martin Luther and John Calvin were central Reformation figures. Their writings had a profound effect on the character of Western Europe, particularly in its economic and religious sphere. Although recognized for their work in helping reform the Catholic church and establishing the Protestant movement, they were also influential in the development of modern concepts of work and play. Luther held that work was a form of service to God and that one should be content with one's "calling." He encouraged people to remain in their social class and seek perfection in what they were doing. He did not condemn profit nor encourage upward mobility, but asked all to be content with their vocation. Luther believed work took on religious significance. He challenged workers not to seek material gains but to develop their own abilities and to seek perfection. His was a philosophy of transition between that of St. Thomas Aquinas and John Calvin.

John Calvin further extended the Reformation and the ultimate development of capitalism with his notion of predestination and election. He held that God had foreordained the role each person was to play, and that no one could change God's plan, only discover and follow it. Furthermore, he held that God had determined the "elect," those who were to be saved. Because no one was certain of *a priori* salvation, each had to work to symbolize favor with God. All people, even the wealthy, were expected to labor; achievement resulted from God's blessing. Within this philosophy, profits became legitimate and so did the seeking of new roles and status. Calvin believed that one should not be content with one's calling if improvement was possible and that upward mobility also reflected God's favor. If through investment and diligent labor an artisan became an industrialist, then God's will was being done. Finally, Calvin held that one's lack of effort should be considered a sign of questionable election; idleness was condemned. Forms of activity such as dancing and card playing, which emphasized sexuality or encouraged gambling, were prohibited.

The teachings of Calvin and the discipline he espoused formed the basis for the Protestant work ethic, which continues to influence Western civilization today. These views offered no support for frivolity and amusement and implied something sinful in seeking pleasure for pleasure's sake or in associating with those who took time out for pleasure. Recreation was acceptable only if it promoted the virtues of work. Otherwise, it was discouraged.

Fortunately, not all reformers were Calvinists. Some even openly proclaimed the value of games and athletics as well as the importance of social occasions and social environments. Such internationally known parks as Kensington Gardens in London, Prather Park in Vienna, and the Tiergarten in Berlin were established. Coffee shops, arenas and theaters, such as the Globe, and public hunting preserves were also available for free-time expression.

By the end of the Reformation, work had emerged as a means to subdue and control nature. It was held to be more valuable than contemplation, since work involved action. Leisure was emerging as the goal of work, a reward for one's effort. Thomas More wrote in *Utopia* of a shorter workday, of a society where all should work, and where leisure was to be enjoyed when work was done.

The Industrial Revolution

The Reformation ushered in the Industrial Revolution. It legitimized investments and capital expansion. Prior to the Industrial Revolution, people had to earn their living largely through agriculture and the trades which required long hours of labor. Through countless inventions and industrial progress over the centuries, people were now able to recapture some of the leisure enjoyed by the free men of ancient civilizations. A reliance upon the clock emerged, however. It allowed people to be paid for their time and moved civilization from the rhythm of nature to the incessant beat of a clock. It synchronized institutions and captured thought. By the end of the nineteenth century, leisure was becoming synonymous with free time, and the industrial work ethic was emerging as the dominant value system. The mechanical and manual arts were being glorified and, in the words of Tilgher (1958), humans had become *"homo faber,* the work animal" (p. 100).

Leisure in America Prior to 1900

Recreation activities in colonial America were not held in high esteem. Idleness was thought to be associated with evil, loose morals, and personal degeneration. In New England, a strict Calvinist doctrine was, in great part, responsible for this attitude. Little opportunity was available for leisure and, when it was "earned," it was to be used for constructive purposes. Efforts were made to control such undesirable practices as gambling and drinking through the enactment of "blue laws" which prohibited these behaviors during certain hours and certain days of the week. Colonial Americans, however, did play. Social life was important to the land aristocracy of the south and the industrialists of the north. The workers and slaves had their folk and ethnic games. Free-time expressions were controlled, but permitted.

The growth of recreation and parks in the United States was the result of a number of developments, including advances in science and medicine, the growth of public education, industrial and technological progress, and the changing of social and political attitudes. Between the beginning and end of the nineteenth century, the United States moved from a pioneering, agricultural nation to an increasingly industrialized society with large centers of population. Urbanization was taking place as people moved from farms and small towns to the cities and suburbs. Mass production of convenience items was beginning to benefit many Americans, freeing them from the routines of daily activity. These changes in combination with growing affluence and better healthcare allowed Americans to enjoy a leisure unknown to their forebears.

With the opening of the frontiers and the rise of urban centers in the nineteenth century, organized recreation activities took many interesting forms. Social dancing was popular in the East; square-dancing flourished in the West. The waltz, polka, and quadrille were popular dances. Participation included sleigh rides, ice skating, and trips to the beach for the daring experience of "public bathing." Travel to Europe and to resorts in wilderness areas, for those who could afford it, increased during this period.

The issue of the "new leisure" was openly discussed by the intellectuals and avant-garde educators of the times. Horace Greeley spoke of the need for the wise use of leisure. The prestigious magazine, *The Atlantic Monthly,* carried articles on leisure's significance. Gentlemen's clubs such as the New York Athletic Club were organized in the larger cities. Billiard rooms and pool halls were opened and well-patronized by middle- and upper-class males. Workers were being freed from long hours of labor, and with their shorter workweek came time for recreation pursuits. Private enterprise responded to the opportunity by encouraging sports, arts, and entertainment opportunities.

Outdoor sports increased in popularity. Turkey shoots, buffalo hunts, and sport fishing were promoted. Professional sports were being organized, particularly boxing, racing, and baseball. The National Professional Baseball League was organized in 1876. College football had its beginning in 1869, when Princeton played Rutgers. Americans were enjoying bicycling, bowling, playing softball, basketball, and volleyball. The YMCA was much involved in the promotion of the latter two sports.

Church leaders, who had been critical of organized play and entertainment, began encouraging and supporting specific recreation activities. The importance of play for proper growth and development of young people was cited by church members. The healthy body was viewed as a living testament. Popularly known as the muscular lyceum movement, the trend toward melding church and leisure activities reached its height during the late nineteenth century. For example, by 1895, there were 1,400 YMCA branches in the United States (Knapp and Hartsoe, p. 15).

Theatrical and literary activities also increased in popularity during the nineteenth century. The newly created legitimate theaters in Boston, Philadelphia, and New York competed with the Iyceum movement for popular support. Minstrel and variety shows were small town favorites; lecture series were also popular. Band concerts in the park, huge holiday celebrations, and taffy pulls and quilting bees were found in most towns throughout the nation. Thanks to the railroad industry and P.T. Barnum, the circus could come to every city. By 1872, Barnum's circus train had 61 cars and was touring sixteen states annually.

Entertainment was going where the people were. The traveling medicine and Wild West shows were second in spectator appeal only to the circus. Amusement parks and penny arcades, forerunners of theme parks and video game arcades, sprang up across the country. America was learning to play, to relax, and to spend money on its pursuit of pleasure. Resort areas such as Saratoga Springs, NY, and White Sulphur Springs, WV, prospered as did a fledgling tourist industry. A popular culture was emerging; it was believed that all Americans could share the same forms of entertainment.

The park movement was enjoying a similar degree of attention and recognition. Although Boston had established its commons in 1634 and the town of Newton, New Hampshire had acquired a community forest in 1710, the first major urban parks did not come into being until the mid-1800s. Central Park, (New York City) in 1853 became the cornerstone for the development of large urban park and parkway systems. The park concept rapidly spread throughout the eastern seaboard and Great Lakes regions. Fairmount Park (Philadelphia) was established in 1867; Washington Park (Chicago) was created nine years later. These new parks and park systems broke with the tradition of the past where simply green areas and forests were provided; the new parks were areas which accommodated a variety of activities including horseback riding, pleasure walking, concerts, and floral gardens. Frederick Olmsted was the genius of this new park idea; his concepts provided the basis upon which modern landscape architecture and park planning were founded.

Concerns for conservation also paralleled the growth of urban areas. For example, the potential development of spas as commercial areas prompted the United States government to reserve the land around Hot Springs, Arkansas in 1832 for public use. This area later became the Hot Springs National Park. In 1864, the United States Congress gave land grants within the Yosemite Valley to the state of California to operate the area as a state park and eight years later established Yellowstone, WY, as the first national park. In 1873, New York State acquired 40,000 acres of land as a forest preserve. This land is generally accepted as the first substantial purchase of forest lands by any governmental unit in the United States. The American Forestry Association was established in 1875 to give direction and leadership to the forestry movement. Four years later, the Division of Forestry was established in the United States Department of Agriculture. In 1885, New York made another significant contribution to the conservation movement by acquiring the lands around the Niagara Falls as a preserve. One year later, the Ontario (Canada) government approved the establishment of a provincial park at Niagara Falls. Both of these purchases of land resulted from an active campaign by leading citizens in the United States and Canada for the preservation of these areas. In 1898 just six years after the Sierra Club was founded by John Muir, the New England Association of Park Superintendents, which became the forerunner of the American Institute of Park Executives, was established. The conservationist movement was beginning to demonstrate power as a political force.

Public recreation in cities, particularly the large metropolitan areas, also began to take shape at the end of the nineteenth century. The movement (Oliva, 1985) started with the sand gardens, an idea brought to America from Europe by Dr. Marie Zakrsewka in 1885. By 1893, the Massachusetts Emergency and Hygiene Association, a Boston charity, was operating ten summer playgrounds utilizing both volunteer and paid leadership. Joseph Lee was one of the pioneers in this effort. Lee believed that every child had a right to play. Playgrounds were furthered by the settlement house movement, the social gospels of religious reformers, and concerns about the effects of urbanization especially on youth.

As the nineteenth century came to a close, small parks dotted the landscape of many communities, public libraries and community centers were being established, and America was entering a new era of social consciousness. Concerns for the less fortunate, for the young, and for the preservation of the environment were a part of this consciousness. These concerns had a significant effect on the parks and recreation movement.

Twentieth-Century Highlights

Opening Years (1900-1914)

The twentieth century began on an optimistic note. A genuine feeling was that the quality of life could be enhanced through programs of social reform. It was an era of philanthropy with dedicated men and women concerned about the future. Although not eliminated, Victorian concepts and ideas were giving way to the views of liberalism and humanism. The provision of proper environments for play and the wise use of leisure were among the major concerns of these philanthropists.

The first decade of the century was an era of expansion and new beginning. The South Park playgrounds of Chicago were opened in 1903 under public auspices. The first playground commission within a municipal government was established in 1904 by the city of Los Angeles. The first public school athletic leagues were organized in New York in 1903 by Luther Gulick who was an early pioneer in youth activity and the first president of the Camp Fire Girls. Psychologists such as Carl Groos and G. Stanley Hall were citing the importance of play in the development of children. Several youth-serving agencies, such as the Boy Scouts, began during this decade.

The year 1906 was an important year for the parks and recreation movement (Dickason, 1985). It marked the beginning of the Playground Association of America (PAA) which later was known as the Playground and Recreation Association of America (PRAA) and ultimately as the National Recreation Association (NRA). As a service organization supported by voluntary contributions, the PAA promoted the cause of community recreation for more than half a century. It grew out of the work of Joseph Lee, Henry Curtis, Luther Gulick and Jane Addams who were the first officers. Howard Braucher served as the first executive secretary; he assumed that responsibility in 1909 and continued in that capacity until the early 1940s. Established as an association comprised largely of volunteer and interested citizens, this early organization serving both the laity and the professional through its field staff and national office. Its contributions to the organized recreation movement were many.

The enactment of the Antiquities Act was another important event that occurred in 1906. This action on the part of the U.S. Congress gave the federal government a tool for protecting scientific and historic areas. The President was given the power to designate national monuments and to protect these areas from destruction. Devils Tower, WY, and the Lassen Peak (Lassen Volcanic National Park, CA) were among the earlier designated monuments. The growing number of national parks and national monuments made imperative the establishment of the National Park Service, which occurred ten years later.

The public schools were also much involved in the development of early organized recreation services. In 1907, staff in Rochester, New York embarked on a program of making school facilities available as community facilities. This beginning had far-reaching effects on the general use of schools for community purposes. The National Education Association in 1911 recommended the use of school buildings and grounds for recreation, and thereby cast the die for the emergence of a community school program. Perhaps none were as successful in this endeavor as was the Milwaukee School System. For years its recreation program, under the leadership of Dorothy Endaris, was nationally acclaimed for its "lighted school houses." After-school programs were offered for both children and adults.

The early years of the twentieth century were also characterized by a marked expansion in the voluntary agency and camping movements. Without the efforts of wealthy philanthropists and social reformers, the growth of recreation opportunities for the urban poor would have been impeded. The settlement houses, which were established in the slum sections in large cities in the East and Midwest, were the first neighborhood service centers. Possibly the most famous of these was the Hull House in Chicago. It was built in 1889 and operated by Jane Addams who felt that recreation could be a powerful force in the prevention of delinquency and antisocial behavior. Youth-serving agency and private camps also increased in number. Although Frederick William Gunn and Dr. Joseph T. Rothrock are credited with having established the first school camp (1861) and private camp (1876) before the turn of the century, over 100 camps were in operation by 1900. By 1916, the camping movement was large enough that those most intimately involved had organized the Camp Directors Association, later to become the American Camping Association.

Increased governmental interest in outdoor recreation occurred during this period. In 1903 the voters of Chicago approved the nation's first five million dollar bond issue to acquire and develop recreational parks. One year later Los Angeles established the first Municipal Recreation Commission which was an appointed board to oversee its playgrounds as an independently governed unit separate from both the school and park boards. Although unpopular for politicians to speak on behalf of such trivia as recreation a few years earlier, by 1906 it was expedient to be in favor of recreation and conservation. In 1908, President Theodore Roosevelt convened a White House conference with the governors of various states to kick off his public conservation program. The National Park Service was established in 1916 to "promote and regulate the use of the Federal areas known as national parks, monuments and reservations...to conserve the scenery and national historic objects of the wildlife therein and to provide for the enjoyment of the same and by such manner and by such means as will leave them unimpaired for the enjoyment of the future generations..." (Act of August 25, 1916).

The expansion of parks and recreation agencies required the development of professional leadership. The first training program for professional directors of play services (later to be known as recreation leaders) was published in 1909 under the title, *The Normal Course in Play*. It was written by Henry Curtis for a committee chaired by Clark Heatherington. Several universities, including Harvard, Columbia, Northwestern and the University of California at Berkley offered courses in play and summer playground institutes. Among the earliest educators were Luther Gulick (1905, New York University), Neva Boyd (1911, Chicago Training Institute, later a part of Northwestern) and George E. Johnson (1915, Harvard). In 1912, the New York State College of Forestry at Syracuse University established the nations first program to train for park administration and city forestry. Professional preparation was on its way (Sessoms, 1993).

A new concept of parks was emerging as active organized recreation programs began to appear. To some extent, the concepts of conservation and preservation were giving way to the people's recreation desires. Distinctions were being made between parks and playgrounds, with the former emphasizing design and the latter stressing places for play. Following the Los Angeles model, municipalities were beginning to organize recreation systems as a complement to their park systems.

World War I (1914-1918)

The growth of municipal recreation and park services was affected by the events preceding and surrounding World War I. Organized recreation was taking on a community focus with attention being centered on neighborhood and community interests. Clarence Rainwater (1922) refers to the 1915-1918 period as the "neighborhood organization" stage of the playground movement in the United States. He said these years were characterized by the development of self-supported, self-governed, decentralized play activities in neighborhoods with funds being solicited for the operation of community recreation facilities. Much of this growth was directly related to the activities of the Playground and Recreation Association of America (PRAA) which by 1917 had twenty field workers promoting recreation services throughout the country.

With the entrance of the United States into World War I and the establishment of a universal draft system, community life underwent tremendous upheaval. Communities adjacent to military installations and training centers which boomed as "war" towns were particularly affected. Suddenly, hundreds of thousands of servicemen and transient workers found themselves in new settings without the traditional support system of the family and small town.

To provide some continuity of normalcy, communities moved to establish recreation programs that would accommodate their new citizens and allow for the "wholesome use of leisure." Under the leadership of the Playground and Recreation Association of America, the War Camp Community Service (WCCS) was organized. In two years of its operations the Association raised over 2.2 million dollars to aid local communities in developing recreation opportunities and services for the military and defense workers. Neighborhood organization was its plan of action. The War Camp Community Service program employed over 3,000 leaders and involved 500,000 volunteers in 750 communities and 47 states during its height. In those states where racial segregation was a legal and cultural fact, the WCCS operated over 100 clubs specifically for the black military (Knapp & Hartsoe, p. 68-70).

In addition to the activities of the war camp program, several religious organizations and the YMCA established recreation programs on military posts. These programs were approved by the War and Navy departments and emphasized both religious and social welfare activities as well as recreation services. They were forerunners of the special programs now provided by the military branches for their service personnel. With the coming of peace, these special war-effort programs were terminated, but their effects were long lasting. They stimulated the interest of many communities in organized recreation services and ushered in the dynamic 1920s.

A Decade of Expansion (1920-1930)

The years following World War I resulted in extensive expansion of all types of recreation services. Stimulated by an era of unparalleled prosperity, Americans sought to enjoy the new freedom of the shorter workweek, the benefits of mass production, and the expansion of the new technology of electronics. In this decade, people enjoyed a higher standard of living than had any previous generation. More people had larger incomes and more opportunity for pleasure than had been known in the past.

Many Victorian ideas gave way to new concepts of morality. Commercial recreation was a growth industry. A marked trend away from the more simple pleasures to those activities which required increased expenditures for facilities and participation was evident. Whereas there were only 5,000 radios in 1920, by 1924 there were over million (Chubb & Chubb, 1981, p. 32). Fads in recreation activity swept the country. Crossword puzzles, miniature golf, dance marathons, bathing beauty contests, and contract bridge were the "activities of the day." Some persisted; others were brief in their popularity. The Jazz Singer (the first "talkie") starring Al Jolson changed the face of the movie industry; the Dempsey-Tunney boxing match grossed the first million-dollar gate. Automobile, horse, and dog races of all types had phenomenal growth, and the legitimate stage (Broadway and the like) enjoyed a rebirth.

Organized parks and recreation was expanding at a rapid rate and so was the demand for paid leadership. The Playground and Recreation Association (PRAA) responded to this leadership need by establishing a series of training programs. From 1920 to 1926, it conducted six-week training programs in various communities throughout the country. In 1926, the PRAA started the National Recreation School. This 34-week, nondegree curriculum, with an emphasis on administrative skills and understanding, graduated over 300 recreation directors within the next nine years. Whereas only 400 communities offered organized recreation services at the beginning of the 1920s, over a thousand were offering them as the decade came to an end.

The Great Depression (1930-1940)

Volumes have been written about the Great Depression of the 1930s. It was a time of unemployment lines, personal tragedies, and economic collapse. It was also a decade of a changing philosophy of economics and government. Many of the programs and approaches introduced in response to the Depression remain today. Though the world was experiencing economic "hard times," it was not an era of decline for organized parks and recreation services. The Great Depression resulted in another decade of expansion in which government became the dominant force in making available public opportunities for recreation and play.

Prior to 1932, the general public solution to industrial unemployment had been charity and unemployment insurance which kept people alive but still unemployed. The New Deal approach of Roosevelt was a radical departure from this philosophy. It was founded on the assumption that any kind of work was better than idleness and that it was the duty and responsibility of government to furnish work when private enterprise found itself incapable of doing so. A variety of public work projects were created that provided jobs for millions. Many of those jobs dealt with the construction of public facilities such as libraries, swimming pools, and community buildings.

Meyer and Brightbill (1964) estimated that the "make work program of the federal government during the Depression advanced organized parks and recreation by twenty-five years" (p. 17). These programs stimulated organized recreation services at every level of governmental responsibility. In 1930 there were less than 25,000 volunteers and professionals engaged in the field of recreation with only 2,500 of these being employed full-time. By 1935, that number had increased to 45,000 full-time workers and the number of communities offering recreation services had doubled. Every county and every state had a director of recreation projects.

The actions of the Federal Emergency Relief Administration positively affected the park and recreation system. Two approaches to recreation services were assumed by the Federal Emergency Relief Administration. One was to employ workers through the construction of facilities; the other was to employ program and activity leadership. For example, writers, musicians, and actors were given jobs through the federal theater. Adult education, group work, and organized recreation services flourished. Both the quantity and quality of recreation and park facilities and leadership expanded within this program.

The Division of Recreation Projects as a part of the organizational structure of the Work Projects Administration (WPA), became a major employer of recreation personnel. These WPA leaders worked under the general supervision of such local tax-supported units as recreation departments, park boards, school boards, and welfare departments. Their work was often integrated into the recreation programs of a local community. To assure an adequate supply of professionally prepared leaders in recreation, the Division of Recreation, under the leadership of Eduard Lindemann, joined with the University of Minnesota in 1937 to sponsor a national conference to develop curricula for the training of recreation leaders. Subsequent meetings were held at the University of North Carolina in 1939 and at New York University in 1941. Largely because of these efforts, the professional preparation of recreation personnel became a responsibility of higher education.

A second major program benefiting parks and recreation during the Depression was the Civilian Conservation Corps (CCC). It was created to give employment and vocational training to unemployed young men. The Corps consisted of unmarried males between the ages of 17 and 28; in the nine years it operated (1933-1942), over 3.5 million young men were involved in the program.

The CCC helped several states to establish their state park systems. It built roads, picnic areas, campgrounds, cabins, and hiking and riding trails for local, state, and federal park and recreation areas programs. It also constructed swimming and boating facilities and upgraded the specialized recreation facilities required by the National Park Service, the U.S. Forest Service, and the Work Projects Administration. The efforts of the CCC added significantly to the number of resources available for outdoor recreation pursuits.

Two other Great Depression programs also merit recognition. One was the National Youth Administration, established in 1935, which provided youth with opportunities for part-time employment in recreation programs. It assisted in organizing local recreation training institutes and offered grants-in-aid to high schools and colleges to establish and operate recreation projects. The second project was the Public Works Administration, which concentrated its efforts on the construction of public facilities.

Separate from the New Deal program, but equally significant, were three congressional actions taken in the mid-1930s that increased the role of the federal government in parks and recreation services. All were somewhat a departure from the traditional national park and historic site approach. The first was the creation of Lake Mead, NV, as the first national recreation area in 1936.

The other two were the designation of areas for pleasure driving and aquatic interests. The Blue Ridge Parkway (NC/VA) was the first national parkway begun in 1936. One year later, Congress designated Cape Hatteras, NC, as America's first National Seashore area.

With so many thousands of persons working as recreation and park specialists, the desire for professional identity among parks and recreation personnel increased. Several new professional organizations were established. The Society of Recreation Workers of America, later to become the American Recreation Society, was created in 1937. The following year, Recreation was added as a division of the American Association of Health, Physical Education and Recreation. Various state recreation associations were established at this time, with many of them affiliating with the Society of Recreation Workers of America.

World War II (1941-1945)

The United States was slowly recovering from the Depression when war broke out in Europe in 1939. By 1941, it seemed inevitable that the entire world would be at war. With the bombing of Pearl Harbor in December of that year, the expectation became reality. For the next four years, the preparation and concerns of war dominated all social and economic behaviors. As during World War I, industrial centers expanded, small towns adjacent to military installations were inundated with the arrival of new recruits, and the federal government assumed a greater responsibility for the social behaviors of all.

Among those programs which had a direct bearing upon the lives of the military were the activities of the various branches of the armed forces and the United Service Organization. Each of the armed forces was encouraged to establish recreation programs. Facilities and services for recreation and entertainment were provided at the various military installations. Millions of dollars were expended for their operation. As Meyer and Brightbill (1964) cited, "Never in the history of the armed forces was so much attention given to recreation as a functional part of the total military operation" (p. 20). Six private organizations—the Jewish Welfare Board, the Salvation Army, the National Catholic Community Services, the National Travelers Aid Association, the Young Men's Christian Association, and the Young Women's Christian Association—combined efforts and formed the United Service Organization. It organized camp shows and provided a range of social and recreation services, primarily for the off-duty military. The USO Center became an accepted part of the American landscape. At its peak, the USO served over one million persons a day in some 3,000 locations.

A second private, voluntary association which contributed significantly to the war effort was the American Red Cross. It operated approximately 750 clubs and 250 mobile units throughout the world. Through these programs, hundreds of thousands of servicemen and servicewomen were able to escape, however briefly, the events of war. Whereas the special service programs stressed athletics and theatrical activities, the American Red Cross effort emphasized social programming. Possibly the most significant contribution to the recreation movement at this point was the Red Cross work in military hospitals. Over 1,500 Red Cross workers functioned with a concern for recreation activity with therapeutic value.

One federal program of nonmilitary nature merits mentioning. During the war, the Federal Security Agency established a Division of Recreation within the Office of Community War Services. The Division was responsible for aiding communities to organize, develop, and maintain adequate recreation programs, especially in those areas affected by the war effort. Through Lanham Act grants, the Division of Recreation assisted communities with the construction of facilities and buildings for recreation purposes. Through field representatives, it offered technical assistance and was directly responsible for the establishment of nearly 300 additional permanent, local tax-supported recreation departments in the United States. Many of the key personnel were on loan from the National Recreation Association. One of them, C. K. Brightbill, later became the head of the Division of Recreation (Knapp & Hartsoe, p. 135). The Division strongly advocated the establishment of state and federal recreation services by providing technical assistance.

The Post-World War II Years (1946-1960)

A host of social changes resulting from the war altered the face of America drastically. The changes resulted in a focus on consumerism during the second half of the twentieth century. A series of explosions occurred in such areas as higher education, births, consumptive behavior, automobile and highway construction, the use of gasoline and other forms of fossil fuels, civil rights, and new residential patterns.

Organized recreation and park services were also a part of this explosion. Following the war, hundreds of towns and cities constructed community centers, swimming pools, playgrounds, and athletic facilities as "living war memorials." Tax-supported public recreation systems increased in number, and states gave greater attention to their responsibility in organizing recreation and youth services. Hospitals established therapeutic recreation services, universities created degree programs in parks and recreation, and tourism became a major industry. Americans were on the go, seeking their pleasure and enjoying their new found leisure. The workday and workweek were shortened; vacation periods were lengthened. Not even the disruptive years of the Korean Conflict could delay these changes.

Among the many events which occurred after World War II that helped establish current patterns of behavior and organizational approaches were:

1. the White House Conference on Aging in 1951, which emphasized the role of recreation for a growing population of older citizens.

2. the creation of the National Association of Recreation Therapists as a separate professional body and its joining with the Hospital Section of the American Recreation Society to establish the Council for the Advancement of Hospital Recreation.

3. the Supreme Court decision that made racial segregation in public schools unconstitutional and thereby opened the system to all citizens, regardless of race.

4. the growth of international recreation services which in 1956 resulted in the establishment of the International Recreation Association (now the World Leisure and Recreation Association).

5. the promotion by the United Nations, primarily through its International Office of Labor and World Health Organization, of recreation interests, particularly those related to tourism and the industrial worker.

6. the establishment of Disneyland in 1955 on 150 acres in Anaheim, California. It was the first major theme park and became the model for subsequent theme parks.

7. the public's discovery and use of natural resources for recreation purposes which quickly resulted in overcrowding in public parks and outdoor recreation areas. In response the National Park Service with its Mission 66 project (1956) and the U.S. Forest Service with its Operation Outdoors (1957) began to upgrade and expand federal recreation and park areas.

8. the establishment of the Outdoor Recreation Resources Review Commission (ORRRC) in 1958 by the U.S. Congress. The Commission was asked to provide estimates of the need for outdoor recreation areas for the years 1976 and 2,000. To accomplish this, both the demand for specific forms of outdoor recreation activity had to be considered along with an inventory of the existing resources that might be used to meet those demands. The Commission then suggested directions for responding to new interests and demands.

9. the passing of the Federal Aid Highway Act in 1958 which created the interstate highway system. This network of superhighways encouraged travel and stimulated the growth of an already expanding motel/franchise quick food industry. In a sense, the highways became the playgrounds for millions; vacation travel became synonymous with recreation.

10. the frequent and significant developments within the fields of electronics. By the late 1950s, most Americans had one or more television sets in their homes. There was an expanding market for component high fidelity sound systems; the computer age was beginning.

11. the establishment of the President's Council on Youth Fitness and the authorization of the National Cultural Center for Performing Arts (Kennedy Center)—two programs which furthered the nation's interest in physical fitness and the performing arts.

As a partial response to the increasing demand for trained personnel in parks and recreation, regional recreation and park training institutes were developed. Primary among them were the Great Lakes Training Institute, the Southeastern Institute on Recreation for the Ill and Disabled, and the Southwest Park and Recreation Training Institute. Modifications in recreation curricula also occurred as both the resource-oriented and program-oriented segments of the profession sought to understand each other's view.

Professionalization was a growing concern among those who provided the parks and recreation service. The National Recreation Association no longer spoke for the movement. The American Recreation Society, the American Institute of Park Executives, and the numerous state and local recreation agencies were advocating professionalism and responding to the public's need for information, advice, and technical assistance. The groundwork for the merger of the many professional interests in parks and recreation was being laid. Many local recreation departments and park departments responded to this trend and became departments of parks and recreation.

The Soaring Sixties (1960-1969)

In many ways, the decade of the sixties was a rerun of the 1920s and 1930s with one notable exception—no Great Depression occurred. Instead, there was a tremendous expansion of commercial and outdoor recreation facilities and a mushrooming of youth-serving programs as the children of the postwar baby boom years entered their adolescence. The boating and camping industries became billion-dollar enterprises. Advances in technology were providing climate-controlled homes, home entertainment centers, and a multitude of gadgets guaranteed to increase the "quality of living."

Governmental involvement in parks and recreation also expanded during this period, particularly in the latter half of the decade. The Bureau of Outdoor Recreation (BOR) was established in 1962 in response to one of the recommendations of the Outdoor Recreation Resources Review Commission. Three years later, Congress established the Land and Water Conservation

Fund and charged the BOR with administering it. Those funds enabled local recreation units to acquire and develop land for outdoor recreation purposes.

This was one of many events occurring in the decade which made the system more available to all citizens. Another one was the passage of the Civil Rights Act in 1964. It made segregation illegal; no longer could providers discriminate according to race. Equal opportunity was to exist; the task was to address prejudices and economic deprivation.

To some extent this was accomplished during the Johnson Administration, when Congress enacted a series of legislative actions known as America's "War on Poverty." Among them were the Economic Opportunity Act with its Job Corps and Community Action programs. The Job Corps was very similar to the Civilian Conservation Corps of the 1930s in that it prepared young people for work, frequently in some public service endeavor. The Community Action effort was an attempt to coordinate local public services for the poor and to complement existing services whenever possible. In many instances, recreation services for the poor were provided through this effort. Other acts included: The Older Americans Act (1965) which provided funds for the establishment of Councils on Aging with recreation and leisure services being among the areas designated by the act to be developed by these councils, and The Housing and Urban Development Act of 1965 which authorized several million dollars, in the form of matching monies, to state and local governments for the acquisition and development of open space.

The federal impact on local and state recreation services was felt immediately. With monies available for planning and expanding services, local governmental units embarked on new program directions. Acquisition and development of land and water resources, coupled with planning for the future, gave organized recreation and parks efforts a boost. Thousands of new jobs were created with an accompanying demand for additional recreation and park personnel. New curricula, particularly at the community college level, were established to meet this demand.

By 1966, several major recreation and park organizations had merged to form the National Recreation and Park Association (NRPA). One of NRPA's first undertakings was to assess the recreation and park employment situation. According to the 1967-68 manpower analysis, some 200 universities and colleges were preparing recreation and park specialists in 1967 (National Recreation and Park Association, 1968). Enrollments in these programs exceeded 15,000 majors. The projected need for annual new personnel in 1980 was twice that figure. Although critics of this report questioned its research methodology and validity, all agreed it did accurately reflect the growing importance of parks and recreation.

In addition to the many efforts to expand the services for individuals with disabilities, and disadvantaged individuals during this decade, an ever-increasing concern for outdoor activity, land development, and land use planning was evident in the 1960s. Local beautification projects were encouraged, an action also supported by the Highway Beautification Act, which provided funds for the control of outdoor advertising along certain highways. Furthermore, Congress in 1968 passed the Wild and Scenic Rivers Act and the National Trails System Act thereby providing some protection of those resources.

Technology was creating new opportunities. Boats, trailers, and motorized campers were increasing in both size and number. Americans were taking their urban culture with them to the outdoors and demanding that the outdoors be shaped to fit their interests. Artificial snow and ice makers added to the availability of winter sports; skiing and ice skating became popular pastimes. The interstate highway system was making the parks of the West more accessible to the population centers of the East and Midwest. Gas consumption was up and increasing, while the cost of it remained relatively inexpensive.

The decade of the sixties ended with a question mark. The Vietnam War, the assassinations of President Kennedy, Robert Kennedy, and Martin Luther King, Jr., and the urban riots of 1967 and 1968 suggested a troubled society, that all was not well with the American ethic. Conflicting lifestyles and aspirations particularly between generations, seemed to threaten the stability of American society. Environmental concerns, especially those related to the potential environmental damage done by such recreation vehicles as snowmobiles, dune buggies, and trail bikes were becoming evident. The increasing amount of pollution caused one to wonder about the virtues of material affluence and superabundance. In partial response, the National Environmental Policy Act was passed in 1968, requiring public officials to prepare environmental impact statements before implementing projects, including recreation ones, that might alter environmental and ecological relationships. Meanwhile, attendance at athletic events was increasing, equipment sales were expanding, and people were taking longer and more expensive vacations. Air travel replaced rail travel; international travel became commonplace for millions. Recreation and park services were being challenged to plan for an uncertain future.

Responding to these demands, parks and recreation professionals began to use new managerial approaches to solve administrative and policy problems. The issues of resource use and conservation caused the National Park Service to close some of its areas to automobile traffic until it could fully study the effect of the automobile on the environment. Youth programs took on a new look with community action becoming a major issue. One statistic overlooked by many recreation professionals and planners at the time pertained to the population. During the early sixties the rate of population growth began a significant decline. Only time would tell how significant this shift in growth rate would be.

The Seventies: Regulation and Reaction (1970-1979)

The decade of the seventies was a transitional decade in which the liberalism of the sixties gave way to the conservatism of the eighties. Throughout the decade, a decided move toward more conservative political and social thought was developing, but not evident until the latter third of the decade. The early years were a continuation of the feelings and actions of the late sixties; the Watergate scandal and the subsequent resignation of President Nixon distracted the nation from the more subtle changes which were occurring in our national character.

The beginning years of the 1970s were still filled with concerns for civil rights, the urban poor, and the disadvantaged. Issues of leisure were very much a part of the 1971 White House Conference on Aging. Equal rights for women, concerns for endangered species, and the elimination of poisonous pesticides from the environment gave rise to numerous causes and special interest groups. Many of these concerns resulted in legislative action that restricted or regulated the nation's political, social, and economic behaviors. Federal bureaucracies grew as the government attempted to enforce regulations that would guarantee the rights of all, protect the environment, and assure a continued rate of economic growth and prosperity. To accomplish these goals, Americans paid higher taxes and seemed willing to do so until the effects of the first oil embargo were felt in 1973-74.

During this period of growing regulations, several significant governmental actions occurred that affected parks and recreation. In response to the recreation interests of urban residents, two urban parks (Golden Gate and Gateway East) were established in 1972 by the National Park Service. Thus, the national park system embarked on an urban parks program which was intensified in 1978 when the Congress appropriated 1.2 billion dollars for the improvement of the urban and national park systems. Some conservationists responded with alarm to the establishment of the urban parks program. They felt urban parks were a deviation from the traditional role of the National Park Service and would draw resources away from the national park system, resources which were desperately needed to maintain their quality and fulfill their mandate to protect and preserve.

In matters concerning human rights, governmental action was equally pronounced. The Congress passed the Education for All Handicapped Act in 1974, which guaranteed equal educational opportunity for handicapped youth "in the least restrictive environment." Public Law 94-142 assured persons with disabilities of opportunities for physical education and recreation in the public schools while Public Law 93-112 required that federal buildings or public buildings with federal support be accessible to all citizens. Physical barriers which prevented accessibility were to be eliminated (Blake, 1981). The field of therapeutic recreation services expanded, particularly at the local level where hundreds of park and recreation departments created special program divisions to serve these special populations. The Bureau for the Education of the Handicapped, Office of Education, did much to stimulate the growth of these programs through its financial support of the training of therapeutic recreation personnel.

Commercial recreation enterprises continued to expand during the seventies, as did the private recreation movement. Jogging and other physical fitness activities, tennis, and video games grew in popularity while land acquisition for recreation areas continued to be a primary concern of public recreation officials. The availability of Land and Water Conservation Fund monies on a matching basis encouraged and supported these acquisition interests. Monies were also available for performing arts programs and for the acquisition and renovation of historic areas. In 1978, the Bureau of Outdoor Recreation was given new responsibilities and a new name. It became the Heritage Conservation and Recreation Service. Conservation was important during the Carter Administration and when the Alaska Lands Bill failed in 1978, (*Controversy...*, 1978) President Carter proclaimed 56 million acres of Alaskan lands as national monuments and wildlife refuges, thereby protecting the area from development. Later, in 1980, the Alaska National Interest Lands Conservation Bill was passed by Congress.

By the end of the decade, it was obvious that Americans were growing somewhat weary of bigness including big government, big corporations, and big automobiles and were inclined to do something about it. Escalating gasoline prices, high interest rates, and a seemingly unresponsive bureaucracy were adding to their frustration. They responded in 1978 in California with the enactment of Proposition 13, which restricted the property tax rate. They elected Ronald Reagan in 1980 on a conservative platform and saw the federal government embark on a policy of deregulation.

Professionalism made giant strides during the seventies. Enrollments in parks and recreation curricula increased and by 1980 had reached the enrollment figures projected in 1967 by the NRPA Manpower Study. Accreditation of recreation curricula had become a reality. Thirty college and university curricula had been accredited by the Council on Accreditation, a body established by the National Recreation and Park Association in conjunction with the American Alliance for Health, Physical Education, Recreation and Dance in 1974. Licensing of therapeutic recreation professionals was established when Utah enacted a registration plan for therapeutic recreation specialists. The profession was preparing to write the next page of its history, a history which would have to take into account a new set of attitudes, populations to be served, and approaches to those services.

The Reagan Years: A Decade of Private Action (1981-1990)

Entrepreneurism best describes parks and recreation in the 1980s. Reflecting the general attitudes towards business and government, the private commercial and not-for-profit sectors of the leisure service delivery system prospered. Even the public sector became more businesslike, developing programs and services which were self-supporting or which assured the agency some recovery costs. Pricing and marketing concepts became a part of the leisure studies curricula as did specializations in commercial recreation/resort and tourism management. Some curricula even changed their names to reflect the trend, becoming Departments of Parks, Recreation and Tourism.

The 1980s were also an era of retrenchment with the federal government reducing considerably its involvement in parks and recreation, particularly in the funding of outdoor recreation developments and acquisitions. It abolished the Heritage Conservation and Recreation Service in 1981 thereby leaving parks and recreation with no single agency voice to advocate at the federal level its needs, but it did not loose its interest in outdoor recreation. Responding to Congress' request for an update of the Outdoor Recreation Resources Review Commission's (ORRRC) report, President Reagan established in 1985 the President's Commission on American Outdoors, asking that it complete its work in one year. Unlike ORRRC, the President's Commission did not undertake a national survey or create a special staff. Rather, it brought together personnel from various federal departments and consultants to do its work with former Tennessee Governor and later Secretary of Education Lamar Alexander to head the Commission. The Commission in its report (1987) recommended a variety of private sector approaches including the development of greenways which would address the increasing demand for outdoor recreation experiences (Tindall, 1987).

One of the characteristics of the decade was the decline in student interest in recreation and other human service fields. Social concerns were passé; making money was in vogue. Enrollments in park and recreation curricula dropped except for those specialties embracing entrepreneurialism and therapeutic recreation, the latter being aided considerably by the passage of the Americans with Disabilities Act and the creation of the American Therapeutic Recreation Association and the National Council on Therapeutic Recreation Certification. Furthermore, for the first time in the history of the profession, more females than males were choosing parks and recreation as a major. By the end of the decade, the ratio was two to one (Bialeschki, 1992).

Professionalism continued to be a high priority. Both the National Council for Therapeutic Recreation Certification and the National Recreation and Park Association created certification examinations and pushed for a mandatory requirement that professionals be certified to practice. Both organizations administered their initial exams in 1990 after two years of study and test construction activity (Dateline, 1991). The NRPA/AALR Council on Accreditation continued to refine its standards and approaches. In 1986 it received approval of its effort by the Council On Post-Secondary Accreditation (COPA). COPA's recognition stimulated more interest in universities in making sure their programs were accredited. By the end of the decade, nearly a hundred universities and colleges had accredited curricula.

As had occurred in previous decades, parks and recreation was influenced dramatically by national and international events. The deregulation of the airlines and banking industries helped stimulate the growth of resorts and shopping malls. Conflicts between developers and environmentalists intensified. Under the Reagan and Bush Administrations the national debt soared to nearly four trillion dollars. The impact of the debt, the break-up of the Soviet Union and the cessation of the cold war affected the defense industry, causing huge employment lay-offs. The building boom became the building bust as America entered its longest recessionary period since the Great Depression of the 1930s.

The Nineties: A New Beginning

Although mixed with a sluggish economy, Americans entered the 1990s with a new spirit and direction. Social liberalism once again became popular with society's concern about the welfare of its children, homeless people and its new immigrants (Sessoms & Orthner, 1992; Kunstler, 1992). The woman's movement, failed savings and loans, and the problems associated with an aging infrastructure had had their impact on the political system. So had the aging of the baby boomers, now in their forties. As a result, concerns for health and welfare became more important than national defense. Although some public recreation departments were finding it difficult to provide equitable services in an era of declining financial support, the public continued its interest in recreation. Electronic games, fitness equipment, and short but frequent vacations remained as major recreation expenditures while concerns grew about its youth-at-risk and its need to address diversity. Americans were preparing for the last decade of the twentieth century, one in which the issue of work and leisure would remain central.

Suggestions and Study Guides

1. Talk with someone born in the 1930s and someone born in the 1960s about their play and recreation patterns during their childhood and teen years. How do those activities and patterns differ from yours? In what ways are they similar? What seems to be the major difference between and/or causative factor of the patterns?

2. History can be an exciting subject, especially when the events of the past are seen as precedents for present-day behaviors. Consider and discuss the role that leisure and recreation played in previous generations, such as the games of ancient Rome, the tournaments of the Middle Ages, the theater of Elizabethan England, and the cotillions of the Old South. What are the modern counterparts of these activities, and what appears to be the underlying motivation of each?

3. Look around your community and see how many facilities and buildings were constructed during the 1930s with WPA support and in the 1960s with federal matching fund grants and which serve a recreation and leisure service function. Imagine what your community would be like if these swimming pools, libraries, community buildings, parks, and athletic facilities were not there. Discuss the role of these public investments in the life of your community. Also, consider the importance of the various administrative systems needed to operate the services and programs which utilize these resources.

4. The next time you visit a historic site imagine yourself living in the time when this area or facility achieved its historic significance. What types of recreation behaviors would you have engaged in at that time, and where would you have gone to seek these pleasures? Consider the role of these historic sites and areas as recreation resources and what society can do to increase their potential as "leisure places and spaces."

References

Act of August 25, 1916 (39 Stat 535).

Bialeschki, M. (1992). The state of parks, recreation and leisure studies curricula. *Parks and Recreation, 27*(7), pp. 72-76, 95.

Blake, K. (1981). *Education exceptional pupils.* Reading, MA: Addison-Wesley.

Carls, G. *Outdoor recreation in North America.* Unpublished manuscript.

Ceram, C. (1971). *Gods, graves and scholars,* quoted in Kraus, R. (1971). *Recreation and leisure in modern society.* Englewood Cliffs, NJ: Prentice-Hall.

Chubb, M. & Chubb, H. (1981). *One third of our time?* New York, NY: John Wiley and Sons.

Controversy over Alaska lands conservation proposal. (1978). *Congressional Digest, 57*(12), pp. 289.

Cross, G. (1990). *A social history of leisure since 1600.* State College, PA: Venture Publishing, Inc.

Dare, B., Welton, G., & Coe, W. (1987). *Concepts of leisure in western thought.* Dubuque, IA: Kendall/Hunt.

Dateline. (1991). Certification: A historical perspective. *Parks and Recreation, 26*(10), pp. 91.

De Grazia, S. (1964). *Of time, work and leisure.* New York, NY: Doubleday.

Dickason, J. (1985). 1906: A pivotal year for the playground movement. *Parks and Recreation, 20*(8), pp. 40-45.

Dulles, F. R. (1965). *Recreation in America.* New York, NY: Appleton-Century Crofts.

Goodale, T. & Godbey, G. (1988). *The evolution of leisure.* State College, PA: Venture Publishing, Inc.

Jensen, C. (1977). *Outdoor recreation in America: Trends, problems and opportunities, 3rd ed.,* pp. 18. Minneapolis, MN: Burgess Publishing Co.

Knapp, R. F. & Hartsoe, C. E. (1979). *Play for America*. Arlington, VA: National Recreation and Park Association.

Kraus, R. (1978). *Recreation and leisure in modern society. 2nd ed.* Santa Monica, CA: Goodyear Publishing Company.

Kraus, R. (1990). *Recreation and leisure in modern society. 4th ed.* Glenview, IL: Scott Foresman and Company.

Kunstler, R. (1992). Forging the human connection: Leisure services for the homeless. *Parks and Recreation, 27*(3), pp. 42-45.

Meyer, H. & Brightbill, C. (1964). *Community recreation, 3rd ed.* Englewood Cliffs, NJ: Prentice-Hall.

National Recreation and Park Association. (1968). *Supply/demand study (Professional and pre-professional recreation and park occupations).* Washington, DC: Author.

Oliva, L. (1985). A Boston sand garden kicks off the playground movement. *Parks and Recreation, 20*(8), pp. 36-39.

Pieper, J. (1965). *Leisure, the basis of culture.* New York, NY: Random House.

Rainwater, C. (1922). *The play movement in the United States.* Chicago, IL: The University of Chicago Press.

Sessoms, H. D. (1993). *Eight decades of leadership development.* Arlington, VA: National Recreation and Park Association.

Sessoms, H. D. & Orthner, D. (1992). Our growing invisible populations *Parks and Recreation, 27*(8), pp. 62-65.

Tilgher, A. (1958). *Homo faber.* Chicago, IL: Henry Regnery Co.

Tindall, B. (1987). PACO Implications for state and local governments. *Parks and Recreation, 22*(9), pp. 45-49, 73.

CHAPTER THREE

The Conceptual Base of Leisure and Recreation

The function, value and relationship of leisure, work, recreation, and play has been the subject of many publications. Each are critical concepts to those who study and/or manage recreation and leisure service delivery systems. Society has long held these activities to be important and has ascribed to each a variety of benefits and functions. No universally agreed upon definitions of work, leisure, recreation, or play exist.

In this chapter, attention is focused on these terms and their relative importance to the park and recreation profession. These concepts undergird and give meaning to the park and recreation movement; the value of what professionals do is directly related to the value that society places upon the function of each of these behaviors.

Social Values

According to sociologists, social values are patterns of behaviors and beliefs held by society to be important to its welfare. Values are reflected in desired experiences and are manifested in the expressed preferences of people. Values give directions for choosing courses of action and are used as a means for evaluating the relative importance of individual acts and society's social structures.

Each of us has different perceptions of what is important and what life ought to be. These perceptions are the product of experience as well as socio-economic and cultural backgrounds. In a heterogeneous society a multitude of value structures exist, yet all of them are influenced by a dominant value structure.

No independent system for addressing leisure values exists. Individual recreation behaviors and priorities are modified by personal, social, and cultural expressions. The dominant value system influences recreation and leisure. The system also reflects the organizational approaches that may be taken in providing park and recreation opportunities for the public.

The list of societal values is too long to mention, but a few dominant values play a critical role in the shaping of leisure behaviors and the leisure service delivery system. Among them are the values of action, vitality, individualism, civil liberties, materialism, and group identity. For example, Western society favors goal-oriented action. Time is of greatest value when something is accomplished; keeping busy is important. Initially, this value was demonstrated in the need to work, but it is also reflected in consumptive activities and behaviors related to recreation. Then, too, we value vitality. Those individuals who are more active are more vital because they can produce and consume more goods and services. A fascination with physical fitness and with physical activity as a high-priority form of recreation expression is directly related to the value of vitality and the need to do something during free time.

Many Americans have long considered the frontier style of life essential to their well-being and have restricted programs and structures which might inhibit individual behavior. Although self-reliance and freedom are important, freedom requires responsibility; the line between individualism and the social good may be clouded. Park and recreation professionals, for example, have often experienced ambivalence in enforcing norms of behavior which inhibit self-expression yet are necessary to protect the environment and the rights of others. Closely related to the concept of individualism is the notion of civil rights. Americans believe in the right of equal opportunity.

Materialism is an approach to life which frequently allows for individual worth to be judged in terms of material possessions. The value of materialism is supported by the desire for immediate gratification. Many individuals can enjoy immediate pleasures through deferred payment by charging goods against future income. The boom in recreation equipment and apparel, accompanied by an increased demand for recreation areas and facilities, has been one result of materialism and consumptive behavior.

Group identity may be another way of describing conformity. Being like others and being liked by others appear to hold great importance to many people. Group identity may be the prime motivator behind the creation of private clubs, associations, and groups. The United States has many associations and organizations. This tendency toward group security and identity, however, does not require conformity to a single set of values or group standards. A diversity of groups and lifestyles exists within society. A complex delivery system has been created to accommodate these many interests. Americans seem to want security; people want to express their individuality but feel most secure with others who share the same definition and expression of that individuality.

This Hispanic Festival is one example of ethnic celebrations organized by the Maryland National Capitol Park and Planning Commission.

M-NCPPC Photo by Steve Abramowitz

Numerous shifts have occurred in the American value system. Some of the values formerly held to be important now seem to be less critical. They are being replaced by other patterns and beliefs. The greatest shifts, however, have not been in the values themselves but in the way they are expressed, and the consequences are now being seen. For example, pollution is a result of a consumer-oriented society. When there is high productivity, few rewards for thrift, and constant encouragement by advertisers to "pamper yourself," ego-centric and immediate gratification behaviors are encouraged.

Self-indulgence and a "no deposit, no refund" philosophy are natural by-products of these actions. Problems arise when the search for pleasure leaves in its wake pollution, a decline of quality, a loss of order, and an increasing number of legislative regimentations. Thrift may reduce waste and pollution, but it may also discourage economic growth. What do we value?

A second interesting and complicating factor is the relationship of recreation and park services and social values. Although the dominant value system affects all groups, many subsystems of values each have an impact. Differing value patterns and expressions often exist between urban and rural groups; the priorities of upper and middle-income people are not necessarily the same as those held by lower-income individuals. Some people express their affluence through housing and recreation equipment, while others enjoy flashy clothing and package tours. Both the activities pursued and the means by which they are pursued are a function of the value system.

Since all societies allow and promote play and recreation behavior, play must serve some social function. People in society place labels upon an activity and determine what activities are play and recreation and which ones are work. In modern societies, those experiences for which one is monetarily rewarded or that result in some good with monetary value tend to be valued and labeled work. When these activities are pursued for their own ends, they are generally referred to as vocations, hobbies, or recreation. Likewise, those activities which tend to be nonpurposeful and produce no tangible goods or earnings are labeled play or recreation unless they become commercialized and then are considered work. Professional sports and the performing arts are illustrations of this commercialized phenomenon.

The role of values is multidimensional. If society is concerned about pollution and increases the relative importance of the value of conservation, then parks and recreation agencies tend to allocate more of their resources for maintenance and control in outdoor areas. If civil liberties is an issue and people are concerned about equal opportunity, then parks and recreation professionals will emphasize more program efforts and activities for people who are disadvantaged. If efficiency is the key and crime in the streets a concern, then cost accounting and law enforcement become important administrative preoccupations of parks and recreation professionals. Values along with administrative and program practices are intertwined as each affects the other.

Leisure and Work: Definitions and Significance

Each generation has asked the question, "Why do we exist?" Most people in this industrial world generally contend that a human being's function is to live a useful and productive life. For several hundred years, paid work generally has embodied all of the duties and virtues of existence. All other experiences were considered secondary or supportive of work. Work has allowed people to be active, to dominate the environment, to have power and status, and to progress.

Social structure has been built around the notion of paid work. Schools, for example, try to teach the tools necessary to survive in the industrial world as well as socialize children to adhere to work schedules and earn good grades and gold stars (the forerunners of wages and salaries). Religious institutions have provided the moral backdrop for social actions and patterns. Since the days of the Reformation, idleness has been suspect while the production of marketable goods has been the criterion of maturity and salvation. Government, too, has supported the work value system. Laws against vagrancy, for example, uphold the virtue of work. We have Departments of Commerce and Labor at the federal level but no Department of Leisure.

Industrial society's need for organizations and compatible work activities led to the concept of free time versus work time. With this division, activities were evaluated according to when they took place and to what end. Activities that did not result in monetary gain or were pursued by children were labeled "play," while those that brought profit and were done during the "workday" were given the honorable title of "work." Leisure time and recreation behaviors were assumed to be the rewards of work but were never given equal status as valuable activities. Neither was equal status given to the tasks performed by females; work at home did not generate income. Because nonwork activities had little status, women and children were not given the same privileges and status afforded males, at least not until after World War II. Perhaps this valuation of work explains why it has taken so long for acceptance of the attitude that leisure and recreation experiences could be pursued for their own right, not for some extrinsic reason.

Until the advent of mass production, leisure was essentially a philosophical ideal. As discussed earlier, the ancient Greeks and Romans thought of leisure as freedom from obligation and the state of being in which people were truly themselves free from all encumbrances. One was at leisure when involved in experiences which were totally his or her choice. Leisure was defined in terms of one's motivation, and the dream of all was to have leisure. No guilt was associated with materially nonproductive activity. In Greek and Roman days, work was considered a drudgery and an obligation that must be fulfilled, but it was never viewed in terms of activity that had to be performed in a specific time frame such as the eight-hour workday.

Clock time is a modern concept, a product of the Industrial Revolution and the need to determine the value of labor. Clock time became a way of organizing the day and integrating the interdependent elements of an industrial order. It provided a mechanism for scheduling activities, for measuring and rewarding behavior, and for assembly and control.

Leisure as freedom gave way to leisure as free or discretionary time after the Industrial Revolution. Leisure became synonymous with nonwork time, time earned through work, or time freed from work to be used for whatever pursuits one desired. Rather than being viewed as polar extremes in a context of obligation, work and leisure became polar extremes in a context of time. One could not be at leisure if one were engaged in activities for which payment was received. Leisure activities or those activities done during one's free time, were rationalized as being essential to the work process because they provided relaxation and refreshment from labor. Recreation and leisure experiences were seen in support of work rather than as ends in themselves. This view was supported by those who subscribed to the compensation theory, which holds that recreation pursuits are motivated by those needs not met through work (Witt & Bishop, 1970). See Figure 3-1.

Figure 3-1
Two Approaches to a Typical Workday

(1) As viewed from a time/activity set approach (segmented)

Work	Subsistence Time (sleeping, eating, etc.)	Free Time
8 Hours	12 Hours	4 Hours

(2) As viewed form an attitude approach (holistic)

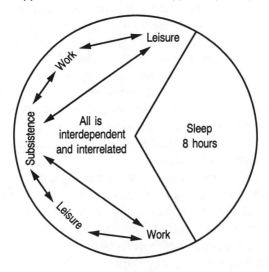

The dividing of life into time segments inevitably destroyed the holistic and integrative aspects of agrarian existence. Priorities of activity, such as how time was to be used, were established. Activities for which one received payment gained the greatest social support; those which tended to contribute to the life of the community, to family life, or result in personal development and growth were second in desirability. Finally, activities which resulted in personal pleasure and for which no visible material or socially beneficial outcomes seemed to exist were disdained and discouraged. Free-time activities took on legitimacy only when they resulted in increased productivity. Time and money appeared to be one and the same.

Something interesting happened as a result of this division of life into work and leisure time. As more free time became available, it became the setting in which people could express their personalities and demonstrate their worth to others. In the words of Thorstein Veblen, leisure became the time for conspicuous display and, in some instances, conspicuous consumption (Veblen, 1899). This display has taken many forms such as the kind of car an individual drives, the type of house, or the size of one's boat and motor. These acts and objects assumed status value, but the ultimate conferral of status was work, one's occupation. Even though work was becoming a drudgery for many people, it had to be done to enjoy those activities which provided opportunities to express one's personality. Work remained central. This attitude began to change somewhat after World War II. For many blue-collar workers, leisure time became equal in value to work; work as an end in itself was questioned. A new value system, which stressed leisure as well as work, emerged. Americans were entering the postindustrial age (see Table 3-1).

Table 3-1
Views of Work and Leisure in Three Eras

	PREINDUSTIRAL	*PRESENT*	*POSTINDUSTRIAL*
The concepts are viewed in terms of:	Attitude	Time	Experiences
The concepts are valued in terms of:	Work to support leisure	Leisure activities support work habits	Both are needed for societal and personal growth
The concepts are:	Intertwined (integrated)	Operationally defined (time and activity)	Intertwined (integrated)
Life is viewed as:	Holistic	Segmented	Holistic

Contemporary Perspectives on Leisure and Work

As stated previously there is no single definition of leisure. It may be defined as an attitudinal state of being, time, activity, or as an integrated experience. Preindustrial societies viewed work and leisure as attitudes toward existence with work seen as obligatory activity and leisure as freedom from obligation. With industrialization came two other definitions of work and leisure. One defined work and leisure in terms of the time in which an activity occurs; the other focused upon the nature of the activity. Definitions of time and activity allowed for scientific inquiry into the measuring of leisure time and leisure behaviors, and for the opportunity to plan and program for leisure. The emerging view of leisure is that attitudes, time, and activities all integrate into the experiences that result in a desired quality of life through work and leisure that each individual seeks.

State of Mind

Contemporary writers defining leisure as a state of being are expressing a view held by most classic scholars and those who interpret life according to the motives of the actors. In the words of Sebastian De Grazia (1962):

> Leisure is freedom from the necessity of being occupied. This includes freedom from the necessity to labor, but it could also embrace any activity one finds necessary to perform, but would fain be free of...Leisure is a state of being in which activity is performed for its own sake or as its own end (pp. 14-15).

John Neulinger (1976) described leisure in a similar fashion, holding that "pure leisure" is intrinsically motivated and is the opposite of the extrinsically motivated work/job. According to Neulinger, "Pure leisure requires freedom in the sense of absence of external control but implies the condition of being able to enjoy satisfaction derived from intrinsic rewards without having to pay attention to potential extrinsic ones" while the work/job activity is "engaged in by necessity and under constraint with no reward in or of itself, but only through a payoff resulting from it" (p. 16). Both Neulinger and De Grazia reflect the classical view that one is at leisure or at work depending upon one's motivation (obligation, rewards) for the activity. John Kelly (1982, 1983, 1987) has also written extensively about the importance of freedom and constraint as they pertain to leisure. The leisure experience, according to Kelly, is more likely to occur when one has a high sense of freedom, when one is "in control," and when the experience is unrelated to one's daily work or obligations. Other researchers (Kleiber, 1979; Crandall, 1980; Mannell, Zuzanek, & Larson, 1988) have discussed state of mind in terms of one's locus of control. That is, when people make choices, they either feel in control of their existence or they perceive that their choices and behaviors are controlled by external factors. Leisure, by definition, is intrinsically decided; therefore, the locus of control is self.

Leisure as Time

When work is defined as the time for which one is paid for an activity, leisure becomes synonymous with free time. It is time freed from work. For homemakers, leisure is freedom from housework and childcare although these activities, often defined as social support work, are frequently not rewarded in the same way as is paid work. In the "leisure as time" context, leisure is earned and may be used at the discretion of the laborer. Work and leisure are polar ends of a time-use continuum; between them is that block of time which is required for personal subsistence. Economists and sociologists tend to define leisure as time. The earlier writings of Joffre Dumazedier (1967) and the time budget studies of John Robinson (1977) and Alexander Szalai (1972) relied upon this concept of leisure. The obvious difficulty with defining leisure in a time context is having to accept a segmented view of behavior; each activity is separate and distinct from every other activity. It emphasizes the time in which activity occurs rather than the motives for and interactions of those activities. In addition, for some people, especially parents, one is seldom free from social support obligations and little time is considered "free."

Leisure as Activity

Leisure may be defined as an activity pursued for pleasure. Its proponents conclude that since certain activities are frequently engaged in during periods of free time for the pleasure derived from those experiences, and since one is not paid to pursue those activities, those activities must be intrinsically motivated and intrinsically "recreational." In this view, leisure and recreation are similarly defined with both concepts being operationalized in terms of activity sets such as sports, games, dance, and social activities (Goodale & Godbey, 1988). See Table 3-2.

Table 3-2
Americans' Use of Leisure Time by Activity
(mean hours per week)

Activity	Total Population			Male			Female		
	1985	1975	1965	1985	1975	1965	1985	1975	1965
Total	**40.1**	**38.3**	**34.5**	**41.1**	**38.6**	**34.4**	**39.6**	**38.3**	**34.4**
TV	15.1	15.2	10.5	15.7	16.2	11.7	14.5	14.1	9.3
Visiting	4.9	5.5	6.6	5.0	5.1	5.8	4.8	5.7	7.5
Talking	4.3	2.3	2.6	3.5	1.9	1.6	5.1	2.7	3.6
Traveling	3.1	2.6	2.7	3.4	2.8	3.0	3.0	2.4	2.4
Reading	2.8	3.1	3.7	2.7	3.0	4.2	2.9	3.3	3.3
Sports/Outdoors	2.2	1.5	0.9	2.9	2.3	1.4	1.5	0.8	0.5
Hobbies	2.2	2.3	2.1	1.9	1.6	1.4	2.6	3.0	2.8
Adult Education	1.9	1.6	1.3	2.2	2.1	1.6	1.6	1.3	0.9
Thinking/Relaxing	1.0	1.1	0.5	1.2	1.0	0.2	0.9	1.2	0.6
Religion	0.8	1.0	0.9	0.6	0.8	0.7	1.0	1.3	1.0
Cultural Events	0.8	0.5	1.1	0.8	0.3	1.3	0.8	0.6	0.9
Clubs/Organizations	0.7	1.2	1.0	0.8	0.9	0.8	0.6	1.5	1.2
Radio/Recording	0.3	0.5	0.6	0.4	0.6	0.7	0.3	0.4	0.4

Source: Americans Use of Time Project, University of Maryland. *American Demographics*, November, 1990.

For the most part, leisure inventory schedules and activity lists tend to include those pursuits that society defines as "recreational." Both leisure activities and recreation activities are assumed to be pursued during one's free time, and typically, in environments set aside for those pursuits. Since golfing generally occurs during one's free time, golfing was defined as a leisure or recreation activity and the golf course as a recreation environment. Also, those activities related to golfing or that normally occurred at the golf course or clubhouse were also viewed as leisure activities. The natural extension of this view was to assume that one could only be at leisure or recreate when in the leisure environment or at the recreation facility during periods of free time.

An Integrated View of Leisure as an Experience

Both the *leisure-as-activity* and *leisure-as-time* notions deny the qualitative aspects of the leisure experience. They also tend to deny a holistic nature. They assume behavior is segmented and stimulated by distinct and separate motives. They are operational and functional, but simplistic. Human behavior is more complex than acknowledged by these two views. For many, the motives which give rise to work and the satisfactions derived from fulfilling one's obligations are no different from those which give rise to leisure expressions. Likewise, leisure activities are not restricted to one set of environments or to predetermined, designated time periods. Consequently, a new understanding and definition of leisure has emerged. It is couched in the attitudes of a postindustrial society where work and leisure assume equal importance as experiences for the individual and for society (Samdahl, 1991).

The emerging view of leisure is an integrated one. It recognizes that no activity is inherently work or leisure, that work or leisure may take place in any time frame, that both are functions of attitude or state of being, and that they occur in any setting, time of day, or day of the week. Leisure is a personal experience that is conditioned by the values of society. The view of leisure as an integrated experience also acknowledges that leisure occurs during activity or at least is expressed as an activity, but is not an activity in itself. The view acknowledges that society tends to view certain activities as work or leisure and has organized itself to foster those experiences. This dynamic concept of leisure accepts the integrative and intangible facets of leisure in a world where the clock still holds an important role in structuring experiences. The concept also acknowledges the meanings and purposes of play and recreation.

Theories of Play and Recreation

Many attempts have been made to explain the meaning and purpose of play and recreation. At first, attention was given to the study of play as it occurred in animals, then play among children, and finally play in recreation and in the daily lives of all people, both children and adults. Play is a subject of interest to biologists, physiologists, psychologists, sociologists, and educators, as well as those who identify themselves as recreation and park professionals.

The theoretical basis upon which the recreation and park movement rests stems from society's notions of play. In a sense, parks and recreation systems exist because of the play impulse; parks and recreation professionals provide the environments and opportunities for selected play and recreation expressions. Theories of play have given direction to recreation programs, to the design and forms of facilities and equipment, and to the rationale for the importance of recreation and leisure in society.

The term "play" stems from the Anglo-Saxon words *plegian* and *plegan* and from the German *pfegen,* which meant to take care of, or bestir, oneself. Play has been used to describe the free, natural, engaging, and satisfying activities of the young. It is synonymous with amusement and diversion to many people. Play is universal; there are no societies in which the young do not play. It may be that people never cease to play, only that play behavior is refined and described by some other label. Play is such a generalized term that many behaviors are included in its definition. For example, people go to see a "play," "play" a musical instrument, are in a "playful mood, and are "at play."

The term "recreation" stems from the Latin *recreare,* which meant to re-create, restore, and renew. It is most frequently used to describe the play activities of adults, although some people define it as being distinctly different from play. The line which distinguishes the two concepts is thin. Both are engaging forms of expression that are freely chosen without concern for external gain or achievement, but for the satisfaction derived from "playing." Both are self-contained experiences with intrinsic rewards.

The understanding of play and recreation is changing. The answer to the question "Why do we play?" is endless; each set of answers is always temporary and relative to its time and situation. Because play and recreation behaviors are only part of the overall pattern of human expression, the theories offered as explanations for them are rarely different from the theories offered to explain behavior in general (see Table 3-3). Recreation and play theories should always be considered in the context of the history and culture in which they were formulated and offered.

Earliest Theories

Prior to the emergence of scientific research, most human behavior was explained in terms of "the spirit." One played "when the spirit moved him or her," just as one supposedly committed an evil deed when possessed by an evil spirit. Explanations for all behavior were simple and direct. This view changed with the coming of scientific methods and the need to have testable hypotheses to describe and predict action.

Table 3-3 Basic Play Theories

THEORY	PROPONENT(S)	ESSENCE	COMMENTS
Surplus or Superfluous Energy	Schiller, Spencer	Play results from the energy not needed to stay alive and reproduce. It is an outlet for surplus energy.	Views play as aimless, which is questionable. Does not account for playing to the point of exhaustion. Offers no explanation of the differences in forms of play among the various species of animal life.
Preparation for Life	Groos, et al.	Play is instinctive and life preparatory. It allows for practice of those skills necessary for survival.	Attempts to explain the form which play takes, but leaves no explanation of adult play.
Recapitulation	Hall	People repeat, through play, the activities their ancestors experienced (running, jumping, throwing and the like); heredity is a large factor.	Does not explain progression in play and tends to ignore or refute the new forms taken by play. Contributes to the attempt to classify culture by cycles or eras, which is debatable.
Instinct	James, McDougall, et al.	Play is wholly instinctive and based on automatic impulses: a result of drive, appetite, and inner urge; play instinct common among humans and perhaps other forms of animal life.	There is disagreement as to what constitutes an instinct in human beings. How can one distinguish the acquired from the innate? How can one distinguish between instinct and impulses or reflexes?
Relaxation	Patrick	Play is pleasurable and sought for its own sake; it is a release from work, compulsion, and the struggle to live; play results in its own satisfactions; it relieves stresses and strains of the individual and is a natural change from work since it refreshes, replenishes, and restores energy.	Applies mainly to play and recreation of adults but inadequate in explaining the play of children.
Self-Expression	Mitchell, Mason, (since modified and refined by others)	Play is the natural urge for action. This theory recognizes the nature and capacity of humans, their anatomical and physiological structure, their psychological inclinations, and their desire for self-expression. Accordingly, self-expression is a supreme need.	Widely accepted and seemingly plausible but it provides no explanation of, or accounting for, play other than that motivated by self-expression. Fails to consider other motives.

Theory	Theorists	Description	Evaluation
Catharsis	GutsMuths	Play is an outlet for the confined emotions; a release for feelings which might otherwise remain suppressed and harmful.	Leaves unanswered the same kinds of questions as does the Surplus Energy Theory.
Compensation and Sublimation	Slavson	Recreation and play behaviors are means of meeting unmet needs and wishes. When work and other activities do not allow for fulfillment, play serves as a compensatory device. It allows the organism to interact with the social and psychological environment in a pleasurable, acceptable way.	This theory assumes the presence of substitute behaviors, each with equal potential for fulfilling unmet needs and wishes. Also, it holds that play is a socially acceptable outlet for certain psychic expressions but seems to exclude the play of children because, for them, play is a way of life.
Developmental and Learning	Erikson, Piaget	There are normal sequences of play experiences basic to the development of the organism. Play is a societal form for the socializing of the young, and through play, children come to know themselves, their relationship to others, and the world in which they live. Play expressions are tied to intellectual and social development; its forms are conditioned by society.	Mastery is the essential element of this theory. It does not explain the play behavior of adults, which seems to be motivated by pleasure seeking and which occurs after the organism has matured. Also, it does not explain the cultural difference of play.
Cultural Determinism	Mead, Huizinga, Caillois	This theory does not offer an explanation for play behavior but cites play as a motivation force in the development of a civilization and a reflector of the culture. To the determinists, play is more than a biological act, it serves social and cultural purposes. Play is viewed as a basic socialization tool.	This theory is important to the development of modern concepts of play but lacks an explanation for why one plays. It is also culturally biased toward Western man's concepts of civilization. The focus is upon society's use of play, not the reasons for universal forms of expression.
Modern Concepts: Arousal and Stimulus-Response	Berlyne, White, Csikzentmihalyi	These theories acknowledge play as an interaction between the environment and the internal dynamics of the organism. Accordingly, one plays to seek an optimum level or balance. Play is an arousal-seeking and maintenance activity and allows for the demonstration of competencies.	The modern theories integrate many of the strong features of several earlier concepts. They avoid the labeling process and cite play as action motivated by the desire to achieve the optimal state. Arousals and exploration are central behaviors to these theorists. Play accommodates these needs.

All theories have consequences: (1) they offer a reason for the observed behavior and stimulate questions about those behaviors and the adequacy of the theory explaining them; and (2) they also become a part of the folk knowledge of the people and remain as a functioning dynamic long after the theory has been replaced by another or even disproven by new information. For example, most people no longer believe behavior is motivated by "the spirit," yet people still talk about playing when "the spirit moves them." Many scientific explanations have been offered during the past hundred years with some proven and others disproven. All remain a part of knowledge and literature and continue to serve as explanations and justifications of actions.

According to Michael Ellis (1973), at least fifteen theories of play can be identified. The essential ingredient to all of them is an explanation for this universal form of expression. Basically, these theories can be grouped into four major schools of thought. They are the physiological (biologic/genetic) theories, the psychological theories, the sociological theories, and the contemporary (psycho-socio-physio) theories.

Physiological Theories

The earliest explanations of play stressed genetic and biological factors. These theories, offered during the latter half of the nineteenth century, reflected much of the thinking of the Darwinians who ascribed all human behaviors to genetics. Schiller and Spencer stressed the role of superfluous physical energy and instincts. Human play was correlated with animal play; Groos concluded that children played because they were genetically programmed for that activity, that it was nature's way of developing the necessary skills for survival, and that they would cease to play or modify their forms of play when it was no longer needed. These theories suggested that children had little to say about what they were going to play since those determinations were biologically and genetically set. Some of the modern notions of letting children "play" to drain off their energies, or thinking that all boys should play sports because "that is what males naturally do," stem from these early explanations of play.

As the inadequacies of the biological explanations became apparent, new schools of thought developed. The first of these were the psychological-biological theories that suggested people had certain basic innate needs and drives which had to be met. These needs could be fulfilled in a variety of ways with play being one of them. Play was assumed to be a compensatory and cathartic activity and a way of releasing energies and psychic tensions, especially for adults. Work was tension-producing and play was the opposite; therefore, play was needed to provide an emotional balance. G. W. T. Patrick was among the first to recognize the importance of play for adults, suggesting that it was necessary for relaxation, that workers needed the pleasures which come from recreation, and that play was not an activity exclusive to children.

Psychological Theories

With the growing awareness of the role played by the environment in shaping behavior, new explanations of the origin and function of play were offered. Many of the early psychological theorists were influenced by the writings of Sigmund Freud; later theorists tended to embrace the views of the developmental psychologists. Both schools of thought cited the relationship of play to growth and development and acknowledged the interaction between play, which was motivated by inner drives and urges, and the social control of society.

One of the more interesting Freudian analyses of play was given by S. R. Slavson (1948), who held that society had legitimized certain forms of play that allowed the individual to deal with internal conflicts and to express basic urges. For example, the death wish might be accommodated and released through automobile racing, whereas exhibitionist tendencies might be handled through acting and dramatic performances. Instead of attacking someone when frustrated, one can hit a ball or chop some wood. Slavson may be the father of activity analysis since he was one of the first to relate specific needs or actions to specific play forms.

Developmental psychologists, Erik Erikson (1950) and Jean Piaget (1962) cited the role of play in the developmental process. Erikson stated that play was essential for the establishment of self and that certain types of play were critical to certain stages of development. He said that pleasures first came from being physically able to engage in activity; later, as the child develops, he or she derives pleasure from being able to manipulate physical objects. Then, in the third stage, the child learns to deal with social relationships through play. In all stages, it is the ability to master that satisfies and moves the process forward. For adults, Erickson suggested play is an escape from reality, but also a means of continuing the developmental process.

Piaget (1962) also acknowledged the development sequence of growth and the role of play, stating that children go from the random and symbolic stages of play to games, as they move through their own developmental process. According to Piaget, play through games, especially, is necessary for the intellectual development of the child. Through play the child learns to assimilate ideas and behavior, makes them a part of his or her own existence, and accommodates the world by adjusting to the external order of things.

Many questions are raised by the developmental theories. To what extent do specific forms of play influence or result in specific behavior? Can activities be used to accomplish specific goals and objectives such as therapy? If so, can play be prescribed as treatment? It is apparent from the study of primates that play is a needed ingredient in the emotional and sexual development of apes. Does the same hold true for humans? Can we ascertain where an individual is in his or her development by the games and activities he or she plays?

Sociological Explanations

Although some sociologists wrote about the role of play earlier in the twentieth century, most sociologists did not devote much attention to it until George Herbert Mead discussed its role in the socialization of young children in 1932. At that point, play became an interesting area of study and has remained so to some extent today. Sociologists, in general, do not attempt to explain why people play, but focus upon the forms of play and its role in maintaining social groups and social organizations. They assume that play is human and institutional, natural and useful, and serves definite societal functions. According to sociological theory, play and recreation are necessary for the maintenance of the social structure; consequently, play reflects the values and controls of society. In a sense, sociologists offer not an explanation for play but statements about its consequences, whereas the psychologists are interested in the motives or drives leading to play.

Possibly no sociologist did more to demonstrate the relationship of play to social development than did Mead (1963). According to him, play is second only to language in the development of the social self. In play, children are allowed to explore various social roles and learn the ethic and morals of a society. This is done through fantasy play; the child assumes and acts out various roles such as father, mother, cowpoke, or firefighter. It is also done through games, since the very nature of the game itself requires the player to "play by the rules" and come to grips with his or her role and the role of others playing the same game.

Whereas Mead wrote of play as a contributor to the socialization of the child, Roger Caillois (1961) discussed its significance in the structuring of civilizations. According to him, play is a social determiner and may be used as an index of social development. Caillois analyzed the play behaviors of various cultures and civilizations and observed the dominant patterns in each. In his scheme there are four major forms of play: *agon* (competition), *alea* (chance), *ilinx* (vertigo), and *mimicry* (simulation). Each type of play is found in every civilization, but advanced civilizations emphasize the games of chance and competition, whereas declining or more primitive civilizations stress the games of vertigo and mimicry.

According to Caillois (1961), play is distinctive and has six basic characteristics:

1. It is separate from other activities and is always acknowledged as such by the players when they begin playing ("Let's play golf." "Let's play hide-and-seek." "Let's play chase, and you're it.").
2. It is uncertain in its outcome with the results being left to the strategy and actions of the player.
3. It is make-believe and enjoys its own reality.

4. It is nonproductive in that no goods are produced nor wealth exchanged (Caillois would not consider art as play).
5. It is governed by rules, and players get in difficulty when they attempt to change the rules during the course of the game or fail to specify what the rules are before the game begins.
6. It is free and unobligated (pp. 9-10).

One of the more recent concerns of sociology as it relates to play behavior is the difference in participation rates of males and females as well as individuals from various socioeconomic, ethnic, and racial backgrounds. The Civil Rights and Women's Movements in the United States have underlined the need to examine whether all individuals have equal opportunities for play and recreation participation and benefits and to determine if there are patterns related to these demographic factors. If so, to what extent are these culturally induced? And what can society do to make sure that the values of equal opportunity are being evidenced and instilled in play behavior?

For parks and recreation systems, the sociological explanations of play are most useful as they emphasize the social functioning of activity and give direction and explanation for the programs offered, the facilities provided and the types of activities scheduled.

Contemporary Concepts

The more modern concepts of play and recreation are a blending of the physiological, psychological, and sociological views into a single explanation. Today's theories hold play to be necessary for human development; play is necessary for the total functioning of the organism and is caused by the need to interact with the environment at an optimum level. Further, play and recreation, as well as leisure, are essential for contributing to the quality of life of individuals, communities, and societies.

Several contemporary writers have explanations and theories of significance for students of play and recreation behavior such as the social psychologists and the cognitive behavioralists. The former group has identified a variety of motives or satisfactions which they feel "drive" leisure behaviors. Among them are the satisfactions that come from adventure, being a part of a group, learning something new, expressing one's creativity, engaging in fantasy, and/or experiencing solitude (Tinsley & Kass, 1979; Crandall, 1980). These theorists argue that leisure experiences are satisfying because of the qualities inherent in leisure; consequently, they hold, research should be focused on the attributes of the leisure experience, not its determinants (Mannell, Zuzanek, & Larson, 1988). The behavioralist school tends to do the latter, citing that responses are conditioned by experience and the stimuli perceived.

Csikzentmihalyi's (1975; 1990) work with "flow" focuses upon a social psychological response to the environment as a challenging set of relationships and elements. He stresses the importance of the *peak* experience, which occurs when one's skills are equal to a challenge. There are eight characteristics of the flow or peak experience. They include clear goals and immediate feedback, a merging of action and awareness, a sense of potential control, a feeling of "here and now," an absence of self-consciousness, a distorted sense of time, intrinsic motivations and the opportunity to match one's skills to the challenge. In the peak or flow experience, the organism is totally involved and the ideal homeostasis is achieved. When the situation (stimulus) is no longer challenging (boring) or exceeds the skill level of the individual (produces anxiety), the response is either to discontinue or not engage in it or change the activity to become manageable. If the game is too complex to play, for example, an individual either develops the skills necessary to play it, does not play the game, or modifies its rules so it is within the range of competency. Csikzentmihalyi cautions, however, that playing does not necessarily guarantee that one will experience flow.

Some contemporary theorists (Berlyne, 1960) have focused more on the role of the environment and the need for sensory input and stimulation while others have concentrated on satisfaction which comes from exploration and learning (White, 1959). Their views are important to parks and recreation professionals since they give direction and a rationale for the design of programs and facilities as well as the scheduling of activities. Programs must be dynamic, challenging within the limits of the participants, held in stimulating and satisfying environments, and offered in a developmental sequence (Wallach, 1983).

Not all theories of play are presented here, nor is the discussion of play a comprehensive one. What has been attempted is a demonstration of the importance of theory to current understandings of play, to the design of recreation programs and services, and to the methods by which opportunities are offered for the recreation/play experience. Parks and recreation planners should pay attention to the writings of the theorists who have much to say about environmental design, programming sequence, and the relationship between skill level and challenge.

Although significant differences exist among the theories, several points of agreement are evident. For example, all of the theories conceive of play as action rather than inaction or idleness. Action does not necessarily mean vigorous physical action, but it does imply the expending of energies in the play pursuit, whether they be psychological, physical, or emotional. In most instances, play requires an individual to be active on several levels of expression. Also, nearly all of these theories suggest that play is pleasurable and somewhat motivated by the satisfactions derived from the experience; otherwise, the activities would not be continued.

The consequences of play are numerous. Play may assist or be a primary vehicle in the social development of individuals. It allows for learning and exploration. Through play, a person develops and tests his or her concepts of self, and is able to test the world and come to grips with it. Play affords opportunities for physical development and for experiencing the consequences of decision making. Attitudes toward play and recreation are culturally molded; the values and traditions of society ultimately shape behavior and determine avenues of fulfillment.

Describing Recreation

The explanations for recreation are similar to those given for play, and the recreation experience is frequently defined as a play experience. In many ways, play and recreation are the same, yet are often treated as separate phenomena. Traditionally, we have referred to play as something children do without reference to time and place. Recreation, on the other hand, has been seen as adult activity that occurs during one's free time.

Two basic views of recreation exist. Some theorists analyze the recreation experience in terms of its meaning and motives. Others view recreation as pleasurable and entertaining activities pursued for their own sake during periods of leisure time. In the former sense, play and recreation serve the same function as play. In the latter context, recreation is more narrowly defined than is play and is viewed most frequently as a diversionary or fun experience. Kando (1975) in his work on mass culture claims that most people perceive recreation to be sports and rarely view it as intellectually stimulating activity. De Grazia (1962) expressed a similar view, defining recreation as diversion and amusement for the masses, something quite different from leisure, a state which could only be experienced by the more disciplined elite. Others define recreation as activity and use recreation and leisure as synonymous terms; both are viewed as nonwork activities pursued for their own pleasure. This activity definition is also the view often expressed by economists who write of the multi-billion dollar recreation/leisure economy.

A unique aspect of recreation is society's concern for the recreative experience and its willingness to develop a social system to accommodate this enjoyment. People recognize the importance of recreation to their well-being and the inherent need for diversionary experiences. They also acknowledge that a diversion is not necessarily nonpurposeful. In fact, diversion may be most beneficial when it is meaningful, and therefore capable of providing the feelings of well-being and satisfaction associated with the recreative experience. Recreation has the following characteristics:

1. *Recreation involves activity.*

    It may be physical, mental, or emotional, but always there is activity. It is action as distinguished from rest or inactivity. In one way or another, the recreation experience involves the exertion of energies, even though they may not be visible to the observer. Action is easily seen when a person swims, hikes, or plays a musical instrument. It is less easy to detect in watching television, listening to a recording, or meditating. Nevertheless, activity is present.

2. *Recreation has no single form.*

    The recreation experience may occur in any form of activity. It is one's motives that give the expression of recreation meaning, not the form it takes. The range of activities that people enjoy as recreation expressions are endless. It is a mistake to define recreation as a given list of activities, even though some activities are pursued more frequently as recreation expressions than others and come to mind first when one is asked what you do for "recreation." Popular definitions of recreation frequently depend upon these activity stereotypes, but the actual recreation expression is not limited to any one listing of activities.

3. *Participation in recreation is entirely voluntary.*

    The recreation experience is a free-choice experience. It cannot be superimposed upon an individual or group. If the activity is required, then the potential for the recreative moment may be diminished. Opportunities for the recreation experience can be provided and activities planned and organized, but freedom of choice and action must be preserved. The concept of freedom of choice may be why recreation is so closely tied to the concept of leisure.

4. *Recreation occurs during leisure.*

    Accepting either the "free time" or "state of mind" definition for leisure, recreation is a leisure experience. Recreation may occur when one is free to make choices, in control of the situation, free from external compulsion. In other words, recreation occurs when one is at leisure.

5. *Recreation is motivated by the satisfaction derived from the experience.*

    Satisfaction may occur in any human experience; feelings of self-worth, achievement, and pleasure are not unique to recreation. What matters are the motives which give rise to the recreation activity, not the benefits or outcomes of the experience. The motivation factor makes a given activity recreation for one person and work for another. Playing eighteen holes of golf on Wednesday afternoon with a group of friends may be recreation for the amateur, but may be work for the professional earning a living playing golf. An activity can be both work and recreation to a person at different times under different conditions.

6. *Recreation is like play; it is serious, purposeful, and uncertain.*

Some authors write of recreation as a human need. Actually, what they are describing is the need for self-directed and self-motivated activity. As such, recreation is both purposeful and necessary. The pleasurable aspect does not deny its seriousness and purposefulness. A fair way to test this contention is to interrupt someone when they are busily engaged in a favorite recreation expression. Watch a fisher neglect chores when the fish are biting, or an amateur gardener plan weekend activities around the garden requirements. These people are not "playing" in the frivolous sense of the word. They are engaged seriously in something that is an integral part of their lives.

7. *The recreative outcomes of the experience cannot be predetermined.*

Although some individuals seem to derive pleasure in the planning and organizing of their recreation experiences, the outcomes are not always known. Possibly one reason why the pursuit of recreation is so pleasurable is because people "write the script" as they go. People expect certain things to happen when they play tennis or picnic with the family because the outcomes have happened before and because society says they should happen. The same results, however, cannot be predicted or predetermined. Opportunities for recreation can be organized or can occur spontaneously. They can be sponsored by private groups, public agencies, or pursued at home, but the individual player has to determine whether the experience was recreational.

8. *Recreation has by-products.*

What we observe and frequently define as the results of recreation are its by-products. Consequently, the recreation experience may be described as a learning activity, a promoter of good health, or stress reliever. These perceived benefits are often used as justification for organizing and supporting some recreation programs and services. They are, however, not the reasons why individuals seek recreation experience. Recreation is done for the intrinsic reward and satisfaction which comes from total involvement and the freedom to participate.

In summary, recreation can be defined as an activity which occurs during moments of freedom for the satisfaction derived from the experience. The relationship among recreation, leisure, and play is complex, with the term "recreation" frequently being used interchangeable with "leisure" or with "play." Play is an activity, as is recreation. Leisure is based on an integrated experience related to one's state of mind during involvement in a free-time activity, as is recreation. Recreation activities are those forms of expression which society tends to assume provide the recreation experience. The parks and recreation delivery system is comprised of those agencies and organizations that sponsor, promote, and offer opportunities and environments for the pursuit of recreation activity. Parks and recreation is a profession which assumes as its mission the provision and management of opportunities and resources for selected recreation, play, and leisure experiences and expressions.

The Recreation/Leisure Experience

A number of aspects influence how an individual experiences leisure or recreation. These factors relate to benefits, constraints, the actual experience, and the systems providing for experiences.

Benefits and Motivations for Leisure and Recreation

Benefits to involvement in leisure and recreation may be manifested in a variety of ways. The benefits that individuals seek are often closely related to their motivations for involvement. Motivations are those inner urges that prompt one to behave in a certain way often based on what the individual expects. Some benefits for recreation and leisure occur within the individual while other benefits relate to the society in general. Driver (1992) has identified and categorized these benefits stating they may be grouped under six headings: physiological, psychophysiological, economic, environmental, psychological, and social cultural.

The physiological benefits of regular exercise are documented scientifically. For example, chronic aerobic exercise reduces serum cholesterol, helps prevent hypertension, and offers other cardiovascular benefits. From a psychophysiological perspective, many of the same physiological benefits result in stress management. These result in mental and physical relaxation as well as positive changes in mood (Iso-Ahola & Weissinger, 1984). Psychological benefits relate to enhanced self-competence, improved sense of self-worth, self-identity, and a better ability to relate to others as a result of being involved in leisure and recreation.

Benefits may also be of a broader social dimension. For example, an economic benefit as a result of recreation occurs in communities where tourism dollars are spent. In other ways, the value of leisure and recreation involvement may result in healthier lives that can result in saving money due to lack of absenteeism on the job. Environmental benefits also exist. Environmental protection has been the outgrowth of a commitment to saving outdoor recreation resources. Further, sociocultural benefits may come through recreation or leisure when one develops pride in one's community and in an ethnic heritage as a result of being involved in a recreation opportunity such as an ethnic festival.

Participants in leisure and recreation experiences ought to be able to identify the benefits or by-products that are evident if a recreation experience it is to be meaningful. From a leisure service delivery system point of view, professionals must be able to program and plan for the positive effects that individuals and society seek from recreation experiences and programs. Much is yet to be learned about such aspects as how pervasive benefits are among different groups in society, what constrains people from realizing benefits, how much certain benefits are worth to people, and how benefits to recreation/leisure experiences can best be optimized.

Constraints to Leisure and Recreation

For benefits to be realized and for individuals to get the most from their leisure and recreation experiences, constraints to leisure and recreation must often be addressed. Constraints are those factors that impact the preference or participation for a particular leisure or recreation experience. They may be either antecedent and intervening constraints. Antecedent constraints are those aspects that may prevent one from being interested in being involved in a particular activity. Aspects such as perceived gender roles or body image may discourage participation. Intervening constraints are generally structural in nature and pertain to the inability to do an activity which one desires. Jackson (1988, 1991) cites that over 100 constraints have been identified by leisure researchers. In general, the intervening constraints can be grouped according to five main types: lack of facilities, lack of awareness of recreational opportunities, lack of time, lack of money, and lack of necessary skills and abilities. Henderson (1991) has suggested that these types of constraints may apply to both males and females, but females may experience constraints in different ways due to quality issues that surround leisure. For example, the expectation that childcare is predominantly a woman's role may reduce the opportunities available for leisure.

Research on leisure constraints has grown greatly in the past five years. The issues that surround constraints negotiation appear to be particularly salient as researchers seek to understand how individuals address the various constraints which often are negatively affecting their recreation opportunities or experiences. Everyone faces various constraints to leisure but some people are better able to manage or negotiate them. By understanding how people make leisure-based decisions and how they seek to overcome obstacles they encounter may help professionals in parks and recreation systems better understand how to plan and program recreation and leisure experiences.

Understanding the Leisure and Recreation Experience

Recreation and leisure experiences do not occur in a vacuum. Individuals typically go through a process of preparing to participate. On the simplest level an individual might anticipate or plan a leisure or recreation experience, participate in the actual activity, and then recollect or reminisce about the experience. Chubb & Chubb (1981) suggest that the nature of the recreation or leisure experience may in fact involve eleven phases: awareness, initial-decision, exploratory, final-decision, anticipation, preparation, outward-travel, main experience, return travel, follow-up, and recollection. All of this suggests that any single involvement in a recreation experience may consist of much more than just the activity or the actual time spent in leisure.

Leisure also relates to what one does as well as why the activities are chosen. Many people view leisure or recreation as a chance to show their own identities and to relate to others. John Kelly (1983) contends that within the leisure experience one is always in a process of developing one's identity and examining interactions. In a sense he is extending the concepts of the developmentalist and behaviorist citing the learning and mastery potential of recreation.

Kelly (1987) also described leisure as a function of the relative freedom of choice and meaning attached to an activity by an individual. He suggested four types of leisure: unconditional, recuperative, relational and role-determined. Unconditional leisure is influenced by high freedom and intrinsic meaning. This type of leisure expression is creative, expressive, and exciting. Recuperative leisure has intrinsic meaning but low freedom. Watching a movie or reading a book, for example, may be undertaken to relax or unwind because one is exhausted from other daily activities. Relational leisure has high freedom with social meaning and is done because one finds leisure in interactions with others. Going camping with friends or picnicking is illustrative of this form. Role-determined leisure expression tends to have low freedom and social meaning since it is frequently found in meeting the expectations of others. For example, you may not really want to watch a ball game on TV but because the family wants to be together, you go ahead and become involved.

Much has been written about the meanings of recreation and leisure experiences that goes beyond the scope of this book, but suffice it to say that leisure is a complex phenomenon with many aspects to consider.

Providing for Leisure and Recreation Experiences

In response to the diversity of motivations, participation patterns, constraints and meanings attached to leisure experiences, a complex leisure service delivery system has evolved as discussed throughout this text. Leisure service professionals are concerned with theories of leisure as they apply to human behavior and as they undergird the mission of the delivery systems. Not all professionals equate leisure studies with parks and recreation, nor do they view themselves as the guardians of the leisure service delivery system. Sometimes they do not hold recreation and leisure to be synonymous. Yet they often rely upon the same explanations and definitions given for leisure as are given for recreation. This is especially true when both recreation and leisure are defined in integrated experiential terms.

Philosophical Approaches

Having offered some explanations for play and some definitions and interpretations of the basic concepts of work, leisure, play, and recreation, the philosophical positions which underlie the park and recreation profession are important to examine. Whereas theory gives direction for research and practice and serves as an explanation for observed behavior, philosophy provides the direction for theory and the value framework for interpreting the meanings of theory.

Philosophers have always attempted to explain the nature of human beings and the universe. Their perceptions of the world have stimulated inquiring minds to offer theories and testable hypotheses. Although no one leisure philosophy exists, many parks and recreation authors have discussed a philosophy of play and activity. Their work has reflected no one dominant school of philosophy but has been eclectic with a combination of several philosophical doctrines. Their views have given direction to parks and recreation services, particularly to its administrative practices and programs of professional preparation. Among the more dominant philosophical positions affecting the leisure service delivery system are the assumptions of idealism, realism, pragmatism, existentialism, and humanism. The following is a brief discussion of each of the five schools of philosophy and some of the philosophers who have contributed to understandings of the delivery system and parks and recreation services.

Idealism

Idealism holds that an eternal set of goals or ideas govern human behavior and that one should seek to understand these truths and work for perfection. According to the idealist, individuals should be goal-directed and that the means employed to achieve their goals should be equal to the ends. In other words, how one plays the game is just as important as the final score.

The earlier writers and thinkers in the parks and recreation movement were idealists. Perhaps the most influential of these pioneers was Joseph Lee, one of the founders of the Playground Association of America. To him, certain forms of play were essential. He believed all play should contribute to the wholesome development of the individual; consequently, play should teach discipline, sacrifice, and moral character as well as be pleasurable (Knapp & Hartsoe, 1979).

Henry Curtis (1917), Luther Gulick (1920), and J. B. Nash (1953) also supported this idealism philosophy of parks and recreation. Nash wrote that participating in a "creative way" was the most preferred form of leisure expression, whereas spectatorism and "getting in trouble" were undesirable pastimes. To him and to the other idealists, being physically active was important and essential to creative participation. Spectatorism encouraged passivity. Many of the earlier programs in recreation services embraced this philosophy; hierarchies of activities based upon a value orientation were established and ideal programs suggested. Regimentation and staff-dominated programs were the result. To the idealist, the ideal way was the only way to conduct recreation programs.

Realism

The development of scientific thought, with the concomitant need to measure and test ideas, forced a modification of the philosophical position of some thinkers. The school of realism emerged with the idea that people must constantly measure their performance against some standard to know what they have accomplished and what their objectives and plans should be. Many of the concepts of scientific management and administration resulted from the realists' position. Examples of realists in parks and recreation are George Butler (1949) who pioneered work in determining park and recreation facility standards and W. C. Sutherland (1948) who studied recreation personnel management and development. Their works are still used by many recreation professionals as a guide for planning for, acquiring, and developing facilities and staff.

Unfortunately, some parks and recreation practitioners have accepted these early standards as unquestionable and have used them even when current practices and patterns suggest otherwise. For example, the early standards for the location of a playground in a small park were based upon different population density relationships than now exist in urban areas. They suggested a playground of four to seven acres for a neighborhood of 5,000 population in which the inhabitants were distributed over a square mile. In today's urban environment, where 2,000 residents may inhabit one super block, the standard is inappropriate. Standards have a way of becoming rules, not benchmarks, and when that occurs they become difficult to change. Although realism is a viable philosophy, data must be continually generated to keep professionals up to date with current research.

Pragmatism

Perhaps the philosophy that has had the greatest impact in the development of parks and recreation systems is that of pragmatism. The pragmatist holds goal achievement to be the critical element; the method by which a goal is reached is secondary. It is a more flexible philosophy than idealism and stresses some of the functionalism of realism. The noted educator, John Dewey, was one of the pragmatic thinkers who influenced parks and recreation thought. He stressed the importance of play and recreation in the learning process. He stated that one learns best by doing and that individuals should have freedom of choice and opportunities for self-expression rather than adhere to a set pattern of behavior imposed upon them by an "authority" (Dewey, 1916). To him, play was a spontaneous activity and an outlet for creative expression and creative development. Each player should find his or her own means for expression through individualized programming. Each community should also provide leisure services to its citizens based upon the unique needs of that community. According to the pragmatist, each community should develop a unique approach to recreation and park services based upon the resources and traditions of the community and the skills and resources of staff.

To some pragmatists, methods and techniques are important only as tools. Pragmatists use standards as guidelines but not as binding laws. They acknowledge that an ideal state exists toward which one should work but the ideal is relative and subject to change depending upon the changing needs and views of people. In recreation practice, the pragmatic philosophy has encouraged decentralized programming. Its major shortcoming has been the expediency factor, which sometimes causes long-range planning goals to be sacrificed for the immediate situation. Individual needs, too, often become secondary to group concerns and an administrative need to get things done.

Existentialism

Existentialism is a relatively modern philosophy that emerged after World War II. Its most noted proponent was Jean-Paul Sartre. It is, to some degree, an extension of pragmatism. To the existentialist, the individual is all-important and there are no absolutes except life itself. It is the philosophy of "now." *Ad hocism,* as an administrative practice, is an existentialist approach; bureaucracies are of little importance since everything is subject to change. How one feels about life is more important than what one does.

Existentialism has had its impact on parks and recreation thinking by returning the individual to the forefront. Consequently, many of the policies of governmental bureaucracies have been challenged by both consumers and professionals. Much therapeutic recreation programming has an existentialist overlay. Possibly, the biggest danger accompanying this philosophy is the tendency to underestimate the future and the ultimate consequence of decision making. The "here and now" has a way of becoming the past, and the decisions of yesterday do affect the present and the future.

Humanism

To the humanist, the human being is the supreme value. The humanist, like the existentialist, focuses upon the individual's potential and advocates the elimination of all social, physical, economic, and psychological barriers that might hinder or restrict growth and development. Unlike existentialism, this philosophy is action-oriented.

Humanism is an attractive philosophy. It stresses purposeful living, higher functioning, and a sense of social consciousness. It forces one to consider the whole person, the interaction between the individual and the physical and social environment, and the limitations that those environments impose upon the individual. According to the humanists, when environments are oppressive, they must be changed. Moreover, the failure to grow is the result of the environment, not the fault of the individual.

Humanism is a contemporary approach, having risen in popularity since the late 1960s. Its advocates are strong supporters of civil liberties, equal rights for women, cultural diversity and the broadening of the scope and mission of the parks and recreation service system. They promote a more individualistic approach to the provision of recreation opportunities, advocating that recreation professionals assume a more humanistic perspective in allowing for individual exploration and self-discovery.

For the mature individual, humanism is a philosophy of sensitivity. For the less mature person, it is a philosophy of permissiveness. For the immature person, it can be a philosophy of hedonism. Among the more articulate interpreters of humanism in parks and recreation are David Gray, Dan Dustin and James Murphy. They believe that it is imperative that parks and recreation assume a humanistic perspective. Others feel that humanism is only one of the many philosophies which can aid parks and recreation's future development.

Toward an Integrated Philosophy

Each philosophical stance has its advocates and there is an element of truth in each position. Likewise, each has its adversaries and shortcomings. Recognizing these contradictions, the authors of this text have attempted to pull together the strengths of the various philosophical positions into an integrated statement about parks and recreation systems.

Individuals and groups differ and, therefore, no single program or approach will meet the needs of all. The resources of each community, the skills of its leadership, and the diversity and desires of the public require professionals to be pragmatic about their goals and objectives. The existentialist and humanistic elements come into play through the recognition of the holistic nature of life and the difference between the objectives of the participant and those of the professional. The participant is concerned about the satisfactions derived from the experience, whereas the professional must consider the administrative and management practices and policies as well as the nature of the activity. Given this understanding, parks and recreation professionals should work (1) to remove those constraints that might prevent an individual from enjoying the recreation moment, and (2) to create optimum environments for leisure and recreation experiences to occur.

Through time and experience, a set of principles for parks and recreation has evolved. They reflect a broad philosophy of recreation and park services.

1. All people, regardless of race, creed, sex, ability, or economic status have a right to pursue the recreation experience. All people seek and enjoy the recreation experience; it is essential to their well-being.

2. A democratic society has the responsibility to provide and maintain opportunities for leisure and recreation experiences. Ideally, these experiences should result in the personal growth and well-being of the individual and add to one's self-concept and sense of worth and satisfaction.

3. The provision of leisure opportunities is primarily the responsibility of the individual and the family. When the requirements for recreation opportunities are greater than what the individual or family can provide for itself, it becomes the responsibility of the community, including social institutions and governmental structures, to provide those recreation services.

4. Where opportunities for recreation are provided on a community basis, they need to be planned and administered with respect to the needs, interests, diversity, and competencies of the people they serve; the resources available; the leadership (both lay and professional) required; and the goals to be met.

5. It is the responsibility of the leisure service professional to promote the values and benefits of the recreation experience, to organize and administer the resources required to provide the needed services, and to work against those constraints that inhibit or limit the possibility of leisure and recreation experiences.

Suggestions and Study Guides

1. Play may be viewed in its purest form when children, puppies, and kittens are at play. Observe and compare the activities and forms of play of children with those of puppies and kittens. In what ways are they similar? Different? Why?

2. Which theories of play seem to hold more credence for you? Why? Discuss your observations and explanations of play with a sociology major; a psychology major; a physical education major. Does one's undergraduate major influence one's understanding and perception of play? How?

3. Prepare a brief statement on your philosophy of recreation. Be careful not to confuse philosophy (belief systems) with theory (the various scientific explanations of behavior).

4. Discuss the benefits of play, leisure, and recreation in terms of your own personal physiological, psychological, and sociological situation.

References

Berlyne, D. (1960). *Conflict arousal and curiosity*. New York, NY: McGraw-Hill.

Butler, G. (1949). *Introduction to community recreation*. New York, NY: McGraw-Hill.

Caillois, R. (1961). *Man, play, and games*. New York, NY: The Free Press.

Chubb, M., & Chubb, H. (1981). *One third of our time?* New York, NY: John Wiley & Sons.

Crandall, R. (1980). Motivations for leisure. *Journal of Leisure Research, 12*(1), pp. 45-54.

Csikzentmihalyi, M. (1975). *Beyond boredom and anxiety: The experience of play*. San Francisco, CA: Jossey-Bass.

Csikzentmihalyi, M. (1990). *Flow: The psychology of optimal experience*. New York, NY: Harper & Row.

Curtis, H. S. (1917). *The play movement and its significance*. New York, NY: Macmillan.

De Grazia, S. (1962). *Of time, work, and leisure*. New York, NY: Twentieth Century Fund.

Dewey, J. (1916). *Democracy and education*. New York, NY: Macmillan.

Driver, B. (1992). The benefits of leisure. *Parks and Recreation, 27*(11), pp. 18-22, 75.

Dumazedier, J. (1967). *Toward a leisure society*. New York, NY: The Free Press.

Ellis, M. (1973). *Why people play*. Englewood Cliffs, NJ: Prentice-Hall.

Erikson, E. (1950). *Childhood and society*. New York, NY: W. W. Norton.

Goodale, T., & Godbey, G. (1988). *The evolution of leisure*. State College, PA: Venture Publishing, Inc.

Gulick, L. (1920). *A philosophy of play*. New York, NY: Charles Scribners and Sons.

Henderson, K. (1991). The contributions of feminism to an understanding of leisure constraints. *Journal of Leisure Research, 23*(4), pp. 363-377.

Iso-Ahola, S., & Weissinger, E. (1984). Leisure and well being—Is there a connection? *Parks and Recreation, 19*(6), pp. 40-44.

Jackson, E. (1988) Leisure constraints: A survey of past research. *Leisure Sciences, 10*(3), pp. 203-215.

Jackson, E. (1991). Leisure constraints. *Parks and Recreation, 26*(11), pp. 18-23, 73.

Kando, T. (1975). *Leisure and popular culture in transition.* St. Louis, MO: The C. V. Mosby Company.

Kelly, J. R. (1982). *Leisure.* Englewood Cliffs, NJ: Prentice-Hall.

Kelly, J. R. (1983). *Leisure identities and interactions.* London, England: George Allen & Unwin.

Kelly, J. R. (1987). *Freedom to be: A new sociology of leisure.* New York, NY: Macmillan.

Kleiber, D. (1979). Fate control and leisure attitudes. *Leisure Sciences, 2*(3), pp. 239-248.

Kleiber, D., & Crandall, R. (1981). Leisure and work ethics and locus of control. *Leisure Sciences, 4*(4), pp. 477-485.

Knapp, R. F. & Hartsoe, C. E. (1979). *Play for America.* Arlington, VA: National Recreation and Park Association.

Linder, S. B. (1970). *The harried leisure class.* New York, NY: Columbia University Press.

Mannell, R., Zuzanek, J., & Larson, R. (1988). Leisure state and "flow" experiences: Testing perceived freedom and intrinsic motivation hypotheses. *Journal of Leisure research, 20*(4), pp. 289-304.

Mead, G. H. (1963). Mind, self and society. In C.W. Morris (Ed.), *Perspectives in the Social Order* (pp. 139-141). New York, NY: McGraw-Hill.

Nash, J. B. (1953). *Philosophy of recreation and leisure.* St. Louis, MO: The C. V. Mosby Company.

Neulinger, J. (1976). The need for and the implications of a psychological conception of leisure. *The Ontario Psychologist,* June, pp. 16-17.

Piaget, J. (1962). *Play, dreams and imitation in childhood.* New York, NY: W.W. Norton and Company.

Robinson, J. (1977). *How Americans use time.* New York, NY: Praeger Publishers, Inc.

Samdahl, P. (1991). Issues in the measurement of leisure: A comparison of theoretical and connotative meaning. *Leisure Sciences, 13*(1), pp. 33-49.

Slavson, S. R. (1948). *Recreation and the total personality.* New York, NY: Association Press.

Sutherland, W. C. (1948). *Recreation leadership standards.* New York, NY: National Recreation Association.

Szalai, A. (1972). *The uses of time.* The Hague: European Coordination Center for Research and Documentation in the Social Sciences.

Tinsley, H. & Kass, R. (1979). The latent structure of need-satisfying properties of leisure activities. *Journal of Leisure Research, 11*(5), pp. 278-291.

Veblen, T. (1899). *The theory of the leisure class.* New York, NY: Viking Press.

Wallach, F. (1983). Play in the age of technology. *Parks and Recreation, 18*(4), pp. 36-38, 63.

White, R. (1959). Motivation reconsidered: The concept of competence. *Psychological Review, 66,* pp. 297-333.

Witt, P. & Bishop, D. (1970). Situational antecedents to leisure behavior. *Journal of Leisure Research, 2*(1), pp. 64-77.

PORTIONS OF CHAPTER FOUR DEVELOPED AND CONTRIBUTED BY
MARK HAVITZ OF THE UNIVERSITY OF WATERLOO, AND
RICHARD GITELSON OF THE PENNSYLVANIA STATE UNIVERSITY

CHAPTER FOUR

Economic Considerations and the Commercial Recreation Sector

For years the business of America has been its business. Today it may be the pursuit of its pleasure. One gets this feeling when reading the parks and recreation section of the *Statistical Abstract of the United States* (1992), looking at the hundreds of special interest magazines at a newsstand, or measuring the thickness of the entertainment and travel sections of a Sunday paper. Americans love to play, and their play urges have been encouraged and sustained by a leisure service industry that in 1992 was reported to generate in excess of 400 billion dollars. In this chapter, attention is given to the significance of leisure, its contribution to the national economy, the nature and scope of the commercial recreation sector, and the burgeoning travel and tourism industry.

As stated previously, the leisure service delivery system is comprised of three major elements: public; private not-for-profit; and commercial recreation. The last element affects the largest number of people and is the focus of this chapter. Although many of the organizations, businesses, and industries that provide the bulk of commercial recreation opportunities may not consider themselves recreation agencies, they constitute the backbone of individual recreation and leisure services. They provide the equipment, the home entertainment technologies, and the recreation travel opportunities for millions of people. They also are beginning to employ graduates of recreation and parks curricula.

The Economics of Leisure

One does not have to be an economist to understand the economics of leisure. Leisure goods and services exist because of the demand for them. The shorter workweek, the acceptance of the right to play, and the satisfaction which comes from the pursuit of pleasure have created the demand. Sensitive entrepreneurs have responded by providing the desired goods and services. As the public benefits from opportunities for personal satisfaction and growth from these recreation experiences, the economy is enhanced as jobs are created, goods are consumed, and tax revenues are increased. The successful leisure service businesses are those that "read" the wants and desires of society and respond to them. This dynamic market has changing tastes and forms. According to the U.S. Department of Commerce, recreation goods and services constitute 7.9 percent of all consumer spending. In 1990 alone, Americans spent $280 billion for fun and this figure did not include the billions consumers spent on recreation travel (approximately $153 billion) or on recreational eating or clothes (Academy of Leisure Sciences, 1993).

The commercial system's relationship to the economy, however, is more than the number of dollars Americans spend for recreation. It also includes financial benefits such the appreciation of property values, the circulation of the tourist dollar, the production and sale of leisure goods and services, and the location of industries. In some communities, commercial recreation businesses are the primary employer or the base industry. In others, commercial recreation is a secondary industry. A prime example of the former are those ski villages and beach communities that depend almost entirely upon tourists for their financial existence. For other cities such as Anaheim, California the contribution of professional sport teams and theme parks are vital to the general economic health of the community. Imagine the consequences to the Orlando, Florida area if Walt Disney World were to terminate its operations. Its 28,000 employees would be without jobs and many of the industries depending upon tourists would be without clients. Property values would drop, unemployment would increase, and local government would find difficulty in continuing the level of services as tax revenues and property values fell because the welfare rolls grew.

Not all communities are as intimately involved in commercial recreation as are Orlando, Florida; Aspen, Colorado; or Atlantic City, New Jersey. But all communities do have their commercial recreation enterprises and may be benefited by recreation travel. Tourists spend money in places they visit; commercial recreation businesses use public utilities, contribute to the tax rolls, and employ workers.

Intangible Effects

Measuring the total economic effects of recreation resources is difficult. For example, a water reservoir may be constructed primarily for reasons such as flood control, irrigation, and electrical power. When fully developed, however, recreation use may become the more obvious generator and sustainer of the local economy. New subdivisions in communities may be developed because of the recreation potential of the lake. Marinas and other businesses depending upon water activity can be established. Motels and resorts accommodating tourists could be built and, without thinking about it, the public grows to depend upon the lake as a recreation and economic resource. Because planners now recognize the economic potential of natural resource development, they account for recreation as a part of the justification and cost of a project. The recreation impact must be considered.

The economics of leisure and recreation are closely related to society's value system. Some years ago George Soule (1957) wrote about two economic developments which have brought more leisure to more people: (1) increases in production, and (2) a reduction in the size of the labor force needed to sustain the population. He held that whatever gains made in leisure under the market system had resulted from the workers' deliberate choice of free time (e.g., attaining the shorter workweek) over real income (e.g., working longer hours for more money). This view is still held by many, however, this choice is not evident among all labor forces. Some workers choose to "moonlight" (i.e., to hold a second job), whereas others choose to spend more time in voluntary services to the community or in adult education programs. Whatever the choice, the economy of the community is affected by those decisions.

Industries generally try to locate their plants near sources of raw materials, near expanding markets, in areas where taxes and costs will be kept to a minimum, where available skilled labor exists, and where employees will be happy (Decker & Crompton, 1990). Leisure services providers may contribute significantly to the last consideration. People usually want to do business and establish their homes where they can live comfortably and where they most enjoy themselves. Family satisfactions cannot be purchased through the paycheck alone. Something more than high pay, good working conditions, and fringe benefits are needed to attract and keep workers on the job. Recreation opportunities often can serve that function. They add immeasurably to the quality of the social and personal environment and, therefore, to the economic life of that environment.

Other Effects

Other economic effects of recreation are evident. Under certain conditions, recreation and parks help increase land and property values, especially when the recreation areas are properly constructed, maintained, and operated. Recreation services also appear to reduce accident and medical expenses by helping to keep the population alert and healthy. Law enforcement authorities have for many years argued that a dollar spent on recreation reduces the number of dollars the public has to spend on crime prevention and correctional rehabilitation. Recreation services also are a generator of tax revenue by bringing billions of dollars each year to the treasuries of municipal, county, state, and federal governments through excise taxes, sales taxes and jobs creation.

Hundreds of thousands of people earn their living from scores of industries producing materials, equipment, clothing, and services designed to meet leisure interests. Little need for a national park system, for local municipal recreation and park departments, or for therapeutic recreation services would exist if people had no leisure interests or hours to pursue their recreational pleasures. Fortunately, individuals interested in parks and recreation as an area of study and a career can take heart in knowing that each generation spends more time and money on recreation pursuits than did the previous one. Leisure services are one of our nation's most valuable economic assets.

Recreation and Leisure Expenditures

Possibly one of the most dramatic ways to portray the significance of parks and recreation is to examine the amount spent each year on selected activities. These figures represent gross sales and demonstrate the extent of the leisure system in terms of goods produced and consumed, jobs created and sustained, profits earned, and taxes paid.

Comprehensive statistics on leisure expenditures are difficult to obtain from a single source. Various professional associations, such as the Sporting Goods Manufacturers Association, keep records on their industries and some data services, like the Roper Organization, periodically conduct expenditure studies. Perhaps the best source is the U.S. Census Bureau's *Statistical Abstract of the U.S.* The following materials were taken from several of these sources to give an indication of the economic impact of recreation pursuits. For example, in the area of musical instrument sales, over two billion dollars were spent in 1987; for one item, video tapes, American's purchased 200 million prerecorded and 300 million blank tapes in 1988. That same year, nearly two million baseball and softball bats (average cost: $35) were bought and Americans spent $3.5 billion on ski lift tickets. More than a billion movie tickets were sold in 1990 to a public willing to spend $4.75 per ticket (average movie price that year).

An indication of the patterns of activity and expenditure for selected recreation equipment and experiences over three decades is shown by Table 4.1. Notice the shift toward home-centered activities and products.

Table 4-1
Expenditures for Individual Recreation Equipment and/or
Admissions to Amusement Centers: 1970 to 1989

TYPE OF PRODUCT OR SERVICE	1970	1980	1985	1989
Total recreation expenditures*	42.7	115.0	185.7	164.4
Percent of total personal consumption	6.7%	6.6%	7.1%	7.7%
Books and maps	2.9	5.6	8.1	11.4
Magazines, newspapers, sheet music	4.1	10.4	13.2	18.5
Endurable toys and sport supplies	5.5	14.6	21.1	30.2
Wheel goods, durable toys, sports equipment	5.2	17.2	26.7	36.2
Radio and television receivers, records, musical instruments	8.5	19.9	37.0	51.1
Radio and television repair	1.4	2.6	3.2	4.2
Mowers, seeds, and potted plants	1.8	4.0	5.5	6.1
Admissions to specified spectator amusements	3.3	6.5	9.5	13.4
Motion picture theaters	1.6	2.7	3.6	5.0
Legitimate theaters and opera, and entertainments of nonprofit institutions	0.5	1.8	3.0	4.9
Spectator sports	1.1	2.0	2.9	3.5
Clubs and fraternal organizations	1.5	3.0	4.8	6.3
Commercial participant amusements	2.4	9.7	15.1	20.2
Pari-mutuel net receipts	1.1	2.1	2.6	2.8
Other	5.1	19.4	38.9	61.9

* in billions

Source: *1991 Statistical Abstract*, p. 231.

In addition to the obvious recreation expenditures, a host of related expenditures are difficult to measure. What percent of the billions of dollars spent for telephone services can be attributed to recreational conversations? What percent of the 200 billion dollars spent for clothing, jewelry, and accessories can be attributed to recreation behaviors? This relationship may be illustrated best by examining the impact of one piece of equipment, the baseball bat.

First, the timber for the bat must be cut. This procedure requires lumberjacks properly equipped, tree farmers and foresters to select the trees to be cut, and people to plan the reforestation of the cleared areas. The lumber must be transported to the sawmill and processed which requires labor and machinery. The finished lumber is then sent to the factory where it is manufactured into a baseball bat. Everyone working at that factory (e.g., the lathe operator, the polisher, the janitor, the bookkeeper, the typist, the salespeople) depends upon the product for his or her living. The product is then advertised, distributed through a wholesaler to a retailer, and sold. Perhaps the bat will be sold to a major league baseball team where it is used by a professional athlete whose salary depends upon his effectiveness with the bat. In that case, all people effected by the play of the professional team (e.g., the groundskeepers, sportswriters, team owners, television camera operators, concession personnel, parking lot attendants) become involved with the baseball bat. Recreation is big business.

Individual Participation

Another way to measure the effect of recreation and leisure on the economy is to analyze the number of participants engaged in specific activities. Participation records are most useful when recent years are compared to earlier ones to see if interest in recreation activities is increasing or declining. If recreation is on the increase, then expenditures for recreation and recreation related items, e.g., types of equipment, clothing, and admission fees needed to engage in these forms of activity, must also be on the increase.

According to the census data, recreation involvements are up in almost every category and activity. In 1990, there were 67 million swimmers, 40 million bowlers, 18 million tennis players, and 22 million golfers. Both college and professional teams reported increased attendance; the figures for football were in excess of 54 million while 56 million attended major league baseball games (see Table 4-2). A picture of a comparison of participation in selected recreational activities from 1960 to 1990 is presented in Table 4-3. With few exceptions, growth has been spectacular and recreation expenditures have increased

Table 4-2
The Leading Spectator and Participant Activities in 1990

Spectator Activities (estimated attendance)*		Participant Activities (estimated participants)*	
Horse racing	64	Walking	71
Major league baseball	55	Swimming	67
College football	37	Bicycling	55
College basketball	34	Camping	46
Dog racing	29	Fishing	54
NBA basketball	19	Boating	40
NFL football	18	Exercising with equipment	35

*in millions

Source: *1992 Statistical Abstract*, pp. 239 and 244.

even in years of economic decline. For example, it was speculated in 1977 that the increasing cost of gasoline would negatively affect many outdoor recreation activities. Some, such as the motor home industry, did experience a decline, but for the most part growth continued. People merely shifted the places in which they recreated and traveled to nearby areas. They did not cease to recreate. A similar fear was raised when the economy took a downward turn in the late 1980s. The fears were unfounded, however, as the figures in Table 4-3 suggest.

Table 4-3
Percent of Population Twelve Years of Age and Older
Participating in Selected Outdoor Recreation Activities 1960-1985

Activity	1960*	1972*	1985[†]
Picnicking	53	47	46
Driving for pleasure	52	34	38
Sightseeing	42	37	47
Swimming	45	•	50
Pool	•	18	•
Other	•	34	•
Walking and jogging	33	34	41
Fishing	29	24	31
Boating	22	15	22
Nature study/walks	14	17	36
Camping	8	•	•
Developed	•	11	35
Backcountry/primitive	•	5	14
Horseback riding	6	5	9
Backpacking	6	5	10
Water skiing	6	5	13
Canoeing	2	3	14
Sailing	1	3	8
Off-road driving	•	7	9

* Source: Heritage Conservation and Recreation Service, *Third nationwide recreation plan (The assessment)*, p. 41.
[†] Source: *1985-1987 public area recreation visitor study*, Outdoor Recreation and Wilderness Assessment Group, Athens, GA.

Governmental Expenditures and Revenues

A third way of determining the economic significance of leisure activities is to view recreation as a governmental expense and concern. Parks and recreation services exist at all levels of government. In 1990, the Department of the Interior received a Congressional appropriation in excess of one billion dollars to operate the National Park Service. The National Endowment for the Arts reported receiving 170 million while the Land and Conservation Fund was granted 150 million. Various states expended nearly 800 million in support of their state park systems. An additional 280 million was spent for arts programs in 1990 which represented a figure up 50 million from 1988. At the local level an additional 7.8 billion was spent for parks and recreation facilities, programs, and services.

Recreation and parks also provided government with a source of income. In 1989, it was estimated that the federal government collected 26 billion dollars in excise taxes. Those taxes provided 2.5 percent of the tax collections that year. Excise taxes grossed from alcoholic beverages alone amounted to 10.1 billion. State-operated lotteries provided 18.8 billion in 1990 and pari-mutuel and amusement taxes generated another 1.2 billion.

Revenue from recreation involvement is produced in a variety of ways. In 1990, revenue from the state park systems was 400 million dollars while the National Park Service grossed 79 million. The revenue developed by both systems increased over 100 percent between 1985 and 1990 (Statistical Abstract, 1992). In addition, 800 million dollars were collected through the sale of hunting and fishing licenses, not to mention the billions from the sale of alcoholic beverages, pet licenses, and permits to contract home swimming pools.

Property Values and Employment

A fourth major measurement of the contribution of leisure service systems to the economy is the impact on property values and the number of persons employed in the delivery of leisure services. There is evidence to support the contention that the presence of recreation facilities frequently has a favorable influence on land and property values. Realtors have understood this phenomenon for years. Real estate developers know that when public improvements are made in a residential area, property value increases. These increases are reflected clearly in the records of the tax assessors. As the market value of the land increases, so does the amount of tax the owner pays. Waterfront lake properties generally have a higher value than do those lots without direct access to water. The presence of a community center, park, or swimming pool will generally enhance the overall property value of a neighborhood, although the property immediately adjacent to these facilities may be negatively effected by the facility's presence.

In a study reported by the Heritage Conservation and Recreation Service [HCRS] (1978), it was observed that the presence of a particular park in Philadelphia (Pennypack Park) significantly affected the value of the land in the neighborhood. The park accounted for 33 percent increase in the value of a lot when the land was located 40 feet from the park; 9 percent when it was located 1,000 feet away; and 4 percent when it was 2,500 feet away from the park. On the other hand, lots adjacent to or less than 40 feet from the park experienced a decline in property value. It seems that those living adjacent to the park felt vulnerable to vandalism, noise, and light distractions while the rest of the community benefited from the park's presence. According to the HCRS report, each acre of park land generated an average of $2,600 in increased property value.

Another well-documented study (Bureau of Outdoor Recreation, 1968) is that of the Pearl River Reservoir near Jackson, Mississippi. The increase in land value of those lots adjacent to, or accessible to, the reservoir were compared with the sale of acreage not affected by the reservoir. The average price paid per acre of land adjacent to the reservoir showed an actual increase of slightly less than 9 percent prior to announcement of the project. After the announcement, prices increased 165 percent during the first year, 191 percent during the second year, 216 percent during the third year, 236 percent during the fourth, and 357 percent during the fifth year. The sale prices per acre for those lots not affected by the reservoir but in the same general area followed the normal price trend during the five-year period. The speculative influence of the project upon land value within the immediate area was obvious.

One of the best sales attractions is to promote the recreation features of a given neighborhood. The real estate sections of daily papers are full of advertisements trying to sell property on the basis of "leisure living." Literally thousands of retirement communities and real estate developments are "sold" in this manner. As one real estate sales agent said when asked about his promotion of a retirement community, "This is not just a lot of tract homes. In fact, we are not building homes at all. This is a recreational development. We are going to put in a small boat harbor, and later a golf course. There will be a beach club to which all lot holders may belong." The literature advertising the subdivision was filled with pictures of sailing, power boating, and sunbathing by the lake. It spoke of the values of recreational living and the potential growth of property value as the result of the presence of the recreation facilities.

Finally, the leisure service delivery system is a direct employer of millions of persons. In the public sector alone, over 500,000 people work for parks and recreation agencies as professionals, clerical workers, maintenance personnel, specialists, and seasonal and part-time employees. The number of individuals working for the private, voluntary sector is equally as large. Consider the thousands employed as camp counselors, camp administrators, employee recreation workers, tennis pros, country club managers, and the like. According to Robert Crandall, Chair of American Airlines, the travel and tourism industry alone employs more than 9 million people in the U.S. (Academy of Leisure Sciences, 1993). Perhaps as many as one-fourth our nation's jobs are somewhat related to leisure services. Every indicator suggests that leisure services will continue to grow in the future with our postindustrial world's emphasis on service economies.

Commercial Recreation

Whereas those working in the public sector are in a more definable segment of the leisure service system and tend to identify themselves as parks and recreation professionals, those individuals involved in commercial recreation often do not identify with the profession. Instead, they see themselves as business people. They provide goods and services, attend their own trade meetings, and judge success on the basis of their profit/loss statements.

Amusements and entertainment are synonymous with commercial recreation. Most commercial recreation enterprises want a satisfied and happy customer who will return again to use their equipment, facilities, and resources. Commercial recreation is not so much a single industry as it is a collection of industries. The range of businesses comprising this sector extends from the local pool hall and video game arcade to the communication conglomerates who own publishing houses, record companies, motion picture studios, and radio and television stations (Crossley, 1990). Commercial recreation includes amusement and theme parks, professional sports, show business (e.g., movies, TV, and the legitimate theater), the tourist industry, manufacturers of recreation apparel and equipment, health spas and sports clubs, and elements of the transportation and food industry. In an attempt to describe and classify the many components of commercial recreation, Bullaro and Edginton (1986) developed a scheme with five categories or domains of services for listing recreation businesses: entertainment services, natural environment based services, retail outlets, hospitality and food services, and travel and tourism services. Examples of businesses from each of these domains are shown in Figure 4-1. Although their classification scheme is helpful in describing the scope of commercial recreation, their domains are not discrete. For example, businesses from any of the five domains, not just travel and tourism services, are sometimes patronized by tourists. In addition, as Gunn (1988) acknowledges, the tourism industry is not solely comprised of commercial recreation businesses. Many of the tourism components such as parks, campgrounds, historic sites, and cultural facilities are provided by the public sector. The Bullaro and Edginton scheme, does, however, provide a way of noting this sector and its contribution.

Entertainment services are those businesses involved primarily to entertain or amuse people such as our amusement and theme parks, agricultural fairs and events, and spectator sports.

Amusement parks began in England in the late 1800s and came to the United States shortly thereafter. They feature lights, moving objects, rides, and games of competition. They are stimulating by appealing both to sensory and psychic pleasures. Coney Island was among the earliest amusement parks in the United States while the Steel Pier at Atlantic City, constructed in 1898,

Figure 4-1
Commercial Recreation Classification Scheme
adapted from Bullaro and Edginton (1986)

Travel and Tourism

Airlines
Tour promoter/operator
Tour boats (cruises)
Tour buses
Travel agencies

Hospitality and Food Services

Catering services
Convention centers
Guest house/inns
Hotels
Motels
Resorts
Restaurants

Entertainment Services

Amusement/Theme parks
Bowling alleys
Carnivals
Circuses
Entertainment bureaus
Movie theaters
Night clubs
Pool parlors
Pool waterpark
Professional athletics
Racetracks (horse, dog, auto)
Rodeos
Special events and festivals
Ticket agencies
Volleyball courts

Natural Environment Based Services

Beach/waterfront
Campgrounds
Hunting preserves
Liveries
Marinas
Resident camps
Ski resorts
Zoo/Aquarium/Wildlife parks

Retail Outlets

Products:
Catalog showrooms
Full line discount stores
Home shopping network
Specialty (recreational vehicles, athletic
    equipment, specialized boutiques,
    audio/video/game rentals)
Shopping malls
Variety/Department stores

Services:
Aquatic centers
Dance studios
Equestrian centers
Fitness clubs
Golf clubs
Ice rinks
Racquet clubs
Roller rinks

Note: This list is illustrative, but not intended to be all-inclusive.

was a prototype for America's resort piers. By 1950, however, most amusement parks, including the Steel Pier and Coney Island, were in disrepair, suffering from a poor public image, and were in financial straits.

Walt Disney revitalized the amusement park industry in 1955 when he opened America's first theme park, Disneyland, in Anaheim, California. Theme parks are what their names imply. Through careful planning, a specific atmosphere is created through the physical and interior design of the park and its component parts as well as the dress and attitude of its personnel. The theme park is successful because it is more than a set of amusing experiences in one location; it allows guests of all ages to escape to become a part of the fantasy. According to Carlton Van Doren (1993), an expert on theme parks, nearly 95 million people attended America's twenty largest parks in 1991.

Top Attendance—U.S. Theme Parks 1991

Walt Disney World (FL)	28.0 million
Disneyland (CA)	11.6 million
Universal Studios Florida	5.9 million
Universal Studios Hollywood	4.6 million
Knott's Berry Farm (CA)	4.0 million

Developers of commercial recreation subscribe to the notion that commercial recreation attractions, such as theme parks, are most successful when other attractions are within the immediate area. Developers encourage rather than discourage adjacent recreation developments. By having a variety of options available to the visitors, the likelihood of tourists staying for several days or coming for a repeat visit is increased. This concept, known as "clustering," has many proven examples such as Orlando, Florida; Branson, Missouri; and Myrtle Beach, South Carolina. This approach is grounded in the theory that the more services and options available, the more the client is stimulated and entranced by the experience. There is great sensory awareness and a "rush" to experience it all. When those options are multidimensional and the accommodations pleasurable, return visits are likely. To develop such clusters, cooperative planning is required, especially between the public and commercial sectors.

Events are a second major grouping within the entertainment services domain with an estimated 6,000 event attractions occurring annually (Getz, 1991). Although the United States has increasingly become urban and suburban, people still take pleasure in such activities as agricultural fairs, rodeos, and folk festivals. For example, Michigan, though often perceived as an industrialized urban state, hosts over 50 agricultural festivals each year celebrating everything from asparagus to blueberries to tulips. Its Traverse City National

Cherry Festival draws over a half million visitors annually (Propst & Combrink, 1991). Events provide guests and local residents with a sense of excitement and opportunity. Three of our more famous annual events are the Mardi Gras, the Kentucky Derby, and the Indianapolis 500.

Promotion of these events takes many forms. Some communities, such as the Galveston, Texas' Strand Festival, combine the area's natural resource (e.g., beaches) with the community's literary interests (e.g., the writings of Dickens). Others capitalize on folk themes. Spivey's Corner, NC, (population 200) has become internationally known for its annual Hollerin' Contest. Each June, thousands of people congregate in Spivey's Corner for a weekend of hollering, folk dancing, and socializing. Other communities have developed longer running theme festivals. Ashland, Oregon, annually hosts a Shakespearean Festival which attracts local residents and tourists for several months each year. Street and neighborhood festivals and block parties provide outlets for local craftspersons, accommodate the creative urges of street musicians and performers, give communities identity, and stimulate business for restaurants and curio shops.

Spectator events are another popular form of entertainment and have enjoyed an extended period of growth despite occasional countertrends such as horse racing, which is down significantly since 1974, and some sports which have struggled to attain a critical mass of fans such as professional soccer. Included in this category are circuses, touring musical groups, and spectator sports. Although recreation professionals tend to program for participation rather than spectator activity, some of these businesses (e.g., sports organizations) do employ recreation professionals to assist with their marketing and management practices. Among those organizations serving professionals in this domain are the International Association of Amusement Parks, the International Association of Fairs and Expositions and the North American Society for Sports Management.

Natural environment based services involve the use, understanding, or appreciation of natural resources as the basis for their existence. Although many people associate outdoor recreation experiences with the public sector, natural environment based services represent a major component of the commercial recreation industry. Commercial campgrounds, alone, provide over half of all North American campsites. Kampgrounds of America (KOA), in business since 1964 operates over 700 franchises (Franchise Opportunities Handbook, 1985). In 1990, over 46 million Americans camped, almost 54 million fished, 11 million downhill skied, 5 million cross-country skied, and 16 million owned recreational boats (Statistical Abstract, 1992). Someone had to provide these participants with goods and services. The sheer scale of these interests make commercial recreation profitable in relationship to resource-based activities. Recent growth areas include rock climbing, hang gliding, wind surfing, and other outfitter type services. Each of these requires areas and managers of resources. When people purchase recreational equipment such as boats, they expect to use them; they also expect someone to provide opportunities and accommodations related to their use. Lakes, lake wardens, guides, marinas, boat repairers and storage personnel are necessary to facilitate recreation experiences. In 1989, alone, it was estimated that 17 billion dollars was spent on boating and boat related facilities and activities (Jansen, 1992). Among the professional organizations serving these natural resource based businesses are the Campground Association of America and the National Ski Areas Association.

Retail outlets are those business offering specialized products and services directly to their customers. Although most recreation professionals consider retail sales as a distinct industry, many retail outlets, especially shopping malls, have a strong recreation orientation or tie. Not only do retailers provide the link between activity and merchandise, many malls provide facilities for recreation performances such as concerts, art exhibits, and dramatic productions. Some malls even contain amusement areas and rides. In many ways, shopping malls and open air markets are second only to homes as recreation facilities. They are places where people go in their free time to look, visit with others, and share a sense of community. They are urban America's answer to the "old world" market square.

Over 35,000 climate-controlled malls are in the United States and Canada. Some are constructed around a theme, whereas others are simply a collection of shops. A recent trend has been to develop shopping areas in renovated mills and warehouses such as The Cannery and Ghiradelli Square in San Francisco. One famous shopping mall, from a recreational standpoint, is Old Chicago. In the center of it is a seven-acre park with nearly three dozen major rides. The Quincy Market of Boston combines shopping and the cultural arts with its street musicians and artists and commercial vendors. It attracts over 10 million visitors a year. Alberta's (Canada) huge West Edmonton Mall is a city within a city. It contains a diverse range of recreation attractions including a water area large enough to accommodate scuba diving, submarine rides, and wind surfing; there are ice rinks, a roller coaster, and several hotels. Most malls planned their development so that shopping becomes a daylong outing. This is done through the orchestrating of shops, theaters, restaurants, and public facilities, and by providing events such as concerts, demonstrations and exhibits, dances, and festivals. Increasingly, malls have employed graduates of recreation and parks curricula as special activities coordinators.

One of the fastest growing sections of the commercial recreation sector is the manufacturing and sales of recreation and sporting goods. Between 1980 and 1990 it tripled in volume from 16.7 billion dollars to 44.1 billion (Table 4-4). Recreation professionals should be encouraged by such activity but unfortunately, evidence suggests many people do not use what they buy. For example, only 45 percent of those who purchase jogging shoes actually participate in jogging. Similarly, only 52 percent of bicycle owners and 49 percent of those who buy weightlifting equipment use them at least once a year (Brooks, 1988). Using sales figures as evidence of recreation and fitness interests, *per se*, would be wrong. Rather, the amount spent tells something about the use of discretionary dollars and how shopping has become a recreation activity. Some retail outlets employ recreation specialists. They tend to rely heavily upon such organizations as the National Sporting Goods Association and the American Recreation Equipment Association for information and support.

Table 4-4
Sporting Goods Sales in the United States: 1980 and 1990

Product category	Unit	1980	1990
Athletic and Sport Clothing	millions	3,127	11,382
Athletic and Sport Footwear (running, tennis, aerobic, basketball, golf, etc.)	millions	1,731	6,437
Athletic and Sport Equipment (hunting, fishing, camping, skiing, golf, tennis, etc.)	millions	6,487	12,073
Recreational Transport (pleasure boats, recreational vehicles, bicycles, snowmobiles, etc.)	millions	5,345	14,248
Total sales	millions	16,691	44,140

Source: *1992 Statistical Abstract*, p. 242.

Service businesses are more commonly associated with the recreation industry than are retail outlets. Aquatic centers, bowling lanes, racquet sports complexes, aerobic dance studios, video arcades, and billiard parlors are illustrations of these businesses. They have enjoyed an increased market share during the past decade utilizing a variety of operating strategies (Warnick & Howard, 1990). Some businesses such as fitness combine activity with information by providing comprehensive services (e.g., nutrition counselling and physical fitness classes) with exercise. Others, like racket sports centers, tend to emphasize one or two activities (e.g., tennis and racquetball) while others are multipurposed (e.g., aquatics, fitness and social events).

To remain viable, commercial recreation professionals must be aware of industry trends. They must be adaptable and responsive to change. Conventional wisdom holds that the fitness boom of the 1980s would continue to increase throughout the 1990s. Longitudinal data from a variety of fitness studies substantiate this belief. However, recreation behaviors are difficult to predict especially if one only relies upon activity data. The motives behind choices are complex and often contradictory. Considerable evidence now suggests

fitness activities may decline. The "baby boomers" who made exercise popular when they were in their 20s and 30s are turning 40 and their preferences
seem to be to purchase fitness equipment, which they may not use, and take
long walks, occasionally, rather than exercise at a fitness center or jog.

A recent analysis of American adult participation in six popular sport and
fitness activities (Howard, 1992) revealed growth in only one (i.e., golf) of the
six major activities surveyed. Tennis actually dropped from 18 million players in 1980 to 14.6 million in 1989 (Table 4-5). Adult joggers/runners declined
from almost 23 million to 14.6 million in the same period. Given the fad aspects
of recreational behavior, commercial recreation professionals need to measure
and accurately anticipate both upward and downward trends in order to stay
successful over the long term. Many racquet sport facilities have compensated

Table 4-5
Frequency of Adult Participation in Selected Sport and Fitness Activities: 1980-1989

	Golf		Racquetball		Tennis		Aerobics		Jog/Run		Weightlifting	
	%*	No.[†]	%	No.	%	No.	%	No.	%	No.	%	No.
1989	12.5	22.2	4.7	8.4	8.2	14.6	6.5	11.5	8.2	14.6	5.8	10.4
1988	13.0	22.9	5.4	9.5	8.8	15.5	7.7	13.6	8.9	15.7	5.8	10.2
1987	10.9	18.9	5.3	9.2	7.9	13.7	7.9	13.7	10.6	18.4	6.1	10.6
1986	11.5	19.7	5.6	9.7	8.7	14.9	8.2	14.1	12.5	21.5	8.9	15.0
1985	8.9	15.1	5.0	8.5	7.0	11.8	N/A	N/A	13.4	22.7	8.8	14.7
1984	8.9	15.0	5.1	8.7	8.0	13.5	N/A	N/A	13.2	22.2	7.5	12.4
1983	8.3	13.7	5.5	9.0	8.8	14.5	N/A	N/A	13.5	22.3	7.4	12.0
1982	8.1	13.0	6.6	10.6	9.1	14.7	N/A	N/A	13.1	21.5	N/A	N/A
1981	8.2	13.1	6.1	9.7	10.2	16.2	N/A	N/A	13.6	21.6	N/A	N/A
1980	8.3	13.0	6.0	9.5	11.4	18.1	N/A	N/A	14.4	22.8	N/A	N/A

* Percent of the total adult population who reported participating at least once in the activity
 in a twelve-month period.

[†] Total number (in millions) who participated at least once within the twelve-month period.

Source: Howard, D.R. (1992). Participation rates in selected sport and fitness activities.
Journal of Sport Management, 6, pp. 191-205.

for the declining numbers of racquetball and tennis players by offering aerobic and weight training opportunities, while others went out of business. The key is to understand the motives which determine behaviors and the forces which modify interests as an individual ages, society changes, and new interests are promoted. Professionals in this domain tend to join industry-specific organizations like the International Racquet Sport Association and the National Golf Foundation to keep informed and remain viable.

Hospitality and food services are devoted to the lodging and feeding of travelers and tourists although local residents also benefit from their presence. Resort communities represent a major component of this commercial recreation domain. Usually planned around a major activity (e.g., performing arts, gambling, the visual arts, skiing, golf, tennis, sailing), they try to give their visitors a total recreation experience. Given their dual nature as a permanent residence for the host and a vacation destination for others, resort communities frequently employ two types of recreation personnel: (a) those whose primary responsibility is to provide services for the permanent residents of the community, and (b) those who are to work with the tourists to make their visit a recreation experience. Ideally, these two groups should work together for a more effective planning and utilization of a community's resources. Both need to be sensitive to the effects of tourism on the resources and social structures of the community, especially when large numbers of nonresidents inundate it (Crompton & Richardson, 1986).

The patterns of tourism development are not always the same. Some resorts are a series of complexes under single management while others develop as resort communities. Salishan, Oregon, and the Homestead, West Virginia, are examples of the former; Park City, Utah, and Sun Valley, Idaho, are examples of the latter. An estimated 1,300 ski communities exist in the United States and Canada. To avoid the seasonal aspects often associated with the ski industry, many of these areas serve as conference centers or have built golf and tennis facilities to attract off-season visitors to make it a year-round business. The Resort and Commercial Recreation Association and Council on Hotel, Restaurant, and Institutional Education are among the groups giving leadership to the growing number of recreation professionals employed in this tourism and hospitality domain.

Another hospitality/resort business which has enjoyed much success recently is the cruise ship industry. Its popularity can be traced to a variety of factors including nostalgia, positive publicity (e.g., the television series, "The Love Boat," which reinvigorated cruise lines in the 1970s), and sociodemographic trends (e.g., more single professionals, more double-income married couples, a rising number of healthy and affluent senior citizens). Cruise ships provide millions of passengers with experiences from traveling the Mississippi on paddle wheelers to island hopping in the Caribbean on luxury liners to scenic and educational tours up the coasts of British Columbia and Alaska. Two of the trade groups serving the professional in this industry are the Cruise Line International Association and the International Passenger Ship Association.

Contemporary Issues Facing Commercial Recreation Professionals

There is some evidence to suggest that commercial recreation professionals differ from their public sector counterparts with respect to organizational motives (Yoshioka, 1990), job characteristics (Yen & McKinney, 1992), and work motivators (Lankford, Neal & Buxton, 1992). In addition, a series of studies on "sector biases" has revealed that many participants perceive differences not only in the types of services and facilities offered by public and commercial sector agencies, but also in the employees themselves (Havitz, 1989; Bogle, Havitz & Dimanche, 1992). In other words, commercial recreation professionals seemingly view the world differently from their public sector counterparts and so do their clients. Their ability to offer high risk activities, respond quickly to trends and offer programs and services to fit changing needs and interests set them apart from the public sector. As a result of these differences, numerous issues and problems face parks and recreation educators and those who wish to join all segments of the leisure service delivery system into one professional voice.

Technology has created entire subindustries. Mountain bikes, bungee cords, Gore-Tex,™ wave pools, video cassette recorders (VCR), video games, and computer technologies have dramatically changed our recreation habits. Commercial recreation professionals are often the first to embrace new technologies for their recreation and market potentials. In some instances, the technologies become the experience. Walt Disney's EPCOT Center (Experimental Prototype Community Of Tomorrow) and Photon Marketing, Ltd. are classic examples of technology as a recreational attraction. Photon franchises provide "a unique experience where a mere earthling is transformed into a Photonian Warrior... a fast-paced adventure where you suit up in space-age battle gear and compete... in a heavily-mazed extraterrestrial planet enhanced with futuristic lighting and sound effects" (*Franchise Handbook*, 1985). The public sector could never have been able to respond to the markets and potential as did Disney or Photon. Rapid response time including the ability to respond quickly, to risk, and to take immediate advantage of innovations is one of the unique features of commercial recreation.

Whereas technology generally creates opportunities, legal and safety issues sometimes limit their use. This duality can be positive or negative, depending upon one's perspective. Trampoline sales and pole vault competitions, for example, have declined because of the physical danger associated with participation and their corresponding legal implications. Commercial recreation operators generally push the risk boundaries more than do their public sector counterparts. Commercial businesses are more likely to perceive leisure and recreation as an end rather than as a means to produce some socially desirable outcome, although these two goals are not necessarily mutually exclusive. They may also offer leisure activities such as drinking or gambling that are restricted or not acceptable as a responsibility of government. This tendency to operate "on the edge" has characterized commercial recreation throughout much of its history (Cross, 1990; Butsch, 1990).

Responsiveness to sociodemographic changes and a market approach characterize most commercial recreation businesses. As cited earlier, the decline in racquet sports in the 1980s can be traced to an aging population that favors golf. Given this information, the sporting goods industry did not become an activity dinosaur; instead, it adjusted production and changed marketing to target a new product and a new sales group. When commercially provided activities decline or no longer attract sufficient participants, they are discontinued or modified. When sociodemographic changes occur, they are often viewed as an opportunity, not a threat. For example, a San Francisco area business reacted to the growing single parent/working women market by creating a summer camp session exclusively for moms. They participated in many of the same activities and in the same settings as did their children. The difference was in who the campers were and their reasons for being there. Similarly, some fitness businesses have reacted to the changing circumstances of the boomer market by offering childcare facilities and services while their parents are exercising or attending nutrition classes.

Some might assume that the commercial sector should be given preference to the public sector for its career potential because of its ability to adapt and generate economic success. The public sector often appears static and unexciting. The two sectors, however, complement each other by playing their separate roles. In recent years, both have relied heavily upon market strategies. Fostered by the commercial sector, marketing strategies have been adopted by other segments of the leisure service delivery system including the public and private not-for-profit agencies. Marketing involves the development and/or provision of select activities or services to satisfy specific needs and wants. Most public recreation professionals feel that if recreation products and activities are to be marketed as public goods, these services ought to have a positive societal and environmental effect. On the other hand, the commercial sector is under less pressure to look at the social consequence of their products; potential participants are more likely to be provided with "exactly what they want." Thus, retailers of jet skis and mountain bikes may have different views on those products than do U.S. Forest Service employees charged both with protecting natural resources while serving visitors.

Commercial sector professionals also have a lesser mandate to reach the underrepresented or financially disadvantaged than do public sector professionals. Commercial recreation providers do not have to serve all; they can target the 5 percent who play racquetball, the 10 percent who play golf, or the 30 percent who swim and not worry about those who do not do any of these activities. Commercial sector marketing efforts generally focus on increasing participation frequency or on attracting participants from other sites so that profits are sustained or increased. They do not have to maintain programs of interest to only a few or those nonrevenue producing programs designed to meet the special needs of some individuals. Each sector has its mission. One is not supplementary to the other. The relationship is complementary, not competitive.

"Golf for the Hungry," organized by the Cleveland [OH] Metroparks, is an innovative fourteen-day promotion that allows golfers to play at any area course for a donation of five nonperishable food items or $3 cash. Proceeds benefit the hungry.

Projecting the Future of the Commercial Recreation Industry

The changing fiscal realities resulting from America's shift from a manufacturing-based to a services-based economy suggests in the future public-commercial cooperation likely will become an everyday event. Cooperation produces obvious benefits by reducing cost and duplication. Nevertheless, differences between the commercial and the public sectors must be recognized and addressed if cooperative efforts are to succeed. Contracted services and franchising are two likely growth areas.

Many commercial professionals have chosen to contract services rather than build and operate large, expensive facilities. For example, American Golf Corporation manages over 145 courses in 22 states and employs over 5,000 people, but it does not own a single golf course. Instead it manages golf courses for both public and private organizations by maintaining courses, operating pro shops, giving lessons, scheduling rounds, and sponsoring tournaments. SKIwees, Inc. is a franchise combining expertise related to skiing, leisure behavior, and education theory to provide specialized lessons for young children. Other recreation entrepreneurs have specialized in providing corporate recreation services, conducting birthday parties, and leisure counselling. Numerous niches are yet to be discovered.

Franchising will also continue to grow beyond the franchising of fast food and lodging establishments. Franchises are now available for miniature golf operations, travel agencies, go-karts, campgrounds, and combination pubs-movie theaters. Many of these are family business; some evolve into major corporations. For example, thousands of small video rental outlets were formed in the early 1980s in response to that technology. More recently, large companies (e.g., Blockbuster Video) have come to dominate the industry. Yet, there seems to be a place for the small business enterprise. The growing number of B&Bs (bed and breakfast inns) is a case in point.

Commercial recreation is an exciting industry with numerous career opportunities. Like all segments of the profession, multidisciplinary training is essential. In addition to a strong understanding of leisure behavior, commercial recreation professionals must have a basic understanding of research methods, marketing, management, finance, accounting, and legal issues.

Tourism

In 1980 you likely would not have found a chapter or even a section that dealt exclusively with "travel and tourism" in a text on parks and recreation. Some reference might have been made to tourism's effects on local economies, but an introductory text in geography would have been needed to learn more about this sector of the leisure services system. Like therapeutic recreation or camping, today tourism is recognized as a vital element of the leisure service delivery system and a specialty within the profession. Several major universities have established tracks or emphases in tourism; some have added it to their departmental title. It is an expanding field, but a difficult one to define with its many facets. Some professionals argue that tourism should be an area of study in business because it is a collection of industries; others see it as a part of the hospitality field. Some view tourism as a profession in its own right. All agree that it is a growth industry and is motivationally tied to our recreation behaviors and interests (Murdaugh, 1984). Because of this tie, students of parks and recreation should know something about tourism.

Travel for trade and religious purposes dates back to antiquity, yet tourism is a modern industry and perhaps the most dominant form of commercial recreation behavior. Its growth as a major economic force and as a leisure interest for millions is due in part to technological advances and affluence. It is also an outgrowth of the desire to see other cultures, visit other environments, and experience new and different things. These reasons have motivated pleasure travel for generations, but only in the last 160 years has tourism become fashionable enough to warrant a system to accommodate it.

Definitional Concerns

When is one a tourist and when does travel become tourism? Tourist behavior ranges from trips to the beach to sunbathe and walk the strand to trips to the Antarctica to study its fragile ecosystem. Tourism involves traveling to an outdoor destination to ski, swim, or hike but it can also mean taking a trip to Las Vegas to gamble, to New York to attend a Broadway play, or to London to sightsee and shop at Harrod's. Tourism may mean visiting friends or relatives or taking a sightseeing trip to Busch Gardens or to the Grand Canyon. Many faces of tourism exist. Given its complexity, most professionals tend to define it by describing its characteristics or elements rather than offering a single, unequivocal statement. The elements most frequently mentioned are: distance traveled, motives of travel, and the time required for the visit.

Distance Traveled. The first characteristic involves travel. How far does one have to go to be a tourist? The United Nations definition requires one to cross an international border while the U.S. Census Bureau defines a trip as traveling one hundred miles away from home. Both definitions are problematic. For example, skiers traveling from New York City to the Poconos in Pennsylvania would go less than a hundred miles, but their behavior and impact on the local economy would be very similar to those coming from points several hundred miles away. On the other hand, it is highly unlikely that the natives of Juarez, Mexico feel as if they are tourists when they cross the border each morning to work in El Paso, Texas.

Motive. The second characteristic is the reason for the trip. Is it work related, purely recreational, or is it both? Is it required or is it voluntary? The U.S. Travel Data Center includes in its definition all motives for travel except those related to commuting to and from work, school-related travel, or travel involved in operating a transportation vehicle such as plane or train.

Time (Duration) of the Trip. The final consideration is the length of time one stays away from home while traveling. Most definitions of tourism include a time frame, such as the U.N.'s definition which requires a stay of at least 24 hours. Such a restriction, however, would eliminate many day trips in excess of a hundred miles for recreational purposes, trips in which the traveler exhibits the characteristics of a tourist. Consequently, most students of travel and tourism are less concerned about the duration of the trip than the motives and distance traveled.

Given these parameters, a tourist is defined as one who travels to a destination for recreation purposes and inherent in that travel is the sense of having taken a trip. This definition allows the business traveler to become a tourist when that portion of the travel is recreational rather than work required (see Table 4-6). In the final analysis, all tourists are travelers but not all travelers are tourists. Perhaps the area which has the greatest tie to parks and recreation is mass tourism. It is that segment of the industry which appeals to the majority of recreational travelers. It requires little of the traveler to adapt to the culture of the host and to go beyond the attractions or to explore. It is "convenient" tourism. Travel may be with a tour group or individually planned and may be organized or spontaneous. Whatever form it takes, it requires little of the traveler. It is highly system-dependent, relying heavily upon travel agents, promotion materials, tour guides, travel organizations such as the American Automobile Association (AAA), and hotel and motel chains.

Table 4-6
Characteristics of Business Trips and Pleasure Trips: 1980 to 1990

Characteristic	Unit	Business Trips			Pleasure Trips		
		1980	1985	1990	1980	1985	1990
Total trips	millions	97.1	133.3	155.6	342.8	384.4	460.5
Average household members on trip	number	1.5	1.4	1.4	2.2	2.1	2.1
Average nights per trip*	nights	N/A	3.6	3.7	N/A	5.6	4.4
Average miles per trip[†]	miles	N/A	1,180	1,020	N/A	1,010	867
Traveled primarily by auto, truck, recreational vehicle, rental car	percent	56	51	58	80	73	77
Traveled primarily by air	percent	42	44	37	16	21	18
Used a rental car while on trip	percent	25	20	14	7	6	7
Stayed in hotel while on trip	percent	66	62	71	34	39	37
Used a travel agent	percent	21	28	21	10	13	12
Also a vacation trip	percent	10	13	17	75	80	82
Male travelers	percent	N/A	67	71	N/A	48	49
Female travelers	percent	N/A	33	29	N/A	52	51
Household income: less than $40,000	percent	N/A	58	42	N/A	73	63
$40,000 or more	percent	N/A	42	56	N/A	27	38

N/A—not available.   *—includes no overnight stays.   [†]—U.S. only.

Source: *1992 Statistical Abstract*, p. 245.

The Travel Industry

Other than the recreational component associated with tourism, it is extremely difficult to separate the tourist industry from the travel industry. Both depend upon the same infrastructure and types of accommodations and services. Travelers of all types need accommodations and a means of transportation. Motels would exist with or without tourists. Likewise, airlines would operate even if no passengers were flying to destinations for recreational purposes. But these industries would not be as significant if there were no tourists, especially the mass tourists.

In addition to these basic elements of the travel industry, tourism requires the additional component of attractions. There must be activities, sites, and relationships which bring the traveler to a given destination for recreational purposes. The activities generally include shopping, sightseeing, dining, active participation (e.g., skiing, horseback riding, attending the opera), and/or structured tours. Travel and tourism is a many faceted industry with success dependent largely upon the successful interaction of the traveler, host, private sector, and governmental policy. Each has its own motives, expectations, and roles.

The traveler. The first perspective is that of the traveler. People expect trips to be pleasurable and to be worth their time and effort. They usually expect amenities at the destination and in a form familiar to those of the home community (e.g., similar food and lodging accommodations). They often want the local population to be open to questions and stop what they are doing to meet their needs of the moment. In short, tourists expect to be accommodated; after all, they are paying for it.

The host perspective. Those residing in tourist destinations often have a different perspective. Depending upon the importance of the tourist industry to them, hosts typically have a love/hate relationship with tourism. Recent research suggests that host community residents are not universally happy to see their area become a "travel destination" (Milman & Pizam, 1988). They understand the economic impact it brings to their communities, but they also know that with the tourists come longer lines at local restaurants, crowded highways, perhaps increased criminal activity, and inflated prices on local goods and services. They understand the symbiotic relationship which exists between the traveler and his or her needs and the host environment with its services and attractions (Hill, 1992). The degree to which local citizens are involved in tourism planning and development is related directly to the attitude the host has toward its visitors and the visitors' view of the community's "hospitality."

The private sector. From a marketing standpoint, local businesses need to differentiate the host from the tourist. By knowing something of the tourists' origins and behaviors (i.e., their cultural traditions, interests, income and motives), local merchants better know how to stock for them; they also know if these same products and services will be needed or wanted by local residents. They can make adjustments accordingly. Many tourism related industries do differentiate tourists from other travelers. For example, airlines and hotels/motels generally use a different pricing policy for tourists and business travelers because business travel is usually less flexible than recreational travel. They have found that it is in their best interest to encourage the tourist to travel midweek and to stay over a weekend when business travel is less significant. Many motels and hotels reduce their rates considerably to attract weekend guests.

Government policy and involvement. Local governmental officials are interested in tourism for a number of reasons. Travelers and guests will have an impact on those services and infrastructure provided by government such as police and fire protection, the transportation system, health and sanitation, water treatment facilities, and operations of local parks and public areas. It is critical that local governments consider the impact of tourism before embarking on a course of action to attract them. It may require, for example, the building of a sewage treatment plant with a capacity many times greater than that required by the local residents but necessary to meet the demands of its visitors as occurred at Rehobeth Beach, Delaware, where its annual population of 6,000 becomes 60,000 on a summer weekend.

The Scope of Tourism

The economic and social impact of tourism is significant. It is imperative that government and industry work closely to assure controlled growth and development and to minimize host community and visitors conflicts. In a society where service economies dominate, travel and tourism is an essential industry. It affects all aspects of life, and, in turn is affected by many forces—political unrest, governmental policy, weather, individuals' motives and the like.

How large is tourism and what is its future? From a global perspective, the tourist industry in 1992 was estimated at $2.9 trillion with a growth potential to $5.5 trillion by 2005. Should that occur, an additional 30 million new jobs will be created globally. At the national level, the statistics are equally dramatic. In 1991, 32,000 travel agencies in the United States grossed over $86 billion in sales. Nearly half of their business was their clients' personal or pleasure trips. International travel to the United States reached an all-time high in 1992 with 18 million overseas visitors including 3.6 million from Japan, followed by 2.7 million from the United Kingdom. Impressive as these statistics are, it is our next door neighbors who give us the largest number of guests: Canada and Mexico, with 21 million and 8.6 million visits, respectively, in 1991. Tourism was one of the few United States industries that year to experience a trade surplus with $85 billion in receipts from foreign visitors compared to the $67 billion expended by U.S. citizens traveling outside the United States. See Figure 4-2 (page 124).

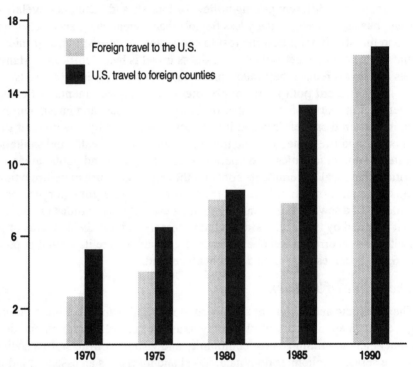

Figure 4-2
Travelers To/From the United States 1970-1990
(excluding travelers to/from Canada)

Sources: *1980 Statistical Abstract*, p. 234 and *1992 Statistical Abstract*, pp. 246-7.

At the local level tourism's impact can be significant. For example, the Charlotte, North Carolina, Chamber of Commerce estimated that the National Basketball Association's all-star game in 1991 had a $15 million impact on the Charlotte region and that the sales tax generated from visitors to the Coca-Cola™ 600 stock car race was equal to having 22 new property owners paying property tax. The businesses and government of Charlotte like the idea of being an event city. The pattern is repeated by hundreds of communities.

From an incidental perspective, consider the laundry operator who has a contract with a local convention hotel, or the food wholesaler who provides hamburger or salad materials to a theme park, or the furniture company which provides beds, carpets and television sets for a regional motel chain. It is doubtful any of these workers (i.e., the farmer, the furniture maker, the local laundry worker) would consider himself or herself being employed in the tourist industry, yet their jobs are directly related to it as are the jobs of travel agent, events manager, or state director of travel and tourism.

Motivations to travel. All the motives and constraints cited for other forms of recreation hold true with travel and tourism. It is stimulated by a desire to learn, to experience, and to have new adventures. Travel is encouraged by the mass media, popular literature, and a perception of high status. Given the opportunity to travel, people generally do. When they do not, it is largely due to the costs involved, a lack of free time, health limitations, fear and safety factors, or family stage. Occasionally not traveling results from a lack of interest or limited knowledge of the pleasures which a travel destination might provide. Some of the barriers are beyond the ability of the industry to resolve while others, such as lack of information about an area and values of traveling, are a challenge to the marketer.

Modes of transportation. Speed becomes a factor in a society which values time. But with speed comes cost. It is three times more expensive to fly the Concorde than it is to fly first class, trans-Atlantic, on a 747. Distance, preference, and income also determine one's mode of traveling. The mobile home may provide great flexibility for a family of four taking the grand tour of the United States. However, it may be a little demanding for an older adult who would prefer someone else to "do the driving" and therefore opt for a packaged Amtrak tour.

Infrastructures. When President Eisenhower signed the bill to create the interstate highway system in the 1950s, few anticipated its size or the impact it might have on the travel and tourism industry. Today, much of the over 40,000 miles of interstate highway is heavily traveled, old and in need of repair. It would take hundreds of billions of dollars to bring the system up-to-date. The same goes for air transportation and rail infrastructures. Massive investments are required to maintain what exists and develop new systems for the coming decade and century. Beautiful islands in the Caribbean might be attractive to tourists, but without a major airport or a port deep enough for large cruise ships, they will not. Communities throughout the United States would like to develop their tourist potential but lack the necessary highways to accommodate the requisite travel.

A healthy infrastructure is required but this goes beyond transportation. A tourist destination must be able to accommodate outsiders with adequate water and sewage systems, police, fire, medical, and other social services as well. Often these require the cooperation of state and local officials in order to assure both visitors and hosts that they are cared for during peak periods of activity.

The hospitality industry. A number of events in the 1950s came together to give the accommodations and food services industries a boost. The improvement of central air-conditioning opened up portions of the southern and southwestern United States to tourism. Improvements in telecommunications allowed flexibility in scheduling accommodations. The Holiday Inn Corporation was one of the first to take advantage of these changes by developing a telephone reservation system and strategically locating its motels along the interstates. Refrigerated trucks helped Howard Johnson maintain quality control over its food production while allowing the centralized process of food preparation. Both actions reduced costs while improving quality. Other chains and franchises quickly followed their lead. The industry prospered. More recent patterns have seen the development of two specialized modes of accommodation to complement the national hotel/motel chains which some feel may have reached their zenith in the 1980s. They are the bed and breakfast inns (B&B) and the megahotels like Excalibur in Las Vegas with its 4,000 rooms.

The role the quick food industry has played in travel and tourism as well as its influence on our dining habits also must be acknowledged. Like the franchised motel chains, they give travelers a sense of security and familiarity. They have also given new meaning to "eating on the run."

Affluence. Mass tourism implies that both the necessary money and time are available in large segments of the population to engage in pleasure travel. The recession of the early 1990s had a negative impact on the travel industry which suggests tourism is more tied to variations in the economy as a whole, than are some other segments of the leisure service delivery system. The more affluent the economy, the more travel and tourism generated.

Destinations/attractions. After World War II, the demand for travel opportunities meant that virtually anyone could open an attraction and be successful. With the maturing of the attractions industry, however, even the most successful tourist operator, including Disney, must plan ahead and market its attractions. The key is having something people want to see or experience and, although there are notable exceptions, being able to attract the capital necessary to build new tourist attractions. Consequently more attention is being focused on existing attractions, natural resources, and the promotion of festivals and events. Tourist areas tend either to promote themselves as destinations because of their natural resources (e.g., mountains, lakes or shores) or their attractions (e.g., theme parks, events, or cultural aspects). With an increasing number of families with two adults working, vacations patterns have changed. A shift has occurred from the two-week traditional summer vacation to a series of shorter trips taken throughout the year. The effect this change has had on destination choices has yet to be determined.

Political stability. Although some individuals will have sufficient reason to travel to places that are experiencing political unrest, recreation and leisure motives are usually not among those reasons. There are numerous examples of once thriving tourism industries that were destroyed overnight by political instability. Lebanon was once a major Mediterranean resort destination before its civil war. Literally overnight, tourism disappeared. Europe suffered an extreme downturn in tourism in the mid-1980s when a rash of terrorism occurred; the industry lost millions of dollars in canceled trips. In 1992, the civil unrest in

Los Angeles after the Rodney King verdict case caused a significant drop in tourism revenues; the civil war in Yugoslavia has almost destroyed it as one of Europe's more popular vacation spots.

Monetary exchanges. One can imagine the earliest travelers trying to barter pigs for a place to stay or exchanging their dollars for local currency. This may work today at Club Meds where guests exchange beads for drinks, but the beads have an established value. Travelers must respond to local systems; they must use the same monetary system as does their host. How many French francs are there in a dollar and what is the value of the British pound? For mass tourism to occur, a consistent, secure and understandable exchange system had to be created. One of the major breakthroughs occurred in the 1890s when American Express introduced the traveler's check. Credit cards and automatic teller machines now threaten to make traveler's checks, and the sometimes expensive foreign money exchange windows at international airports, obsolete.

Like all international businesses, the exchange process is tied to the international monetary system. The monetary system changes daily and can make or break a tourist destination or create problems for world travelers negatively affected by the devaluing of their currency. For example, the devaluation of the peso by Mexico several years ago made Mexico an attractive destination for Americans while making it extremely expensive or, in many cases, prohibitive for most Mexicans to vacation outside their country.

Governmental policy and stability. Freedom of movement is taken for granted in the United States. But, this freedom is not a universally practiced right. Even the U.S. government restricts the travel of its citizens to certain countries during periods of unrest or when there are political disagreements. Cuba, for example, in the 1950s was a major tourist destination for thousands of Americans, but was placed off limits to travelers once our government broke off diplomatic relations. Government approvals can change without warning. When the Chinese decided to close Tibet to tourists in the 1970s, it was immediate; arriving travelers were told they could not enter the country. Thus, individuals who had planned their trip for months and who had paid considerably for travel were out of luck. International tourism requires numerous agreements covering air and ground transportation, what products can be taken across borders, and what tariffs must be paid. Even in the U.S., travelers between California and Arizona are routinely stopped at the border by Agricultural inspectors and asked to dispose of select fruits or vegetables they may be transporting.

Seasonal weather. Last but not least, the success of a tourist experience or the ability of an area to become a tourism destination is somewhat dependent upon its weather. After several years of marginal snowfalls, the ski industry of the Northeast received a boost in 1992 with some unusually heavy snows. But what nature gives it can take away as it did that same year. Two hurricanes, one in Florida (Andrew) and one in Hawaii (Iniki) caused billions of dollars damage and negatively affected these tourist destinations. Even a single event can have an impact. For example, in 1990 Florida had an infestation of mosquitoes which carried a deadly disease; people were forced to stay inside at night. The effects on the industry were negative. Tourists have the choice to go or not to go to a locale, but the destination itself cannot move due to weather or natural disasters.

Issues Facing the Tourist Industry

Like all industries undergoing growth and change, travel and tourism has its challenges. One of the issues confronting the United States' tourist industry is the role of the federal government. Most industrialized nations have a cabinet office responsible for travel and tourism, but not the U.S. Only one agency at the national level, the United States Travel and Tourism Administration, gives leadership to the industry. Both the Bush and Reagan Administrations in the 1980s wanted to eliminate or severely curtail its efforts, but the USTTA continues to promote travel to the United States and is looking for ways to reduce international travel constraints. It also hopes to use its resources to develop tourism as an economic strategy for rural areas, but this goal has not been financed. Some politicians believe that tourism promotion should be left to the individual states or to the private sector and not involve the federal government.

A second problem confronting the industry is its diversity. The tourism industry is fragmented and comprised of many sectors or subsystems. For example, at least thirty federal industrial codes have been developed by different agencies related to travel and tourism. At the local level, each state has its own

New Westminster [British Columbia, Canada] greets visitors with well-manicured gardens.

set of laws governing operations. Coordination among levels of government, among the various interdependent industries, and between these industries and governments is critical to the operation and growth of the travel and tourism industry. This coordination does not exist today.

The effects that tourism has on a destination's social system, environment and culture is a third issue. Many people view tourism as a savior for economically depressed areas, especially if the region has a strong natural resource base and/or a degree of "quaintness" as one of its attractions. But there are potential negative costs which must be considered as well as economic gains. Pollution, infrastructure costs, increased social problems, and seasonal unemployment issues are important considerations. Tourism promoters must also consider whether an area really has destination potential given the competition, and the choices travelers have. Often overlooked by local officials is the concept of clustering as a necessary ingredient to generate enough attractions to entice travelers to change destination preferences. An underdeveloped infrastructure or poor labor market can negatively affect a destination in much the same way that undercapitalization may negatively affect a start-up industry.

Numerous cases exist where tourism has transformed or destroyed local traditions and crafts. Rather than reflecting the values and interests of the community, local traditions can come to reflect the market. The designs of many Amish quilts, for example, no longer have meaning to the Amish; they are the designs most popular with the tourists. Dance rituals once performed for their own sake are now done at specific times for monetary reasons. Female dancers in Bali now wear bras so as not to offend the tourists. Commercial rugs are often advertised as Indian designs implying they were made by Native Americans; in many instances, trinkets have replaced the native crafts or the demand for inexpensive souvenirs caused a decline in craftmanship. Before a community embarks on the path of becoming a tourist destination it should carefully weigh the gains and losses.

The Future of Tourism

Every indicator suggests that travel and tourism will increase in popularity. Postindustrialism and a growing service economy are having their effects as are political and social changes. The dissolution of the Soviet Union is a case in point. Travel to areas, countries formerly restricted by the USSR, is now permitted, but it will take huge sums of investment and time to build the necessary infrastructure for tourism to help these newly independent nations in a dramatic fashion. Once the infrastructure is in place, new markets for the U.S. travel industry will be available.

Changing attitudes and values are also affecting the industry. As more states modify their laws to allow gambling, new destinations have appeared. Las Vegas and Atlantic City no longer have a lock on gambling activity. Several states such as Illinois and Iowa have actively promoted riverboat gambling; recreation professionals are divided as to what degree they should promote or condemn this trend (Stubbles, 1992). With the "graying of America" every indication is that it will grow in popularity. On many Native American reservations, Bingo has become a major attraction.

Both successes and failures will be common. Tourists have become sophisticated and unless the promoters can convince them that they will get a quality experience at a reasonable price, local developers are certain to lose out in this volatile market. One of the fastest growing segments of the industry are those companies which have capitalized on a select target market such as whitewater, or birding enthusiasts. Between 1989 and 1992, for example, adventure travel grew eight to ten percent annually with some 8,000 outfitters being ready in 1992 to assist the outdoor recreationist. Shopping, educational travel, and cultural travel are other select markets. Shopping will continue to be a major motivation for tourist travel whether it be to an outlet center such as Lightfoot, Virginia; a specialty market such as Pike's Place in Seattle, Washington; or a super mall like Bloomington, Minnesota's Mall of America with a yearly visitation of 40 million shoppers.

With the aging of America, the tourist industry likely will provide more package tours; that is, having the travel agent attend to all the travel details. Considerable evidence suggests that even the more seasoned travelers are turning over the lodging and transportation details to the travel professional so that they might spend more of their energies and time enjoying the pleasures of the destination. Perhaps this is one of the reasons why the cruise ship industry has experienced such success.

Given the dimensions of the tourism industry, it is highly likely the federal government will become more involved in travel and tourism. The large amounts of capital required to build the necessary infrastructure and attractions to sustain tourism suggest this will happen. This government involvement should encourage more public debate and a clarification of government's role in travel and tourism, especially at the local level. The Main Street Program is an example of building local involvement in the tourist development process. Through the program, residents are asked to identify what is unique about their community and what aspects should and should not be promoted. They are invited to aid planners at every step of development. Typical is the community of Jim Thorpe, Pennsylvania, which was designated as a pilot project for the Main Street Program in the early 1980s. Several attempts had been made previously to revitalize the community but had not succeeded, not until Main Street with its mandatory requirement of community involvement.

The Relationship of Tourism to Other Sectors of the Industry: Commercial and Public

Tourism is a major industry and involves a variety of corporations and Fortune 500 companies: airlines, rental car companies, hotel and motel chains, and entertainment groups. There are the Marriotts and Walt Disney Worlds, but the majority of the tourist operations in the United States (up to 90 percent) are "Mom and Pop" operations employing 25 or fewer persons. The major theme parks may get our attention, but it is the small operators who serve as the backbone of the industry. Within tourism, countless opportunities exist for individuals who want to test their entrepreneurial skills, whether it be providing travelers with information, services en route to their destination or home, programming for tourists at their destination or during their travels, or memories (e.g., video tapes, photographs, etc.) of their experience.

Often overlooked is the role local parks and recreation systems play in providing activities and services. Working cooperatively with their chambers of commerce or tourist bureaus, local systems are able to schedule events that are easily marketed as an attraction; they can sponsor cultural activities, street fairs, and sporting events as well as make their aquatic areas, tennis courts, and golf courses available to their guests. They may even receive a percentage of the "guest" taxes charged tourists by local hotels and restaurants to expand or support those programs and facilities that have tourist appeal.

Tourism affects all. Like so many forms of commercial recreation, it is often criticized as being a contributor to pollution, immorality, urban blight, and related social problems. It also has the potential for bringing to the public some very creative, stimulating experiences and aesthetic surroundings. The latter can be maximized when government and industry work cooperatively as partners to provide quality recreation opportunities. Through trade controls and local ordinances, some gains have been made but the future of tourism lies in cooperative planning.

Almost on a daily basis we are either a tourist or a host interacting with those visiting our home communities. Tourism has the potential to create more understanding between people and to infuse life into morbid economies. Its positives far outweigh its negatives. Every time a community develops an attraction for its visitors, it also is providing additional recreation opportunities for its citizens. Every time a community develops its public recreation areas or encourages private entrepreneurs to operate an attraction, it adds to the attractiveness of the area as a tourist destination. The systems are interactive and interdependent. The benefits to a recreating public are enormous.

Suggestions and Study Guides

1. Most individuals involved in the delivery of leisure services (other than those associated with parks and recreation agencies) do not consider themselves to be recreation professionals. Test this contention by talking with the managers of various commercial recreation enterprises. What do they see as their relationship to parks and recreation? their profession? the nature of their agency's mission?

2. Discuss with a realtor and/or someone in business the importance of recreation facilities and programs to their business. How do they utilize recreation resources to further their business operation or to achieve their business goals? What evidence do they have that recreation has impact on land values and employee morale?

3. Consider your own spending habits. Keep a log of your expenditures for one week. See what percentage of your expenditures are related to your "pursuit of pleasure." Consider the monies spent for junk food, pleasure driving, pleasure reading, and so on as recreation expenditures. Do not limit your record to only those costs associated with admission charges, equipment purchases, records, and tapes.

4. Visit a commercial recreation attraction or reflect upon your last visit to one. What made the experience pleasurable? What kinds of resources and support services did you expect or use? Will you return there again? Why or why not?

References

Academy of Leisure Sciences. (1993). *Issue papers.* Unpublished materials.

Bogle, T., Havitz, M. E., & Dimanche, F. (1992). Sector biases in adults' recreation fitness facility selection. *Journal of Park and Recreation Administration, 10*(3), pp. 49-74.

Brooks, C. (1988). Armchair quarterbacks. *American Demographics, 10*(3), pp. 28-31.

Bullaro, J. & Edginton, C. (1986). *Commercial leisure services: Managing for profit.* New York, NY: MacMillan.

Bureau of Outdoor Recreation. (1968). *Recreation land price escalation,* pp. 10-11 Washington, DC: U.S. Department of Interior.

Butsch, R. (1990). *For fun and profit: The transformation of leisure into consumption.* Philadelphia, PA: Temple University Press.

Crompton, J. & Richardson, S. (1986). The tourism connection. Where public and private leisure services merge. *Parks and Recreation, 21*(10), pp. 38-44, 67.

Cross, G. (1990). *A social history of leisure since 1600.* State College, PA: Venture Publishing, Inc.

Crossley, J. (1990). Multi-ties programming in commercial recreation. *Parks and Recreation, 25*(3), pp. 68-73.

Decker, J. & Crompton, J. (1990). Business location decisions: The relative importance of quality of life and recreation, park and cultural opportunities. *Journal of Park and Recreation Administration, 8*(2), pp. 26-43.

Franchise opportunities handbook. (1985). Washington, DC: United States Department of Commerce

Getz, D. (1991). *Festivals, special events and tourism.* New York, NY: Van Nostrand Reinhold.

Gunn, C. (1988). *Tourism planning (2nd ed.).* New York, NY: Taylor & Francis.

Havitz, M. (1989). The empirical development of a taxonomy for classifying recreation participants based on their attitudes toward the public and commercial sectors. *Leisure Sciences, 11*, pp. 229-243.

Heritage Conservation and Recreation Service. (1978). *The Assessment,* p. 13. Washington, DC: U.S. Government Printing Office.

Hill, B. (1992). Sustainable tourism. *Parks and Recreation, 27*(9), pp. 84-89, 130.

Howard, D. (1992). Participation rates in selected sport and fitness activities. *Journal of Sport Management, 6,* pp. 191-205.

Jansen, W. (1992). Marina development in the public sector. *Parks and Recreation, 27*(11), pp. 49, 75.

Lankford, S., Neal, L., & Buxton, B. (1992). An examination and comparison of work motivators in public, private/commercial, nonprofit, and armed forces leisure service organizations. *Journal of Park and Recreation Administration, 10*(4), pp. 57-70.

Milman, A. & Pizam, A. (1988). Social impacts of tourism on central Florida. *Annals of Tourism Research, 15,* pp. 191-204.

Murdaugh, M. (1984). Tourism: America's burgeoning industry and its challenge for tomorrow. *Parks and Recreation, 19*(10), pp. 39-42.

Propst, D. & Combrink, T. (1991). The interrelations of agriculture and tourism. In D. M. Spotts (Ed.), *Travel and tourism in Michigan: A statistical profile.* East Lansing, MI: Michigan Travel, Tourism, and Recreation Resource Center.

Soule, G. (1957). The economics of leisure. *The Annals of the American Academy of Political and Social Science,* September, pp. 16-24.

Statistical Abstract of the United States: 1980. Washington, DC: U.S. Government Printing Office.

Statistical Abstract of the United States: 1991. Washington, DC: U.S. Government Printing Office.

Statistical Abstract of the United States: 1992. Washington, DC: U.S. Government Printing Office.

Stubbles, R. (1992). A question of gambling. *Parks and Recreation, 27*(4), pp. 61-64, 83.

Van Doren, C. (1993). Personal correspondence.

Yen, T. & McKinney, W. (1992). The relationship between compensation satisfaction and job characteristics: A comparative study of public and private leisure service professionals. *Journal of Park and Recreation Administration, 10*(4), pp. 15-36.

Yoshioka, C. (1990). Organizational motives of public, nonprofit, and commercial leisure service agencies. *Journal of Applied Recreation Research, 15*, pp. 59-70.

CHAPTER FIVE

Public Recreation and Parks Services

Government is the process we use to carry out societal functions in an orderly fashion. Without government, anarchy and chaos likely would engulf us. The United States has chosen a democratic form of government to meet the needs of its people, and although the patterns vary from time to time and from one level to another, ultimately government does for people collectively what they are unable to do individually.

Since democratic governments are concerned with the well-being of their citizens, and since recreation experiences contribute to that well-being, it is not surprising that park and recreation services have become a responsibility of government.

Government is the only agency that is supported by, and can serve all segments of the population, without discriminating according the age, sex, race, and economic condition of those served. It alone has the financial resources to acquire, establish, improve, and operate recreation and park facilities to meet the public's need. Government has the power of eminent domain which means it is the only agency that has the right to take, or authorize the taking of, private property for public use when such action is in the best interest of the public. Furthermore, government is continuous and permanent. It is in the best position to develop the basic policies upon which effective recreation and park services depend and it can do so at a minimum unit cost. The mission of government is to serve the public without excluding anyone from its programs.

Local Service

Organized recreation and park systems are largely an urban phenomenon. As cities grew, so did the need for park and recreation services; the issue of the quality of life of living in an urban environment could not be avoided. Over 80 percent of the U.S. population lives within its metropolitan districts. The attitudes associated with city living dominate the thinking of nearly every citizen. Urban dwellers enjoy being entertained and having opportunities for leisure expression. Since the immediate living environment often restricts their activities, they have turned to the private and governmental sectors. Commercial and private not-for-profit recreation services is one response to their need; local parks and recreation departments is another.

For the most part local public park and recreation departments are financed by the general fund of the community (monies which come from taxes levied on property) or from a special recreation tax. The funding sources are determined by state and local laws and ordinances. These monies are supplemented by revenue derived from fees and charges, grants, gifts, and special assessments. In addition to these sources of support for daily operation, departments generally rely upon bond issues to fund their capital (facility and land acquisition) development projects.

Although local governmental services do not purport to meet the recreation interests for every facet of public life, they do guarantee a basic level of support and opportunity. Communities tend to mandate their expectations, and parks and recreation are a part of that mandate. The public expects them to provide certain types of facilities, opportunities, and services where they can meet and play. Communities create their recreation and park systems, although the organizational structure by which these recreation provisions are made vary considerably. They reflect the historical origins of the recreation and park movement, the attitudes of the profession, and the experience and traditions of each community.

There is no single pattern for the administering local recreation and parks systems. Each is determined by the type and wording of the legislation which allowed the community to become an incorporated body. These charter or enabling acts permit municipalities and local units of government to decide how recreation and parks, along with other public services, are to be provided.

In some communities, local recreation and park services are administered as separate functions of government, each independent of the other. In other localities, public recreation and parks are operated jointly as a combined department or district. Some communities administer recreation services in conjunction with the school system, whereas others operate recreation and parks as a unit within their Department of Community Services. Some idea of the diversity and trend among managing authorities for local public recreation and park departments can be seen in Table 5-1.

Table 5-1
Select Municipal and County Government Expenditures 1988

Service	County		Municipal	
	Amount*	%	Amount*	%
Police	5.6	5.3	15.8	9.0
Fire	•	•	8.2	4.7
Highways	8.4	8.0	10.7	6.2
Health	6.4	6.1	8.0	4.6
Public buildings	1.7	1.7	1.7	1.0
Financial administration	3.0	2.8	3.8	1.9
Parks and recreation	1.9	1.9	6.4	3.7
Total general expenditures	105.4	100.0	133.9	100.0

*in billions

Source: *1991 Statistical Abstract*, pp. 298-99.

The most dominant pattern of organization is that of the combined park and recreation department. It has been the "structure of choice" since the early 1960s. Prior to that time, the most frequent pattern was that of having parks and recreation function as separate, independent departments (a parks department and a recreation department). The choice of the administrative structure is that of the local community. The profession tends to recommend the combining of parks and recreation into a single unit but recognizes that even the "best structure" can fail if the people responsible for its services are uninterested, unwilling, or are unable to make it work. Conversely, the "right people" can often make a poor structure succeed.

Types of Operating Structures

The type of structure employed has no specific relationship to the political subdivision responsible for parks and recreation services. Recreation or park services may be administered by independent districts, commissions, municipal, or county recreation governments (see Figure 5-1, page 141).

A brief description of the major structures employed and the pros and cons of each follows:

Systems in which recreation and parks is administered as a single administrative unit. Independent park and recreation authorities are characterized by a focus on parks and recreation as an integrated function. In this structure, parks and recreation services are seen as interrelated and equally important—the best approach to maximize the natural relationship which exists between programs and facilities. Proponents of this structure argue that when park and recreation services are administered jointly, coordination of maintenance and program schedules is enhanced. Also, the combining of the two broadens the base of political support since each facet of parks and recreation has its own constituent groups (conservationists, naturalists, sports enthusiasts, social advocates). The combined approach also allows for a more effective utilization of specialists. For example, recreation practitioners are typically prepared to create programming services, whereas park planners and administrators know how to design and maintain resources and facilitate their use. The "marriage" of parks and recreation seems to be "made in heaven."

Arguments against this type of administration suggest that under such auspices, one of the two elements of program or facilities receives secondary consideration to the other. Generally, the program component is short-changed. The problems of land acquisition, development, and maintenance are more visible and seem to be more pressing; consequently, they receive a higher priority. When parks and land use is given priority, the human side of recreation services can be negatively affected, especially in services to people who are disadvantaged. The funds needed for recreation services may be diverted for park purposes or vice versa. In either case, if both aspects are not given appropriate resources, either the program or the facilities will suffer and ultimately the people of the community.

Some conservationists feel that the merger of independent recreation and park units into a single service negates the ability of park officials to function effectively as conservationists. The utilitarian approach of recreation seems to run counter to the desires and beliefs of the preservationists. They argue that the recreation element with its concern for the disadvantaged, might sell short the long-range objectives and actions of the parks manager when the department is in search of immediate program solutions. According to some conservationists, recreation professionals appear to be social crisis-oriented. They are more closely related to social service personnel than they are to the planners and designers, the kindred groups for resource managers.

Finally, it is argued that the professional background of the administrative director of the park and recreation unit will dictate the focus of that system. If the director is a recreation professional, programs will be emphasized; if he or she

Figure 5-1
Types of Managing Authorities for Recreation and Parks

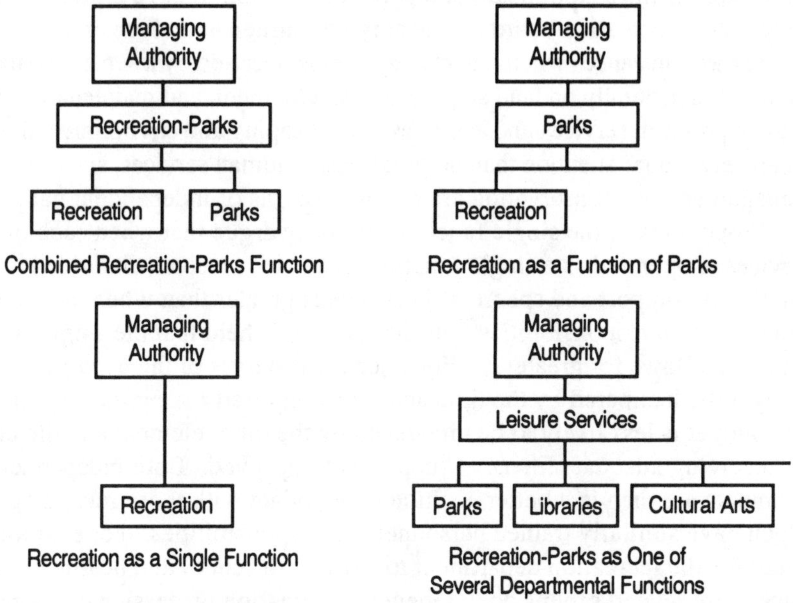

Combined Recreation-Parks Function

Recreation as a Function of Parks

Recreation as a Single Function

Recreation-Parks as One of
Several Departmental Functions

is trained in resource management, facilities and maintenance are emphasized. Leadership is the key. When park and recreation administrators fully understand the interdependence of programs and natural resources, however, the critical balance of the two is protected. Many park authorities have demonstrated their ability to administer public recreation services effectively. Likewise, many recreation administrators have furthered the importance of a quality environment when they assume responsibility for both parks and recreation services. Comprehensive planning, relevant programming, and sound financial management are essential to the success of the park and recreation mission. When parks and recreation interests are combined into a single unit, the potential for understanding and support is increased.

Systems in which recreation or parks is administered as a single function. This type of structure has as its single function the provision of either a recreation service or a park service. The two functions are independent of each other and are not administratively related. There is a department of parks and a department of recreation.

When recreation services are being provided as a single function, the emphasis is on programs and leadership rather than on the acquisition and maintenance or property. The independent recreation unit generally will attempt to use the resources of other governmental units such as those managed by the park department or the school system to expand its services. It is not unusual, therefore, for the school board and park commission to have representatives on the local recreation board or advisory committee and vice versa.

In those instances where the park system is operated by a separate park unit, the focus is generally on land acquisition, development, and maintenance rather than on program services and activities. Landscaping and environmental protection receive more attention than do programs of human services, since resource management and conservation are major concerns of independent park units.

Proponents of the single function authority argue that when each of the services is operated as a single function, each unit receives undivided attention and that its support and sphere of influence is greater than when one department has both responsibilities. Furthermore, it is held that the single-purpose approach allows for greater quality since the progress of the department is not likely to be hampered by the time and effort required for another function. The budget is less likely to be threatened by the other element and the chances for receiving adequate financial support are improved. Both independent departments are then in a better position to negotiate with those related agencies which have similarly trained personnel and responsibilities. For example, it is easier for the recreation department to work with school and health authorities since these related groups do not view the recreation professional as a resource person who has little interest in social services. Similarly, park officials are in a better position to work with those who have responsibility for the development and maintenance of physical resources when they are perceived as "hardware" persons, not "whistle blowers in tennis shoes." Finally, it is argued that accountability is easier to determine when an agency has a specific mandate and focus; it is easy to identify when the agency is succeeding or failing in the management of its responsibility.

Arguments against this type of structure point out that having two departments rather than one adds to overhead and burdens an already top-heavy local government structure; it creates an unnecessary expense. They also compound the problems of coordination and long range planning. Why have two separate units when a combined single unit could handle both functions effectively? Furthermore, the single function structure is contrary to national trends and the preference of the profession.

Systems in which recreation is administered in conjunction with schools (boards of education, school districts). In some states school laws make it possible for boards of education to administer public recreation services. When schools do this, the parks are generally administered by a separate park board or park department. Joint planning of parks and recreation may occur, but the recreation program is viewed as a function of the school system, not local government, and the recreation professionals are school employees.

Arguments for encouraging school authorities to administer local recreation services suggest that the schools are in the best situation to provide programs on a neighborhood basis. Schools are accessible and generally have many of the facilities (e.g., gymnasiums, auditoriums, art and music rooms) needed for recreation activities. They are publicly supported and serve the entire population, not just children. Finally, they are a respected institution and with the growth of the community school concept a logical administrative unit to administer recreation services.

Those who oppose the administering of local recreation services by the school system argue that the school already has more than it can properly handle in meeting the formal educational needs of the school population. Also, they feel that when the public recreation service is administered by the school system, it is a secondary function to the formal educational program and may be neglected, especially the periods of economic difficulty. They also argue that when recreation is administered by the schools, recreation services tend to become synonymous with physical education. Cultural arts and other popular leisure programs tend to be minimized.

Recreation professionals generally recognize that the formal school system plays an important role in providing recreation services to a community. This can be done whether the school administers the recreation system or not. Among those activities the school can do which enhance the leisure life of the community are (1) making school facilities available for community recreation purposes

Day camps can be administered in conjunction with school districts.

during and after school hours; (2) educating for leisure; (3) providing recreation through extracurricular and scholastic sports programs; and (4) cooperating closely with other departments, agencies, and organizations in the promotion of recreation and leisure services.

Systems in which recreation and park services are administered as one of several responsibilities. In recent years, the need for more coordination of governmental services at the local level has stimulated interest in a new design for administering recreation and park services. This approach brings together various units concerned with cultural programs, social services, information, education, and related free-time activity. Such agencies are frequently known as departments of community services or departments of leisure services. They typically administer the libraries, the park system, the cultural arts programs, senior citizen programs, community buildings, and the recreation services. The primary function of these agencies is to provide leisure services; the term "recreation" is generally not a part of their title.

The advantages of this structure are largely economical and political. By combining several units into one, administrative costs are reduced. More effective planning and a greater utilization of existing facilities can be achieved. All of these services (i.e., libraries, parks, art centers, and so on) are community-based efforts and exist to meet the free-time interests and expressions of the public. Each has its specific focus and clientele so by combining these groups a broader base of public support is established. One variation of this approach is to divide parks and recreation, placing each function in a larger system. When this occurs park operations are generally placed with public works while the recreation function is administered as a human service program.

Some problems are evident with this approach. The traditions of the various departments and their vested interests may make mergers difficult to facilitate. The creation of one large administrative unit also increases the potential for a bureaucracy unresponsive to the public's needs. Program and facility priorities and the inability of one agency to generate as much support for the total effort as would be achieved through each unit appealing to a particular constituency are concerns. Some resource-oriented professionals have held that this community services structure tends to minimize the importance of the development and maintenance of natural resources. They hold that the behavioral components of the program and its service aspects tend to dominate. Many of the more conventional recreation professionals are threatened by this approach since their identity as recreators is lost, even though their responsibility for the provision of a leisure service is enhanced.

The viability of this trend towards the merger of these related services is unknown. The concept has support, but the uncertainty of the future and the tendency toward the bureaucratic nature of this structure may discourage some communities from moving in this direction. Problems are related to modifications of any system, but the changing nature of the social structure suggests that the future will not be a mirror image of the past and many types of structures are likely to be.

Local or Community Governments

Public recreation systems are administered in a number of ways by different types of governments that provide them. For the most part, local recreation services are provided through the offices of municipal government (see Figure 5-2). Municipalities draw their power from their state constitutions. In most instances, recreation is recognized by state legislatures to be a local government responsibility. These states have enacted enabling (i.e., permissive) legislation that gives local communities the power to create municipal park and recreation departments. Most municipalities have such a unit.

A second local government approach to the provision of recreation services is through a special recreation and/or park district (Toalson, 1980). These districts function as separate governmental units with the power to levy taxes for

Figure 5-2
Typical Organizational Structure of a Local Government Recreation and Park Service

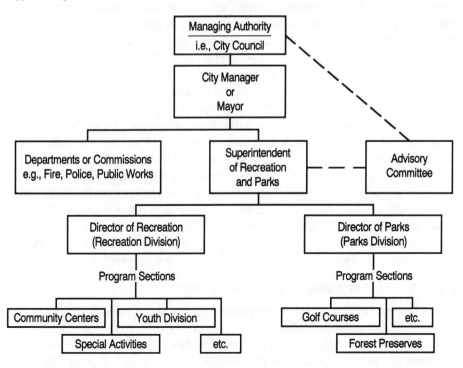

recreation and park services. The amount of the tax money varies from state to state and is usually determined by state law. Illinois and Missouri have used the district approach extensively in the development of their local recreation and park services.

These districts function like municipalities except that they have only one responsibility: to provide recreation and park services. They may or may not conform to the boundaries of a municipality. They generally have their own managing authority and assume whatever responsibilities are necessary for the protection and maintenance of their areas, facilities, and services. The district approach is flexible, but not popular with city managers and other public administrators. Coordination with other local governments is sometimes difficult since the districts are autonomous. Where there are several independent districts such as water, fire, and recreation serving a region, the problems of political jurisdiction, cooperation, and control increase tremendously.

A third and growing approach to the provision of local recreation and park services is the county recreation and park approach. Counties, like municipalities, draw their power from the state legislature and constitutional documents. Traditionally, counties have not been a force in the provision of recreation services although many have operated park systems for years. But with the growth of suburbia, parks and recreation has become an accepted function of county government. Although similar in structure to municipal recreation services, county recreation and park systems have a slightly different orientation because the geographic area served is much greater and the population density is much less than that of a municipality. A general discussion of county recreation services is presented later in this chapter.

A fourth approach is to administer local recreation services through the public school system. In rural areas, the school unit is frequently the basic provider of public recreation services. School districts function much like recreation and other special districts with the power to tax and administer services. The role of the school as a provider of leisure services is discussed in Chapter Six.

Regardless of the type of local government agency that provides the services, management patterns for recreation and park services are basically the same. They are either under the direction of an independent commission or board with policy responsibilities or they are a department of local government where the director is responsible to the mayor or city manager. In the latter case, recreation advisory committees may or may not be present.

Policy and Advisory Boards and Commissions

In the first half of this century, independent recreation or park units with board and commission members appointed or elected to office were popular. Recreation districts, park districts, and municipal recreation and park services all followed this pattern. Administrators viewed recreation as a service similar to public education, and therefore modeled the administration of park and recreation services after the educational system. Since the school boards tended to govern the school system, it was believed that policy boards should guide recreation and park units.

The arguments for the policy board approach are straightforward. By having citizens elected or appointed to direct the public recreation services, citizen input and control is assured. The recreation and park system is directly responsible to the community; citizens, not professional administrators, set the direction for the recreation and park service. Having several persons involved in the determination of policy tends to make policy decisions more acceptable and politically appealing than when policies are formulated by a single individual (the director) or by a group (a city council) which may not have recreation and parks as its primary concern.

The arguments against the commission/board approach to managing recreation and park systems are equally straightforward. Opponents to this system argue that parks and recreation units rely heavily upon the cooperation of other units of municipal government such as public works, personnel, and accounting. These units are under the general direction of the town's chief executive officer, usually the city manager. When the city manager is able to coordinate the functions of the recreation and park department with those of other city departments, a better administration is assured. When he or she has to deal with a separate independent authority, such as a policy board, the efficiency of operation is sometimes affected. There may simply be too many bosses. Furthermore, recreation and park systems with policy boards frequently incur additional expenses by having to duplicate some of the administrative services such as the accounting department normally provided by a town government for all the units administered by the city manager. This additional cost reduces the department's resources that could be used for programming and capital development. The opponents to independent recreation boards and commissions have offered the stronger case since most local park and recreation departments now function with advisory rather than policy boards.

Regardless of the administrative structure, the need for some type of citizen representation is universally accepted by park and recreation professionals. Because parks and recreation is often viewed as an important but not essential governmental function in the same context as are police and fire services, advocates are needed and this advocacy is often achieved through advisory boards and committees. They serve to interpret the value of parks and recreation to the political structure as well as to influence the programming views and thinking of a professional park and recreation staff.

Recreation boards and commissions, both policy and advisory, are political entities. Members are appointed or elected. Consequently they, rather than the recreation and professional staff, should be involved in the political process.

Recreation and park professionals may assist in the determination of policy and the development of program strategies, but they should avoid engaging in partisan politics. Professionals need to be politically astute but not politically involved whereas commission and board members need to be politically involved.

Intergovernmental Cooperation

Recreation and park authorities have found it beneficial to work cooperatively with other units of government, especially school and public housing officials, to aid the recreation and park department with its political and planning processes. For example, many recreation and school authorities are now using the park-school concept. This popular device brings park and recreation and school authorities together for the purpose of planning, acquiring, developing, and operating their respective facilities at a common location. Certain school facilities (e.g., gymnasium, music rooms, libraries) are made available for community use; the adjacent outdoor recreation facilities are available for school use. Each unit supplements and complements the activities and functions of the other so the community gets more for its money.

The same type of cooperation is observed with recreation and public housing authorities. The public housing authority provides space that may be utilized by the recreation department for program purposes, especially in communities with housing units for the elderly. In some instances, the recreation and parks department will work cooperatively with other governmental agencies, such as the Department of Health and Social Services, to provide a comprehensive program. The recreation agency may coordinate the entire effort in the public housing facility; the health and social services departments will provide nutritious lunches and health information while the public school system offers adult education classes. All of these programs are done in an environment where people come to socialize and interact. The task of working cooperatively with other agencies challenges the professional at all levels of government but especially at the local level where the direct services are provided.

One of the most noticeable areas requiring cooperation exists when citizens living in one jurisdiction, say in a county, use the recreation facilities of a neighboring municipality. Political entities have jurisdictional boundaries, but people do not restrict their activities to those boundaries. They go where the opportunities are. The picnicker does not care who manages the picnic area; all he or she wants is an attractive environment for a picnic.

To address the problem of the nonresident, local recreation authorities have attempted various policies and programs. Special surcharges for nonresidents have been levied, special recreation districts have been established, and special contractual arrangements have been made. Some of the contracts have involved agreements between different governmental units such as the municipality and the county. Other contracts have been between private recreation bodies and local governmental units. The intent is to make sure the local citizen has access to recreation resources. This problem of nonresidents partaking of programs is most acute in areas where suburban growth and urban sprawl are most apparent.

Local Recreation Services

A tremendous range of services is offered at the local governmental level. They vary from elaborate park systems, such as those in New York City, Boston, and Portland, to the direct involvement of local municipalities in professional athletics. For example, Durham, North Carolina, owns the athletic park in which professional teams play. In Phoenix, Arizona, the library system is administered by the Recreation and Park Department; in other cities, community theater is a function of local recreation agencies.

The type of program and services offered is dependent upon many factors including tradition, other service providers, public expectations, and the philosophy and preferences of the professional recreation and parks staff. Community athletics and youth sports have been the most generally accepted responsibilities of local park and recreation systems as have community parks and play areas. More recently programs for the elderly and greenways have become essential features of most public park and recreation departments. Services and programs for those who are disadvantaged, sometimes referred to as "special populations," is a feature of most departments. Less frequent are those programs which carry some "risk" possibility for the participants such as skydiving and rappelling. They are generally left to the private sector to provide.

The relationship between the private and public leisure service agencies is a dynamic one (Murphy & Smith, 1991). In some communities it is cooperative while in others it is more adversarial. Some park and recreation professionals believe it is their responsibility to provide a variety or cafeteria of activities and services to the public without much regard for possible competition with the programs and actions of the quasi-public and private not-for-profit sectors. Other professionals say their mission is to complement those sectors while still others approach the issue in a more supplemental way of only providing those programs NOT being offered by the other sectors.

With the growth of a business approach to the provision of public recreation and park services, the relationship between the public and private has been more complementary and sometimes even competitive. Public leisure service agencies have developed market strategies to assure program success. Operating stables, marinas, golf courses, and fitness centers, which have middle and upper middle class appeal, can provide public recreation and park units with some recovery costs, be totally self-sufficient, or may even make a profit that can be applied toward other activities. Public providers have also contracted with the other park and recreation systems to have them develop and operate such services as concessions or provide high risk adventure activities. These arrangements expand the offerings of the local department without adding to the operational costs or liability of the unit.

Recreation programming is the heart of any leisure service agency. Its scope and content are dependent upon the facilities available, the mandate of the agency, and the interest and philosophy of its leadership. Through research and experience, a set of programming principles have evolved. Chief among them are:

1. Wherever possible, involve those to be served in the planning and conduct of the programs;
2. Have well-stated objectives so everyone including participants and staff know what is to be done and how;
3. Realize that no one program or approach will be accepted by all. Know the limits of appeal and the demands for a given service or program; and
4. Effective programming requires sound leadership, adequate financial support, and an appreciation of the forces such as local traditions which condition it.

Promoting Rural and Suburban Recreation Services

The focus of rural and suburban recreation services is essentially one of organizing local resources. No adequate program can exist without some organizational structure to give the effort direction and permanency. The creation of the operating unit or the managing authority is the first step.

The adoption of the County Park Act of 1895 by the New Jersey legislature was one of the most significant legislative achievements in the history of the public recreation and park movement. It made possible the establishment of the first county park system, Essex County, New Jersey, and paved the way for the enabling legislation that gave local municipalities the right to levy a tax for the support of their recreation services. This also occurred first in New Jersey in 1915.

From this point in the early part of the twentieth century, a varying pattern of administrative alternatives for providing recreation and park services to rural and suburban areas developed. Among them are:

1. The establishment of *separate county recreation and park departments* or independent recreation or park districts;
2. The creation of a *quasi-public recreation and park council* with representatives from various communities or hamlets to be served; and
3. The use of a *contract system* whereby a community or political subdivision enters into a contract with a legal recreation authority of another political subdivision or private recreation agency to provide recreation and park services to the community for an annual fixed sum.

Of these three, the most frequently used is the first. Typical of it is the Northern Virginia Park Authority which provides a host of services and facilities for the citizens of several communities and nonincorporated areas adjacent to the District of Columbia. The least used is the second pattern. The one which has experienced the greatest growth has been the contractual approach. An example of the contractual approach is the agreement which exists between Arvada, Colorado, and the North Jeffco Park District. The city has contracted with the District to operate its pools and other facilities in such a manner that both its citizens and those of the District are served. The resources of the District were expanded by their agreement, and the cost of recreation services for the citizens of Arvada was reduced. With the nation's growing interest in decentralization of government and the greater involvement of the private sector in providing community services, the council and contractual approaches will likely increase in popularity (Long, 1989).

Federal and State Governmental Involvements

Recreation and park services traditionally have been considered a function of local government. For the most part, federal and state involvements have been limited to the management and operation of park and recreation lands and to the activities of regulatory agencies. Federal and state governments have assisted local recreation departments through financial grants, planning and technical assistance programs, and data and informational services. During the 1970s both federal and state governments became more active as direct providers of recreation experiences particularly in the urban environments.

Although the Constitution of the United States does not mention recreation and parks, it does discuss the right of each individual to pursue pleasure (i.e., "life, liberty and the pursuit of happiness" in the Preamble) and implies the responsibility of government to protect the environment and the natural resources of the nation (i.e., provide for the common good). The government's concern for health and welfare and the necessity to use natural resources carefully have become the legal basis for involvement in recreation and parks. The federal government is a major supplier of outdoor recreation opportunity through the programs of the Departments of the Interior (e.g., U.S. Park Service) and Agriculture (e.g., U.S. Forest Service). It has been a stimulator of culture and creative interests and an advocate of cultural heritage. Although not a major employer of professional recreation and park personnel, the federal government has been a dominant force in influencing public opinion on matters pertaining to leisure, recreation, and conservation.

Each state government draws its power from the federal constitution and may provide those activities that citizens deem vital to their well-being. The state pattern of services of recreation and parks has been similar to that of the federal government. Management of natural resource areas, the establishment of natural resource policy, and the distribution of information about various recreation and leisure opportunities within the state boundaries have been the primary activities, although some states have established zoos, symphony orchestras, and performing arts centers. Except for occasional grants-in-aid, neither the state nor the federal government has provided financial support for local recreation and park systems and has exercised minimal control over those services. The controls which have been established have dealt with such issues as employment practices, environmental protection, and civil rights.

The Federal Government and Parks and Recreation

Federal involvement in recreation services is not new. It began in the nineteenth century with the establishment of Yellowstone as the first national park. In 1990, over 70 federal agencies had programs that dealt with some aspect of recreation and park systems. The role of the federal government has been dynamic and ever changing. In the earlier years (1916-1926), it was a promoter of preservation and encouraged states to establish their own park systems. During the Depression and war years, it was active in developing recreation programs and services for youth. Later, in the 1960s and 1970s, it became very involved in grant activities and financial support for outdoor recreation and programs for those with disabilities. It has expanded the scope and operations of the park service, the Smithsonian Institution, and programs for the military while enacting laws to make all public facilities and services available to all.

Even so, questions concerning policy, what role it should assume in parks and recreation, remain unanswered. The optimum relationship between state, federal, and local units is still to be determined. There are those who advocate a policy of federal and state financial involvement with recreation while promoting the rights and autonomy of local agencies. Others suggest that the federal government should be setting standards and monitoring the quality of local services if it is to be involved financially in parks and recreation. Still others hold that there should be no state or federal involvements with local recreation programs; they believe recreation and parks is a highly individualized service and should respond directly to local needs, resources, and demands. These differing opinions reflect the public's view of recreation and parks as a governmental responsibility and the growing concern for environmental and consumer protection. Consequently, the public can be assured that both federal and state government will continue to be involved in parks and recreation as they have been in the past. The needs for recreation and parks remain the same, although the roles of those who provide it may change.

A complete description of the recreation and park involvements of the federal government would require a volume in itself. The following is a brief description of some of the major federal programs involving parks and recreation. It is by no means a thorough analysis of the federal park and recreation system.

U.S. Department of Agriculture

The U.S. Department of Agriculture (USDA) has been one of the federal government's major providers of recreation services. It has done this primarily through the U.S. Forest Service, the Federal Extension Service, and the Soil Conservation Service. It has provided technical and educational assistance, outdoor recreation resources, and encouraged and enacted regulatory policies to protect the quality of the environment and the recreation experience.

Although established to serve rural America, the USDA has many urban program thrusts. A major landowner, the U.S. Forest Service maintains nearly 200 million acres. There are National forests in nearly every state available for various forms of recreation including sites for picnicking, camping, hiking, and boating.

Millions of persons visit the national forests each year to engage in their favorite outdoor recreation activities. Through the Forest Service philosophy of multiple use of resources (i.e., compatible activities occurring simultaneously at the same resource), private investors are able to develop resorts on public lands. Many of the better-known winter ski and sports resorts are located in national forests. Hunting and fishing in national forests, except in a few areas, are controlled by state laws. The Forest Service Organic Act of 1897 and the laws subsequently passed authorized the recreation functions of the Forest Service.

The Federal Extension Service (FES) and Cooperative Extension Services of the USDA provide a wide range of technical and educational assistance programs. Among these are technical information on the design and development of recreation areas, the means by which crop lands can be converted to recreation use, and the operation of tourist attractions. The Extension Service functions only in an advisory and consultative role. Much of its activities are implemented through its 4-H clubs, the work of county agents, and the activity of the extension programs of land-grant colleges and universities. The Extension Service of some states includes the employment of full-time recreation specialists. The Federal Extension Service draws its power largely from the provisions of the Smith-Lever Act of 1914 (Section II) and the subsequent acts of Congress that deal with activities of the FES.

The major purpose of the Soil Conservation Service (SCS) is the conserving of the land, but this federal organization also encourages camping, picnicking, hunting, fishing, and other forms of outdoor recreation. Most of its service facilities are for public day use. Under the provisions of the Watershed Protection and Flood Prevention Act (P.L. 566, 83rd Congress, as amended), the Soil Conservation Service was able to enter into cost-sharing arrangements with local organizations for the development of certain lands for public recreation or fish and wildlife usage. SCS was one of the earlier federal programs offering direct financial assistance to local organizations for the development of recreation resources.

In addition to those services mentioned above, the USDA has conducted a variety of research activities directly related to outdoor recreation behavior and natural resource management of recreation agencies through its agricultural experiment station network. As a group, the U.S. Forest Service operates one of the more comprehensive recreation research programs. Their findings have influenced the design, maintenance, and construction of various recreation sites and have offered direction for recreation resource management.

Department of Defense

The Department of Defense is one of the few federal agencies that provides direct recreation services. The only major exception is the activities of the Army Corps of Engineers. The recreation programs operated by the military branches are similar to those normally found in a local recreation and park department or an employee recreation service. Many of the issues confronting local recreation and park agencies are experienced by civilian park and recreation professionals employed by the Department of Defense. Matters of programming and finance are major concerns.

Since World War I, the military has been concerned with "morale, welfare, and recreation programs" needed to promote the physical, social, and mental well-being of its personnel and their families. Each branch of the service has its own pattern of recreation administration. All attempt to serve both the military and their families with recreation sports, library services, arts and crafts centers, musical and theatrical programs and youth and family services. In many instances, civilian employees and retired military personnel are hired who work or reside on or near a military installation. All rely heavily upon monies appropriated by Congress and self-generated revenue (nonappropriated funds) resulting from the operation of post exchanges and on-base clubs. The military has been assisted in its program efforts by both the American Red Cross and the United Service Organization (USO). To understand the place and function of recreation within the armed forces, it is important to know the services being provided by the different military units under the direction of the Department of Defense.

ARMY

The U.S. Army Recreation Service program, Special Services, is directed by the Office of the Adjutant General. The Army, like the other three military branches, holds that a good special service program is an inducement for enlistment and that it offers the prospective soldier a recreation program comparable to or better than that offered by the typical community. The program tries to compensate for the loneliness that military personnel experience when they are assigned to an isolated post. The Special Services Division employs civilian personnel as recreation specialists. Their qualifications and salary range are defined by the Office of Personnel Management.

AIR FORCE

The recreation program sponsored by the U.S. Air Force is similar to that offered by the Army. Operated by the Air Force's Special Services and administered at the installation or base level, the Air Command attempts to coordinate its programs with those communities adjacent to the air bases.

NAVY

The recreation program of the U.S. Navy is provided by the Recreation and Physical Fitness Branch of the Bureau of Naval Personnel. The major objective is to develop and execute programs to increase levels of productivity and sustain morale throughout the naval establishment. In general, the programs include a wide range of activities, services, and facilities both aboard ship and onshore and may include both naval and civilian personnel for its operations.

MARINE CORPS

The recreation program of the U.S. Marine Corps is similar to that of the Navy. It is operated by the Morale Support Activities Branch of the Personnel Services Division and involves both military and civilian specialists. The responsibility of the conduct of the U.S. Marine Service program remains with each local commander.

Due to the large number of civilian personnel, family members of the military, and retired military personnel who use their recreation facilities, many military recreation facilities are overused. Some special services specialists have advocated a fee system to reduce demand, especially for retired military. Others hold that their operations, especially their maintenance and capital improvements budgets, should be a line item in the military's general budget. Then there are those who argue that the military should not be involved in the provision of recreation except aboard ship, in isolated areas, or in combat zones, that our military personnel should be integrated into the general community (e.g., county and municipal, private not-for-profit) recreation programs and not have a separate military recreation system.

CORPS OF ENGINEERS

The Corps of Engineers, a branch of the Army, differs in its civilian function from the other units of the Department of Defense that are involved in the recreation enterprise. Its functions are similar to the U.S. Forest Service and National Park Service. The Corps is a provider of outdoor recreation opportunities through the development and maintenance of recreation areas. Although the primary responsibility is to develop and maintain rivers and waterways in the interest of flood control, the Corps of Engineers has built picnic areas, hiking trails, public boat launching and docking facilities, campgrounds, and other recreation facilities for public use. The Flood Control Act of 1944, as amended by the Flood Control Act of 1962, authorized the Chief of Engineers to construct and maintain public park and recreation facilities at Corps water resource and development projects. Also, the laws provide that the Corps financially assist local groups and governments in the development, operation, and maintenance of project land and water areas for recreation, fish, and wildlife enhancement. The Corps' programs have added considerably to the fishing and boating opportunities of the public.

One other program of the Department of Defense merits mention. The federal government does assist state and local governmental agencies in obtaining surplus equipment that might be suitable for playground and recreational purposes. Surplus equipment, including tanks, airplanes, and the like, may be obtained without charge, although the receiving agency must bear the cost of handling and transporting the various items.

Department of Education

Prior to 1979, the federal responsibility for education was a part of the Department of Health, Education, and Welfare. Under the Carter Administration, those programs coordinated by the Department of Education were grouped together and a new cabinet position, the Secretary of Education, was established. The purpose of the department is to promote the cause of education throughout the nation. This responsibility is discharged in a variety of ways including the collection and dissemination of information, the awarding of grants, and the provision of consulting services. Recreation and play are recognized as a significant part of education and the involvement of the public school system in the provision of adequate recreation opportunities is encouraged.

Three programs of the Department of Education have had a special relationship with park and recreation services. The Office of Special Education has offered training grants for the preparation of recreation personnel to work with youth with disabilities since 1969. It also supports some recreation research activity, particularly those studies which have focused upon the development and improvement of the delivery of recreation services to people with disabilities.

Second is the Office of Rehabilitation Services. It was among the first federal agencies to offer financial support (1963) for the development of graduate study in the field of therapeutic recreation and has actively supported the effort to elevate the role of recreation as a significant area of service for special populations. The inclusion of recreation services in rehabilitation centers, sheltered workshops, and other special facilities designed to strengthen the habilitation skills of individuals with disabilities, have been provided by this office. It has encouraged state and local institutions to provide recreation opportunities as a part of the treatment and rehabilitation of people who are hospitalized and/or chronically ill.

The final program is the Community School Act of 1975, which authorized millions of dollars of support for varied community education projects including recreation. Its enactment has encouraged recreation development in rural areas but has tended to discourage the establishment of county recreation services. The impact on municipal recreation and park services has been minimal.

Department of Health and Human Services

Within the Department of Health and Human Services are several bureaus and programs that impact upon the recreation and park system. The most prominent are the Administration on Aging, the Children's Bureau, and the Public Health Service.

The Administration on Aging was established in 1965 as a part of the Older Americans Act to encourage and financially assist the establishment of comprehensive program services for older persons. The provision of recreation opportunities has been a prime element of that effort. Under the Older Americans Act, funds have been expended for recreation related purposes such as the renovation and repair of facilities, payment of salaries, and the operation of continuing education, recreation, and outreach programs.

Established in 1912, the Children's Bureau is one of the oldest federal agencies involved in the recreation enterprise. It has largely concentrated efforts in the development of literature pertaining to the play and play environments of children. It has worked cooperatively with state, federal, and private not-for-profit national agencies and organizations to promote services for youth.

The United States Public Health Service addresses recreation when matters of health are involved. It also offers therapeutic recreation services in the hospitals, such as at Saint Elizabeth's in Washington, DC. Funds for research and training through the various national institutes of health are provided. The major contribution to recreation is in the areas of safety and environmental care. Any federal or state agency may call upon the Public Health Service for technical assistance concerning the development, planning, operations, or maintenance of a recreation facility in which communicable diseases might be transmitted and where sanitary services are needed.

Department of Housing and Urban Development

The Department of Housing and Urban Development (HUD) is primarily concerned with the comprehensive planning and development of American cities. Recreation concerns are part of the planning process. HUD has encouraged the development and use of planning standards for recreation and parks and the necessity for effective evaluation of park and recreation delivery systems. It has made efforts to include space for recreation in public housing areas, but has not assumed responsibility for administering recreation programs within these areas. Those programs have been retained by public recreation and park agencies.

Department of Interior

Without question, the Department of Interior is the major federal agency concerned with parks and recreation. Through several bureaus, it affects the recreation behavior of the American public in a variety of ways. The providing of resources, the regulating of hunting and fishing activity, the caretaking of cultural and historic sites and ceremonies, and the managing of those specific facilities designed primarily for recreational purposes are some of the responsibilities. In addition to these activities, the Department of Interior also offers technical assistance to local and state governments, conducts research investigations, and has stimulated the development of recreation resources through various grant programs. The park and recreation interests of the Department of Interior are coordinated through the activities of the Undersecretary of Interior.

Prior to 1960, few federal programs had a direct relationship to local recreation and park services. Federal agencies were generally mandated to maintain national recreation and park areas or to regulate recreation behaviors through game and wildlife legislation or gambling laws. This pattern changed in the 1960s when the Bureau of Outdoor Recreation was charged with the responsibility of coordinating federal recreation research and planning activity particularly involving state and local recreation and park units. The BOR, later known as the Heritage Conservation and Recreation Service (HCRS), developed and maintained a nationwide outdoor recreation plan, began to disseminate information on recreation behaviors, and implemented a federal outdoor recreation policy. Each state was encouraged to establish an outdoor recreation planning body and develop a state wide comprehensive outdoor recreation plan (SCORP). These state components encouraged local planning and served as a focal point for the collection of data on outdoor recreation behaviors (McCormick, 1991).

In 1965, the Bureau of Outdoor Recreation assumed responsibility for administering the Land and Water Conservation Fund (LWCF). This was a major step toward more federal involvement in local recreation park services because land and water conservation monies could be used by local recreation and park departments for the acquisition and development of outdoor recreation areas and, although the Fund is considerably smaller in the nineties than it was in the sixties and seventies, the federal government is still providing matching grants to local communities for development purposes. For a local political subdivision to acquire a federal LWCF grant, it has to file its outdoor recreation plan with the appropriate state agency. Grants to the local subdivisions must be approved by the state outdoor recreation planning unit. This network assures a close working relationship between federal, state, and local services.

The Land and Water Conservation Fund monies primarily come from three sources: (1) the proceeds from entrance admissions or user fees and charges at federal recreation areas; (2) receipts from the sale of surplus federal real property and offshore drilling leases; and (3) taxes from the sale of motorboat fuels. Hundreds of municipal park and recreation systems have benefited from these grants; the total acreage available for outdoor recreation opportunities has been increased considerably.

In 1981, the Heritage, Conservation, and Recreation Service was eliminated although many of its functions were transferred to the National Park Service. Through the Bureau and the Outdoor Recreation Planning Process (SCORPS), the federal government had influenced significantly the direction and planning of local park and recreation systems and aided thousands of communities in the expansion of their physical resources for recreation and park purposes.

NATIONAL PARK SERVICE

The National Park Service (NPS) was established in 1916 and has played a prominent role in providing outdoor recreation opportunities. The system includes national parks and monuments; national historic areas and memorials; national seashores and lake shores, parkways, riverways, and recreation areas; the National Capital Park System; and the Wolf Trap Farm Park for the Performing Arts and the John F. Kennedy Center for the Performing Arts (see Table 5-2. page 160).

The National Park Service was established, according to the Organic Act (August 25, 1916, 39, Statute 535), to "promote and regulate the use of the federal areas known as national parks, monuments, and reservations...by such means and measures as to conform to the fundamental purpose of the said park, monument and reservation, which purpose is to conserve the scenery and natural and historic objects and the wildlife therein and to provide for the enjoyment of the scene in such manner and by such means as will leave them unimpaired for the enjoyment of future generations..." The mission of the National Park Service is set in the Organic Act. Its dual responsibilities of preserving and interpreting our national areas while also making them available to the public for its enjoyment has created, at times, some interesting conflicts. A variety of other acts, such as the 1935 Historic Preservation Act and the 1936 Park, Parkway, and Recreation Area Study Act, have expanded its areas of responsibility. In 1990, the National Park Service was managing some 350 units, encompassing 76 million acres with over 260 million daily visitations (see Table 5-3, page 161).

Table 5-2
National Park System by Type of Area* 1988

Type of Area	Number of Areas	Federal Acreage (thousands)	Recreation Visits (millions)
National Park System	354	78,176	282.5
National parks	50	45,955	56.7
National historic parks	29	96	23.3
National monuments	79	4,637	23.2
National military parks	9	33	4.4
National battlefields	11	10	1.7
National battlefield parks	3	8	1.8
National battlefield site	1	1 acre	N/A
National historic site	68	17	11.7
National memorials	23	8	18.3
National seashores	10	476	19.3
Parkways	4	161	42.0
National lakeshores	4	144	3.9
National rivers	14	260	4.4
National Capital parks	1	6	9.0
Parks, other	10	32	7.4
National recreation areas	18	3,339	54.5
National trails	3	93	N/A
National preserves	14	20,904	0.1

*excluding the National Mall and White House

Source: *1991 Statistical Abstract*, p. 229.

The NPS system is organized according to basic functions. The five essential functions are:

1. *Resource management.* These include the management of land, water, and wildlife resources within a given administrative unit and its surroundings, the general ecology of a park area and its surroundings, and the relationship of use to resources as a major concern of the resource manager.
2. *Visitors' services.* Included are those activities which insure the comfort and protection of the user while visiting the park. Among the services are concession (food and lodging), safety, and traffic control operations.
3. *Interpretation services.* One of the major responsibilities of the national park system has been to stimulate the public's interest in the historical, geological, biological, and cultural aspects of a given area or resource through interpretation services. They take many forms including tours, exhibits, film presentations, publications, museums, and demonstrations. Interpretation services is one of the two major responsibilities of the National Park Service as specified in the Organic Act which created the system; the other is the protection of the environment.

4. *Maintenance and development.* Well over half of the financial resources of the National Park Service are devoted to the maintenance and development function. Trail systems, roads, visitor and information centers, and historic buildings must be maintained in a reasonable manner if they are to provide the visitor with a heightened outdoor experience. The quality of the National Park experience is related to the extent and quality of its maintenance operations.

5. *Administrative services.* This area of responsibility includes management of personnel, planning, budgeting, interagency cooperation, public relations, and the development and dissemination of data.

The National Park Service is administered by a director and administrative staff, which includes a deputy and several associate directors, the central office personnel, and the regional office staffs. Each park has its own superintendent and both seasonal and permanent staff.

For the past several years, the NPS has vigorously attempted to upgrade and expand its facilities, camping areas, and resources. In doing so, it has encountered resistance from those who feel that the park areas are being inundated by users and suggest that the Park Service restrict admissions and use. On the other hand, the NPS has received criticism from those who feel it is not making its facilities as accessible to the public as it should. The latter group has demanded the development of more urban recreation areas and urban parks.

As stated earlier, the National Park Service is concerned with areas other than the national parks. Only the Congress can establish a national park, whereas national recreation areas may be designated by the President or the Interior Secretary. Because of the power and the actions of recent presidential administrations,

Table 5-3

Recreation Visits* to National Park System Units by Type of Unit: 1982, 1986, 1990

Type of Area	1982	1986	1990
All Areas	244.1	281.1	258.7
National parks	49.6	53.5	57.7
National monuments	16.2	21.2	23.9
National historic areas	62.3	65.5	57.5
National parkways	36.1	41.6	29.1
National recreation areas	49.7	54.8	47.2
National seashores	17.2	23.0	23.3
National capital parks	5.3	6.9	7.5
Miscellaneous areas	7.7	14.5	12.5

*in millions

Source: *1991 Statistical Abstract*, p. 232.

a new controversy has arisen. In response to the demands for recreation areas, various presidents and/or secretaries have increased the number of areas within the NPS system. Unfortunately, appropriations for the Service have not kept pace with expansion and demand; consequently, some of the resources which might have been used for the maintenance and development of our national parks have been expended for the development and operations of national recreation areas. Despite the general feeling that the services provided by the National Park Service are important, not enough money has been allocated to the continued maintenance and operation of park areas. In 1993, some national parks are being restricted due to the lack of personnel available to supervise and control park areas and was the subject of a CBS News feature.

This policy of support for urban outdoor developments and areas has come under the attack of such groups as the Conservation Foundation, which called for the Park Service to return to its traditional role of administrator and preserver of our unique natural areas and get out of the "recreation business." The Sierra Club has asked the National Park Service to close certain sections of our national parks to motorized vehicles and to restrict the number and type of camping units permitted in the parks.

At the same time that these demands are being heard, the Park Service is being urged to modernize its camping program with advanced registrations and more lighted areas to reduce vandalism and related crime. During peak periods of activity, national park and recreation areas exhibit most of the characteristics of urban America including concerns for convenience and security. Added to this is the pressure of the concessionaires who wish to add to their "sales" potential by expanding their line of goods and services, thereby making the parks an even more urban environment. Traditionally, concessionaires have obtained leases from the Park Service for the operation of canteens, cafeterias, lodges, and convenience shops. Typically only one concessionaire receives a lease per park. During the latter part of the 1970s, the National Park Service attempted to control the quality of the concessionaire operations so that their quality was at the same level as services provided by the Park Service. In the 1980s, efforts were made to liberalize these policies and to give the concessionaires more freedom by letting public demand determine quality. Unfortunately, it is difficult to envision the operation of the free enterprise system in a park area where only one concessionaire has a lease.

The role of the national parks will continue to be debated in the coming decades as conservationists, concessionaires, and the manufacturers of recreation equipment advocate their positions. So will discussions about funding and future outdoor recreation acquisitions and operations. One of the more recent proposals is the creation of a National Trust using private gifts and a manufacturers excise tax (a special tax on the sale of recreation equipment) to support it (Crompton & Decker, 1989).

BUREAU OF INDIAN AFFAIRS

The Bureau of Indian Affairs (BIA) was established at the turn of the century primarily to oversee Indian reservations and maintain a positive relationship between Indians and non-Indians. The BIA has a strong commitment to recreation services. It has developed and operated various recreation facilities such as campgrounds, museums, restaurants, hunting, and fishing areas on Indian reservations. These services are primarily for the tourists who happen to be visiting Indian lands. It also operates a more typical community recreation program for Native Americans with community centers, playground facilities, and programs for special populations.

BUREAU OF LAND MANAGEMENT

In 1946 the Bureau of Land Management (BLM) was established to oversee all federally managed public lands not under the jurisdiction of other agencies, such as the Park Service, the Forest Service, and the Corps of Engineers. The BLM was empowered to sell unreserved, nonmineral lands to other political subdivisions for recreation and park purposes. It also leases or sells small tracts of land to individuals for camps, cabins, and other recreational use. Prior to the enactment of the Alaska Lands Bill which designated the National Park Service as the "caretaker" of much of the Alaska area, the Bureau of Land Management was responsible for those Alaskan holdings. Like the U.S. Forest Service, the BLM has a multiple-use philosophy that suggests the simultaneous development and utilization of areas for recreation, mining, and resource exploration. The BLM seeks a balance between conservation and controlled development. In a sense, it is both a real estate and a conservation agency.

BUREAU OF RECLAMATION

Although it was established primarily to oversee the development of water resources in the western states, the Bureau of Reclamation has encouraged the recreational use and development of its resources for over five decades. Active participation in outdoor recreation activities, especially those related to water sports such as boating, fishing, and swimming are encouraged. The Bureau works closely with other federal agencies, since it is the policy of the Bureau to transfer "those reservoir areas which qualify as national recreation areas" to the Park Service for operation. It also works jointly with the National Park Service and various states in planning, developing, and promoting of outdoor recreation facilities. State or local government organizations may administer or develop recreation resources on Bureau lands.

FISH AND WILDLIFE SERVICE

The Fish and Wildlife Service (FWS) is both a regulatory and a resource management agency. It has two major responsibilities: (1) the protection and development of fish and wildlife resources which includes the enforcement of federal game laws; and (2) the management of recreation areas associated with national wildlife refuges and national fish hatcheries. The refuges protect a variety of wildlife including migratory water fowl and other migratory birds; the fish hatcheries are devoted almost entirely to the preservation and development of fresh water game fish and salmon. These refuges and fisheries are open to visitors; photography, picnicking and sightseeing are encouraged. Some recreation facilities are provided by FWS; others are developed by concessionaires or through agreements with local governmental or civic groups.

A variety of federal legislative acts have endowed the Fish and Wildlife Service with the responsibility of protecting migratory birds and game animals. One act allows the Service to give financial assistance to state fish and game departments for projects to restore, conserve, and manage fish and wildlife resources. These programs are supported primarily by excise taxes from the sale of firearms, ammunition, and fishing equipment; the funds are distributed to states on a prescribed formula. In 1990, the Fish and Wildlife Service operated over 400 nature preserves encompassing some 53 million acres of land and water.

Department of Transportation

A limited number of programs within the Department of Transportation have direct bearing on parks and recreation. One of these is the Bureau of Public Roads. It works cooperatively with the U.S. Forest Service and National Park Service in the construction of roads in national forests and parks and also with various highway departments in developing major and secondary roads to serve recreationally motivated traffic. Travel to hunting, fishing, picnicking, and camping areas as well as to golf courses, winter sports sites, and water areas is critical to the recreation experience. Erosion control, adequate parking facilities, turnouts for scenic, historic and rest areas, and roadside parks are concerns of the Bureau. Several federal aid highway acts provide the authority for its program.

A more recent program of the Department of Transportation allows local park and recreation departments to utilize the right of ways of federal highways if those highways become permanently closed. These spaces provide excellent areas for drag racing and bike races. Under Title III of the Public Law 89-285, the Highway Beautification Act of 1965, the Department of Transportation may approve as part of the construction of federally aided highways, the cost of landscaping and roadside development including the acquisition and construction of recreation areas and rest facilities.

Other Federal Programs

In addition to the previously mentioned federal departments that have programs impacting upon park and recreation systems, several other agencies and activities merit mentioning:

THE NATIONAL ENDOWMENT FOR THE ARTS

The National Endowment for the Arts assists individuals and nonprofit, tax-exempt organizations in the development and promotion of arts, dance, literature, music, and theater. This program was created in 1965 to aid local communities in the creation and support of performing arts activities. Although its funding was reduced by the recent administrations, the program remains vital with private philanthropic support. Its efforts to stimulate cultural arts programs in such areas as the inner city and correctional facilities merit special mention.

THE PRESIDENT'S COUNCIL ON PHYSICAL FITNESS

The President's Council on Physical Fitness was established in 1956 as a result of a series of recommendations by various groups concerned with the apparent lack of fitness of American youth. Since then, the President's Council has aggressively promoted the cause of fitness and sports in the United States. It disseminates information on the importance of fitness to general well-being, sponsors various national forums, and encourages the development of fitness programs throughout the school system. It works primarily through existing agencies and organizations rather than by providing direct services.

THE TENNESSEE VALLEY AUTHORITY

The Tennessee Valley Authority (TVA) was established in 1933 to oversee the development of hydroelectric power in the Tennessee Valley and to monitor the flood control and navigation aspects of the Tennessee River. The TVA has been a significant force in the development of recreation resources and activities in that region. It has created a wide range of recreation facilities including boat docks, fishing camps, resort sites, and lots for vacation cottages. Through its recreation resource development program, the TVA has made land available to other federal agencies, state and local agencies, private organizations, and individuals. Within the TVA region, the Fish and Wildlife Service maintains more than 100,000 acres of game refuges. Since its creation, over 200,000 acres have been transferred by the TVA to various governmental authorities for recreation use.

Although recreation was not a primary concern when the TVA dams were developed, it has become a major interest of the Authority. The presence of these resources has stimulated private recreation development, particularly those activities related to tourism, and has aided in the Tennessee Valley region's economic development. The Land Between the Lakes recreation area in western Kentucky and Tennessee is one of its better known projects. The TVA conducts studies and demonstrations, provides technical assistance on matters pertaining to the development of outdoor recreation resources, and encourages the support of the performing arts and cultural heritage of the Appalachian region.

THE VETERANS ADMINISTRATION

The Veterans Administration operates therapeutic recreation programs at each Veterans Administration Hospital and Home. Programs include a wide range of activities and services directed by a professional staff of therapeutic recreation specialists. As a therapeutic recreation program, its objectives are to aid the patient in adjusting to hospitalization and treatment, to contribute to the morale of the patient during hospitalization, to facilitate the patient's recovery and rehabilitation, and to aid in the patient's return to a "normal" life in the community.

Unmet Needs

At present, six basic types of federal involvement in parks and recreation are offered: (1) the direct management of federal lands for outdoor recreation purposes; (2) the provision of technical assistance and promotion of recreation activities through private industry, commercial recreation enterprises, and various state and local governmental services; (3) the provision of financial assistance to state and local governments through various grant programs; (4) the offering of programs and services directly to such selected groups as the military, inmates in federal institutions, and patients in Veterans Administration hospitals; (5) the provision of direct services (programs and activities) such as those of the Smithsonian Institution with its national zoo, national art gallery and related programs; and (6) the enactment and enforcement of those regulations for the protection and continuation of our natural resources including plant and animal life, with particular attention being given endangered species.

Despite the numerous programs and services which currently exist, no single federal agency is uniquely concerned with recreation and leisure. Some feel that a federal agency primarily concerned with leisure activities and services should be established to coordinate the overall effort of the federal government. Furthermore, they argue that that agency should have cabinet rank; there is a Department of Labor, why not a Department of Leisure? Others argue that the present system of "many" federal agencies involved in recreation and parks is ideal. It guarantees a variety of options and support although the problems of duplication are acknowledged.

The growing concern with the preservation of natural and cultural resources, the acceptance of leisure as a major economic and social force, and the expansion of tourism ensures further discussion of the appropriateness of a federal recreation and leisure service agency. Before its demise, the Heritage Conservation and Recreation Service was moving in that direction. Should such a program be initiated in the future, it should emphasize the technical assistance, planning, applied research, and information dissemination functions.

State Government Involvement in Parks and Recreation

The role of state government in parks and recreation is an interesting one. Through fairs, parks, and museums, states are a direct provider of program services; through regulatory legislation, state governments influence recreation behaviors. State involvement is more similar than dissimilar to the federal government in organizational structures and policy statements.

In the United States, the Tenth Amendment to the Constitution guarantees to the states "the powers not delegated to the United States by the Constitution, nor prohibited by it to the States, are reserved to the States respectively, or to the people." This amendment gives those responsibilities to the state that are not specifically stated as federal responsibilities. Parks and recreation is one of those areas of state activity.

The initial role in parks and recreation assumed by most states was that of protecting the natural resources. The state park movement began in California in 1864, several years before Yellowstone was established as a national park. Concerns within states for game regulations, forestry management, and state fair operations were also shown before the turn of the century. In general state involvements in parks and recreation have followed or been patterned after federal actions.

Possibly the most significant development of state governments in recent years has been the expansion of public services including recreation and parks. The promotion of tourism has resulted from a growth of state interest in recreation and as a public good. The range of services provided vary from state to state but they generally embrace the following activities:

1. The acquisition, development, and management of land and water resources for conservation and outdoor recreation purposes.
2. The advertising and promotion of recreation resources and attractions by state tourist bureaus and development commissions.
3. The enactment of permissive legislation that enables communities and districts to mobilize their resources for recreation services.
4. The establishment of state recreation or state recreation and park commissions, boards, departments, or divisions as a unit of state government to coordinate the development and management of state recreation and park services and opportunities.

5. The employment of recreation and park personnel in such state departments and agencies as state youth commissions, departments of public instruction, departments of natural resources, state hospitals, and training schools where responsibilities are broader than that of providing recreation services.
6. The enactment of laws and the establishment of policies designed to protect natural resources and wildlife and to regulate certain individual recreation behaviors.
7. The development of technical assistance programs to aid local communities in the establishment, improvement, and development of their park and recreation facilities and services.
8. The appropriating of public funds for the management of a state recreation and park system and the granting of funds to local communities for the supplemental support of their park and recreation system.

In summary, state contributions to recreation and parks are fourfold: legislation, resource management, technical assistance, and direct service.

Legislative Function

State governments impact on recreation services through the legislative process. All local recreation and park programs, services, and facilities supported with tax monies have their foundation of authority in state laws and local ordinances. Leisure services, whether under governmental auspices or not, are influenced by state laws. For example, a commercial recreation facility such as a theme park must adhere to the health and sanitation laws of the state. Likewise, the seating capacity of a motion picture theater must conform to state or local laws and ordinances such as fire regulations and hours of operation. The very function and operation of our tax-supported recreation and park systems are specifically defined and authorized by law.

There are four general types of laws enacted at the state level which have bearing on recreation systems. The first are the state *enabling laws*. These laws are found in the State Park Code of Laws, the State School Code of Laws, and/or in the State Recreation Enabling Legislation. All states have such laws, and efforts are being made to broaden and liberalize them. Enabling legislation, in a single act, grants the local community the right to establish, organize, administer, and conduct recreation and park programs under any one of several authorities. These enabling acts are permissive and not mandatory; they do not require the establishment of a recreation and park system but allow local governments the right to expend public monies for parks and recreation purposes.

In some states, local park and recreation systems function under local ordinances which result from the enactment of municipal charters. In those instances, the municipal charter serves as the document which directs and defines the power of the municipality. Regardless of an enabling or a charter law, the authority, the geographic jurisdiction of the managing authority, and the responsibilities and functions of that authority are detailed.

Service laws are a second type of legislation which influences recreation behavior. These laws authorize state agencies and departments to provide and operate services and facilities. They determine the scope and focus of state agencies. For example, they may assign the function of recreation services to an agency such as a Youth Commission or detail the authority and structure of an agency established totally for the provision of park and recreation services such as a state department of parks, recreation, and tourism.

A third set of laws, the *regulatory laws,* are enacted for the purpose of regulating, controlling, licensing, censoring, or supervising recreation activities in the best interest of the public's health, safety, and welfare. One of the primary examples of this type of legislation are those laws establishing the dates for hunting and fishing and setting limits the number of species killed or caught. Health and sanitation codes are also types of regulatory acts.

Finally, some laws authorize actions or the expenditure of funds for projects of interest to a given locality, and for which state wide authority is neither requested nor required. These *special project laws* give local groups the right to act on a specific matter that is of no interest or consequence to other communities in the state. For example, if a community wanted to receive a special dispensation of a use permit from the state for certain public lands, it would need to have a special projects law enacted.

An understanding of the relationship between law and recreation and park services is essential because all recreation programs are affected by the legislative process.

Resource Management

With the creation of the National Park Service and the formulation of the National Conference on State Parks in 1921, the legitimacy of state government in outdoor recreation was established. Each state operates its own network of parks and other outdoor recreation facilities and resources. The total expenditure for capital expansion and operation approaches a billion dollars annually. Over nine million acres of public lands are managed by state park departments; an additional 19 million acres are managed by state forest systems. State governments contribute significantly to the availability of outdoor recreation opportunities.

No single approach for the provision of state park and recreation services exists. Philosophy of service, patterns of organization and management, and the responsibilities assigned to state agencies vary from state to state. For example, in South Carolina, state government activities in parks and recreation are administered through the State Department of Parks, Recreation, and Tourism. In Michigan, the parks are administered by the Park Division of the Department of Natural Resources: tourism is the responsibility of a separate state agency. In Oregon, the state park system is administered by the Highway Department of the State Department of Transportation; roadside parks are included as state park units. In other states, roadside facilities are not included as a state park operation.

Several factors enter into the organizational pattern of a state park and recreation system. They relate to political trends, intergovernmental relationships, historical events particularly related to the time the state park system was established, and current management concepts. Prior to 1950, the primary function of the state park system was that of preserving state lands. Areas were relatively undeveloped; recreation was not seen as a critical element in design and management of these resources. During the 1960s, a number of states began to modify their philosophy of operation. Some states such as Kentucky, West Virginia, and Oklahoma, developed extensive accommodations for tourists in their state parks. Their lodging and dining facilities are comparable to those of commercial motels and restaurants. Policymakers in these states hoped that their state park systems would add to the economy of their regions. The parks took on a resort quality; golf and tennis facilities were constructed along with the more conventional picnic and aquatic facilities. Initially this pattern was most prevalent in the Appalachian region but with public entrepreneurialism and an emphasis on private/public partnerships, it has became common nationwide (Meyer, 1990).

Other variations which might be noted pertain to use and acreage. Jones Beach in New York State accommodates a quarter of a million persons per day. In Vermont and New Hampshire, the state park systems have encouraged the development of the ski industry by making state land available to commercial firms on a long-term lease basis. More recently state agencies have indicated a growing interest in the preservation of wild and scenic rivers and trail systems. Some states such as Michigan have established wilderness areas. Most have become extremely interested in the general planning and coordinating of state and local resources as they relate to the outdoor recreation movement.

Technical Assistance and Consulting Services

The role of state governments concerning the nonresource aspects of recreation planning and development is relatively new. It began in the late 1940s with the establishment of independent recreation commissions in North Carolina (1946), Vermont (1946), and California (1947). These agencies were created primarily to assist local recreation and park units in the development of their systems. Their relationship to state park systems was minimal.

With the creation of the Bureau of Outdoor Recreation and the availability of federal grants to local communities for the acquisition and development of outdoor recreation resources, most state park agencies expanded their technical assistance and consulting capacities. For most, this responsibility was assumed by the state's department of parks; in other states, particularly those where a state recreation commissions had been established, the commission was given that task. Organizational specialists quickly concluded that the best approach to assure interagency cooperation and a systematic development of state park and recreation resources was to combine the resource management and technical assistance functions. Most states followed the national trend and created a separate department of parks and recreation, generally under the administration of the state's Department of Natural Resources. The independent recreation commissions were eliminated or became a bureau with the state's department of parks and recreation.

Organizations that provide technical assistance have helped stimulate local governments in expanding their park and recreation services. Regional and state planning has also been enhanced through the efforts of these agencies, especially those related to travel and tourism. They influence the legislative process, provide both federal and local departments with needed data, and increase the public's awareness of the recreation and parks field as a profession. The need for some type of consulting and technical assistant agency has been proven; the question is one of structure. Should technical assistance be provided by an independent agency or should it be one of the many services provided by a state department of parks and recreation? Those supporting the more independent operation argue that their approach provides greater flexibility and allows them to interact more freely with nonresource-oriented agencies. Those who favor being a part of a state department of parks and recreation cite the advantage of professional identity and the strength drawn from being seen politically as a part of a larger organization. Regardless of one's view, state governments need some type of planning and advisory services. Each state also needs some type of agency to foster good working relationships between the various levels of government, between state agencies, and between the private and public sectors related to recreation and park services. To date, technical assistance encompasses all of these activities. In the future, it may be expanded to include financial assistance from the state to local park and recreation departments.

Direct Services

The fourth major responsibility of state governments in recreation and parks includes a variety of direct service activities. Many of these are of a cultural and social nature; others involve the health and higher educational systems of the state.

Many states operate fair or exhibition centers. The most common type is the state agricultural fair, generally held on state-owned grounds and operated by the state department of agriculture or a special fair commission. Some

states have developed extensive facilities to be used year round to accommodate commercial shows and exhibitions such as boat shows, horse shows, and
music concerts. Many of these are located on state fair ground property while
others have been built as a part of state-operated exhibit complexes.

Although not everyone agrees that gambling is a recreation pursuit, various forms of gambling have state approval; in fact, many states now provide
or license one or more forms of gambling (see Table 5-4). Millions of people
purchase lottery tickets each month in the thirty-four states which have authorized lotteries, and in one instance, Colorado, lottery funds are used to support
other recreation endeavors, i.e., the acquisition and development of outdoor
recreation areas.

Some states such as New Jersey, have created major sports areas. Others
such as North Carolina, have established a state-operated zoo. Most states
have state botanical gardens and state historic museums; some support a state
orchestra or dance group. Cultural arts programs are most often seen when the
state does not have a metropolitan area large enough to support these cultural
programs as a local government or private, philanthropic activity.

The other major direct service component involves various state institutions.
Nearly every state has established therapeutic recreation programs within state
hospitals and training centers. Recreation has been accepted as a legitimate
responsibility of the state when it administers to those it has incarcerated, or
those who have voluntarily sought treatment and rehabilitation.

Nearly every state has at least one state-supported institution of higher learning which offers a park and recreation major. These university curricula are not

The St. Louis County [MO] National
Steeplechase attracts 6,000 people each
year to raise money for the Cystic
Fibrosis Foundation.

Table 5-4
Legalized Gambling by State and Type of Gambling Allowed 1990

State	Horse Racing	Harness Racing	Dog Racing	State Lottery	Casinos	Off-Track Betting
Alabama			•			
Arizona	•		•	•		
Arkansas	•		•			
California	•	•		•		
Colorado			•	•		
Connecticut			•	•		•
Delaware	•	•		•		
District of Columbia				•		
Florida	•		•	•		
Idaho	•		•			
Illinois	•	•		•		•
Indiana				•		
Iowa	•		•	•		
Kansas	•		•	•		
Kentucky	•	•		•		
Louisiana	•			•		•
Maine		•		•		
Maryland	•	•		•		
Massachusetts	•		•	•		
Michigan	•	•		•		
Minnesota	•			•		
Mississippi				•		
Montana	•			•		
Nebraska	•					•
Nevada					•	•
New Hampshire	•		•	•		
New Jersey	•	•		•	•	
New York	•	•		•		•
North Dakota						•
Ohio	•	•		•		
Oklahoma	•					
Oregon	•		•	•		•
Pennsylvania	•	•		•		•
Rhode Island			•	•		
South Dakota			•	•	•	
Texas	•		•			
Vermont			•	•		
Virginia				•		
Washington	•			•		•
West Virginia	•		•	•		
Wisconsin			•	•		
Wyoming	•					•

Source: *Sports Illustrated*, April 22, 1991.

only engaged in the preparation of students for the park and recreation profession, they frequently are a major contributor to the state's responsibility for technical assistance. For example, North Carolina State University and the University of Illinois operate technical assistance programs through their university extension divisions. In addition to providing recreation services for students and faculty, the university system also provides hours of entertainment and recreation for citizens through various athletic, cultural, and entertainment programs.

The future role states are to play will depend largely upon the role played by local and the federal governments. If the federal government once again offers grants in the magnitude it did in the 1970s, then state agencies may again serve as intermediaries. If there are no major federal grants and if local governments find it difficult to expand their recreation and park resources through bond issues and increased tax sources, state governments may be asked to help. Such aid might come in the form of grants funded by lotteries as is the case in Colorado (Waldo, 1983), or through a special Park and Recreation fund as enacted in Kentucky in 1982. New enabling legislation may be required to give local government the right to create special recreation districts or to expend public funds to assist private developers and nonprofit agencies to expand recreation services and opportunities.

Regardless of the role that governments assume in parks and recreation, their involvement and acceptance as a necessary ingredient in the recreation system has been established. Just as no governmental subdivision alone can clean up a polluted river which flows through it, the problems of urban planning and recreation resource development must also be approached on a statewide or regional basis. Recreation is the responsibility of government at all levels.

Suggestions and Study Guides

1. Government is by far the major provider of organized recreation and park services. Visit your local park and recreation department and discuss with someone with administrative responsibilities the goals and operations of the department. Be sure to focus upon the policy issues, administrative problems, and long-range plans of the agency. Consider these in light of current patterns of activity and change.

2. Repeat the assignment above with a state or federal agency. Compare the views of those at this level of governmental responsibility with those whose primary concern is the delivery of recreation and park services at the local level.

3. If you were responsible for the selection of the members of a park and recreation board or advisory commission, what criteria would you use in choosing the members? How important are such items as access to the power structure, name recognition, previous committee experience, and personal philosophy of recreation services? How important is an interest in recreation, active participation, or being representative of a special interest or age group? Which factor do you consider to be the most important? Why?

4. Inasmuch as public recreation is largely supported from general tax revenues, develop a policy to govern admission fees to public recreation and park areas. Also consider the pros and cons of public recreation and park agencies becoming self-supporting, or partially self-supporting, revenue producing agencies. Examine your feelings on these points; justify your position.

References

Crompton, J., & Decker, J. (1989). Establishing a federal recreation trust fund. *Journal of Parks and Recreation Administration, 7*(1), pp. 1-14.

Long, P. (1989). Reaching rural communities with recreation. *Parks and Recreation, 24*(9), pp. 82-86.

McCormick, S. (1991). Funding the next five years. *Parks and Recreation, 26*(1) pp. 58-63, 84.

Meyer, P. (1990). State parks in a new era. *Parks and Recreation, 25*(4) pp. 28-32.

Murphy, W., & Smith, D. (1991). Expanding opportunities through private partnerships. *Journal of Physical Education, Recreation and Dance, 62*(10), pp. 45-46.

Statistical Abstract of the United States: 1991. Washington, DC: U.S. Government Printing Office

Toalson, R. (1980). …Special districts. *Parks and Recreation, 15*(7), pp. 29-30.

Waldo, B. (1983). Colorado lottery enriches parks and recreation. *Parks and Recreation, 19*(4), pp. 50-52.

CHAPTER SIX

Membership and Private Not-for-profit (Quasi-Public) Recreation Services

Having considered the public section of the leisure service delivery system, attention is now turned to those organizations and groups that comprise the quasi-public and private, not-for-profit sector. Many of the elements of these services have a public character in the way that they approach recreation programming. Those organizations such as the scouts that tend to solicit financial support from the community at large are known as quasi-public. Those such as swim clubs which depend upon their members for their fiscal operations and make their services almost exclusive, for their members only, are defined as private. For purposes of this chapter we will refer to both as private sector agencies.

Historically, it was the private sector that first offered organized recreation services. Today, its contributions are varied and extensive. In some communities, private recreation providers supplement the public recreation and park offerings; in others, they may be the basic provider of the community's organized recreation service. Among the many community organizations and groups comprising this system are the youth-serving voluntary agencies; employee recreation groups, special interest groups (such as Sierra Club, Audubon Society), religious organizations; specialized recreation associations (such as neighborhood clubs, soccer clubs, running clubs); education institutions; and those facilities and services provided by families and/or individuals for their own recreation pursuits. Common to nearly all are the concern for their members and the use of volunteers. For some, especially the quasi-public groups, their success is highly dependent upon their understanding and use of community organization techniques.

Community Organization Efforts

The process of organizing, mobilizing, and using the many resources of a community toward achieving some predetermined objective is known as *community organization*. It involves a variety of strategies and undertakings. It is a means for achieving goals; not an end in itself. Its intent is to maximize the resources of the community toward the improvement or betterment of the life of its citizenry. Widely used to coordinate and integrate local social service programs or to implement a program of general community development within some rural areas, community organization involves a commitment on the part of many individuals and interest groups to work together. It acknowledges individual concerns and priorities while acting for the good of all.

Public recreation and park committees are one of the ways communities coordinate their park and recreation services. Unfortunately, these committees tend to be more concerned with the coordination of governmental efforts than with the bringing together of all deliverers including the quasi-public, private not-for-profit, and voluntary agencies. The coordination of these private service providers is usually left to one of the major fund raisers such as the United Way.

The United Way

The United Way, also referred to as the Community Chest, United Fund, or United Campaign, is primarily concerned with the fund-raising efforts of its member groups. The United Way is a system for caring and joining together in an organized effort to enhance the community's capacity to meet the human service needs of people. These agencies raise and distribute monies to member groups through a united campaign once a year in cities or areas. Funds are distributed based on a prioritized basis to those agencies that meet the funding criteria established by each community.

In most communities, an organized and united fund-raising effort is the most effective way of raising money for social service agencies. Billions of dollars are raised through these "united campaigns" annually. Although most of the groups that constitute membership in the United Way are private, not-for-profit agencies, public agencies sometimes participate. Occasionally a local recreation department will obtain supplemental monies from the United Way; nearly all youth-serving agencies look to it for partial support of their operations. The basis for funding, for example, for the United Way of East Central Iowa are based on the following visions of a caring community: providing for basic needs (food, healthcare, shelter, safety, clothing, education/training, and access to services), strengthening families, promoting health and wellness, nurturing children and youth, supporting older adults, respecting diversity and ending discrimination, and access to supportive community resources (*Opening the door...*, 1992).

Coordinating Groups

Frequently local chapters of national organizations, such as the Sierra Club, will take an active role in the development and protection of local recreation and park resources. These groups often provide recreation opportunities as well. In addressing issues of development and protection, groups sometimes will form a coalition with other private, not-for-profit recreation and park interests to work for the enactment of key legislation to protect the environment, thereby adding further to the leisure potential of the community. These federations generally include garden clubs, conservation groups, and Friends of the Parks alliances. Although they may be primarily concerned with ecological issues, their representation and participation in recreation community organization efforts is desired. Similar systems exist with federated sports groups or cultural arts groups. They may or may not have representation on local park and recreation councils but their presence in a community affects the way services are delivered.

Among the tasks most frequently performed by these recreation coordinating groups are:

1. The exchange of information about recreation and park services and operations within the community.
2. The publication of recreation directories, pamphlets, and annual reports.
3. The operating of a recreation and leisure service information exchange.
4. The planning and promotion of recreation and park capital development.
5. The avoidance of unnecessary duplication of services.
6. The promotion of joint sponsorship of program and services.
7. The joint training of volunteer leadership.
8. The promotion and monitoring of standards.
9. The programming of some recreation opportunities and services such as street festivals or recreation trips.

The Volunteer in Recreation Services

Just as the private, not-for-profit and quasi-public organizations rely primarily upon the United Way and other local coordinating councils to assist them in the developing and financing their efforts, they also rely heavily upon volunteers for the operation of their programs. It should be remembered that the organized park and recreation movement was begun with volunteer leadership and that most public recreation and park programs still involve volunteers, especially at the advisory board and neighborhood council level. Within private, not-for-profit and quasi-public agencies, volunteers often provide much of the leadership and labor, at least in the provision of direct services to members and participants.

Volunteers are essential to the operation of many recreation and park systems as well as being a recreation activity for many individuals. Two major types of volunteerism can be found: structured and unstructured. These types may be classified as regular versus lend-a-hand volunteers, or short-term (single event) versus long-term volunteers (Tedrick & Henderson, 1989). Some of the changes in volunteerism over the past two decades have been largely due to a change in the orientation of people from service-oriented to self-serving (Watts & Edwards, 1983). People are generally looking for volunteer positions which meet their personal needs as well as can contribute to an organization or a cause in which they believe. They may be seeking to change the system or keep it intact; to work for themselves or for others; to give monetary gifts or help solicit from others; to work occasionally or to seek some type of continuous volunteering.

Volunteers can assist leisure service systems in a variety of ways: teaching activities and skill classes, serving on policy or advisory boards or commissions, advocating through education or fund-raising for certain causes, assisting in

Two volunteers from Anaheim, California plant a parkway tree on a residential street for the Releaf Anaheim project.

the carrying out of office routines such as distribution of pamphlets and other informational materials, serving as sponsors or advisors of recreation clubs, or providing transportation for people in special recreation services to and from recreation centers. Volunteers add vitality to the park and recreation system (Tedrick & Henderson, 1989).

Who are the volunteers? Anyone may be a volunteer. They may be recruited from former recreation workers, program participants, retired persons, hobbyists, parents of children participating in the program, schoolteachers, business and professional leaders—the list is endless. In addition to individual participation, many groups can be used in volunteer services. Organizations such as the American Legion, the Rotary Club, and the Junior League are often looking for specific projects for members. Several recreation programs, such as American Legion Baseball, originated because of the efforts of these groups; they have served as sponsors for teams, underwritten the financial operations of tournaments, and donated and developed land for park purposes. It is estimated that voluntary corporate giving to recreation services alone adds millions to their operational budgets each year (Duwe, 1981).

The Retired Senior Volunteer Program (RSVP) is an example of a volunteer program that involves thousands of older adults over the age of 60 in a variety of human service programs in over 800 locations throughout the United States. The purpose of RSVP is to create meaningful opportunities for persons of retirement age to participate more fully in the life of their communities through volunteer service. To this end, RSVP matches senior volunteers with meaningful volunteer assignments, provides insurance for volunteers, provides transportation/meal reimbursement, and provides recognition and social events for volunteers. The volunteers provide expertise and experience to meet community needs and determine the activity and time commitment that is compatible with their interests. Local RSVP programs receive money from ACTION (the federal domestic volunteer agency) as well as from state governments and local United Ways.

In addition, numerous other opportunities exist for volunteering in communities through the Voluntary Action Centers and Volunteer Service Centers that serve as clearinghouses for linking interested potential volunteers with possible volunteer opportunities. The needs of volunteers to find "satisfaction" through the productive use of free time does not exceed the variety of opportunities that exist in working in various aspects of human and social services.

When working with and through volunteers, several key ideas should be kept in mind:

1. Everyone is a potential volunteer and the field of recreation and parks offers opportunities to all who wish to volunteer. Marketing volunteer programs applies and is as important as marketing any kind of recreation program.

2. Volunteers are multi-talented but frequently they need professional staff to organize and facilitate their work. The job descriptions of volunteers and paid staff should be distinct as each has special talents to offer an organization.
3. The volunteer is a participant; volunteerism is a leisure activity for many.
4. Budgets of private, not-for-profit and public recreation agencies are generally limited; the use of volunteers tends to increase the scope of services without increasing the budget.
5. Advantages and disadvantages exist in using volunteer leadership. The advantages should be stressed; the disadvantages minimized.
6. Volunteers need training, supervision, and guidance.
7. Volunteers require recognition for services well done; it is their "payment."
8. The efforts of volunteers and the volunteer program itself require continuous evaluation.

The Family

Families, like volunteer groups, contribute significantly to the recreation opportunities of the community. They provide activities and programs for their own members, teach their children skills and activities, and spend billions of dollars for recreation equipment. By doing so, they supplement the programs and resources of park and recreation agencies.

Family forms and structures have undergone dramatic changes in the United States in recent years. The traditional family of the "bread-winner" husband, a homemaker mother, and children represent only a small minority (less than 20

"Playground Olympics" for children fourteen years of age and under is designed to give youngsters an opportunity to compete with others in Westchester County, New York.

percent) of families today (Shaw, 1992). An increased number of nontraditional families including single-parent families, gay and lesbian families, "blended" families, and childless families exist. In many instances, couples and groups are living as families outside of the traditional and legal social definition of the family, yet their behavior is very similar to that of traditional couples living in an extended family situation. They seek recreation opportunities as a unit for themselves and their children. Furthermore, regardless of one's economic, racial, or ethnic background—all of which may affect family patterns—the need for group support and sharing experiences, including recreation, remains, regardless of how one defines "family."

Since World War II the number of unmarried men and women has risen considerably. According to Kraus (1982), there are over 16 million single adults in the United States. They live alone but not like their predecessors, the "old maid" or "stodgy bachelor." Private recreation interests have accommodated them with a variety of clubs and agencies (e.g., Parents Without Partners) and commercial operations (e.g., singles bars). A wide range of life styles are evident within this population; their recreation resources and interests are considerable and data do not suggest a reduction of this trend.

Modifications in sex roles have also had an effect on patterns of family recreation. In recent years, it has become acceptable for men to spend more time in the kitchen, sharing culinary responsibilities. Women are no longer discouraged from pursuing sports and woodwork activities; the equality of opportunity in work has been followed closely with a belief in the equality for opportunity in play. Just as recreation activities can contribute to courtship, as a means of "getting to know each other," they can also contribute to the nurturing or deterioration of a marital relationship.

Shaw (1992) has identified several benefits as well as problems that may be associated with family leisure. The current research suggests:

1. Many adults consider family leisure to be an important part of their leisure lives.
2. A positive relationship exists between marital satisfaction and shared or joint leisure.
3. Participation in joint wife-husband recreation activities are shown to lead to greater marital stability.
4. Most families have to negotiate how much time they want or need to spend together.
5. For some people, particularly women, family time together is not always associated with leisure. This finding may be due to the amount of work that women continue to have to do for family occasions (e.g., cooking meals, organizing the family for leisure) even when they also have work outside the home.

6. Competition exists for the time that families set aside for family recreation pursuits due to peer expectations, outside responsibilities, dual career families, and differing interests among family members.

For millions of middle-class families, in particular, the home remains the basic recreation center. Many free time moments are spent watching television, playing video games, reading, or pursuing hobbies. This home-based recreation has affected the participation patterns of a community as well as the offerings of the leisure service system. In many neighborhoods, playground programs have declined in popularity as children elect to stay in their air-conditioned family rooms, enjoying the equipment and opportunities available to them, rather than going to a playground during the heat of the day.

Leisure service providers are beginning to accept the home as a recreation resource, one that can be used in a decentralized program approach. Roving leaders, mobile recreation units, cable television programs, and individualized instructional videotapes and videodiscs allow people to enjoy their leisure where they live rather than having them come to a designated place for "recreation." Public park and recreation services can be a catalytic agent for family recreation services. The provision of information about recreation opportunities in the community and the importance of recreation in the life of each family is one of the responsibilities. Another one is assistance to individuals in their choices of equipment and toys. Individual family members often come to park and recreation professionals seeking information about places and opportunities to recreate and use their equipment. They do not necessarily wish to have the recreation department plan their activities, but they do need information about available opportunities; they also want to know more about the care and maintenance of their recreation investments.

Leisure service agencies can be of service to families in a variety of ways. They can sponsor special family events, street fairs, festivals, and neighborhood recreation programs. They can operate organized camping for family units, provide facilities for family camping, and encourage family experiences which require all family members to participate, rather than segregating by age-based activities. In some instances, staff in leisure service agencies have established a family recreation advisory service to give assistance on children's activities, games the family can play as a unit, information about hobbies, guidelines for the purchase and care of toys and equipment, and tips on vacation travel. They have recognized that family recreation patterns change with the age of the family and the life stages of its members.

In general, recreation activities have the potential for strengthening family unity (Orthner & Mancini, 1990). They may also contribute to the growth of the intellectual, spiritual, social, and moral character of the family. This potential is most frequently realized when the activity needs of each stage of family development are understood. For example, the needs of young couples living in cramped quarters who are on a meager income are different from those of a single parent attempting to begin a new life; the neighborhood ties of the pre-school child and the extended school activities of the elementary school years are not the same for families who are dealing with the challenges of adolescence; the empty next stage and the retirement years have their peculiarities. Each stage requires a different set of understandings, program strategies, and methods for the delivery of recreation services. Each stage has its own patterns, priorities, expectations, and circumstances. When programming for family recreation, an understanding of life cycles and life stages is critical (Witt & Goodale, 1981).

The family can function only in relationship to a larger social order. Each member is inevitably affected by the stability of society. The social values and controls centered in other institutions such as government and business also influence family life: in turn, modifications in the family structure affect community behaviors. Families as well as the larger social order are also affected by other social institutions including formalized religious groups.

Religious Organizations

With over 400 separate denominational organizations and sects, with membership in excess of 147 million (National Council of Churches..., 1989) and with a corporate wealth in the billions, organized religion in the United States is a powerful social institution. Religious bodies tend to shape people's values and attitudes; they are a critical force in the lives of millions of people. Their land holdings are considerable. They are a major element of the private sector because they are a primary provider of recreation and fellowship experiences for many of their members. All three major coordination religious bodies—the National Council of Churches of Christ in the United States, the National Catholic Welfare Conference, and the Jewish Welfare Board—have proclaimed recreation to be an important part of the church members' concern and service.

Churches have assumed three basic responsibilities in relationship to leisure services. First, they have aided and shaped the development of the public recreation and park agencies through the positions they have taken on recreation issues and their attitude toward specific recreation experiences. Second, they are a provider of direct recreation services for their members with their recreation centers, recreation activities, and recreation programs. Finally, they also provide a community service and a variety of programs for the public at large, especially by making their facilities available for youth and civic groups and through the public use of their camping programs, music and pageant activities.

Influences on Attitudes and Public Policy

The objectives and purposes of organized religion and the public recreation service are in many respects similar and complementary. Churches are concerned with the personal development of the participants through their satisfying uses of leisure. The compatibility of religion and recreation is best seen in the effort to achieve an abundant and meaningful existence for all. The effects of religious teaching and the ethics of the community are frequently demonstrated in the play and leisure behaviors of the public.

Church members often look to the clergy for advice on community matters that influence their daily lives. Consequently, the clergy can rally support for civic activities as well as act as the community's representative. Churches can lend their support to securing adequate play areas for children in neighborhood housing developments and can urge congregations to support local festivals and contribute to the United Way. Their members can appeal before the city council as individuals or, in cooperation with colleagues, plead the case for a senior citizens program. They may urge a congregation to join with others and shape national policy on programs of entertainment such as the "moral majority" attempted to do in the early 1980s.

Some people hold that if community and individual practices are not up to the church's standard of wholesomeness and decency, churches have an obligation to object. Churches serve as society's moral conscience. Their task is to create a proper environment and stimulate those attitudes that encourage and promote individual growth and development. Another view is that the church does have the responsibility to speak out on issues but not to invoke censorship or impose its view of morality on others. The church is in a unique position to influence opinions.

The Church as a Provider of Activity

Recreation and social activities are an appropriate part of the church program. Church officials often combine recreation with their education and worship programs; the religious environment lends itself to the promotion of certain types of recreation pursuits. Probably no group in the community is more involved in music and drama than are church groups. Likewise, religious holiday celebrations are among the fundamental threads of recreation fabric of many communities.

Many variations of the church's involvement in recreation are evident throughout the United States. Some groups, such as the Southern Baptist Convention, have a staff of recreation consultants and have developed a comprehensive set of recreation resources that are available to member churches. Other groups such as the Church of Latter Day Saints and the Catholic Church, have their own youth-serving organizations (the Mutual Improvement Association and the Catholic Youth Organization, respectively). Some have urged a policy of exclusiveness; their programs are basically for their members only. Others have encouraged the integration of the church's programs and resources with those of the other social institutions of the community.

Not all forms of recreation expression have been accepted as legitimate activities to be sponsored by some churches or are encouraged by some religious groups. Some denominational groups have historically opposed dancing, horse racing, and gambling. Others have spoken out against motion pictures and card playing. Some have strongly opposed the church's involvement in such matters as civil rights, women's rights, and environmental issues. Some have taken an active role in censoring the content of television shows, movies, and popular magazines. All of these concerns obviously do not have the same level of consequence.

Services for the Public at Large

Although primarily concerned with the recreation opportunities provided for its members, the church's involvement in recreation services goes beyond the individual member's interests. Church facilities are meeting places for the many youth-serving groups such as the Boy Scouts, Girl Scouts, and Camp Fire Boys and Girls. In some communities, churches are active in providing day-care facilities for elderly and individuals with disabilities. They may operate programs for preschoolers, such as Head Start, or childcare services for the children of working mothers. They may join with secular groups to offer adult education and senior citizen programs. Many churches have taken an active role in the preservation and conservation of historic and natural areas, speaking out on the quality of life issue and urging communities to preserve their heritage and natural resources. Church congregations have initiated action to establish local recreation authorities and have sought representation on those policy and advisory boards that direct public recreation services. They operate conference groups, camps, and other outdoor recreation facilities. Many local churches have constructed gymnasiums as part of the church facility and have operated youth sport leagues and teen clubs. Some employ full-time recreation professionals to direct their programs (Epperson, 1983).

Because of the long-standing tradition of the separation of church and state, some communities have been somewhat hesitant to have their religious institutions get involved in social issues. Likewise, they have been hesitant to have their governmental agencies use church facilities and church resources in a secular manner. Although these patterns have broken down, these attitudes still affect the role that religious bodies assume in providing recreation and park services to their members and to the larger community. Among the problems which have resulted from these attitudes are the issues of Sunday observance, the disapproval of certain forms of recreation activity and entertainment, the use of churches for recreation purposes, the use of church programs as a means of proselytizing, and the competition and duplication of programs and facilities.

Churches that are pressured to allow the use of their property as an available space for community recreation programs face special problems. Among them are: (a) the church's desire to be a good neighbor and contribute to the life of the community while at the same time keeping the sanctity of the church; (b) some members' objections to the normal wear on the building and its furnishings when the building is open for general public use; and (c) the question of accommodating those who are of different faiths or religious views, even when religious traditions do not prevent the use of church property for certain types of activity. Although churches today tend to be more liberal in the offering of their facilities to the community for general use, the problem of censorship and "exclusive rights" remains.

The issue of proselytizing is a difficult one to analyze. Most groups want to expand their membership and scope of influence as a sign of healthy growth. If, however, the principal motive of sponsoring recreation opportunities or participating in the community recreation program is to attract members for a particular church or religious body, the question of proselytizing arises. A thin line exists between proselytizing and being a good neighbor.

In any case, where the church does make its facilities available for community recreation activities, it should avoid the duplication of services and activities. Competition between recreation departments, public schools, youth-serving groups, religious groups, and other organizations functioning in the recreation field has negative affects. This competition is costly. Cooperation between leisure service providers and churches benefits all; it tends to add to the quality of life in the community and assures the partnership between spirituality, play, and recreation.

The Voluntary Youth-Serving Agencies

Recreation services were initiated largely because of a concern for youth. The social welfare movement of the late nineteenth and early twentieth centuries served as an impetus for public recreation development. Sensitive philanthropists responded to the needs of urban workers by creating agencies and services for children and youth. Although recreation was not the central reason for the development of many of these programs, it was one of the essential ingredients and has remained a major thrust for more than 100 national youth-oriented organizations in the United States.

The voluntary youth-serving agencies are a major part of the private not-for-profit sector. They join with the public agencies in serving an age group that society has deemed to be a primary target for recreation programming. These youth-serving agencies draw support from private not-for-profit donations, the

United Way, other philanthropic groups, and from agency membership fee structure. Educational groups, family life agencies, fraternal and patriotic orders, and religious bodies have youth programs. Probably the best known of these are the YMCA and YWCA, the Boy and Girl Scouts, Youth Councils, Camp Fire Boys and Girls, the Catholic Youth Organization, and the Young Men's and Young Women's Hebrew Associations.

A large proportion of the youth movement is primarily directed by youths themselves with organizational support from public school and public recreation agencies. Literally thousands of teen centers and youth-directed programs exist throughout North America. Most of these appeal to the older teenager, whereas the programs of the more established national organizations have a younger youth constituency. Parental involvement with these more youth directed services is less than it is with the nationally affiliated groups. Most of these programs have a strong middle-class appeal.

In addition to the above-mentioned youth service groups, some organizations stress services to minority groups, the urban poor, and "youth-at-risk." Several federal programs, particularly those associated with the "war on poverty" efforts of the late 1960s and early 1970s, emphasized services to these groups. Private organizations such as the Police Athletic League and the Children's Aid Society are found primarily in metropolitan areas working almost exclusively with these groups. These recreation activities are generally used as a means for preventing delinquency and enriching the lives of less fortunate people.

No segment of the population has been targeted for more services than has the youth of America. It is assumed that, left unattended, youth will get in trouble; consequently, recreation services are necessary to prevent delinquency.

The Monmouth County [NJ] Park System offers children the opportunity to re-create life as it was in the early 1900s at Longstreet Farm.

No evidence supports the assumption that organized recreation services will prevent delinquency. What is obvious, however, is that recreation activities are important to all age groups, and that youth is one group that has an abundance of resources and energies available to pursue its recreation interests.

Regardless of the motivations of the public in developing youth services, unnecessary competition, duplication, and overlapping of youth programs sometimes occurs. On closer analysis, however, the duplication does not seem to be a problem, since most youth-serving organizations have a well-defined role, clientele, and support structure. Only those groups which tend to be more general in their programs run the risk of program overlap, competition, and duplication. The dangers of duplication are minimized when an effective community organization structure is in place.

Numerous ways can be used to analyze and describe the youth recreation system. The end result of each is the same: a classifying of efforts and services. Youth-serving groups can be viewed in terms of their service focus (outdoors-oriented, social service-oriented, church-oriented, educational-oriented); their appeal to one sex or the other or to both; their organizational structure (national affiliation, local autonomy); their management approach (group work-oriented, facility-based); or their leadership structure (volunteers, professional staff, adult-led or advised and youth-led). The leadership factor is the key for grouping the following major types of youth-serving agencies currently providing recreation and leisure services (see Table 6-1).

Adult-Led Organizations

A number of youth-serving agencies have policies and organizations established by adults, programming decisions made by adults, and employed professional staff to administer the program services. These groups are best known by the public and are the older organizations. They have a general appeal, often

Table 6-1

A Comparison of the Facility-Based and Program-Based Approaches to Services

Type	Agency Type	Leadership Structure	Role of Agency Personnel	Program Thrust
Facility-based	YMCA, CYO, BGCA	Organizational hierarchy	Administrator, leads activities and supervises facilities	Centralized, uses own buildings and grounds
Program-based	B.S.A., G.S.A., CFG	Group-work oriented	Develops group leadership, supervises volunteers	Decentralized, uses facilities of sponsoring agencies

operate their own facilities (facility-based programming), and have a religious, nondenominational focus. Among them are the Boy Scouts and Girl Scouts of America, the Boys' Clubs and Girls' Clubs of America, the Camp Fire Boys and Girls, and the YMCA and YWCA.

Boys and Girls Clubs of America

The Boys Clubs of America is currently a national federation of over 1,200 clubs serving some two million youth. Originally two organizations, the Boys Clubs of America and the Girls Clubs of America merged in 1990 to become the Boys and Girls Clubs of America (BGCA). The purpose of the organization is to guide urban boys and girls in their physical, intellectual, emotional, and social development. The national organization furnishes services to individual Clubs on matters pertaining to the organization, administration, and operation of the club facility. Each club functions with its own policy board and depends largely upon voluntary leadership to supplement its professional staff. The BGCA are largely urban-oriented, offering a wide range of services including tutorial programs, family counseling, and the more conventional athletic and crafts programs.

The organization is supported by contributions, income from contributions and endowments, and membership fees. These clubs offer facility-based programs which means that most of their services and programs are centered in a single building or set of buildings owned by the Club. Consequently, professional staff generally are concerned with the operations of the building, its maintenance and care, and the programs offered.

Boy Scouts of America

The Boy Scouts of America (BSA) is the largest organization for boys in the United States and was established in 1910. The original intent was to promote character building and citizenship training for young males through a variety of outdoor recreation and nature activities under trained, professional and volunteer leadership. Today, Boy Scouts has broadened its base of concern and now provides urban-oriented programs and activities; some programs and troops accept female members. Programs are planned for specific age groups: Tiger Cubs and Cub Scouting for younger boys, Boy Scouting for older boys, and Exploring for older boys and girls. It is basically a group-oriented program as opposed to a facility-based one. In other words, the program is not restricted to a specific facility or agency. Boy Scouts seek sponsorship for local troops; church, service, and educational groups tend to provide sponsorship and the meeting place for troop activities. As a group-centered agency the professional scout leadership is not as concerned with the problems of maintenance and facility care as are those professionals working with facility-based organizations.

Boy Scout troops function through local councils, have a membership in excess of five million scouts, and operate over 600 camps. In addition to the program in the United States, over 110 countries support the scouting program with an international office in Switzerland.

The major program focus is to prepare the scout for adult life through various outdoor living experiences and citizenship. Basic leadership comes from parents and other interested adult volunteers, and this leadership is coordinated through the efforts of the professional scout executives. Much emphasis also is placed upon the concept of citizenship which is reinforced through a variety of community service projects. Although the Boy Scouts have been regarded as a middle-class organization, they do have an active program in the inner city and have even developed troops for individuals who are disabled and who reside in public and private not-for-profit institutions as well as in communities.

Financial support for the Boy Scouts of America comes primarily from troop fees, private donations and United Way giving. The most famous camping facility is the Philmont Scout Ranch and Explorer Base in New Mexico. This area has more than 100,000 acres and provides opportunities for hiking, camping, horseback riding, and wilderness survival experiences.

CAMP FIRE BOYS AND GIRLS

Although traditionally the oldest of the organized youth programs for girls, the Camp Fire program is less well-known than are its Girl Scouts and YWCA cousins. Originally established to promote the spiritual ideals of the home and stimulate the development of good health and character for girls, Camp Fire programs now have a more outdoor recreation and community service focus for both boys and girls. The name was changed and "boys" were incorporated into the name and the program in the late 1970s.

The organization relies primarily upon volunteer leadership with support from paid professionals. Over 600,000 boys and girls belong to Camp Fire across the United States. It is group-oriented with programs designed for four different age levels. Many Camp Fire programs are operated through school systems and are developed on a short-term, activity specific or event centered basis today rather than through a traditional club structure.

CATHOLIC YOUTH ORGANIZATION

Established as a national organization in 1951, the Catholic Youth Organization (CYO) emphasizes programs that have social, physical, and spiritual value for Catholic youth. Leadership generally is provided by the parish priest and adult volunteers. It is designed to attract and involve young people in the life of the parish; athletics is regarded as a basic program to achieve that end. In some instances, the program is facility-based; in others, it is not. When it is facility-based, the facilities are administered and financed by the diocesan headquarters. In addition to athletic programs, the CYO promotes music activities, day camps, young adults clubs, and scouting activities.

4-H Clubs

Although not a private, not-for-profit-voluntary association, 4-H Clubs do merit special mention under the category of youth-serving organizations that rely heavily upon adult leadership. Leadership comes primarily from Cooperative Extension Service staff who are employed in virtually every county in the United States through cooperative agreements between the U.S. Department of Agriculture, the state land grant university, and county governments. On the local and county level, volunteers are heavily used to provide club and event leadership.

The four Hs stand for Head, Heart, Hands, and Health, and the association was founded as a self-improvement group for rural young people at the turn of the century. Today, it serves over two million boys and girls in both rural and urban areas and involves them in a variety of educational and service activities. It is no longer restricted to rural environments; camping and social activities are as much of a part of 4-H as are poultry raising and sewing. The 4-H program is basically a group-centered approach to youth services. Its support comes largely from government appropriations at the federal, state, and local levels.

Girl Scouts of the United States of America

The largest of the voluntary organizations serving only girls, the Girl Scouts of the USA has over three million members in nearly 400 councils. Established in 1912, it is primarily a group-oriented program with emphasis on nature, outdoor recreation, and community service activities. Membership is divided by age group into Daisies, Brownies, Juniors, Cadets, and Seniors. Leaders are both professionals and volunteers.

Like most organizations in this classification, it has a national office but provides most functions through its regional and local units. The local councils are relatively autonomous and draw support from United Way giving, membership fees, and voluntary contributions. The organization aims through a series of developmental experiences to provide a program to make members useful, responsible citizens. Like the Boy Scouts, the Girl Scouts operate day camp and residential camp facilities sponsored by local councils or troops throughout the United States. On an international level, Girl Scouts of the United States are a member of the World Association of Girl Guides and Girl Scouts. Over eight million girls belong to the organization worldwide (see Figure 6-1, page 194).

Figure 6-1
The Girl Scout Connection

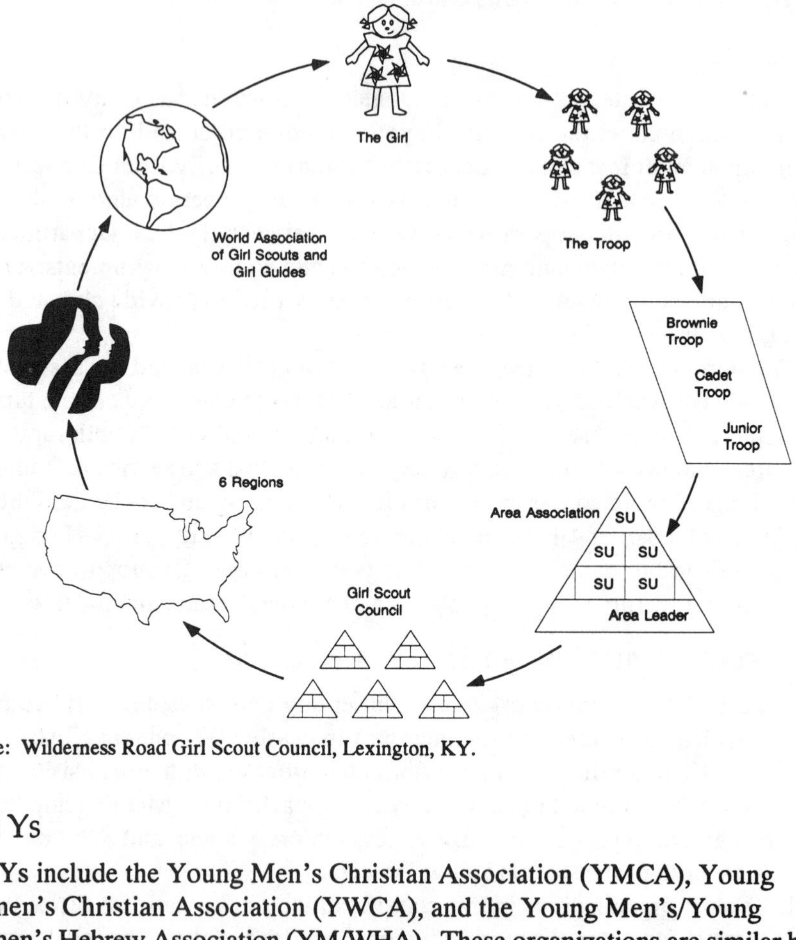

Source: Wilderness Road Girl Scout Council, Lexington, KY.

THE YS

The Ys include the Young Men's Christian Association (YMCA), Young Women's Christian Association (YWCA), and the Young Men's/Young Women's Hebrew Association (YM/WHA). These organizations are similar but vary from locality to locality concerning structure and approach. Most are facility-based and rely heavily upon a professional staff to operate their services. They have traditionally served primarily as general youth-serving and family organizations, not as recreation agencies, although the provision of recreation services and activities is a major component of their programs. All have some element of religious orientation and often address family values and activities as well as services to youth.

The Young Men's Christian Association is one of the oldest youth-serving organizations, having been established in England in the 1840s. The first U.S. operation was in Boston in 1851. Currently there are nearly 2,000 member associations in the United States serving some 13 million members. Each YMCA functions autonomously but with a strong relationship with its national council. Although YMCAs were established as Christian groups, primarily Protestant, with a restricted membership based upon one's sex and age, they no longer function in that capacity. Approximately one fourth of the membership of the YMCA is female, and a rather high percentage is over the age of 21. The mission now reads "to put Christian principles into practice through programs that build healthy body, mind, and spirit for all." Originally established to serve urban poor and transient youth, the YMCA has moved away from that orientation to serving families through its "progressive programs" approach to providing services. The range of services includes educational programs, opportunities for recreation, and physical fitness and aquatic programs.

The Young Women's Christian Association emerged in the United States shortly after the YMCA. It was originally designed to meet the needs of young women working in urban environments. Today the YWCA is the world's largest multi-racial women's movement and the major goal is the empowerment of women and the elimination of racism. The program promotes the good health, education, and social awareness of its members. The YWCA now has male members although the primary focus is on girls and women, and does not stress a sectarian affiliation as a prerequisite for membership. Over two million members are involved in the United States. YWCA facilities vary greatly from community to community but may include housing opportunities, multi-purpose recreation centers, camps, and social activity areas.

Both the YMCA and the YWCA regard professional leadership as essential for their success. Volunteers are important to local organizations in determining policy and aiding with fund raising, but the basic program service is provided by professional staff specialists. Both have active organized camping programs. Many of the finest residential camps in the United States and Canada are operated by YMCAs and YWCAs. Both have strong high school programs such as the High-Y and the Y-Teens. Their basic support comes from United Way giving, membership fees, and foundation grants. In recent years, they have relied increasingly upon membership fees for support and, in the minds of many, have made it more difficult for the economically disadvantaged, in particular, to participate fully in the life of the YMCA.

Apart from their strong Jewish culture component, the Young Hebrew Associations are very similar in approach and structure to the YMCA and YWCA. They do not consider themselves recreation agencies, but service agencies with a strong religious component. Social group work concepts and educational concerns are traditional with the YHAs. A typical YM/WHA operates social, cultural, and athletic programs for all age groups. Culture and performing arts activities are also stressed, as are programs for teens designed to strengthen their religious and cultural heritage. These groups are frequently associated with Jewish Community Centers in some communities.

OTHER GROUPS

A variety of youth groups sponsored by adult organizations merit mentioning. Many of these are auxiliary groups. All are characterized by the leadership given them; they are directed by volunteers, members of the parent organization. Typical among them are fraternal and patriotic societies and national civic organizations. Examples are the Junior Order of Elk, the Order of DeMolay of the Masons, branch organizations of labor unions, the Junior American Red Cross, the Junior Legion of the American Legion, and the Key Club of the Kiwanis International. These programs range from sponsoring a youth recognition day to actively supporting a comprehensive youth service organization. Although recreation is not the basis of these programs, it is a key element. The parent organizations have found their youth programs to be a way to promote citizenship and introduce to youth the values and benefits of the parent organization. Few, if any, of these groups employ professionals to administer their youth services.

Youth-Directed Groups

Some youth programs and organizations are planned and directed by youth. Generally these groups are a program of the parks and recreation service or a program of the mayor or county commission. Occasionally they are autonomous. All emphasize the self-directed aspects of the program, with youth providing their own leadership with a minimum of adult advice and supervision. They are known by a variety of names but the most frequent terms used are Teen Centers and Youth Councils (Bennett, 1980). No single national federation exists for these groups. They generally operate in a church, school facility, neighborhood recreation center, or have their own clubhouse. There may or may not be an adult advisory board; they may or may not have adult supervisors or leaders. They rely heavily upon private not-for-profit contributions and membership fees. Their programs are varied but always with a strong social and community awareness function. They may sponsor their own radio and TV shows, have their own newspapers, or operate community service programs. Experience suggests that youth do respond to the challenge of having their own organizations. Adult support may be necessary to provide some continuity, but the program must reflect the interests of youth.

Problems of Youth Services

A variety of issues and concerns confront voluntary youth organizations. Paramount among them is the issue of finance. Those organizations established to serve economically disadvantaged youths and youth-at-risk have found it increasingly difficult to provide the types of programs that are needed. To survive, some have become programs directed more toward the middle class. This evolution is neither good nor bad, but a reflection of the economic times. In some instances, public park and recreation agencies have taken up the slack of service to low income people, but not always. An expectation on the part of the public for private not-for-profit agencies to work with underprivileged individuals still exists, especially when those agencies receive financial support from the United Way.

A shift in role of these voluntary youth-serving agencies is issue number two. As these agencies have become more generalized in their service, less tied to a specific age, socioeconomic, or sex group, they have found themselves in competition with public and other private not-for-profit agencies serving middle-class youth. Each group, in its own way, has attempted to establish itself as a basic provider of youth services to obtain the broadest base of financial support possible. In the process, specialized needs are sometimes overlooked and not provided even though the need for these services remains. The need for more coordinative planning and a better-articulated role of service is apparent. Roles continue to exist for female-only organizations or for agencies serving specific ethnic or racial groups.

A third issue is directly related to population changes. The percentage of children and teenagers is less than it was during the 1950s and 1960s when programs for youth expanded. However, the 1990 U.S. Census shows that number of children between the ages of 5-13 has increased by almost ten percent from 1980 as the Baby Boomers are now becoming parents. With the reduction of the potential client population in the 1970s and 1980s, youth-serving organizations were forced to look for new population groups to serve if they were to survive. The middle-aged and older adult population were a natural target group but with the Boomers' children reaching youth organization age, we will likely see more emphasis placed on youth again. Many organizations, however, will face the challenge of balancing their programs to provide needed services for both youth and older groups.

Program viability is also a persistent issue for these traditional youth-serving organizations. The needs of families and youth are constant, but the means by which they find fulfillment and by which society meets these needs are ever changing. This year's teen group wants a program different from last year's. It is difficult to establish a continuity of service that is meaningful when the clients continually perceive themselves to be different from those who came before them. The values of the young are not necessarily in agreement with those of their parents or recreation professionals. The potential for conflict between those being served and those financially supporting the service exists, and the professional may be caught in the middle.

Some trends are discernible in services to youth. Youth serving organizations are seeking a broader base of support. In addition to working with youth-at-risk, more attention is being given to co-recreational activities, to family activities, to nonathletic activities, and to short-term projects and activities rather than long-term club membership. Youth are being involved in planning and conducting those programs and services designed for them. More utilization of group dynamic and community organization techniques are being employed by leisure service professionals. The issues facing youth in the United States related to drugs, peer pressure and gang activity, and sexual behavior create the need for a continued dialogue among the many public and not-for-profit agencies concerning the best ways to meet the needs of this growing, and often disadvantaged population (Kleiber & Richards, 1985).

Private Membership Organizations

One of the most extensive and difficult elements to describe within the leisure service delivery system is the private membership-oriented recreation movement. No precise record of the number of country clubs, recreation associations, or special interest groups such as swimming or stamp collecting clubs exists in the United States. Yet these groups offer recreation opportunities for millions of individuals; combined, these groups may be the largest single provider of organized recreation services.

For many individuals, recreation has always been a private concern. They have organized clubs and groups to facilitate their recreation interests and opportunities. These organizations are highly individualistic, may be formally or informally structured, and generally are not part of some national organization. What is characteristic of all organizations is that they are member-centered and respond to the interests of those who "belong."

Sociologists suggest a relationship between the extent of these private programs and the affluence and freedom enjoyed in a society. The presence of these semi-exclusive opportunities is directly related to economic conditions and the desire for activity with selected friends in an environment of one's own choosing. Recreation interests provide the vehicle for this kind of interaction and expression.

As stated earlier, the exact nature and magnitude of this segment of the recreation system is largely unknown. Many of these associations employ professional staff; others rely totally upon their membership for leadership. Some of these organizations have extensive property holdings and elaborate programs; others hold no property, have no set schedule of activity, but do meet periodically in homes of friends and members, or use the facilities of the public or other private not-for-profit recreation organizations. All rely upon membership fees and donations for financial support and tend to emphasize either a single activity or interest, such as tennis, or sustain a particular social relationship, such as a women's club.

Among the more obvious private clubs are those which exist for social reasons, such as country clubs, civic organizations, and fraternal orders. Other clubs promote and encourage specific athletic or recreational interests such as tennis, golf, track and field, soccer, skiing, and boating. Hunting and fishing clubs, sky diving and flying clubs, motorcycle and snowmobiling clubs are also found in many communities. The list is endless. Any recreation activity has the potential as a club activity.

Some clubs may organize for one reason but continue for another. For example, a garden club may be formed to support the garden interests of its members, but the members may continue to come because of the club's civic and social involvement in the community. Some groups exist to provide membership services, such as the American Automobile Association (AAA) clubs, whereas others represent a neighborhood interest, such as the Westside Development Club. Rarely does one go through life without being a member of a private, not-for-profit club.

Some social and behavioral scientists question the benefits of the private recreation association movement. They see the development of these programs as a divisive factor, further segregating people into isolated and exclusive groups. They hold that the natural extension of this trend is the relegation of public recreation to serve only people who are socially disadvantaged, disabled, or economically deprived. Private profit and not-for-profit interests then would serve the rest of the population.

On the other hand, many individuals who participate in private profit and not-for-profit recreation opportunities also use public recreation facilities. When they do develop their own facilities, they tend to be selective in what they construct. The presence of the private groups generally supplements the community's recreation effort rather than detracts from it. Private recreation is not a substitute for public recreation, but a reaffirmation of the democratic system and an opportunity for people to have many recreation choices and opportunities.

Employee Recreation and Corporate Fitness Programs

For the thousands of American industries and businesses providing recreation services for their employees, employee recreation is an important element of the private sector. For many employees and their families, employee programs are the key providers of organized recreation services and fitness opportunities.

The term "employee recreation" (formerly called "industrial recreation") does not mean any special brand of recreation services. Employee recreation is the application of recreation services to a particular clientele (employees or a particular company and their families) by a specific sponsor (the corporation itself). Employee recreation may be provided by the employer and/or by the workers themselves. This type of employee services has been in existence for over a hundred years having its origin in the industrial reform movements of the mid-nineteenth century. According to recreation historians, employee recreation programs began in the United States when the Peace Dale Manufacturing Company of Peace Dale, Rhode Island, established a community library in 1854 (Murphy, 1984). Today, it is estimated that American companies and labor organizations spend over three billion dollars annually on employee recreation services.

Employee recreation does not occur only in large industries and manufacturing plants. It applies equally to such commercial enterprises as banks, insurance companies, department stores, private utilities, transportation lines, service firms, and other business organizations. Many of these smaller organizations have well-organized recreation programs; they sponsor athletic teams, operate camps and park facilities, stage dramatic and musical productions, provide preretirement and leisure counseling, and offer tours or special travel arrangements for their employees.

Corporation executives, labor unions, and industrial sociologists generally agree that recreation activities contribute to worker productivity and well-being. Some data exists to support this assumption, and logic tends to dictate its validity. The stress of modern technology with its specializations, monotony, automation, and health hazards suggests the provision of recreation programs may be a diversion from work. If employee recreation and fitness programs reduce absenteeism, worker turnover, and industrial accidents, then it is a benefit to the company and a good business investment. If these services add to the life of the worker, enhance the quality of the environment, and provide opportunity for personal fulfillment, then it is profitable both to business and to the community. Some advocates of employee recreation claim it does all of this; others are less charitable in their assessment of its contribution. Nearly all agree, however, that recreation is of value and should be a concern of industry (Finney, 1984).

Types of Employee Recreation Services

Employee recreation programs are administered in a number of ways. Some programs are sponsored entirely by management; management provides all the areas and facilities and operates the program with little or no cost to the worker. In other instances, management provides capital for the areas and facilities and the employees provide the leadership and conduct the programs. A third approach is to have the employees assume total responsibility for their recreation service; they plan, finance, and operate the entire service. A fourth approach is to have some other organization—a public or private not-for-profit agency—provide the services. In the past, YMCAs have often filled this role. More recently, public recreation agencies have organized employee sports leagues or made available facilities to industries on a special lease arrangement (e.g., a

Rockwell International, 1990 corporate champions, lead the parade during closing ceremonies for Anaheim's [CA] Corporate Challenge, an Olympic-style competition for corporate teams.

municipal park would be reserved exclusively for a company picnic). In a number of communities, joint action is undertaken for the building of various facilities and the operation of a recreation program. Essentially, for those communities, employee recreation is community recreation. In some situations, industries and commercial organizations provide neither areas nor facilities nor operate a program; instead, they make liberal contributions to the community program through voluntary leadership, financial gifts, and company-sanctioned programs and events.

The pattern varies according to the historical traditions, the industrial base of the community, and the size and nature of the industries. Employee recreation is also a concern of labor organizations. Like corporations, unions have found that recreation contributes to the well-being and life of their members. The pattern with unions, both in terms of sponsorship and program scope, is similar to that with companies.

From the very beginning, sports and athletics were a major staple of employee recreation. Such companies as Goodyear, Phillips Petroleum, Firestone, and Caterpillar Tractor fielded outstanding semiprofessional sports teams. During the early 1960s, the pendulum of programming swung from athletics and spectator events to more individual participant interests. Company teams became a program of the past; intramural and employee sports leagues replaced them (see Table 6-2, page 202).

Many companies offer different services. Texas Instruments, for example, operates country clubs, golf courses, and camps for their employees. Other companies purchase and distribute admission tickets to theme parks to their employees. Many underwrite employee travel and tour programs. Employee clubs, lunchtime recreation activities, physical fitness programs, and

Table 6-2
On-Site Fitness Equipment Available at 132 Industrial Recreation Centers

Type of Equipment	% Who Have Equipment	Quantity Available			
		1-2	3-5	6-9	10+
Variable resistance machines	68%				
Multistation weight machines	70%				
Free weights	77%				
Exercise bikes	92%	46%	23%	19%	16%
Rowing machines	77%	83%	11%	4%	3%
Treadmills	84%	69%	16%	7%	7%
Stair climbers	84%	60%	29%	8%	2%

Source: *Employee Services Management*, April, 1992, p. 32.

special programs for the children of employees are also often offered. The range of recreation facilities is equal to the scope of programming. Companies have built YMCAs and community centers, golf courses and athletic fields, playgrounds, and parks. In recent years, the trend has been toward the development of fitness centers and programs and the development of employee recreation areas on tracts of land away from the company rather than adjacent to or on the plant property. Other than for fitness activities, industries have found their employees use their facilities more frequently when their recreation areas are nearer the employee's home or located where people generally go to recreate, such as at the beach or a lake. For example, Springs Mills owns and operates a beach complex at Myrtle Beach, South Carolina for its employees.

Methods of Finance

A variety of ways exist to finance employee recreation. As previously indicated, some employee recreation programs are totally financed by the company. Recreation and employee services is a line item in the company's budget. A second major source is the revenue generated by employee recreation association dues. Employees join their recreation association as they would any other private not-for-profit recreation group. Some advocates feel that this is the best means of financing the service, since those who use it are also the ones who support it. A third method is to utilize the profits from vending machines, snack bars, canteens, and other concessions. According to Frank Guadagnolo (1978), a company of 20,000 employees or more can realize up to a quarter of a million dollars of profit a year from vending operations. A fourth method is to charge admission or activity fees. This is the pay-as-you-go plan. Most companies have found a combination of all four methods to be advantageous.

Professional Organizations

Professionalism is a concern of employer recreation specialists. In response to the growth of employee recreation as a bona fide concern, the National Industrial Recreation Association (NIRA) was organized in 1941. Its major objective was to promote and assist in the development of employee recreation programs. In 1981, in keeping with the changing focus of industrial recreation programs from sports to employee leisure-time services, NIRA changed its name to the National Employee Services and Recreation Association (NESRA). Some 900 major companies are members of NESRA. It is estimated that these organizations employ over 1,000 employee recreation directors and administer some 600 park and recreation centers. The Association has been a strong advocate of program quality and has worked diligently to upgrade personnel standards.

A second association serving industries and their employees was formed in the 1970s. In response to the growing interest in physical fitness and reports which related physical fitness to general health and productivity, industries began employing physical fitness directors to develop and supervise exercise programs and administer employee health and fitness areas. They may or may not be a part of the employee recreation program. The directors of these fitness programs have created their own association—the American Association of Fitness Directors in Business and Industry.

Issues

As with most private not-for-profit, voluntary agency programs, employee recreation has had to face the issue of duplication of services when justifying the continuation of recreation services in light of expanding government park and recreation services. To some, the provision of successful programs appears to be an unnecessary expense, since industries and their employees are taxpayers, and because the local park and recreation programs are supported by tax funds. Why, then, should the industry or labor groups provide services that are legitimately the responsibility of the community? On the other hand, employee services and recreation programs generally are not a duplication of the public recreation service. They have a specific clientele and program thrust. They are designed primarily for the employees and their families; they are a form of private recreation.

Industrial and employee recreation services have been a major element of the leisure service system for several decades. The role is changing, and advocates are increasing in number. With the need for more programs in which workers can identify with their employers and have a sense of partnership and community, the attractiveness of employee recreation service increases.

Other Private Interests

Most private organizations and agencies exist to provide a direct service for their membership. The provision of opportunities for recreation is a major reason for their existence (see Table 6-3). Some organizations, however, impact upon parks and recreation through their advocacy programs or through their willingness to allow the public to use their resources for recreational experiences. In the latter group are the public utilities, which often make their land and water resources available for outdoor recreation experiences. Also included in this group are the ranchers and farmers who offer their lands for hunting and camping. It is estimated that 347 million acres of forest lands are in private ownership (*Statistical Abstract of the United States*, 1991). Add to it billions of acres of farmland and you have a major resource for outdoor recreation. Finally, some recreation opportunities are afforded the public through industrial tours. Such companies as Anheuser-Busch, the Christian Brothers, and Hershey Chocolate open their plants to visitors. They encourage these tours; it is good public relations and provides a recreation and educational experience for their guests.

Socially concerned advocacy agencies are also important to the recreation and park movement. Among them are the environmental organizations such as Nature Conservancy, which purchases ecologically significant lands and holds them in escrow until those lands can be acquired by governmental organizations

Table 6-3
A Nation Of Joiners
A select list of popular associations Americans join (1988)

Association	Members (millions)
American Automobile Association	29.0
American Association of Retired Persons	28.0
YMCA of the USA	14.0
National PTA—National Congress of Parents and Teachers	6.1
National Wildlife Federation	5.1
4-H Program	4.8
Boy Scouts of America	4.8
Women's International Bowling Congress	3.7
American Bowling Congress	3.3
Girl Scouts of the USA	3.1
National Rifle Association	3.0
YWCA of the USA	2.0
U.S. Youth Soccer Association	1.4
Rotary International	1.0
Junior Achievement	1.0
Mothers Against Drunk Driving	1.0

Source: *American Society of Association Executives,* 1989.

as parks and preserves. The National Trust for Historic Preservation operates museums and advocates the acquisition and preservation of historical areas. The National Audubon Society also offers educational programs, lecture series, and support for wildlife sanctuaries. The National Easter Seals Society with its camping program, the Joseph P. Kennedy, Jr. Foundation, known for its work with mentally retarded persons through Special Olympics, and the National Council on Aging, advocating services to senior citizens and promoting the role and importance of senior centers and adult education programs are typical of the program-oriented groups.

The School and Its Role in Recreation

No discussion of membership and private, not-for-profit recreation services would be complete without an analysis of the school's role in recreation. Although most schools are publicly funded, their involvement with the recreation system is included in this chapter, rather than in the chapter on governmental services, since it has a specific clientele (its students) and approaches its role of service much like that of a membership group. Yet its programs are significant to the provision of leisure opportunities for all and its support comes from both the public and private sector.

A close relationship exists between learning and recreation. Both areas stem from a desire to understand and master the world. The early Greek scholars were aware of this relationship and considered leisure an opportunity for learning and a time for exploration. They knew that discoveries resulted from pleasure seeking, and that the memory is enhanced when the learning environment is satisfying.

Public and private school systems have played a vital role in providing recreation opportunities for nearly two centuries. In 1821, the Latin School in Salem, Massachusetts opened its outdoor physical education facilities for recreation use; in 1888, the New York School System opened its buildings to the public as evening recreation centers. Since 1911, the worthy use of leisure has been recognized as a cardinal principle of education by the National Education Association. More recently, the Department of Education, through the Community School Act, has provided monetary grants to state and local school systems for the establishment and expansion of their community school programs.

The degree to which school systems are a provider of recreation services varies from community to community. In some states, school law and codes are liberal in their support of recreation services through the public school system. This is especially true in Pennsylvania, Wisconsin, and California. In other states, such as North Carolina, the laws limit the schools in providing public recreation service. Although not all school systems are sensitive to their role in education for leisure, growing interest exists in the cooperation between local public recreation systems and boards of education and school authorities.

Because the school is an essential and influential institution in every community, school officials and authorities cannot avoid dealing with the issue of leisure. Nor can they avoid providing direct services for the millions of children and adults who spend a major portion of their lives each day within the confines of school facilities. As institutions that purport to develop understanding and learning, schools must deal with the issue of leisure and prepare students for that aspect of life. The role of schools involves shaping attitudes, developing leisure skills, and providing opportunities for practicing those skills.

In addition to the educational mandate, the public school system is a significant owner of public facilities. School property holdings are enormous. Most schools have gymnasiums, auditoriums, arts and music facilities, playgrounds, park areas, and athletic fields. Some have swimming pools, stadiums, and well-equipped industrial arts areas. Most of these facilities can and should be made available for recreation pursuits. Essentially, the school has five major responsibilities in parks and recreation:

1. *To educate for leisure.* This responsibility includes the development of leisure attitudes and values, activity skills, knowledge of the resources of the community available for leisure expression, and an understanding by the individual of his or her interests, motivations, and leisure aptitudes and appetite.
2. *To provide recreation opportunities and services.* The school has the responsibility to provide recreation opportunities for the school population, and, where feasible, recreation services to the entire community. It may provide services through direct programming or by opening its facilities for after-school and weekend use.
3. *To advise, counsel, and guide leisure behaviors.* Just as the schools make available counseling services on academic, vocational planning, and personal matters, the school should advise on matters related to the recreative use of leisure.
4. *To prepare individuals for serving in recreation leadership capacities.* The school is the institution to which society turns for training in any field of service and because recreation and parks needs both professorial and volunteer leaders, opportunities for leadership development and practice, as well as curricula for the preparation of park and recreation professionals, are essential.
5. *To be an advocate of leisure.* School officials and administrators can play a critical role in the support of public and community recreation and park services. They can demonstrate their concern for "quality living" through joint planning and development efforts. Whenever possible, the school system should be represented on recreation advisory boards and vice versa. Two-way communication is essential.

Three basic methods are used by schools to fulfill these roles. They are the community school and school-park programs, contractual agreements with public recreation and park agencies, and leisure education and extracurricular programs.

Beginning with the work of the Charles Stuart Mott Foundation in Flint, Michigan in the late 1930s, the *community school* concept has enjoyed considerable success. The concept holds that the school is the major governmental institution serving neighborhood areas and, as such, its programs should go beyond the traditional formal education services to provide adult education, recreation programs, and related activities. Its proponents state that school facilities should be used as community centers, available to the public for meetings and recreation activities. Furthermore, they believe that the schools should be the catalytic agent to further community growth and development. They advocate that this responsibility be a legitimate part of the budget of the school system and that a separate faculty is employed to operate the community school program after the formal hours of instruction are completed.

Although many local school boards are somewhat hesitant to expand their services or seek additional funds for a community school, the concept does have merit and suggests that school buildings, like all other public facilities, should be available to the public. In rural areas, the school is often the only public agency which has the resources to provide community services. The community school concept is ideally suited for this setting.

The *school-park* concept is a more urban-oriented notion (see Figure 6-2). It is defined as "a situation where a school has been built in or immediately adjacent to a park, and the design and operation of the two amenities are coordinated so that the school's students benefit from the park's recreation and education resources while the park and recreation department uses school facilities to enhance its program" (Chubb & Chubb, 1981). To implement this concept effectively, recreation and park agencies and school officials must coordinate their planning and development activities. Contractual arrangements are generally entered into, thereby formally committing each unit to a set of responsibilities and services. The community school-park concept has been most successful in those communities where the lines of responsibility of education and recreation are well-defined and where separate administrative organizations have been established to carry out those responsibilities.

In no area is the public more likely to duplicate its resources for organized recreation and leisure activities than in its construction and operation of school facilities. The school is an excellent recreation resource just as play is a wonderful medium in which to learn. Probably for that reason alone, some have advocated that the school be the administrator of public recreation systems. But the systems are complex and have their own unique mandate. What is needed is an understanding between recreation and school officials so that public lands

Figure 6-2
School-Park Concept at Work, Chapel Hill, NC

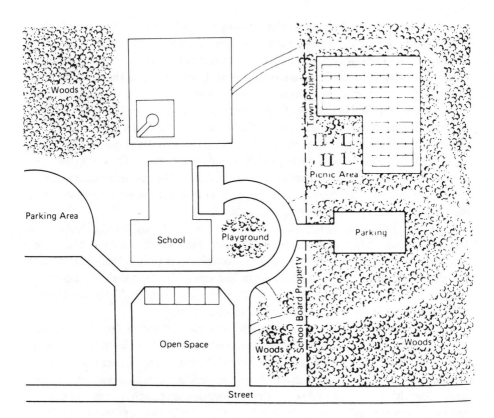

and buildings can be used by the public, and by those agencies serving the public regardless of who manages them. Little is to be gained by including various kinds of public recreation facilities in a school building unless the building is open and available to the community. Community use cannot have a prior claim over the school use of school facilities, but too many school buildings have recreation facilities that could be used after school and on weekends but that are inaccessible to the public.

Even under the best of circumstances, when schools are used for the dual purpose of education and community recreation, it is a challenge to schedule and coordinate the use in a way that best serves both interests. The most common way this coordination is accomplished is through *contractual agreements* between school officials and other governmental bodies like recreation and park departments and libraries. Similar to the school park concept, these arrangements require cooperative planning and administration. It seems foolhardy for a community to build an athletic stadium for high school athletic use when its park and recreation department may already have a stadium which could serve the school's needs. Likewise, constructing a neighborhood playground seems superfluous when a neighborhood school complex already has such a facility. Through contractual agreements, the recreation department might assume responsibility for the operations and maintenance of the school grounds for specific periods of use. It might even pay the school system fee for that privilege. Similarly, the school board might enter into an agreement with the recreation department for the exclusive use of its athletic stadium for specified dates. The school's responsibility for the supervision and maintenance of that facility during those periods of time would be specified, as would the financial arrangements.

Obviously, schools provide recreation opportunities for their students. Recess and extracurricular activities, including interscholastic sports programs, are prime examples. Schools also teach the basic skills vital to leisure expressions. In school, people learn to read, draw, develop athletic and artistic skills. Unfortunately, some of this education is frequently not related to its potential for leisure expression, nor is it offered in a systematic and developmental sequence. This occurs only when the school system is committed to a program of *leisure education*.

Leisure education is more than the learning of lifelong sport skills. It involves the development of values and attitudes toward leisure and the integration of leisure moments and activities with other life interests and experiences. It is not a course or a series of courses entitled "leisure education," nor is it restricted to the public school system. Advocates feel it should be integrated in the learning experiences which already exist in schools as well as other recreation activities.

Closely related to leisure education is the concept of continuing education. Learning is a lifelong experience, one which can be quite pleasant. Largely promoted by adult education specialists, continuing education does not necessarily follow the traditional mode of "taking courses for academic credit." It is concerned with both the furthering of professional or vocational learning and personal growth and development (e.g., life enrichment). Continuing education has been demonstrated through innovative and flexible learning models, and for many has become a recreative experience. With an increasing older population, the school can be expected to devote more of its resources to continuing and adult education than it has in the past.

Finally, through *intramural and extracurricular activities* and interscholastic athletic programs, schools provide a wide range of recreation opportunities and experiences. Millions attend college and high school sporting events. Millions of students work on school newspapers and yearbooks, and sing or act in school musical or dramatic productions. Millions participate in college intramural and student union programs, services often administered by parks and recreation graduates. Schools are most active in providing direct leisure services for their constituents through this role. Schools are an important element of the leisure service delivery system, as are all the organizations, institutions, and agencies which comprise the membership and private not-for-profit recreation service grouping.

Summary

The private not-for-profit sector, with a focus on membership interest and an ability to respond to special interest groups, is a critical element in the leisure service delivery system. Portions of this sector are similar in form and structure to the public recreation and park system. Other segments are more characteristic of the commercial sector. Both elements complement and supplement the organized park and recreation service.

The role of the private not-for-profit sector has varied depending upon public attitudes, fads and leisure interests, and patterns of governmental involvement. To date, the private not-for-profit sector has not considered itself a part of the park and recreation movement. The more traditional groups, such as the youth-serving organizations, have identified with the social welfare movement; they have relied upon their own programs of professional preparation or have sought graduates with a background from one of the social or behavioral sciences. Management skills are critical for the administrative personnel but so are the skills of fund-raising and public relations. The religious bodies have sought leadership with an activity orientation; those affiliated with religious institutions generally see themselves as religious educators who also have a responsibility to provide recreation and fellowship to their members. The degree to which these elements will eventually turn to the park and recreation profession for personnel or identify with the profession's programs of certification and accreditation is undetermined.

The other segments of the private, not-for-profit sector are moving closer to the organized park and recreation service. Increasingly, private recreation clubs, employee recreation services, and university student activity programs are employing graduates of parks and recreation curricula. Like the public agencies, they need personnel with management and program development skills which are emphasized in parks and recreation curricula. The services they provide for their specific constituents are not dissimilar from those provided to people by public park and recreation agencies. In the coming decade these elements may become major employers of park and recreation graduates, and their identification with the recreation and park movement may become stronger. Certainly, their role in the delivery of leisure services will not diminish in the near future.

Suggestions and Study Guides

1. Visit one of the many facility-based youth-serving agencies. Discuss with a chief administrator his or her philosophy of service, professional affiliation and the goals and hopes of the agency. Discuss the various issues which confront the operation of the agency; explore the agency's mandate and strategies for support. Compare these views with those expressed by the public recreation and park professionals whom you have met and interviewed.

2. Repeat the assignment for question one, except this time talk with an administrator or professional affiliated with a group-oriented youth-serving agency. Compare his or her views with those of the facility-based administrator.

3. What role do you see the private recreation sector playing in the immediate future? On what basis have drawn this conclusion? In what ways is the private not-for-profit sector influenced by or does it influence the role of the public recreation and park agencies? How does it differ from those of the commercial sector ?

4. Draft an argument or position statement for the use of public areas by private recreation services. Consider the benefit and problems one might encounter when making public lands and resources available to private not-for-profit groups to operate or use exclusively. Develop an argument against such use. Finally, what do you consider to be the appropriate relationship between public and private not-for-profit interests in the provision of recreation and leisure opportunities for the public?

References

Bennett, J. T. (1980). The Youth Council approach: An alternative to the street. *Parks and Recreation, 15*(6), pp. 34-36.

Chubb, M. & Chubb, H. (1981). *One third of our time.* New York, NY: John Wiley & Sons, p. 711.

Duwe, M. J. (1981). Coaxing the corporate dollar. *Parks and Recreation, 16*(9), pp. 58-60.

Epperson, A. (1983). Recreation's potential partners. Church and the public sector. *Parks and Recreation, 18*(3), pp. 60-62.

Finney, C. (1984). Corporate benefits of employee recreation programs. *Parks and Recreation, 19*(8), pp. 44-46, 71.

Guadagnolo, F. (1980). Employee recreation. In G. Godbey (Ed.), *Recreation, Park and Leisure Services,* (p. 183). Philadelphia, PA: W. B. Saunders.

Kleiber, D. & Richards, W. (1985). Leisure and recreation in adolescence: Limitations and potentials. In Wade, M. (Ed.) *Constraints on Leisure.* Springfield, FL: C. C. Thomas.

Kraus, R. (1982). Singles, a large (and largely ignored) target population. *Parks & Recreation, 17*(5), pp. 48-51.

Murphy, M. (1984). The history of employee services and recreation programs. *Parks and Recreation, 19*(8), pp. 34-39.

National Council of the Churches of Christ in the United States of America. (1989). *Yearbook.* New York, NY: Author.

Opening the door to the future: Community VISIONS. (1992). Cedar Rapids, IA: United Way of East Central Iowa.

Orthner, D. & Mancini, J. (1990). Leisure impacts on family interaction and cohesion. *Journal of Leisure Research, 22*(2), pp. 125-137.

Scheier, I. (1980). *Exploring volunteer space: The recruiting of a nation.* Boulder, CO: Volunteer Readership.

Shaw, S. (1992). Family leisure and leisure services. *Parks and Recreation, 27*(12), pp. 13-16, 66.

Statistical Abstract of the United States 1991. Washington, DC: U.S. Department of Commerce.

Tedrick, T. & Henderson, K. A. (1989). *Volunteers in leisure: A management perspective.* Reston, VA: American Alliance for Health, Physical Education, Recreation, and Dance.

Van Doren, C. (1993). Personal communication.

Watts, A. D. & Edwards, P. K. (1983). Recruiting and retaining human service volunteers: An empirical analysis. *Journal of Voluntary Action Research, 12*(3), pp. 9-22.

Witt, P. & Goodale, T. (1981). The relationships between barriers to leisure enjoyment and family stages. *Leisure Sciences, 4*(1), pp. 29-49.

PORTIONS OF CHAPTER SEVEN DEVELOPED AND CONTRIBUTED BY
LEANDRA BEDINI
OF THE UNIVERSITY OF NORTH CAROLINA AT GREENSBORO

CHAPTER SEVEN

Special Recreation Services

Parks and recreation has held from its very beginning that its services are for all people. The necessity for activity, for the recreation experience, is well-documented and the pursuit of happiness, including the right to recreate, is guaranteed to all. Recreation and park services were never meant to discriminate against any segment of the population.

Unfortunately, not all citizens have had equal opportunity to participate in its services. Because of a variety of conditions such as limited economic resources, racial and ethnic prejudices, transportation difficulties, age and gender discrimination, and physical and mental disability, some segments of the population have been discriminated against and have not enjoyed the benefits of recreation programs. The recreation and park profession recognizes this situation and has responded to it by developing services for these groups.

The history of recreation services for people with special needs paralleled the growth of recreation services in general. In addition to their concerns for underprivileged youth, early recreation advocates sought to include play and recreation in mental hospitals and schools for the retarded (Frye, 1962). Recreation programs for children with illnesses and disabilities existed in pediatric units in the 1920s where the workers were known as "play ladies." Their work was seen as having "therapeutic value" which "hastened the cure of the child." Not until the 1940s, however, did recreation for hospitalized adults became a reality largely due to the experience of the Veterans Administration (VA) and military hospitals during World War II.

By 1950 most state mental hospital systems were employing "hospital recreation" specialists, many of whom were former Red Cross hospital workers. The Red Cross had been asked by the War Department to provide recreation in its military hospitals. These recreation workers, along with their VA hospital counterparts, urged the American Recreation Society in 1948 to accept hospital recreation as a legitimate specialty. Four years later, a similar special interest section entitled "therapeutic recreation" was established by the American Association of Health, Physical Education and Recreation. A third and independently separate professional body, the National Association of Recreation Therapists, was created the following year. All promoted the need for specialized training for hospital recreation personnel and wanted this specialty to be recognized as a distinct field of practice.

In response to their concern, several universities and colleges established special options in hospital recreation for the preparation of personnel to work in these settings in the 1950s. The University of Minnesota, the University of North Carolina, and New York University each held regional institutes on hospital recreation to further this effort. These institutes were designed to upgrade the skills of recreators working in these medical settings.

In time, the term "hospital recreation" gave way to the concepts of "medical recreation" and "recreation for the ill and disabled." Hospital recreation no longer seemed an appropriate title as an increasing number of therapeutic-oriented programs were taking place in community mental health centers, sheltered workshops, and half-way houses. Recreation specialists were working in a variety of health-related settings and they wanted a title that reflected their broad interests; their cause was aided by a training grant program of the Vocational Rehabilitation Administration. This federal agency was the first, in 1963, to offer financial support to those universities and colleges interested in preparing recreation specialists to work with people with disabilities.

The "ill or disabled" term proved to be somewhat cumbersome in describing a specialty which used recreation services as a therapeutic modality. Those professionals working with people with disabilities within communities also found it awkward in describing their interests. "Therapeutic recreation," "recreation therapy," and "recreation for special populations" seem to better describe their programs. These terms, along with "special recreation services," have become widely accepted to describe the specialization concerned with recreation services for people who are disadvantaged, disabled, deprived, or undergoing medical treatment. Specialists in this area may be found working in the more traditional hospital and medical settings, but they also function as staff members of municipal recreation department and state and federal recreation and park agencies. They work with individuals who have special needs and who are often denied equal opportunities for participation because they are visually impaired, mentally retarded, elderly, homeless, incarcerated, or economically disadvantaged.

Definition of Terms

Differences exist in programming for people with disabilities residing in the community and those who are in institutions. In the institutional or medical setting, program efforts are directed by the major objectives of the institution, whether it be therapy, protection, or rehabilitation. There, activities are usually prescribed by medical personnel or approved by correctional officials; the recreation service does not function independently but is related to the activities of other therapies and program services. Recreation services in medical facilities are usually referred to as recreation therapy. Such functions as assisting with the patient's therapy and rehabilitation, providing leisure education, and offering recreation programs and services are performed by the recreation therapist. Today, due to pressures for reduced length of stay in the hospital and third party reimbursement issues, most therapeutic recreation units within a medical facility tend to address only the first two functions, except when dealing with children.

In the community, recreation for people with disabilities is no different from recreation services for any other citizens. The term "special populations," which is still widely used today, originated because people with disabilities frequently received services considered to be compensatory. Additionally, it was perceived that people with disabilities required a special understanding of the conditions which result in disability and deprivation. Because of this perception, the approaches used by professionals working with people with disabilities were originally more like the methods employed by social group workers than like the techniques used by other recreation professionals.

Recreation for people with disabilities in the community is similar to, but not the same as, recreation therapy. The latter is prescriptive while most recreation for people with disabilities in the community is not. Those involved in offering recreation therapy are attempting to modify or reinforce behaviors through recreation and play experiences whereas special recreation in the community is a general recreation service extended to all populations. Its main function is not to be prescriptive or rehabilitative. If better health and personal development occur through recreation and play, it is because of the play process, a by-product of the service rather than the intent of the service.

Because many people with disabilities reside in institutions, it was natural for the recreation and parks professionals to turn to specialists in these institutions to help the profession in "making even the unevenness of the recreation and park delivery system." This decision has had both negative and positive effects upon recreation services for people with disabilities and upon therapeutic recreation services. The two approaches are not philosophically the same, and both have struggled with their identities. Lee E. Meyer (1977), in his writings about the origins of therapeutic recreation services and the professionalization of therapeutic recreation, argues that therapeutic recreation has little to do with the setting in which it is practiced. He holds that therapeutic recreation is clinical by nature and therapeutic in intent. When recreation and park specialists in the community develop special programs for postcardiac patients to assist them with their recovery to health, they are providing therapeutic recreation services just as much as are recreators in mental hospitals when they conduct leisure education sessions with people with psychiatric impairments. Meyer also contends that recreation for people with disabilities has little to do with the setting in which it is practiced. Recreation for people with disabilities is not prescriptive; it is the provision of general recreation services to those who may require special consideration or understanding (see Figure 7-1).

Figure 7-1
Program Integration: A Continuum of Services to Special Populations

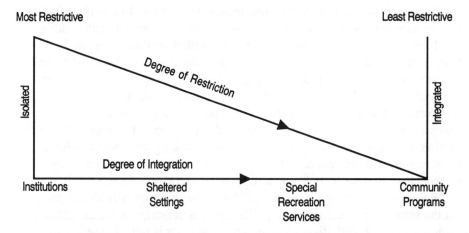

Therapeutic Recreation in Medical Settings

Hospitals, training schools, rehabilitation centers, and other treatment institutions exist because those being served by them cannot be helped effectively in the community where they live. They require rehabilitation, treatment, or constant care in a setting which is designed primarily to offer that care. The uniqueness of this environment forms the basis for understanding recreation services in medical and institutional settings.

Several assumptions exist about therapeutic recreation in medical settings. First, patients are in the institution because of some physical, mental, emotional, or social illness (such as drug abuse or crime). Whereas general recreation services in the community can expect only a small percentage of the participants to be health impaired, in the institutional setting the majority have health problems. Second, the patient population is not a homogeneous one; there are a variety of illnesses and levels of functioning within each diagnostic grouping. Furthermore, there are a variety of institutions—military, state and tax-supported hospitals, private hospitals—catering to specific disability groups; some serve "long-term" patients while others only deal with acute, short-term illnesses and situations. Finally, recreation intervention, treatment, and techniques must be facilitated by personnel specially trained in therapeutic recreation. Because the function of the hospital is to treat patients, no activity should be scheduled without medical approval; no patient should participate in an activity without clearance.

In the institutional setting, recreation services are just one of the many rehabilitative therapies including physical therapy, occupational therapy, social work, nutrition, speech and audiology, volunteer services, and religious activities. These therapies provide a wide range of expressions and activities that address the normal functioning of the patient when at home and in the community. Therapeutic recreation programs in the institutional setting are also diverse as they range from activities conducted on a ward or in a dayroom to tours in the community and leisure education. To be most effective, therapeutic recreation services must be integrated into the general treatment program of the institution.

As noted, the need for recreation services has long been recognized in hospitals for the mentally ill, particularly state institutions, in state schools for the mentally retarded, and in those settings operated by the Veterans Administration. Although there have been recreation opportunities in some state institutions for many years (i.e., the Lincoln, Illinois, State School and Colony since the early 1930s), it has only been within the past four decades that therapeutic recreation programs have begun to expand to most institutions. The work of the American Psychiatric Association's Committee on Leisure Time Activities, and the concerns of the American Red Cross for the hospitalized military encouraged its earlier growth; today, that role is being assumed by professional recreation organizations such as the American Therapeutic Recreation Association (ATRA) and the National Therapeutic Recreation Society (NTRS).

Contemporary recreation programs in medical settings are designed to treat, rehabilitate, and educate people with different disabilities to empower them to identify and incorporate leisure independency in their daily lives. Specific areas of treatment might include stimulating the resocialization processes, developing self-awareness and self-expression, and aiding in community reintegration.

Objectives of Therapeutic Recreation

Essentially, the purpose of the therapeutic recreation services in the medical setting is fourfold:

1. To provide treatment and/or rehabilitation of the patient.
2. To assist in the patient's adjustment to hospitalization/institutionalization of the patient; to provide him or her with opportunities for the continuation of "normal" life patterns.
3. To aid in the prevention of further difficulties which might lead to rehospitalization.
4. To aid in the education of patients regarding using their leisure toward their own self-actualization.

The degree to which any one or all of these objectives are emphasized in a given setting depends upon the philosophy and function of the institution. Likewise, the importance of any of these objectives in the treatment of specific individuals varies according to individual needs. The therapeutic recreation specialist must assume a variety of roles to carry out each of these objectives effectively. Those roles involve providing programs and activities; teaching activity skills; facilitating prescriptive treatment techniques; developing leisure education programs; being a leisure counselor; developing agency relationships, especially with recreation professionals in the community to which the patient will return; and interpreting and advocating the importance of recreation within the institution and community (Laudick, McGovern, & Cosgrove, 1982).

Many physicians accept that the major responsibility of recreation services in the medical setting is to concentrate on the "well" side of the patient. Others allow the recreation therapists to become intimately involved in the patient's treatment. When that occurs, the treatment responsibilities of the recreation therapists are the same as other therapists and medical personnel. Therapeutic recreation specialists are involved in patient assessments, goal writing, designing individualized treatment plans, program implementation, documentation and progress notes, patient and program evaluation, and discharge planning. Therapeutic recreation specialists conduct group and individual sessions and often function as role models for specific patients.

Leisure education is often one of the components of therapeutic recreation services. It is initiated to help prepare individuals for their discharge and transition home and exists in the majority of facilities (Bedini, 1990). Originally, leisure education was simply the imparting of information about recreation resources and the type of skills and equipment needed to engage in leisure activities. Within the framework of therapeutic recreation service today, however, leisure education includes helping patients develop the skills necessary for successful integration into their communities after discharge. For example, leisure education can help individuals increase their leisure awareness, identify leisure attitudes and values, develop decision-making and problem-solving skills, and become knowledgeable of the leisure resources of their communities. According to Dattilo and Murphy (1991), leisure education is the application of select educational models and techniques "to enhance the individual's leisure lifestyle."

The third and final component of the recreation service model, first described by Peterson and Gunn (1984), is the provision of opportunities for recreation participation. In addition to conducting programs and activities for the institutional patient, recreation specialists are in a position to work with community agencies and assist with their transition to home. Whereas therapeutic recreation services traditionally provided activities for diversion and enjoyment, today's focus is intervention and leisure education so that recovering patients or clients may enjoy the programs and services offered by their communities more fully. Cooperative programming between medical and community facilities is instrumental to successful integration.

In several institutional settings, recreation therapy assumes a less medical/ therapy approach than it does in the more conventional treatment-oriented settings. These settings include nursing homes, military hospitals, and in some general hospitals, particularly within the pediatric and medical-surgical services. There recreation is normally viewed as a part of the daily routine of the patient and is so offered. For example, the nursing home is the resident's community; the convalescing soldier must be combat-ready when returning to his or her unit, so hospitalization is frequently required even though the treatment phase has ended; play is an essential item of daily life for a child and must be provided. When recreation services are not offered in these settings, or when the quality of the program is less than optimal, morale and behavioral problems may develop. The entire institutional staff is affected by these difficulties. Recreation is essential in these settings for the social well-being of the entire institution.

Special Recreation Services in the Community

Although one could trace recreation services to people with different types of special needs as early as the turn of the century, it was the deinstitutionalization movement of the late 1960s and early 1970s that accelerated its growth. The federal government spearheaded the movement with funding (Hillman, 1969), and the belief that the institutionalized should be "one of the nation's priority goals" (Pomeroy, 1974). Hospitals and institutions serving people with disabilities were encouraged to help their clients to "re-enter" their communities, to be normalized; that is, those with disabilities should be allowed the same opportunities as others, to become as "culturally normative" as possible.

Two other important developments for people with disabilities occurred during this period. One was the creation of the Special Olympics in 1967; the other was the White House Conference on Handicapped Individuals which took place ten years later. Partially in response to the President's Council on Physical Fitness and partly because of the limited number of recreation opportunities for the mentally retarded in the community available, the Joseph P. Kennedy, Jr. Foundation established the Special Olympics, a program of activity and competition for the mentally retarded. The White House Conference on Handicapped Individuals stressed the need for adequate funding for recreation programs to serve people with disabilities, the need for coordinators at the state level to promote recreation services for people who were disadvantaged and disabled, the removal of architectural and transportation barriers, and the training and employment of people with disabilities as recreation personnel.

Despite the enthusiasm and encouragement experienced in the early 1970s, many communities were not prepared for the numbers of people with special needs. It took time for community recreators to respond, to develop programs for these "special" individuals, to integrate them into their activities as many of those being released from the institutions had some type of developmental disability. Although studies from the late sixties and early seventies identified that services to people with disabilities in the community doubled from 23 percent in 1970 to 47 percent in 1979 (Edginton & Neal, 1981), they remained in the minority.

It took several legislative acts to rectify the situation, including the Architectural Barriers Act of 1968, the Education for All Handicapped Children Act, 1975 (now called the Individuals with Disabilities Education Act), and the Americans with Disabilities Act of 1990. The later is perhaps the most powerful piece of federal legislation to affect recreation services for people with disabilities in the community. It states that no one, specifically people with disabilities, should be denied opportunities, segregated, or otherwise discriminated against based on their disabilities. Along with housing, employment, and transportation, the law specifically identifies recreation as an area of potential discrimination. Public services (state and local such as city and county parks and recreation programs), public accommodations (restaurants, hotels, movie theaters, museums, zoos and "other places of recreation") must assure that people with disabilities are not unnecessarily separated, omitted, or discriminated against. As a result, programs which previously separated people with disabilities from those without disabilities may have to reevaluate their services to assure equity of opportunity and establish that they are not separating solely based disability. Unfortunately, the enforcement of the ADA is only a beginning effort. To make leisure services truly accessible, recreation services and facilities must not only be designed for all people, but also public attitudes toward the role of recreation in meeting the needs of people with disabilities must be modified.

In the 1990s, however, people with disabilities are not the only individuals who have been traditionally underserved in communities. Others include those who are economically disadvantaged, youth-at-risk, and the homeless.

Programs are now underway to serve then as well as our new immigrants and our traditional "special populations." The work of the Vocational Rehabilitation Administration, the Office of Education (especially the Bureau for the Education of the Handicapped), and the Law Enforcement and Assistance Administration have given added impetus to these program concerns. Their cause has been furthered by the actions of such private groups as the National Committee for Urban America and local philanthropic organizations.

Several major problems have been associated with development and expansion of recreation and play services for people with special needs. Many still exist. They include misconceptions about the nature of recreation for people with disabilities and special needs, concerns about financing these programs and facilities, the issue of special preparation of recreation and park personnel, and the public attitude toward individuals with disabilities or other "out-of-the-mainstream" conditions.

The Nature of the Recreation Services

Whereas the major objective of recreation services in the institution is to aid in the rehabilitation, treatment, and recovery of the patient, the objectives of programs for people with special needs in community programs is to provide them with the same opportunities for involvement in meaningful and satisfying recreation and leisure experiences as are afforded other segments of the population. In some instances, those who provide these services do establish other objectives such as goals of social integration, the overcoming of prejudices, improving the participants' general living conditions, or developing vocational and habilitational skills. These may be achieved as by-products of the recreation experience. They are not, however, the purpose of play and recreation. Because of these concerns some recreation and park professionals inappropriately view recreation services for people with disabilities as a quasi-social service operation rather than as a primary recreation function. That is a misconception. It is recreation and park services for those who have special needs.

Cost of Programs for People with Disabilities

A second misconception is that the provision of leisure services programs for people with disabilities and other special needs is more expensive than for other programs. Opponents of the programs argue that to design facilities to accommodate all people and to employ specialists to direct those programs costs money that must come from the public treasury. A related argument is since most people who use parks and recreation facilities and services are not disabled or disadvantaged, the cost for providing services to these special groups is disproportionately high.

The reality does not support this view. People with special needs are not the small minorities we think they are. People with disabilities alone make up 17 percent of the U.S. population. When one combines people with disabilities with those who are elderly, socially disadvantaged, and economically deprived into one group, they constitute over one third of the population. Programs for people with disabilities become expensive only when they are add-ons to the general recreation and park services. In some instances, however, providing specific recreation services to some people with disabilities may cost additional monies. For example, it sometimes requires more personnel to supervise camping programs for those with physical disabilities or the mentally retarded than it might for the people without disabilities. Often, some of these personnel are volunteers and therefore, do not increase the department's financial outlay for programs, but even their use does have an economic effect since more professional staff time must be allocated to their recruiting, selecting, supervising, and training.

The enactment of the Americans with Disabilities Act of 1990 will help prevent unnecessary spending by encouraging professionals to evaluate their facilities and services before renovating them and to think proactively about architectural changes and modifications to include people with disabilities. When buildings are planned in the construction stage, the cost factor to make them accessible is nil. Less than one percent of additional expense is incurred when ramps and accessible rest rooms are included in the initial construction phase.

It is important to note that many special recreation services for people with disabilities do not require special appropriations. These citizens can be easily integrated into the normal services of the recreation agency if the agency actively promotes its services for them as a part of the total community. The basic programs service to these special citizens should be a part of the general recreation and park budget.

Specialized Personnel and Program Integration

When departments are embarking on a program to make their services available to all, questions of staffing and program philosophy arise. Does the program require specialists, a certified therapeutic recration specialist, or can it be supervised by a "regular" staff member? Should there be special programs only for those with disabilities or special needs, or should the participants be mainstreamed into existing programs and services? The nature of the needs will often determine the approach but there is little data which says it is always necessary to hire a specialist, although the trend seems to be in that direction.

Leisure service professionals must be careful in initiating programs of social integration for integration is more than placing people with disabilities in a group of people without disabilities. According to Wolfensberger (1972), integration involves social interaction as well as physical integration. Recreation programmers can meet the needs of people with disabilities by attempting to provide choices of both integrated and segregated programs. A well-conceived and well-implemented recreation program for those with disabilities in the community should do both. For most individuals and groups, special programs are not needed if program accessibility is truly provided through the elimination of the economic, physical, and social barriers which often deter participation. For those individuals and groups that require services beyond those normally provided by the community, special segregated programs should be developed. The provision of these specialized services, however, should not be in conflict with the agency's philosophy of leisure services. Most recreation agencies program for special groups as well as those who have general recreation interests and use a variety of approaches to accomplish their mission (Schleien & Green, 1992).

Alternative program structures for people with disabilities, in particular, have been successful in recent years. Montgomery (Maryland) County Parks and Recreation Department created its "Mainstream Initiative," a program which focuses on integrating rather than separating people with disabilities in recreation programs. For those participants who might have difficulty participating in activities alone, the program offers recreation "buddies," volunteers who work with and assist the participants with their specific needs. Many programs have moved to integrated summer camps, no longer separating campers with disabilities from campers without disabilities. The Easter Seals Society of North Carolina disbanded its segregated camp programs for people with disabilities after 25 years of operation to adopt a "Progressive Mainstream Model." The new program provides year round programs of camping and leisure activities in segregated, modified mainstream, and mainstream environments in an attempt

For most individuals and groups, special programs are not needed if accessibility is truly provided through the elimination of economic, physical and social barriers.

to serve *all* people. Similarly, the Easter Seal Society of New Hampshire adopted a model of integrated residential camping after 20 years of segregated camping. The integrated model, directed by a certified therapeutic recreation specialist, is a collaborative program that stresses an inclusionary environment to all participants, with and without disabilities.

Although some parks and recreation professionals are concerned that these integrated programs may increase chances of accidents and liability risk among those with disabilities, experience suggests these problems are more imaginary than real. Similarly, the fear of lack of knowledge about how to "deal" with people with disabilities or with special needs is not realistic in many cases. The recreation professional does not have to function alone. Parks and recreation programmers should plan to use the many professionals within the community who can act as advisors and consultants to facilitate services to those with differing needs.

When park and recreation students are made aware of the needs for accessible facilities and services for people with disabilities in the community, the need for specialized personnel is diminished. The failure of recreation professionals to offer experiences which create or add to the quality of life of people with disabilities and other special needs that is the problem. Citizens and professionals, not people with disabilities, have created the problem (Bedini & McCann, 1992). The challenge is to correct society's past behavior, to make sure the leisure service delivery system no longer neglects these citizens (see Table 7-1).

Attitudes Toward Disability and Other "Out-of-the-Mainstream" Conditions

As suggested, attitudes can be the strongest barrier to inclusion and equity that individuals in communities may encounter. It is important to note that disability is the only "minority" group that *anyone* can join. Whereas most people are born into most other minorities, people without disabilities are only "TABs" or "temporarily able-bodied." At any moment in one's life, an individual can become disabled and experience some of the fears and negative attitudes traditionally imposed by society.

Western societies tend to place great emphasis on the appearance of things. People are socialized to seek perfection; when things are attractive and unblemished, we feel we must be doing something right. We do not like wrinkles; we do not like gray hair; we do not like sagging waistlines, distorted features or anything which suggests any imperfections. Huge industries have been built to aid in covering up these natural processes and other industries glorify a world where these conditions do not exist. Billions of dollars are spent in support of the cosmetic, movie, and television industries. Traditionally, to be different in our society meant being unattractive as well. Consequently, we have not

Table 7-1
Perceived Benefits of Community-Based Special Recreation Services by Participants

Physical Competence
Increased self-confidence due to activity
skills learned
Improved physical coordination
Improved strength and/or endurance

Social Competence
Improved social interactions in the home
Acquired friends with disabilities
Increased comfort in the work place
Improved activities of daily living
Acquired friends without disabilities

Community Integration
Acquired leisure activity skills
Increased comfort in public places
Acquired social skills
Increased independence in the community
Acquired interests and skills which he/she
engages in at home or in the community

Affect
Improved emotional expression or mood
Increased awareness of events, people, and
places
Reduced boredom at home
Reduced general anxiety or irritability
Increased self-confidence due to social
skills and experiences

Personal Competence
Improved decision-making skills
Improved self-concept
Increased concentration in tasks
Increased sense of personal responsibility
Increased interest in learning new things

Source: *Therapeutic Recreation Journal*, Fourth Quarter 1992, p. 13

encouraged people with disabilities or other "out-of-the-mainstream" conditions to mix with those without disabilities or disadvantages, especially in areas of fun. These attitudes are perhaps the greatest barrier of all.

Fortunately park and recreation services can facilitate equal opportunities in recreation for all individuals when a clear philosophy of inclusion underlying services, facilities, and staff exists. Kennedy, Smith, and Austin (1991) suggest that to include all people, parks and recreation staff must be careful to not omit anyone. They explain that most barriers to recreation participation for people with disabilities result from doing something which encourages exclusion due to professional insensitivity. For example, by using only written advertisements for programs, persons with visual impairments are omitted. The lack of role models (i.e., staff members with disabilities) may also be a barrier of omission. Whereas people without disabilities have a wide range of role models, children with disabilities see only a few adults with disabilities who are successful with recreation endeavors.

Program accessibility is a concern that involves both access and omission. When organizations charge admission and entry fees to their programs, they minimize the likelihood of the economically deprived participating. Likewise, when programs are scheduled some distance from residential areas, transportation problems are created for participants who may be young, old, and/or poor.

Without realizing it, the location of programs and financial policies are as great a barrier to participation as are the architectural barriers. One of the reasons recreation and park agencies may not see disadvantaged individuals in their programs is because they have not made their programs accessible to them.

LABELING

Attitudes of professionals are just as important as attitudes of the general public. Inherent in an organization's attempts to make facilities and programs more accessible is the danger of making people with disabilities or some other condition appear to be "different." The messages imparted by the parks and recreation staff through their actions and their program design are essential to promoting acceptance and normalization. Large segments of the sixty-five and older population, for example, do not want to be identified with programs for the older adults. Likewise, many parents of people with mental retardation frequently avoid enrolling their children in programs labeled "for the retarded." It was quickly observed by the National Park Service that people with visual impairments were sometimes offended when special interpretative trails were created for them. They did not wish to be singled out by having special attention called to their disability; they much preferred the park service to treat them as they would any other segment of the population. This problem was remedied by having both Braille and printed characters placed on the stands where people normally went to receive instruction. Also, it was accomplished by having cassette tape recordings available to all visitors at various sites. The information presented through these recordings were of a general informative nature beneficial to all, and did not call attention to those with visual handicaps (Seven, 1979).

PHYSICAL BARRIERS

Architectural (human made) and ecological (natural) barriers can pose severe restrictions to the pursuit of leisure for individuals with disabilities. When the mobility needs of the those with physical disabilities are disregarded in the planning phase of building construction, these individuals may be prevented from participating in the programs which occur in these areas. By providing ramps, doors large enough to accommodate wheelchairs, and smooth, well-defined walking areas, people with orthopedic and visual impairments are partially accommodated. The avoidance of architectural barriers deprives no one of the recreation experience, yet it enhances the opportunity for thousands, including nondisabled populations such as parents with strollers. These open design features require little or no additional cost in construction and they benefit everyone (Servedio, 1979).

Many communities, unfortunately, have major investments in recreation areas and facilities, many of which are not barrier-free. This problem is not an insurmountable one. For example, many recreation programs such as arts and crafts classes and card and game tournaments do not have to take place in a recreation center. If there are public buildings in the community that are barrier-free, they can be used for these programs. Proprietary feelings about facilities should not block the recreation and park department's program efforts for equal access for people with disabilities.

Complying with the Americans with Disabilities Act's requirements for accessibility will help professionals determine ways to facilitate all its citizens in recreation programs (Oestreicher, 1990). To assist with this the federal government has developed guidelines to aid individual park and recreation departments with their assessment of the facilities and services; their guidelines also offer guidance in initiating cost-efficient changes.

Other "Special Populations"

Although people with disabilities are the group that is traditionally considered when one hears the term "special populations," professionals today recognize a new diversity within our communities. As a result, recreation programs are evolving to meet the needs of all diverse groups ranging from different cultures to various financial statuses and all ages. Several other "special" groups will be described in this chapter but it is important to note that this by no means covers all the diverse groups which might exist in any given community or area.

Older Adults

People over 65 years of age are the fastest growing segment of our population. According to the Administration on Aging, by the year 2030, almost 22 percent of the population will be over the age of 65. Advanced technology and medical care have greatly increased life expectancy.

Many myths exist about older adults in American society. First, not all older adults are feeble and live in nursing homes. In reality approximately 95 percent of older adults live in the community while only 4-5 percent live in nursing homes. Similarly, not all older adults are poor. Financially, they make up one of the more affluent segments of our society. Additionally, older adults constitute a significant political and social force and, other than the very young, they are the only major population group which has an abundance of free time. Like all other groups, older adults make up a heterogeneous collection of individuals with differing interests, values, experiences, health, status, income, and education.

Legally, aging is defined in terms of the number of years lived, but is that an accurate determiner? Many people are "old" when they are 60, whereas others are "young" at 80. Each individual ages at a different rate, just as the organs in one's body age at different rates. Some individuals are psychologically old while still physically vital; for others, the opposite is true. Physical capacities clearly demonstrate the aging process, but the mind and spirit may suggest something much different. It is dangerous to label individuals "old" or assume that all who are 65 or older have common characteristics. Nothing can be further from the truth.

Other variations exist with older adults as well. Many are economically independent. Some live with their families at home; others may reside in a retirement community or nursing home. Some are still employed while some live on a pension. Even within these categories, there are numerous differences based upon individual preferences, past lifestyles, and current opportunities (McAvoy, 1979). Again, as noted with people with disabilities, older adults are individuals, first; their age is just one aspect of their being.

Although community parks and recreation programs sometimes include programs for older adults under their "special populations" category, it is important **not** to consider older adults as part of a disabilities group solely because of their age.

Leisure Interests of Older Adults

No activities are specific only to older adults (Godbey, Patterson & Brown-Szwak, 1982). Their recreation behavior is as diverse as are their economic, cultural, health, and educational backgrounds.

In recent years, many programs have been developed on the assumption that leisure services agencies ought to provide organized recreation opportunities for older persons through such structures as the golden age clubs. These programs have been largely facility-oriented and are an extension of the traditional

Ballroom dance is a favorite pastime at the Long Beach [CA] Senior Center.

community center recreation programs offered to youth and children. These offerings have been diversionary and routinely scheduled, but experience suggests there may be a better way to serve the elderly. Most of their recreation takes place at home or in their neighborhood. Given this, it seems logical that leisure service providers should approach the elderly using a decentralized model of service delivery; that is, take programs to them where they live rather than forcing them to come to a central location. Diversity is the key.

It is also important when programming for older adults to recognize the value systems at work and the lifestyles of those being served. Developing programs and approaches consistent with one's lifestyle and in keeping with the rhythms of the specific life stage is essential. Successful programming requires a sensitivity to where people are, what their interests are, the barriers which prohibit them from participation, and the strategies which may be implemented to bring about the best possible quality of life.

Among those agencies with specific interests and concerns with services to the older adults are the National Council on Aging, the American Association of Retired Persons, the Administration on Aging (U.S. Department of Health and Welfare), and local councils on aging. They are valuable resources when recruiting volunteers, developing financial support, and interpreting the recreation services to the older population.

PROGRAM EMPHASES FOR OLDER ADULTS

Today, most community programs that serve older adults have a "senior specialist" who is in charge of the coordination and programming for this population. Public recreation departments have responded to the challenge of providing services by developing a wide range of activities and events. Among them are Senior Games, an Olympics-like program for those over 55 years of age. In addition to competitive athletic events, Senior Games activities include contests in art, dance, music, and other forms of recreation expression. Other programs offered through parks and recreation which tend to have great appeal are senior citizens clubs, adult leisure education services, and outreach programs. Rather than develop segregated programs, however, most departments have attempted to integrate the older adults into their general program services by eliminating architectural and economic barriers.

Recreation programs for older adults are sometimes a part of a larger comprehensive service package for older persons offered by a senior center where older individuals receive counseling services, healthcare, hot meals, legal and employment advice, and educational services. These senior centers may be sponsored by local and state recreation and park departments, local and state departments of health, the mayor's office, or private associations such as the YMCA, the Salvation Army, or a religious group. They are not recreation centers, per se.

Some senior citizen programs and commercial retirement community programs, however, do focus entirely on the leisure interest and desires of the older adults. They offer movies, tours, arts and crafts activities, and instructional programs. These centers may be located within a general recreation complex or may be specifically constructed and maintained for the older adults alone. Inasmuch as local councils on aging, urban programs for the older adults, and healthcare facilities and homes have recreation components, any plan for the organization and administration of recreation services for older people by a local recreation and park department should take into consideration these and other existing facilities and programs within the community. The local park and recreation department is only one of the agencies attempting to meet the free-time expressions and interests of this group.

Many communities have found recreation activities and programs to be an excellent avenue for introducing other services to older citizens. The older adults may come to the recreation center or senior center because of the recreation opportunities afforded by it but find other services they need and which might not otherwise be sought out. In this context the recreation and park department may find itself becoming a catalytic agent assuming some roles and responsibilities unknown in its traditional patterns. Likewise, it may be asked by other social service agencies to cooperate in providing recreation experiences in their settings, whether they be hospitals, nursing homes, or multiple purpose centers. The main concern should be programs for the older adults, not the space or place in which the activities take place.

Recreation and the Criminal Justice System

Recreation and park professionals have had a long-standing interest in providing recreation services in hopes of preventing delinquency and criminal behavior and in the rehabilitating of those convicted of crimes. Recreation professionals hold that participation in socially acceptable forms of recreation expression tends to negate deviant behavior. Through participation, incarcerated individuals are able to get positive reinforcement, may be more likely to develop a healthy self-image, and have less need for antisocial acts.

Crime has risen steadily over the last 30 years. At the end of 1988, there were over 600,000 adult men and women in American prisons. If one includes, however, all juvenile offenders, individuals on parole, and those on probation with those incarcerated, the total reaches 3.4 million (Kraus & Shank, 1992).

A major controversial issue for recreation service providers to this population is the determination of whether recreation in correctional institutions should be rehabilitative or whether it should be a reward/punishment (Schleien & O'Morrow, 1981). When recreation is viewed as an instrument of punishment, it is difficult to sell people on the value of programs that provide pleasure. On the other hand, correctional officials are quick to embrace the use of recreation as a means of prisoner control. Consequently, and unfortunately, some prison officials have used recreation activities and programs as a reward for good behavior rather than accepting it as an essential element in the life of all individuals, prisoners included. This view has come under legal scrutiny since various court cases have identified the absence of exercise or recreation as cruel and unusual punishment and a violation of the Eighth Amendment (Barbee & Calloway, 1979).

Probably the most significant legal decision concerning the responsibility of the state in providing recreation services for its inmates occurred in Alabama when the U.S. District Court ordered a drastic reform of the Alabama Correctional System, including the employment of a full-time recreation director at each correctional institution. The judge ordered that these recreation professionals be qualified and possess at least a bachelor's degree with training in parks and recreation.

Current approaches for providing recreation services to incarcerated individuals seem to embrace a more holistic philosophy. Munson (1991) suggested that the application of an ecological approach to recreation for adjudicated youth was useful in that it combined clinical and social models of recreation toward changing undesirable behaviors. Similarly, Stumbo and Little (1991) proposed ten principles for leisure service delivery within the prison setting for women in particular. They are based on the assumption that leisure and recreation services should be built on rehabilitation principles and considered a right of all individuals. With a rehabilitation focus, the recreation services are directed toward the eventual release and community reintegration of the individual.

According to Hormachea and Gulak (1980), recreation services provide several important functions within the correctional system. Among them are:

1. It is a vital link for the inmate with the outside world and helps to maintain his or her identity.
2. It allows the inmate to work off aggressions and therefore lessens the pressures associated with incarcerations.
3. It assists in keeping the inmate alert and helps to prevent physical and mental deterioration.
4. It may be a primary force in behavior modification through the enhancement of one's self-image and as a motivator to change one's lifestyle.

An effective delinquent prevention and rehabilitation program requires the cooperative effort of all involved—the home, the school, the judicial system, the correctional institution, and the community. Recreation has been an effective tool in working with youth-at-risk, an accepted mode of intervention especially when working with youth gangs as reported by Robinson-Young (1992).

Likewise, there is no substitute for teamwork when it comes to rehabilitation. The challenge is to educate the public to the values of recreation programs, to see the institution as a setting for rehabilitation rather than punishment and revenge.

The specialized nature of recreation services for the incarcerated has given rise to a subspecialty of correctional recreation. Many of those employed in the correctional setting are members of the American Correctional Association (ACA). The ACA has worked to improve program standards as well as upgrade professionalism. As a result of the work of the American Correctional Association, the American Bar Association, and the professional recreation societies, especially the National Correctional Recreation Association and the National Therapeutic Recreation Society, recreation and leisure services for the criminally incarcerated have improved. The recognition of recreation as a legal right of the inmate and the acceptance of the ACA standards by the courts have had considerable influence.

Worldwide, there is increasing interest in the operations of correctional institutions. The United Nations has enacted a set of standards that suggest each inmate should have at least one hour of suitable exercise in open air daily, that young prisoners should receive physical and recreational training during the period of exercise, and that recreation and cultural activities should be provided for the physical and mental benefit of all incarcerated individuals.

Recreation for People Who Are Economically Disadvantaged

SERVICES TO INDIVIDUALS WHO ARE HOMELESS

People who are homeless is another population segment which warrants the attention of recreation and parks services. Like other populations, there is great diversity among the group. Some are alone; others are in family units. Many have physical, social, and/or mental disabilities and could benefit from some custodial care; others find themselves only in short-term crisis situations (Redburn & Buss, 1986).

Regardless of the cause, the homeless face a difficult situation. They have low status, lack power, and are often treated as if their problems are their own fault. People often act as if the homeless do not exist or at least wish they would go away. They also suffer from low self-esteem, poor social skills, the inability to enjoy life, fear of intimacy, and avoidance behavior that may result in social isolation (Krinsky, 1992). Kunstler (1991) suggested, however, that social isolation and negative attitudes of society can be overcome through recreation participation. To accomplish this she proposes that recreation, medical, and social services agencies work cooperatively to:

1. Establish task forces on local, state, and regional levels to determine responsibilities of leisure service providers within the human service delivery system;
2. Develop a continuum of service links from institutions to day treatment to shelters;
3. Integrate the homeless into community recreation as equal partners rather than segregating them;
4. Develop referral networks for identification and placement of individuals who are homeless; and
5. Create programs to address the issues of self-esteem, illiteracy and lack of independent living skills.

Addressing the problems of the homeless will take community wide efforts, but leisure services has no less of a role in addressing the social problems associated with homelessness than it does with other groups experiencing deprivation and unequal opportunities.

RECREATION FOR PEOPLE OF LOW INCOME

During the late 1960s and early 1970s, park and recreation agencies implemented a variety of programs designed to improve the quality of life for the urban poor and economically deprived. Many of these were funded by grants from the federal government as a part of its war-on-poverty effort. More recently they have been sustained by local and foundation support; large corporations have become increasingly involved. For example, in response to budget cuts due to the enactment of Proposition 13, the Los Angeles County Recreation and Park Department received sizable gifts from such groups as Atlantic Richfield, Coca-Cola,™ and Pepsi-Cola™ to continue support of those inner-city programs which might have otherwise been eliminated. Unfortunately, they were not enough and with little federal support after 1981, most public recreation programs for the urban poor were discontinued or dramatically reduced. Considerable evidence suggests that the urban riots of central Los Angeles in 1992 were due, in part, to the lack of social services, including parks and recreation, available to the poor according to statements made by the 1993 National Congress. The economically disadvantaged continue to be marginal participants in the "good life" enjoyed by most Americans. Their recreation behaviors have been affected by their lack of resources and their leisure activity interests have often been in conflict with the basic value system and morals of the majority. A lack of understanding of their needs has negatively affected many of our program efforts.

Most leisure service systems are staffed by college graduates with middle-class value orientations. They tend to program for people like themselves. Consequently, many of their programs have not been accepted by potential

participants who want activities more akin to their own interests and traditions. This is particularly true when the poor also happen to be members of a
well-defined ethnic or racial group. To overcome these program biases, many
park and recreation departments have established special programs to deal
with the disadvantaged.

Among the most successful programs for people who are economically deprived have been those which utilize the leadership within the community. Portable pools and other mobile recreation units have helped reduce some recreation
facility deficiencies. Busing programs to transport large numbers of urban
children and youth to municipal and county parks have also been successful.
Neighborhood youth programs and the employment of neighborhood youths as
program specialists have added to the validity of the recreation offerings.

Although recreation is certainly no panacea for social ills, recreation and
park services have been used throughout history to maintain social order, especially when neighborhoods are involved in determining their own programs
and services. Empowering people has many benefits. It aids in the development of self-esteem, gives a sense of community and enhances one's coping
skills (Fryer & Payne, 1984).

Cultural Diversity in Leisure Services

The United States has taken great pride in its melting pot tradition, its ability
to mold immigrants into "Americans." During the 1920s, Americanization
programs were quite prevalent in most big cities, with organized recreation

The Maryland National
Capitol Park and Planning
Commission combines
learning and fun with their
computer camp.

M-NCPPC Photo by
Steve Abramowitz

services playing an important socialization role. Children were taught to play the games of their new country, to sing our songs, and the like. To a great extent, the national policy of the United States was to discourage minority and ethnic identification. All were expected to accept the same ideals—the American way of life. Regardless of one's ethnic background, the basic program of services was the same for all citizens, although the concept of "separate but equal" also existed. This seemed to be both acceptable and expected until the Civil Rights movement took on a more militant character. There had been a dual approach to the provision of park and recreation services for some minority groups, particularly African-Americans and Hispanics. In the South, racial segregation was openly accepted with the public recreation and park departments essentially operating two systems: one for whites, and one for blacks. In fact, the National Recreation Association had maintained a special program, a Bureau of Colored Works, from 1919 to the early 1940s.

The enactment of the Civil Rights Act of 1964 and the actions of the Supreme Court which held that segregation was illegal ended the dual approach of providing recreation services and, with the demise of the segregated system, a variety of social changes occurred. Minority groups and people of color began to proclaim their identity and uniqueness. New criteria were applied to measure program success and effectiveness as various groups demanded more participation in the decision-making process. America became aware that its citizens were not alike and did not want to be treated alike. In community after community, recreation and park administrators were asked to develop special recreation programs and services for African-American and Spanish speaking neighborhoods. Black cultural centers were established, Native American programs were developed, and bilingual staffs were employed. Major construction programs were undertaken as compensatory program efforts were put into effect.

By 1980 a philosophy of programs for diverse groups had become an accepted part of the public parks and recreation mission. The success in translating the philosophy into action, however, was largely dependent upon the approach taken by a local community. According to Foley and Pirk (1991), the more successful ones have provided equal access to high quality services, developed a user-fee policy based upon the residents' ability to pay, utilized neighborhood leadership and employed indigenous leaders, provided sound programs of staff development, established effective networks and coalitions, and enlisted the cooperation of other service providers. The bottom line was that communities were mobilized with a sense of ownership, partnership, and social responsibility. They experienced a sense of pride and empowerment.

Given the fact that racial and ethnic minorities are growing at a faster rate than other population groups, that their concentration in the inner city encourages the maintenance of their cultural identity, and that traditional programs and services—even organizational and financial approaches—are inadequate, park and recreation professionals are facing challenges not seen since the migration of Central Europeans to America in the 1890s. New systems and understandings are required if racial and ethnic groups are to be served adequately (Dwyer & Gobster, 1992).

Programs must be conducted where the people are and program approaches must be "natural," based upon the typical behaviors of the constituents. If people who are poor or older adults cannot come to the recreation site, the recreation department should take the program to them. If the users do not speak English, staff and instruction, including signs, should be in their native language. By having some swimming periods available to all free of charge, while also having at the same location some swimming sessions for which there is an admission fee, park and recreation departments can accommodate both those who want a degree of exclusiveness and those who cannot afford such an economic luxury. When a department offers a standard set of activities reflecting what the staff knows and enjoys rather than the activities known and desired by the people of the community, it effectively eliminates those who do not share the same cultural values and biases. Ethnic and other social conditions must be considered in the program planning phase if recreation and park agencies are to extend services to *all* populations. Systems must be created and that means outreach, leadership and program development.

As stated in some cases, recreation and park agencies must take programs to selected segments of a population. An outreach effort may be one of two types. It may rely upon mobile recreation units or employ roving leaders. The

Volleyball is one activity in Long Beach's [CA] International Sea Festival.

Photo by Donna Holtz

mobile unit concept is not new; it has been used by public health and public library officials for years. When used by recreation departments, it requires equipping a trailer or mobile vehicle with the necessary recreation facilities and supplies. Once accomplished, the unit may be driven to those neighborhoods void or deficient of recreation resources, where the recreation specialist can program directly from the mobile unit to conduct art, music, and related skill classes as well as bring recreation equipment to those who do not possess it. Although the mobile unit concept has been most successful when working with economically and culturally deprived groups, this concept is effective with older adults or people with disabilities who are "homebound" due to lack of transportation or health related barriers.

The second outreach effort, the use of roving leaders, may be programmed in conjunction with, or independent of, mobile unit schedules. In application, the concept is similar to that of the "worker priest" and the detached social worker who works in the homes and neighborhoods of the clients (Bannon, 1973). It has been found to be especially effective when working with youth-at-risk. These outreach workers are recreation specialists who do not have an office or central recreation facility which they must supervise. They serve as initiators, facilitators, and stimulators of activities and programs. They go where the citizens are and utilize the resources available in those neighborhoods, often developing peer education programs and working cooperatively with police and social service personnel. They are to recreation and parks what a visiting nurse is to public health. In some communities recreation personnel have provided roving leaders as consultants to school systems working particularly with their developmentally disabled students. As community programmers or consultants, they are able to provide guidance for those who teach these students or work directly with the students to meet some of their recreational interests. Neither of these concepts of outreach should be restricted to people with disabilities alone. They can and should be made available to all citizens. In many instances, program accessibility requires increased sensitivity, not a major modification in the delivery system or the facilities which are a part of that system.

Leadership and Professional Preparation

Leadership is the key to successful programming for all people with special needs. Those professionals working with these groups must be sensitive to their condition, able to affect positive programs and approaches to services, and, at the same time, deal with them as they would any other segment of the community's population. For the most part, this sensitivity can be developed among all staff members. It certainly must be present among the administrators who are ultimately responsible for the services of the organization, as well as those individuals who work specifically with these populations. One does not necessarily have to be professionally trained in recreation services for people with disabilities or older adults to possess this sensitivity, but professional preparation is suggested.

It is recommended by the Council on Accreditation that coursework in recreation for special recreation services should be a part of the general curriculum of all recreation and park majors. For those who wish to work specifically with these disadvantaged groups, courses in psychology, sociology, special education, and adaptive physical education should be pursued. Although not required for most special recreation positions, certification as a therapeutic recreation specialist is recommended. For most clinical settings, it is necessary. The National Council on Therapeutic Recreation Certification, an independent body with headquarters in New York, sets the standards for certification which include both the successful passing of the Therapeutic Recreation Certification Examination and the completion of certain educational requirements, including a supervised internship under a certified therapist.

Technological Advances and Special Recreation Services

The combination of technology, legal requirements and an acceptance of people with disabilities and other special needs has facilitated many opportunities to participate in activities ranging from outdoor and wilderness activities to competitive sports—activities previously denied to most people with disabilities. Many services and facilities can be adapted or special equipment can be provided to enhance the leisure experience of all people. Museums and theaters have headphones and tapes which describe the objects of art in a gallery or the movements of dancers on the stage for those with visual impairments. Ski resorts now rent pull sleds, outriggers, and monoskis (ski equipment that does not require the use of legs) as regular pieces of equipment for skiers with orthopedic disabilities, e.g., amputations and paralysis. Wheelchair designers have streamlined and adapted chairs to facilitate wheelchair activities such as tennis, basketball, and marathon racing. A marathon wheelchair weighs only 14 pounds as opposed to the hospital chair that weigh upwards of 30 pounds. Similarly, adaptations exist for computers that allow people without the use of their hands to type or those who cannot speak to communicate, thus increasing their opportunities for social interactions.

The enactment of the Americans with Disabilities Act should provide more programs for all with minimal attention being given to their disability. Several exemplary programs currently exist. For example, Mammoth Cave and National Park in Kentucky allows those in wheelchairs and older adults who need aid to descend to the caves by elevator and then take a two-hour trip through a dry passageway through the gypsum and crystalline formations. In the Everglades National Park, hard-surfaced interpretive trails have been developed so that any visitor can go into the park and experience the mango groves and native wildlife. In New Jersey, a nature trail has opened on the campus of the new Lisbon State School for the Mentally Retarded that accommodates all types of handicapping conditions. Tape cassettes are available so that people with visual impairments can take full advantage of the resource.

Various special interest groups such as the National Wheelchair Athletic Association, the National Amputee Golf Association, and the National Easter Seal Society, have promoted recreation services and programs for people with disabilities such as the Paralympics, a international competition for people with physical disabilities. Additionally, multi-sensory art museums and gardens have been developed that involve more than one sense so that a visitor can fully appreciate the displays. Having highly fragrant flowers and plants of different textures which may be touched as well as seen, an issue of the sensory deprivation of some is not obvious. A national park guide which describes the levels of accessibility of all the national parks has been developed by Wendy Roth, who uses a wheelchair, and Michael Tompane (Roth & Tompane, 1992). Similarly, many state departments of travel and tourism have similar documents for their state park users.

ACCESSING TECHNOLOGY IN COMMUNITY PARKS AND RECREATION PROGRAMS

Community parks and recreation programs can apply technological advances to enhance the leisure experiences of people with special needs in the community by considering several things. First, adapted recreation equipment such as those mentioned above are expensive, but may be worthwhile as they create new possibilities for those people with disabilities. Second, it is the responsibility of all park and recreation professionals to become familiar with what adapted equipment is available and act as a resource to provide this information to participants who might benefit from the items but do not know about them. Third, based on the assumption that park and recreation departments have little money for the purchase of large pieces of expensive equipment, several strategies might be employed, including the solicitation of gifts, the writing of grants, or plans which allow the use of any budgetary surpluses which might exist at the end of a fiscal year.

Finally, it is important for the professional to become an advocate for all participants by encouraging other leisure service delivery systems, such as bowling establishments and movie theaters, to purchase equipment so that the general public can benefit. A bowling ball ramp can help anyone, from small children to those with temporary back problems, to continue bowling. It would be a small investment for the operator but a big benefit to the community. The advocacy role is important for the recreation professional.

Summary

The task of creating and implementing effective recreation and park programs for all facets of America is continuous. Society is ever changing. Being an effective leisure service provider requires not only an understanding and appreciation of the conditions which make individuals or a group of people "special," but also a sound program of action which takes those conditions into account when attempting to fulfill the objectives of providing recreation and parks services to all. It is a challenge to the profession.

Suggestions and Study Guides

1. To develop a sensitivity to the problems encountered by those with physical disabilities, try the following role plays. Have half of the class wear blindfolds or stuff cotton in their ears to simulate being blind and deaf. Let the sighted and hearing members go with those who are visually or hearing impaired on a tour of the campus. If a wheelchair is convenient, let different members of the class navigate the campus in a wheelchair. Then, reverse the roles so everyone has an opportunity to experience deprivation. Collect information on your reactions, the reactions of others, and the number of architectural or ecological barriers you encounter. Discuss the experience and the effect these barriers have as deterrents to leisure activity.

2. Interview a therapeutic recreation specialist who works in a medical setting. Discuss with him or her the problems he or she encounters in providing therapeutic recreation services. See if the recreator differentiates between therapeutic recreation and recreation therapy and if so, how does he or she characterize each?

3. Interview a recreator who works with people with disabilities in the community. Compare his or her views of recreation services with those of clinical recreation specialists; with those of the recreation administrators you have previously interviewed.

4. Discuss the proposition that "Recreators working with people with disabilities or in a therapeutic environment need a different type of professional preparation than do those recreators working in other settings." Justify your arguments. Is the provision of recreation universal or does it depend upon the setting to give it meaning and structure?

5. Survey three local parks and recreation departments. Collect information about how they address the special needs of the populations discussed in this chapter. Discuss what their strengths and weaknesses are. Ask if any of their staff has a disability. Find out how representative their advisory board is of their community. Then, if needed, design a plan to incorporate more equity and diversity in their programs.

References

Bannon, J. (1973). *Outreach.* Springfield, IL: Charles C. Thomas, Publisher.

Barbee, J. & Calloway, J. (1979). The courts and correctional recreation. *Journal of Physical Education and Recreation, 50*(2), p. 40.

Bedini, L. (1990). The status of leisure education: Implications for instruction and practice. *Therapeutic Recreation Journal, 24*(1), pp. 40-49.

Bedini, L. & McCann, C. (1992). Tearing down the shameful wall of exclusion. *Parks and Recreation, 27*(4), pp. 40-44.

Dattilo, J. & Murphy, W. D. (1991). *Leisure education program planning: A systematic approach.* State College, PA: Venture Publishing, Inc.

Dwyer, J. F. & Gobster, P. H. (1992). Recreation opportunities and cultural diversity. *Parks and Recreation, 27*(9), pp. 22-31, 128.

Edginton, C. R. & Neal, L. L. (1981). Municipal park and recreation services for special populations in Canada and the United States: A comparative analysis. *Journal of Leisurability, 8*(4), pp. 25-29.

Foley, J. & Pirk, H. (1991). Taking back the parks. Part 2. *Parks and Recreation, 26*(4), pp. 22-27, 78.

Frye, V. (1962). Historical sketch of recreation in the medical setting. *Recreation in Treatment Centers, 1*, p. 40.

Fryer, D. & Payne, R. (1984). Proactive behavior in unemployment: Findings and implications. *Leisure Studies, 3*, pp. 273-295.

Godbey, G., Patterson, A., & Brown-Szwak, L. (1982). Rethinking leisure services in an aging population. *Parks and Recreation, 17*(4), pp. 46-48.

Hillman, W. (1969). Federal support of recreation services related to mental retardation. *Therapeutic Recreation Journal, 3*(3), pp. 6-12.

Hormachea, C. R., & Gulak, M. (1980). *Recreation in local jails: A model program.* Richmond, VA: Virginia Commonwealth University.

Kennedy, D. W., Smith, R. W., & Austin, D. R. (1991). *Special recreation: Opportunities for people with disabilities.* Dubuque, IA: Wm. C. Brown, Publishers.

Kraus, R. & Shank, J. (1992). *Therapeutic recreation service: Principles and practices (4th ed.).* Dubuque, IA: Wm. C. Brown, Publishers.

Krinsky, A. (1992). Therapeutic recreation and the homeless: A clinical case history. *Therapeutic Recreation Journal, 26*(3), pp. 53-57.

Kunstler, R. (1991). There but for fortune: A therapeutic recreation perspective on the homeless in America. *Therapeutic Recreation Journal, 25*(2), pp. 31-40.

Laudick, B., McGovern, J., & Cosgrove, S. (1982). Linking the hospital and the local recreation agency. *Parks and Recreation, 17*(4), p. 45.

McAvoy, L. H. (1979). The leisure preferences, problems, and needs of the elderly. *Journal of Leisure Research, 11*(1), pp. 28-39.

Meyer, L. E. (1977). A view of therapeutic recreation: Its foundations, objectives and challenges. In G. C. Zaso (Ed.), *Dialogues in Development—Concepts and Action,* pp. 1-27. Durham, NH: University of New Hampshire.

Munson, W. W. (1991). Juvenile delinquency as a social problem and social disability: The therapeutic recreator's role as ecological change agent. *Therapeutic Recreation Journal, 25*(2), pp. 19-30.

Oestreicher, M. (1990). Accessible recreation 20 years behind the times. *Parks and Recreation, 25*(8), pp. 52-55.

Peterson, C. A. & Gunn, S. L. (1984). *Therapeutic recreation program design: Principles and procedures.* Englewood Cliffs, NJ: Prentice-Hall.

Pomeroy, J. (1974). The handicapped are out of hiding: Implications for community recreation. *Therapeutic Recreation Journal, 8*(3), pp. 120-128.

Redburn, F. & Buss, T. (1986). *Responding to America's homeless: Public policy alternatives.* New York, NY: Praeger Publishers.

Robinson-Young, P. (1992). Recreation's role in gang intervention. *Parks and Recreation, 27*(3), pp. 54-56.

Roth, W. & Tompane, M. (1992). *Easy access to national parks.* San Francisco, CA: Sierra Club Books.

Schleien, S. & Green, F. (1992). Three approaches for integrating persons with disabilities into community recreation. *Journal of Park and Recreation Administration, 10*(2), pp. 51-66.

Schleien, S. & O'Morrow, G. (1981). Recreation for the incarcerated: Treatment or privilege. *Parks and Recreation, 16*(2), pp. 47-51.

Servedio, W. (1979). Eliminating mobility barriers in recreational areas and facilities. *Parks and Recreation, 14*(11), pp. 69-74, 86.

Sessoms, D. & Orthner, D. (1992). Our growing invisible populations. *Parks and Recreation, 27*(8), pp. 62-65.

Seven, S. (1979). Environmental interpretation for the visually impaired. *Therapeutic Recreation Journal, 13*(1), pp. 12-17.

Stumbo, N. J. & Little, S. L. (1991). Implications for leisure services with incarcerated women. *Therapeutic Recreation Journal, 25*(2), pp. 49-62.

Wolfensberger, W. (1972). *Normalization: The principle of normalization in human services*. Toronto, ON: National Institute on Mental Retardation.

PORTIONS OF CHAPTER EIGHT DEVELOPED AND CONTRIBUTED BY
DEBORAH BIALESCHKI
OF THE UNIVERSITY OF NORTH CAROLINA AT CHAPEL HILL

CHAPTER EIGHT

Outdoor Recreation

In recent years no segment of the park and recreation movement has experienced as much scrutiny and study as outdoor recreation and the environment. The political, social, and economic significance of outdoor activities have been analyzed, debated, and recorded. Many manuscripts accepted for publication in the *Journal of Leisure Research* and *Leisure Sciences* have addressed the outdoor recreation phenomenon. A comprehensive national review by the federal government in the late 1950s and early 1960s focused specifically on opportunities and facilities for outdoor recreation. During the 1980s a similar national study was undertaken as a part of The President's Commission on Americans Outdoors.

As an outcome of the growing awareness about outdoor recreation, a debate between advocates for commercial and industrial development of natural resources and proponents who want to preserve them has intensified. During this same time, outdoor recreation has taken many forms and experienced a variety of fads. Continued interest in outdoor recreation and the environment by society has resulted in the emergence of recreation resource management as one of the recognized specialties within the park and recreation profession. No introductory text in parks and recreation would be complete without a review of the scope, forms, and the concerns associated with the management and provision of outdoor recreation.

Definition of Outdoor Recreation

The term "outdoor recreation" has been used to describe those activities of a recreational nature that normally take place in a natural environment and depend primarily upon that environment for satisfaction. Most park and recreation professionals make distinctions in outdoor recreation activities based on the degree to which the environment is the focus of the activity. Some professionals adhere to a restrictive definition that requires a focus on the natural environment while others use a broader definition, one which includes almost any activity done in the outdoors. These differing views make getting accurate data on the extent of outdoor recreation participation difficult, thus contributing to some agency misunderstandings and political posturing as well as affecting our educational approaches to the preparation of park and recreation specialists.

Outdoor recreation activities that depend on the use of natural resources for the activity are usually classified as *resource-oriented outdoor recreation*. Within this category are further divisions of outdoor recreation. For example, *primitive resource-oriented activities* are those activities that use basic outdoor skills, are nonmotorized, and generally perceived as isolated "close to nature" activities such as backpacking and mountaineering. *Intermediate resource-based pursuits* require some moderate skill development and have a balance between nature and the social aspects of the activities such as car camping. *Modern resource-oriented activities* offer opportunities to develop and use skills in supervised and controlled environments where the participant has feelings toward nature but not necessarily close to it. Examples of this type of outdoor recreation are skiing at a commercial resort or swimming in a lake controlled by the local park and recreation department. In all of these resource-oriented outdoor activities, the environment is a critical component to the pursuit even though it may be somewhat controlled.

Certain activities such as softball, golf, tennis, and other outdoor sports are often included as outdoor recreation activities. This type of activity is classified as *activity-oriented outdoor recreation*. The emphasis of these pursuits is on the activity; the environment is of secondary concern. Many of these activities can be done indoors as well as outside.

In this text, the resource-oriented definition of outdoor recreation is used. It includes all those activities of a recreational nature that results from our interest in the environment and our relationship to it. Games such as football that take place outside are excluded but included are such sporting events as sailing regattas and bass tournaments. Ranges in activities are acknowledged

Table 8-1
Sale of Select Outdoor Recreation Products: 1980, 1985, and 1990
(in millions of dollars)

Product	1980	1985	1990
Athletic and sports clothing	3,127	3,378	11,382
Athletic and sports footwear	1,731	2,610	6,437
Firearms and hunting equipment	1,351	1,899	2,295
Golf	336	730	1,204
Camping equipment	646	724	1,072
Bicycles (multiple speed)	N/A	975	1,092
Fishing equipment	539	681	813
Snow skis	379	593	606
Archery	149	212	265
Water skis	123	125	88
Pleasure boats	2,718	6,753	7,524
Recreational vehicles	1,178	3,515	4,007
Snowmobiles	216	162	294

Source: *1992 Statistical Abstract*, p. 242.

from the more urban forms of walking for pleasure and picnicking to the more traditional wilderness experiences of backpacking and primitive camping. Outdoor recreation may be individually pursued or may take place in an organized manner; it may involve minimum equipment as for bird-watching and gardening, or it may require expensive and highly specialized apparatus as for fishing and snowmobiling (see Table 8-1).

A Brief History

As mentioned previously, the history of outdoor recreation as a formal set of expressions and resources goes back to antiquity. The Sumerians had parks (2340 BC) and the Egyptians had hunting preserves for the Pharaohs, public gardens, and trips on the Nile. England developed a park and garden charter by the late 18th century that spread throughout north and south Europe.

Aspects of this park tradition came to America with the early European settlers. In North America, the Boston Common, generally recognized as the first municipal park, was established in 1634 as a common grazing ground for livestock; by 1728, that function had been replaced by the community's need for a common place to socialize and a place to train its militia. The Common's role as a park was assured. The Massachusetts Bay Colony passed legislation (the Great Ponds Act) in 1641 that allowed public hunting and fishing on open bodies of water of ten acres or more. As early as 1799, Congress set aside $200,000 to purchase timber lands. Through similar public interests and legislative supports, other conservation and preservation acts made natural resources available for recreation. During the mid-1800s, a series of urban parks designed primarily by Frederick Olmsted were created in New York (Central Park, 1853), San Francisco (Golden Gate, 1863), Philadelphia (Fairmount Park, 1867), and Chicago (Washington Park, 1876). The first national park in the world was established at Yellowstone in 1872. The creation of these parks reflected the public's interest in the preservation of land and the growing awareness of the importance of outdoor recreation. These actions also suggested that people were aware that population growth and industrial expansion could easily tip nature off balance and damage beyond recovery.

The conservation movement became a major social focus at the turn of the 20th century. This movement grew from a concern over commercial development that was opening up natural resources to support expanding industries. For the first time, power tools were being used heavily in the lumbering and mining industries with little concern by businesses for conservation; land erosion, droughts, and floods were the natural consequences of these exploitative patterns. These wanton acts of destruction incensed many citizens who banded together, developed political muscle, and became the first lobbyists for conservation. They advocated for legislation that continues to influence our ability to enjoy outdoor recreation pursuits today. For example, the Reclamation Act (1902) provided government aid to develop water resources; the first wildlife refuge was established in Florida in 1902, and the National Park Service was established (1916) to preserve natural resources as well as provide the public with opportunities to engage in outdoor recreation in the national parks.

A number of important conservation groups also were created during that time: the Sierra Club (1892), the Scenic and Historic Preservation Society (1895), and the National Audubon Society (1905). Two organizations representing professionals concerned with the management of resources were also established during this period. They were the American Forestry Association in 1875, and the New England Association of Park Superintendents in 1898, the latter being the forerunner of the American Institute of Park Executives created in 1921.

The decades of the 1920s to the 1950s marked a continued interest in the development, management, and operation of outdoor recreation resources by professionals. The period during and immediately following World War I and the middle years of the Great Depression were boom years for outdoor recreation. The Civilian Conservation Corps and the Works Progress Administration, alone, employed approximately 26,500 people during the Depression in jobs created to build outdoor recreation facilities (Jensen, 1985).

In the 1950s many Americans seemed to discover the great outdoor playground that had been created during the past 100 years. The demand for outdoor recreation environments and services far exceeded the capacity of the many public agencies that comprised the outdoor recreation system. In 1958, the United States Congress created the Outdoor Recreation Resources Review Commission (ORRRC) to study the present and future outdoor recreation needs of the American public. The Commission made its report to the Congress and President in 1962 with recommendations for the conceptualizations and planning bases for nearly all of the governmental outdoor recreation programs. Among the recommendations were: the expansion of the National Park system, the establishment of the National Wilderness system, the start of the Land and Conservation Fund program, the establishment of the Wild and Scenic Rivers system, the initiation of the National Trails system, and the authorization of state and local land acquisition programs. A similar Commission (The President's Commission on Americans Outdoors) was established in 1985 to update the information on current outdoor recreation concerns and demands. While not as influential as the ORRRC report, some good outdoor recreation data were gathered, along with several recommendations for the expansion of outdoor recreation opportunities through the expansion of public/private cooperation, the use of the private sector, and the creation of greenways (President's Commission, 1987).

These tangible activities reflected the attitudes of the American people that developed as the culture moved from an agrarian, subsistence-based society to one of industrialization. The early pioneers viewed the natural environment as a dangerous unknown that needed to be tamed with resources that were thought to be limitless. There was the belief in Manifest Destiny and the God-given right to dominate nature, to use it for society's benefit. By the mid-1800s, however, the transcendentalist movement was underway. This philosophy viewed nature as the vehicle to inspire intuitive thought and lift the consciousness to greater spiritual wisdom—to learn to relate to nature rather than exploit it. The great transcendentalist writers such as Emerson and Thoreau inspired future naturalists as well as the general public to respect and preserve the natural world.

By the early 1900s, naturalism emerged. In keeping with the philosophy of realism, these naturalists-scientists observed nature and recorded their observations in ways that promoted a reverence for the natural world that was based on scientific fact. Their efforts spearheaded a preservation movement that gained momentum in the mid-1900s and is still in the mainstream of today's society. From these movements came the pioneer practitioners who put into practice the concepts gained from the transcendentalists and the naturalists-scientists. Practitioners such as Frederick Olmsted, Aldo Leopold, Gifford Pinchot, and Stephen Mather laid the foundations for such institutions as the National Park Service and the U.S. Forest Service, and shaped the roles of park and recreation practitioners. Also from these two approaches, Manifest Destiny and Transcendentalism, evolved two different patterns of outdoor recreation—

those activities in which people seek to dominate nature through power (e.g., motor boats, off-the-road vehicles and jet skis) and those based upon understanding and relating to nature (e.g., sail boating, canoeing, birding).

A Complex Set of Relationships

It has long been held that the nature of the recreation experience is directly related to the quality of the resource. Excessive use of the resource tends to diminish the quality of the experience for both present and future users. The resource-based and activity-based outdoor recreationists are concerned with the resource, but from different perspectives. The resource-based individual, such as the whitewater canoeist, needs an understanding of how to relate to the resource. The activity-based recreationist, such as the trailbiker, is less concerned about the resource but is interested in the administrative policies which govern its use. Therefore, managerial policies and style of the agency affect the resource as well as the participant's satisfaction.

Outdoor recreation experiences are dependent upon the environment with different settings offering distinct types of experiences. Some recreation activities are dependent upon the climate and temperature. For example, it is difficult to snow ski in the Sandia Mountains of New Mexico in mid-July. Others, such as mountain climbing, are dependent upon the physical geography of the area. Still other pursuits, e.g., fossil and mineral collecting, are tied to the natural history of a place as well as its geology. The type of water resources available, the type of vegetation and wildlife present, the amount of open space available, and the general ecology of an area all serve as determinants of outdoor recreation behaviors.

The role of government in outdoor recreation is a traditional one, making available a wide range of activities, environments, and interests through the public system. Some settings require protection and control of the resource; other sites require planning for high intensity use. The ideal is to develop a system which provides optimum satisfaction to the user through effective and efficient management while providing optimum protection of the resource. To accomplish this goal, recreation and park professionals have developed classification systems so that the available resources might be appropriately developed and managed.

Classification Systems

A variety of classification systems are used by state planing agencies, municipal recreation departments and various federal agencies. Some, like those employed by local park and recreation units, deal primarily with the acreage requirements for specific facilities and areas while others emphasize the nature and quality of the environment in relation to select activity use. The latter types are more frequently used by outdoor recreation agencies and specialists. Three are presented here.

The Clawson-Knetsch Classification System

One of the early writers to effectively deal with policy and problems of outdoor recreation was Marion Clawson. As a land economist, he wrote extensively on the economic significance of outdoor recreation activity and the need for an analytical approach to the questions of supply and demand. His economic planning model, a systems approach to the development and management of outdoor recreation resources, was the first to be used (Clawson & Knetsch, 1966). In it outdoor recreation areas were conceptualized as one of three types: resource-based, intermediate, and user-oriented. For each category, Clawson and Knetsch described the intended use of the area, the management and operation concerns, and the level of government primarily responsible for the provision of the area. They also suggested the ratio or percentage of each type of resource to be needed in the future.

RESOURCE AREAS

Resource-dependent areas were defined as our "great outdoors," areas that should remain in this natural state, unchanged and unimproved. Clawson and Knetsch held that people come to these areas because of the resource itself. In this classification they listed the national forests and parks which are generally remote from the nation's population centers and are managed by federal agencies. They felt this form of management was appropriate but suggested more resource areas should be acquired in the eastern United States where the population concentration is denser. They estimated that only 10 percent of outdoor recreation pursuants will utilize these areas; the acreage needed for their activities far exceeds that of the other categories.

INTERMEDIATE AREAS

Intermediate areas were defined as natural resources that should be moderately developed and within a reasonable drive from the populations they serve. These areas should contain some of the features of a resource-oriented facility to accommodate that element of the public which seeks a degree of privacy and solitude. At the same time, the intermediate areas require development so groups seeking activities such as camping accommodations, picnicking, and boating can find appropriate sites and facilities. Clawson and Knetsch believed that the need for intermediate areas would intensify as the demand for outdoor recreation increased. All levels of government will be required to provide these areas, although traditionally, the responsibility has rested with state and federal agencies.

USER-ORIENTED AREAS

These areas are characterized by intensive regular use. Some people have described them as "people places." They are designed and constructed to accommodate the more physically active forms of outdoor recreation such as swimming, skating, skiing, and cycling. They should be easily accessible and located near population centers as 60 percent of the outdoor activities will occur there. The space requirements for these areas, however, are not as great as the intermediate and resource-oriented spaces. Development is essential for these areas, and the problems of management are critical. Many users come to these facilities because they need space and an opportunity to engage in their favorite forms of activity but not for the natural resource itself. As indicated, the demand for user-oriented areas is the greatest, and these facilities have been typically the responsibility of local governmental agencies.

ORRRC Classification System

Although the Clawson-Knetsch classification was a pioneering effort, their system has had limited use, primarily because of the wide acceptance of the ORRRC report (*Outdoor Recreation for America*, 1962) and the creation of the Bureau of Outdoor Recreation. The ORRRC report recommended a classification scheme that included historical and cultural sites as outdoor recreation resources. This system was recommended by the Bureau of Outdoor Recreation to states for use when inventorying and categorizing recreation opportunities for their State Comprehensive Outdoor Recreation Plans (SCORP). Unfortunately, this classification system has some built-in difficulties because of the high degree of subjectivity when trying to place a specific facility into a class. The six classes used by the ORRRC are:

CLASS I, HIGH-DENSITY RECREATION AREAS

These areas are intensively developed, managed for large numbers of users, generally located close to urban areas, and most frequently administered by municipal and state agencies. Examples include beaches, picnic areas, trailer camps, and boardwalks. Natural resources used for these facilities often compete with residential and commercial uses.

CLASS II, GENERAL OUTDOOR RECREATION AREAS

Developed for a wide variety of specific recreation activities such as hiking, camping, and skiing, these resources are generally some distance from major urban areas. They may have highly developed sections such as ski facilities and family camping sites, but also have areas of relatively undeveloped land. Examples include campsites, ski areas, resorts, and hunting preserves.

CLASS III, NATURAL ENVIRONMENT AREAS

These areas with relatively few and simple facilities are generally suitable for recreation in their natural state. Large, undeveloped areas such as state parks, state and national forests, and the national park buffer areas qualify for this classification.

CLASS IV, UNIQUE NATURAL AREAS

The outstanding scientific, scenic and natural areas such as the geyser basins at Yellowstone or the Petrified Forest of Arizona characterize this category. Few facilities exist and only if they enhance the protection of the natural feature. Nearly all of these areas are managed for preservation by the federal government.

CLASS V, PRIMITIVE AREAS

These areas are undeveloped, roadless, and characterized by undisturbed, natural conditions. With the exception of trails, the lack of facilities preserves the primitive conditions. Primitive areas are generally remote and large enough to give an individual a sense of solitude and distance from civilization. Examples are found in wilderness areas such as the Gila Wilderness, most of the Rocky Mountain National Park, and the Quetico-Superior Boundary Waters Canoe Area.

CLASS VI, HISTORIC AND CULTURAL SITES

Areas of major historical or cultural significance are included in this designation. They may be of local, regional, or national importance. The emphasis is on restoration and preservation of the historic features with facilities used for protection, access, or interpretation. They may be historic sites or buildings that are characterized by the human event which gave them meaning rather than their natural uniqueness. Examples include such areas as Mt. Vernon, Tippecanoe Battlefield, and Petroglyphs National Monument.

The Forest Service System

Some federal agencies such as the Forest Service have developed their own system to meet their specific situation and need. The Forest Service classifies areas according to the experience level or type of experience sought by its users (Douglass, 1982). There are five levels ranging from the wilderness experience (level 1) to trailer camps (level 5). For each level, the expected activities and carrying capacity are identified. The five levels are:

LEVEL 1

No public mechanized access; a bare minimum nonwilderness development with basic site protection facilities principally, but minimum facilities for visitor comfort and convenience; requires well-developed camping skills by user.

Level 2

Usually a primitive road access; minimum development with limited controls; hunter camps and boat landings are typical.

Level 3

Good roads; typical medium-density forest campground or picnic area; flush toilets and water supply.

Level 4

Very good accessibility; not rustic, having contemporary facilities and convenience features. Flush toilets and water supply.

Level 5

Excellent accessibility; designed for convenience of users, heavy site modification and contemporary design; associated with trailer parks and regional parks; showers and flush toilets used (Douglass, p. 84).

There are advantages and limitations to all classification systems. In practice, most outdoor park and recreation specialists prefer to classify areas according to their activity use and benefits rather than the environmental characteristics of the area. Consequently, they enumerate the number of campsites, picnic areas, ski runs, and marinas. These data are easily tabulated and analyzed to provide outdoor recreation managers a numerical indicator of use and demand but do not acknowledge the qualitative aspects of the environment.

A comprehensive recreation system should include elements from all the classes or types of areas as well as opportunities for nonoutdoor recreation pursuits. The degree to which each of these elements is needed will vary according to the social factors which influence individual and community behaviors. Among them are traditions and values, population composition and trends, availability of resources and time, interests and past experiences of the users, and skills of the participants. While outdoor recreation opportunities are complemented by the private and commercial interests, the bulk of the responsibility for recognizing and meeting the outdoor recreation needs of the public rests with government sponsorship.

The Outdoor Recreation Experience

Outdoor recreation interests have increased for a variety of reasons. Concern for the environment, the affluence and mobility of our society, the frontier tradition, and a need for diversion are some of the most apparent explanations. Beyond these, however, it is the outdoor recreation experience itself. The vitality, diversity, and psychological satisfaction are qualities that make outdoor

Table 8-2
Visitations* to Federal Recreation Areas by Major Federal Land Management Units
(in millions of visitor hours)

Agency	1980	1985	1990
Fish and Wildlife Service	17	65	53
Forest Service	2,819	2,705	3,157
Corps of Engineers	1,926	1,721	2,280
National Park Service	1,042	1,298	1,322
Bureau of Land Management	68	208	518
Bureau of Reclamation	407	282	280
Tennessee Valley Authority	87	79	10

Source: *1992 Statistical Abstract*, p. 232.

recreation pursuits meaningful and fulfilling. While many writers have tried to explain why North Americans love the outdoors, Clawson's (1959) explanation seemed the most comprehensive. He discussed outdoor recreation activities not as a single occurrence, but as a multifaceted experience with satisfactions coming from any one of a combination of its component parts. Subsequent research has verified the validity of Clawson's idea (Hammitt, 1980) and have been applied to travel and tourism, to any type of recreation trip.

According to Clawson, *five* distinct stages or phases are involved in an outdoor recreation experience (see Figure 8-1, page 260). The first phase is planning which entails the preparation for the trip, the planning and anticipation of what will occur, and the satisfactions to be derived. This phase is often the most enjoyable for many people. The second stage is the travel to the site where the activity will occur. Being on the move or just going somewhere is often sufficient justification for the total experience. The third phase involves the activities engaged in while at the site. This stage is the intense involvement with the environment. This phase is the most important aspect for many people, because it is the "doing" stage. The fourth phase, returning home, is similar to the second stage. Pleasure comes from being on the move and the anticipation of "getting home." This phase has a different focus, however, because the activity is over and reflection replaces anticipation. The final stage is the memory of the experience. In this stage individuals reminisce about what happened, thoughts about the next trip, or perhaps show slides and movies. All of these stages provide satisfaction and add to the motivation and enjoyment of the actual experience. The benefits of any one stage may be enough to sustain interest in the activity.

Other psychological concepts of leisure also have been discussed within an outdoor recreation perspective. The concept of "flow" (Csikszentmihalyi, 1988), perceived freedom (Neulinger, 1974), and "peak experiences" (Maslow, 1962) all have meaning within the highly personal outdoor recreation context.

Figure 8-1
The Outdoor Recreation Experience and Its Component Parts

Adapted from: "The Crisis in Outdoor Recreation" by Marion Clawson, *The American Forest*, March/
April, 1959.

"Peak experience" and "flow," described earlier in this text, are extremely focused experiences; some suggest the outdoor recreation experience is one setting in which all the elements come together. Among the psychological benefits frequently associated with outdoor recreation are an escape from urban pressures, achievement, challenge, autonomy and freedom, communication with nature, reflection on personal values, nostalgia, risk-taking and excitement, and physical fitness (Ibrahim & Cordes, 1993).

Regardless of why one goes to the outdoors, few environments can equal its ability to offer a pleasurable recreation experience. The versatility of the settings accommodate both the skilled participant and the novice. For example, parents and children can enjoy fishing together at their own level of understanding and skill. Families have rediscovered their unity and a commitment to one another in such common projects as gardening or going camping together. The multifaceted aspects to the outdoor recreation experience provide an environment for self-discovery, for sharing, and for learning. Two of the movements that have capitalized upon this fact are organized camping and environmental education.

Organized Camping

Like so many aspects of organized park and recreation services, the organized camping movement began in the late 1800s. It has gone through several emphases ranging from an earlier concern for physical fitness and activity to a more recent concern for environmental awareness. During the 1920s and 1930s, organized camping emphasized the educational aspects of outdoor living while the period during the 1950s promoted it as a setting for "democratic living." Today, it takes many forms and offers a wide range of experiences and benefits.

Organized camping has been portrayed as the outdoor merging of recreation and education. This conceptualization includes the fundamentals (recreation, education, and nature) which make up camping, but additional characteristics should be added to further identify the activity as organized camping. These aspects include the presence of trained leadership, an administrative organization that provides the camping opportunity, and a program which occurs over an extended period of time in contrast with other types of camping, most of which are planned and initiated by the camper. The American Camping Association [ACA] (1990), the professional association for people involved with organized camping, defines it as:

> A sustained experience which provides a creative, educational opportunity in group living in the out-of-doors. It utilizes trained leadership and the resource of natural surroundings to contribute to each camper's mental, physical, social, and spiritual growth (p. 3).

This definition of organized camping requires an interaction with the natural environment, but some contemporary organized camps ignore this element. Activity camps which stress the pursuit of a specific activity such as basketball, music, dance, or cheerleading camps generally do not meet the definition associated with traditional camp programs, even though the living arrangements may be similar.

Potential benefits, however, can be found in any organized camping experiences that occur in the outdoors. Developing interpersonal skills, testing one's ability to make choices and accept responsibility, and having to care for oneself and others are all important lessons to be learned from any camping experience. When these experiences do take place within a traditional organized camping situation, an awareness of the environment and our relationship to the ecosystem is an added learning outcome.

It is difficult to provide accurate camp statistics because the scene is constantly changing. Surveys show that approximately 8,500 day and resident camps serve an estimated 5.3 million children during the summer. Approximately 5,500 of these camps are residential camps. An equal number or more of youth and adults may attend camps during the fall, winter, and spring seasons for outdoor education programs, retreats and winter activities (American Camping Association, n.d.). When you add the millions who trip camp, camp overnight in a national and state park facility, or attend day camps, the numbers of campers are enormous.

Organized camping encompasses a vast array of organizational structures and programs. Sponsors can include governmental organizations, private and voluntary agencies, civic and fraternal organizations, corporations and labor unions, and private enterprise. Some camps operate for profit; others do not. Some camps are used only during the summer while others are operated throughout the entire year. Certain organized camps are only for boys and men, others are only for girls and women while still others operate a coed system or have a family orientation. The majority of camps have programmed for people without disabilities, but with the implementation of the Americans With Disabilities Act, most camps are responding to the needs of people with disabilities. Concerns for access and safety are two of the aspects of a camp considered by the ACA when it accredits. Other elements considered are staff qualifications and staff-camper ratios, health and sanitation, program quality, transportation and facilities.

Since the variety of camps is almost endless, different classification systems have evolved. One approach is to classify by agency sponsorship. Four general types are typically identified: agency camps, independent camps, church camps, and public camps. The following description details these types of camps:

1. *Agency camps* sponsored by such nonprofit organizations as the Boy Scouts, Girl Scouts, YMCA, YWCA, 4-H, Camp Fire Boys and Girls, and the National Easter Seal Society.
2. *Independent camps* sponsored by individuals or corporations and operated as business enterprises or for a select membership group such as a labor union or for a targeted market group.
3. *Religiously-affiliated or church camps* sponsored by religious organizations and usually operated as nonprofit enterprises.
4. *Public camps* sponsored by tax-supported agencies such as schools, municipalities, recreation and park districts.

It should be noted that in this classification system, the term "independent camp" is used to describe what would normally be thought of as the commercial sector of the leisure service delivery system. It should not be confused with the concept of private recreation, which stresses membership and voluntary associations.

A second way of looking at organized camping is to classify the type of camp according to its organization and administration (duration of operation). This classification would result in the following designations:

1. Day Camping: In this type of camping, campers are taken daily to the campsite where the program is conducted and returned to their homes in the afternoons. This form of camping, begun by the Girl Scouts in 1929, has become popular with municipal and local recreation departments.
2. Short-term Residence Camps: Short-term residence camps, the most popular form of camp, accept the camper for one-, two-, or three-week periods. Most agency camps operate this type of camp and will normally run four to six different sessions during the summer.
3. Long-term Residence Camps: Long-term camps generally operate sessions that are at least one month long. The usual pattern is from five to seven weeks of residency. Most independent camps are long-term residency but frequently will operate both a short- and long-term program.
4. Trip Camping: As the name suggests, this type of camping involves covering a specific distance over a period of time. Canoe, bike, motorcamp, and backpacking trips, are illustrative of trip camping. Youth organizations such as the Girl Scouts, Boy Scouts, and YMCA, tend to promote and utilize the trip-camping concept.

Finally, camps may be classified by function or program emphasis. There are special interest camps (basketball, music, etc.), special needs camps (camps for those with disabilities), family camps, and general purpose camps. Fortunately, the concept of organized camping is broad enough to include all types of camping with diverse program philosophies and approaches to service. Organized camping has grown because of the satisfying experiences provided to children and adults. The magic of camping is the opportunity to enjoy oneself, one's friends, and the environment simultaneously. Experts have ascribed a variety of values to camping and its positive effect on health and personality. It is a unique setting for the recreation experience.

Elements of Organized Camping

The success of the camp program, as with all forms of organized recreation, depends upon the quality of its *leadership*. Nearly a quarter of a million people are involved annually as camp leaders. They range in experience and backgrounds from high school students who may serve as junior counselors to experienced professional camp administrators. Most frequently, camp leaders are college students, schoolteachers on vacation, or public and private recreation personnel who function in other professional capacities during the noncamping season. Among the positions and jobs most frequently found in camps are camp director, assistant camp director, program director, aquatic director, counselor (senior and junior), program staff (such as arts and crafts, nature, sports, trips, sailing), nurse, dietitian, cook, camp secretary, and maintenance personnel. Occasionally, camps will have a physician in residence, but a physician on call is more common.

The second element, *type of facilities* needed, depends largely upon the purpose of the camp. Program emphases and camp philosophy dictate the number and characteristics of facilities desired. In general, however, the planning principles governing location, design, and operation of recreation areas and facilities apply equally to the camp setting.

The third element of organized camping is the *program* itself. Good programming involves the careful planning, execution, and evaluation of activities and experiences. The program is a reflection of the camp philosophy and is conditioned by the camp leadership, facilities, clientele, and organizational and administrative structures. Successful camps take individual needs into consideration while offering the campers a set of professionally selected experiences and programs. Camp programmers acknowledge the dynamic interaction between the camper and the environment, the need for rules and regulations without regimentation, opportunities to enjoy both organized and unorganized activity, and a need for time for personal reflection and exploration.

The final element of a successful camping program is its *financial structure*. Most camps operate on agency appropriations, camper fees, and to some extent, grants. The degree to which the camp is sustained by camper fees depends upon the type of camp and its purpose. With most agency and organization camps, the camping program is underwritten by the general budget and funding of the agency. The campers' fees supplement those appropriations. With independent camps, camper fees are the primary source of revenue. They must be great enough to cover operational costs and provide the needed profits and reserve for capital improvement.

Environmental Education

Considerable interest has developed during the past twenty-five years in protecting the environment from pollution, unneeded industrial and residential development, and wanton destruction of the natural resources. This movement has taken many forms. Special interest groups such as the Sierra Club, Defenders of Wildlife, and the Wilderness Society, have mounted large public information efforts. These campaigns have been directed toward congressional legislation such as the National Environmental Policy Act and the Clean Air and Clean Water Acts; the activities of such regulatory governmental units as the Environmental Protection Agency and their enforcement of public laws; and various departments of public instruction through their educational efforts such as those provided by outdoor education and resident outdoor school programs.

Although all of these efforts have had an impact on the recreation and park movement, the resident outdoor school and environmental education efforts have had the closest relationship to park and recreation systems.

The terminology used to describe various environmental education efforts is often confusing because people tend to use the terms interchangeably. The following definitions are provided by the Council on Outdoor Education (1989):

Environmental education: education about the total environment, including population growth, pollution, resource use and misuse, urban and rural planning and modern technology with its demands on natural resources. Environmental education is encompassing, while outdoor education is seen by some to relate to natural resources and not to include the wide sense of the world environment. Many people, however, think of outdoor education in its broadest sense and prefer the term outdoor/environmental education.

Conservation education: the study of the wise use of natural resources that tends to focus on animals, soil, water, and air as single topics in relation to their use for timber, agriculture, hunting, fishing, and human consumption. It is not usually concerned with preservation, recreation, or human relations and as such is more narrow than outdoor education. This term has declined in use since the 1960s.

Resident outdoor school: the process of taking children to a residential camp during school time for a period of usually three to five days to extend the curriculum through learning in the outdoors. This process was originally called camping education. It was later referred to as school camping, but these phrases were discontinued when parents and taxpayers believed they meant the same thing as summer camp, which seemed to be more recreational than educational.

Outdoor recreation: a broad spectrum of outdoor activities participated in during leisure time purely for pleasure or some other intrinsic value. Included are activities such as swimming, boating, winter sports, cycling, and camping. In many countries and to some extent in the United States, these activities are called outdoor education when they are taught in the school as a part of the curriculum.

Outdoor pursuits: generally, nonmechanized outdoor recreation activities done in areas remote from the amenities of telephone, emergency help, and urban comforts. To many people, the terms outdoor recreation and outdoor pursuits are similar.

Adventure education: activities into which are purposely built elements perceived by the participants as being dangerous. The activities are not inherently dangerous as taught (under qualified instruction), but they appear to be so to the participant, and therefore generate a sense of adventure. Adventure activities include such things as rope courses, whitewater rafting, mountaineering, and rock climbing.

Experiential education: learning by doing or by experiencing. Many experiential education activities are synonymous with adventure activities and outdoor pursuits; however, experiential education can also mean any form of pragmatic educational experience. In many ways, outdoor education may be viewed as experiential, especially when learning takes place through outdoor experiences.

Environmental interpretation: usually associated with visitor centers administered by national park or forest service centers. The term refers to a technique used to help visitors understand the meanings of the phenomena on display while simultaneously arousing curiosity for more information.

Nature education and nature recreation: learning or leisure activities related to natural resources. The terms were used from the 1920s to the 1950s, and the activities were not usually interrelated, nor did they focus on the overriding concerns of ecology and stewardship of the land. They were usually isolated, individual activities using natural resources for equipment and facilities, and involving knowledge of nature.

The basic assumption of the outdoor education movement is a simple one: that outdoor education best occurs in the outdoors and that nature has provided the best learning environment for the study of nature. The philosophy is based on four premises: (a) the development of a land ethic that treats the land and its resources with respect and results in ethical ecological action toward stewardship of the land, (b) development of the cognitive aspects of knowledge about the interrelationships of all facets of the ecosystem; this includes a basic understanding of ecological, sociological, and cultural principles that prepares the person to weigh the impact of action on the environment, the culture, and humanity, (c) knowledge of how to live comfortably in the outdoors and how to recreate with a minimum impact on the environment, and (d) the belief that outdoor education must be taught at all levels and pursued throughout life— not as a one-time field trip or one week at an outdoor school (Council on Outdoor Education, 1989).

While public schools have been a focal point for much of the early education in the outdoors, several nonschool agencies offer educational experiences for adults. The most widely recognized programs are Outward Bound and the National Outdoor Leadership School. Outward Bound is an adventure-based program that provides challenging opportunities in wilderness settings that foster self-discovery and leadership training. The National Outdoor Leadership

School (NOLS) offers courses that develop the fundamental knowledges, skills, and experiences necessary for minimum impact use and enjoyment of wilderness environments by emphasizing safety, judgment, leadership, teamwork, outdoor skills, and environmental studies. These courses are specifically tailored to people who want to work professionally as wilderness educators. Some universities and colleges have embraced these outdoor leadership and training programs by offering college credits to participants. These trainings, as well as a variety of other experientially-based programs, continue the efforts to offer outdoor learning experiences throughout the adult years.

A 35-foot climbing wall is used to foster self-confidence and teach rock climbing skills.

Issues Concerning Outdoor Recreation

Interest in outdoor recreation and the environment has paralleled the growth and development of the interstate highway system, the travel and tourism industry, and the sports equipment industry. As one expanded, so did the others. As more people turn to the outdoors to pursue some of their recreation interests, stress on fragile environments has been exerted by the very people who most often want the benefits of these outdoor areas. Simultaneously, the environment is under extreme pressures from industries, developers, and citizens who demand the amenities provided by the exploitation of the natural resources. This clashing of perceptions about the environment ultimately results in heated debates about how best to manage the natural environment. Eight issues of current interest to professionals in outdoor recreation to be discussed briefly in the following section include: use vs. preservation of natural resources, the influence of the Americans with Disabilities Act on outdoor recreation, nature and spirituality, liability and risk recreation, public/private relationships, funding options, gender and cultural influences on outdoor recreation, and ecotourism.

USE VS. PRESERVATION

This issue deals with accessibility and use of the natural resources in contrast to the preservation of these areas. The problems related to this issue focus on the amount of use an area can withstand before severe or irreparable damage is done (*carrying capacity*), whether an area should be left entirely in its natural state or developed for recreational or business enterprises (i.e., timber harvest, mining, oil exploration), and visitor management.

The concept of *carrying capacity* implies that a resource has a natural level of productivity within which use must be controlled in order to be sustained. Recreational carrying capacity refers to the relationship between the recreational experience sought and the recreation resource. This relationship can be translated into the maximum number of people and type of use an area can sustain over a specific time without impairing the environment or the visitor experience (Fogg, 1975). The importance of this broader perspective of recreational carrying capacity is that the role of social capacity as well as the ecological capacity is acknowledged. It also means that the determination of recreational carrying capacity becomes a sociopolitical process as well as a biophysical one (Burch, 1984). Therefore, carrying capacities are the product of value judgments as well as science where the values of managers and users are used to reach a collective judgment (Hendee, Stankey, & Lucas, 1990).

Convenience and accessibility determine to a great extent the amount of use an area will receive. In some of the popular National Parks such as the Great Smokey Mountains, Yosemite, Yellowstone, and the Grand Canyon, people come to these natural areas every year by the millions. The focus is directed toward visitor management. The impact of these large numbers of people is manifested in pollution from vehicles, large amounts of garbage and sewage, crime and vandalism, deterioration of facilities and areas from use, and emergency medical care and rescue. Park managers are confronted with increasingly complex management decisions at a time when fiscal and human resources have been dramatically cut. Policies such as daily visitor quotas, access by permit, a reevaluation of facilities needed to be located within the park, and traffic plans are among the possible solutions to the problems of high use.

Politicians and recreation and park professionals also note that many national parks are inaccessible to the majority of the population. The majority of national parks are in the western half of the United States where the population density is low. The parks are basically out of reach of the urban masses, particularly less affluent people. The National Park Service reported that 21 percent of the recreation visits in 1990 were to national recreation areas which are primarily in suburban and urban areas; however, these national recreation areas only comprise four percent of the total acreage of the national park system. In that same year, 22 percent of the total visits were to the large, primarily western national parks which comprise 60 percent of the total acreage (*Statistical Abstract*, 1991). Therefore, while a small number of federal areas may be subjected to heavy use, other tracts are virtually unreachable to the general public.

The second aspect of this issue of how natural resources should be used is centered around the perceptions of preservation and conservation. Preservation of natural environments is concerned with the maintenance of long-term ecological processes (Hendee, Stankey, & Lucas, 1990) and implies the status quo for ecosystems, nonrenewability, and management to protect the resource from human influence (Jensen, 1985). Conservation is usually associated with renewable natural resources and implies the use of resources in the most beneficial manner over time while avoiding waste. Conservation involves a cycle of intelligent use and timely replenishment of resources as they become damaged or partially depleted.

The conflict between the use and preservation of natural areas is apparent. Some individuals would like to see all of the natural areas, particularly wilderness areas, be preserved for all time (LaPage & Ranney, 1988). Wildernesses are defined as areas where their primeval character and influence have been primarily affected by "the forces of nature," where the imprint of humans is "substantially unnoticeable," and where the opportunities "for solitude or a primitive type of recreation" are significant. Although certain types of minimum-impact outdoor recreation may occur in these settings, management would be for the natural environment. For example, wilderness areas may be used for backpacking trips under primitive conditions but the management focus would remain with maintaining the integrity of the environment when using the resource for recreational purposes.

Other people would like to see these natural areas conserved with recreation being one of the many uses of these renewable resources. A broader selection of outdoor activities would be accommodated, as would more supportive facilities to provide a balance between human activity and the environment. An application of this view can be seen in most national parks where a central core area of the park is developed to meet visitor needs. These accommodations may include lodging, stores for buying supplies as well as souvenirs, equipment rental, educational areas, and structured recreational activities. There is a recognition that some economic gain may accrue to local communities through wilderness recreation but the key is to balance tourism with conservation. The partnership requires an understanding of the needs of the recreationists, outfitters, and resource managers (Wallace, Tierney & Haas, 1990).

Lastly, some people would advocate for the human uses of the natural resources as the leading priority. The development of extensive facilities and the maximized use of the resource to meet the demands of people would be the first priority. Resorts and commercial outdoor recreation facilities that offer a wide variety of amenities are examples of this type of perspective. Controversies such as the proposed development of the Arctic Wildlife Refuge for oil production are also examples of the desire to put human needs as the priority when a conflict arises between use and preservation.

THE AMERICANS WITH DISABILITIES ACT

The Americans with Disabilities Act guarantees access to every critical area of life to people with disabilities, including rights to public and private recreation opportunities. The meaning of the ADA for outdoor recreation providers is that a potential participant or user may not be excluded from services on the basis of disability alone. Participants with disabilities have a right to engage in outdoor activities and gain the same benefits as persons without disabilities. For example, transportation systems that take people to local parks need to be accessible to all people; facilities such as restrooms, telephone systems, and welcome centers should be usable by people with disabilities; and, where possible, the environment should be "opened" so those with disabilities are able to experience its benefits. The issue is how much development should occur in order to make it more accessible without negatively affecting the environment or altering the experience.

While the ADA is designed to maintain the rights of persons with disabilities, some considerations for the effects of the Act on the natural environment have been addressed in design and program guidelines by the National Park Service and U.S. Forest Service (*Interagency Guidelines...*, 1990). According to these guidelines, "All recreation visitors should have the opportunity to participate in programs and services to the highest level of access feasible for persons with disabilities (considering the diversity of recreation opportunities and experiences) when compared to that offered other visitors" (*Interagency Guidelines...*, p. 1). As described in the guidelines, the extent of physical accessibility depends on the degree to which a site or facility is to be developed. Highly developed sites like a picnic area or interpretive and visitor services should provide for a high degree of accessibility, but an undeveloped site, still in its natural state with no significant modifications, should have few, if any, modifications purely for the sake of accessibility. While the intent of the ADA is to provide access, natural areas that are undeveloped need not be modified in ways that would result in significant damage or alteration to the natural environment.

NATURE AND SPIRITUALITY

Two broad views toward the environment can be found in the culture of the United States. These views reflect the heritage and the spiritual connection of the people who contributed to the development of our society. The first is located in the Native American and transcendentalist tradition where nature was celebrated in ways that sought harmony with all life and natural elements. The second view emerged from the Western tradition that promoted a belief in the superiority of humans to all other life and the belief that the universe exists to serve human needs. The difference is dominance versus relating.

The Native American philosophy toward the spiritual experience was intimately tied to the environment. These experiences were personal as well as communal. Most indigenous Native Americans viewed themselves not as the master, but as a part of a balanced universe. In this belief system, they often perceived an imbalance caused by humans, so they developed ceremonies that would retain and reestablish the harmony with nature. These rituals and ceremonies were important for maintaining a belief in unseen powers and the unity with fundamental life forces inherent in all things (Ibrahim & Cordes, 1993).

The Western view often portrayed nature as dangerous, or there to be used. Other life forms were important only in terms of their usefulness to humanity, especially when development and profit motive were at work. Spirituality became tied to various religious doctrines and the belief that civilization, not nature, conveyed the sacred lifestyle. Ritual became inferior and was not incorporated into daily living, because people's language-bound mentality promoted the belief that symbols were too simplistic (Ibrahim & Cordes, 1993). Nature as a spiritual connection became further removed from daily existence.

Currently, a renewed interest in the spiritual side of life — moral values, compassion, and respect for other humans and life forms—is emerging in American culture. In reaction to urbanism, impersonal transactions and industrialism, a growing number of people are exploring their inner feelings, trying to develop a sense of belonging, and are discovering values that arise from direct contact with the beauty, complexities, and mysteries of nature. A recognition seems to exist that modern technical knowledge has neglected the natural at the expense of a basic human need. This new "eco-spirituality" stresses a reverence for the living and nonliving in all their diversity. For some, outdoor recreation has become a forum for spiritual attainment with activities like camping being central to the experience. Others see the movement as antidevelopment, unrealistic, another idealistic cause of the intellectual community. To them camping is spending the weekend in a park, using the mobile camper as home base, enjoying the portable TV, and propane cooking unit. It is a continuation of their urban values, using nature as a backdrop, not as an integral part of their experience. To accomplish both perspectives is a challenge to the outdoor recreation professional.

LIABILITY AND RISK RECREATION

Liability is another issue confronting outdoor recreation specialists and while an in-depth discussion of this topic is beyond the scope of this chapter, certain aspects of the issue are pertinent.

Previously, laws of sovereign immunity protected public agencies from potential lawsuits. Today, however, government is not immune and is expected to provide safe recreational experiences and environments. Liability occurs when a condition exists of being justly or legally responsible for an individual's welfare as opposed to being morally responsible. Most cases in outdoor recreation involve negligence which means that a person in charge failed to perform responsibilities at the expected level of a prudent person under the same circumstances (Ibrahim & Cordes, 1993).

The focus of this issue is on how to provide opportunities or environments for risk outdoor recreation such as rock climbing, hang gliding, and whitewater paddling without being in constant jeopardy from lawsuits when accidents do happen. Discussions center upon the use of waivers; the distinctions between trespassers, licensees, and invitees; and the level of duty owed by the owner/ manager. Many outdoor recreation enthusiasts argue their right to risk during their pursuit of recreational experiences, but managers continue to strive for a clearer interpretation of their obligations and reasonable options for risk recreation. The values of adventure programming are well understood (Zook, 1986); the challenge is to offer them in a way that allows excitement but with controlled risks.

PUBLIC AND PRIVATE RELATIONSHIPS

The report of the President's Commission on Americans Outdoors (1987) called for a greater involvement of the private and voluntary sectors in the expansion of outdoor recreation opportunities. Given that over two billion acres of land and water (about 60 percent of the total acreage in the U.S.) is in private ownership, that only 6 percent of our national shoreline is under public auspices, and with less governmental funds available for capital development, it is essential that the private sector be involved in outdoor recreation planning and management (Sampson, 1986). Many issues are involved in the public and private relationships. For example, who is to maintain private areas when they are opened to the public—government or the private land owner? Why should the private sector become involved and what costs will the public assume in the form of incentives (tax credits, etc.) to encourage their involvement?

The views of the private sector are mixed. Some corporations and individuals feel it is their civic responsibility to make their outdoor resources available to the public when the activities pursued are not injurious to the resource (see Table 8-3). It is good public relations and a potential source of income, assuming they are able to assess a fee or operate a concession. Others argue that it negates their privacy, interferes with the resource's current and primary use, and often results in vandalism. The reality of these assumptions has not been tested as little research on the subject exists. It is obvious, however, that without the private and commercial sectors' involvement in outdoor recreation, further expansion of opportunities and services will be unlikely. The options are simple: to continue to rely upon government to provide and maintain the resource, have the private sector make available its resources for public use, or allow private development on governmental property for both private and public use.

Outdoor recreation on private lands can be divided into two categories: (1) those areas that are unimproved for recreation such as privately owned forest lands, lakes and farms; and (2) those areas especially improved for recreation, such as resorts, commercial beaches, skiing areas, and vacation farms. These are usually operated as businesses or as private facilities for the exclusive use of a group such as the employees of an industrial firm or a social club. Most opportunities are within a relatively short drive from the homes of the primary users. These areas, along with the development of the intermediate-use areas to use Clawson's classification system, could possibly relieve the pressure currently being placed upon federal recreation areas and the national park system. If so, then the more ecologically fragile areas might be reserved for more ecologically compatible activities like hiking, canoeing, cycling, and tent camping.

Table 8-3
Public Land-Use Policy by Private Landowner

Rank	Reasons for Use Policy	Reasons for Non-Use Policy
1	Helps public relations	Preserves privacy
2	Too much trouble to close or post "no trespassing" signs	Interferes with current use
3	Provides income	Reduces vandalism
4	Part of multiple-use plan	Protects wildlife
5	Reduces vandalism	Avoids lawsuits
6	Public pressure to use	Prevents fires and garbage
7	Required by law	Land not suitable for use

Source: U.S. Department of Agriculture, *The Private Outdoor Recreation Estate*, 1979.

FUNDING

Closely tied to the issue of private/public relationships is the funding of outdoor recreation programs and services. Traditionally parks and national resource areas have been viewed as "commons"—available to all with no or few fees or charges. Lands were acquired through bond issues, the use of eminent domain, or as a line item in the annual budget. Tax dollars have been used to pay for the operational costs but this is not the case in the 1990s. Demand often exceeds supply and appropriations are stagnant; new sources of revenue must be developed.

A variety of options are available. Trusts can be created and funded by special taxes such as a land transfer tax, a percentage of governmentally operated lotteries can be designated for parks and recreation, a surcharge on the purchase of outdoor recreation equipment can be enacted, the use and level of user fees can be increased, a heavier reliance on concessions and private entrepreneurs can be encouraged, and/or admission and use of the resource can be restricted thereby reducing operating costs (Mertes, 1985; Crompton & Decker, 1989). Each approach has its advocates and opponents. Many people like the idea of some type of trust for capital expansion and the use of a user fee or some other entrepreneurial approach to expand operations. Most are opposed to any action which would further diminish access and use by the people who are economically disadvantaged. Finally, there are those who are for limiting admission to, or participation in, select areas and activities based upon some type of lottery, reservation system or first-come, first-served basis for a fixed number of users.

How many people should be allowed each year to raft through the Grand Canyon, be admitted to Yosemite on a given day, or drive the Blue Ridge Parkway on a fall foliage weekend? And, at what cost? How much private development should occur in a natural recreation area? At what cost? To what extent should park and recreation operations become entrepreneurial, a business rather than a service, to continue to provide quality operation? At what cost? The issues are many and complex. Any action taken will have serious consequences but action must be taken to keep the system vital.

Gender and Cultural Influences on Outdoor Recreation

Another topic of current interest is the influence of gender and cultural differences on outdoor recreation. Contrary to popular notions, women's involvement in outdoor recreation is not a phenomenon of the past twenty or thirty years. Since the earliest beginnings of outdoor recreation activities, women have been involved in these pursuits although their accomplishments were often obscured by the exploits of their male counterparts, by their relegation to the role of helpmate, and by their achievements being questioned or minimized (Bialeschki, 1992). For example, soon after the Sierra Club was founded in 1892, women made up nearly half of the club memberships, went on group expeditions, and comprised a third of the mountain climbers (Kaufman, 1986). Outdoorswomen were likely not anomalies, but rather were no more uncommon than their male counterparts. History, however, has not acknowledged the accomplishments of these females.

Currently the outdoor environment is often used by women as a source of empowerment, particularly when they participate in all-female groups. Women often chose all-women's outdoor groups because they felt they would have a better opportunity to learn and practice skills and share common interests, to gain self-understanding, to live in "stereotype-free" environments, to gain a sense of renewal or spiritual connection, to work on fear and safety issues, and to be in a supportive group environment (Yerkes & Miranda, 1982). The benefits that result from these experiences were often a result of increased self-esteem that lead to feelings of empowerment (Mitten, 1992) and have spurred a similar development for males (The Men's Movement) and for many of the same reasons. Programs offered by outdoor groups such as Outward Bound or Woodswomen often have specific courses designed for older women, women who have been battered or abused, and women who have been victims of sexual assault. These programs build upon the values attributed by women to experiences in the natural environment.

The influence of cultural heritage is only beginning to be addressed by researchers interested in outdoor recreation (Allison, 1988; Chavez, 1992; Hutchison, 1987, 1988; West, 1989). A great deal of debate exists on why cultural and ethnic differences are experienced in outdoor recreation. According to some studies the rates of participation are quite significant. For example, African Americans are less likely to go hiking or camping than European Americans but have a high rate of participation in many of the more urban-outdoor activities such as sports and picnicking (Dwyer & Gobster, 1992). Speculations focus on the differences in socioeconomic backgrounds ("marginality") or to other factors related to inherent cultural, ethnicity explanations.

Current research topics include environmental and development preferences, social patterns of participation, and racial and ethnic variations. Only recently have researchers begun to examine the role that recreation and leisure may play in the acculturation process as participants become integrated into the dominant culture and the ways that recreation may also encourage the maintenance of traditional culture.

Another area of study just beginning to attract attention is the need to address discrimination and equity issues in recreation. All of these research efforts are designed to increase awareness and understanding about diversity issues in recreation and to provide information that will be useful in policy development and management techniques.

ECOTOURISM

The private provision of outdoor recreation has resulted in a new type of recreational experience called ecotourism. In the broadest sense, ecotourism is based upon a philosophy that closes the gap between intentions and actions toward the environment. The Ecotourism Society defines it as responsible travel that conserves environments and sustains the well-being of local people (Jones, 1993). Ecotourism means more than carrying a camera instead of a gun; it means that revenues generated through user fees and royalties are used for the protection of the area and are injected into the local economy so the local people perceive the importance of the preservation of the environment (Jones, 1993). The message then becomes the acknowledgment that nature is valuable and local people see that environmental conservation is economically profitable.

Ecotourism is often associated with sustainable tourism in developing countries where the environment is seen as a means of survival. Ecotourism can be a positive force in these areas as guiding, lodging, and other tourist support services are developed. Even in developed countries, ecotourism can promote environmental knowledge, activism, and cooperative tourism planning (Hill, 1992). Ecotourism's success depends on the preservation of the natural features and the power and responsibility assumed by tourists who become ecotravelers.

Summary

This chapter has provided an overview to outdoor recreation in the United States. The development of these activities were discussed from historical perspectives that included the interest in environmental preservation as well as the use of these areas for recreational pursuits. The classification systems established by Clawson-Knetsch and ORRRC were described to provide an understanding of the ways in which areas are defined and managed for use. Organized camping and environmental education were specifically discussed to illustrate the types of experiences to be gained from organized outdoor recreation opportunities. Lastly, six current issues were identified and summarized as examples of some of the critical issues facing participants and providers of outdoor recreation.

Suggestions and Study Guides

1. Reflect upon your most recent vacation or outdoor recreation experience. What was the most exciting phase or aspect for you? Why?

2. Debate the issue: "Environmental education should be included in the curriculum of all elementary and secondary students." Justify your arguments.

3. Alaska is America's last frontier and unspoiled wilderness, rich in natural mineral resources and unlimited recreation potential. Develop a national policy on Alaska lands from the view of (a) a conservationist, (b) a recreationist, (c) an oil executive.

4. Describe your environmental ethic. What similarities and differences do you find in your ethic when compared to a Native American view or a Western view?

5. Read about a current environmental issue in your community or state that has implications for outdoor recreation. Develop your perspective about the issue then write a letter to an appropriate government official to relay your concerns.

6. Select one of the current issues identified in this chapter. Develop a position statement and debate your view with a classmate who has a different perspective.

References

American Camping Association. (n.d.). *How to choose a camp for your child*. Bradford Woods, IN: American Camping Association.

American Camping Association. (1990). *Standards for day and resident camps*. Bradford Woods, IN: American Camping Association.

Allison, M. T. (1988). Breaking boundaries and barriers: Future directions in cross-cultural research. *Leisure Sciences, 10*, pp. 247-259.

Bialeschki, M. D. (1992). We said, "Why not?"—A historical perspective on women's outdoor pursuits. *Journal of Physical Education, Recreation, and Dance, 63*(2), pp. 52-55.

Burch, W. (1984). Much ado about nothing—Some reflections on the wider and wilder implications of social carrying capacity. *Leisure Sciences, 6*(4), pp. 487-496.

Chavez, D. (1992, May). *The wildland/urban interface: Hispanics in the national forest*. Paper presented at the Fourth National symposium on Society and Resource Management, University of Wisconsin-Madison.

Clawson, M. (1959). The crisis in outdoor recreation. *The American Forest*. March & April, reprint no. 13, Washington, DC: Resources for the Future, Inc.

Clawson, M. & Knetsch, J. (1966). *Economics of outdoor recreation*. Baltimore, MD: The Johns Hopkins Press.

Council on Outdoor Education. (1989). Outdoor education—Definitions and philosophy. *Journal of Physical Education, Recreation, and Health, 60*(2), pp. 31-34

Crompton, J., & Decker, J. (1989). Establishing a federal recreation trust fund: An analysis of the options with special emphasis on a manufacturer's excise tax. *Journal of Park and Recreation Administration, 7*(1), pp. 1-14.

Csikszentmihalyi, M. (1988). *Optimal experience: Psychological studies of flow in consciousness*. New York, NY: Cambridge University Press.

Douglass, R. (1982). *Forest recreation, 3rd ed.* New York, NY: Pergamon Press.

Dwyer, J. & Gobster, P. (1992). Recreation opportunity and cultural diversity. *Parks and Recreation, 27*(9), pp. 22-32, 128.

Fogg, G. (1975). *Park planning guidelines.* Alexandria, VA: National Recreation and Park Association.

Hammitt, W. (1980). Outdoor recreation: Is it a multi-phase experience? *Journal of Leisure Research, 12*(2), pp. 107-115.

Hendee, J., Stankey, G., & Lucas, R. (1990). *Wilderness management.* Golden, CO: North American Press.

Hill, B. (1992). Sustainable tourism. *Parks and Recreation, 27*(9), pp. 84-89, 130.

Hutchison, R. (1987). Ethnicity and urban recreation: Whites, Blacks, and Hispanics in Chicago's public parks. *Journal of Leisure Research, 19*(3), pp. 205-222.

Hutchison, R. (1988). A critique of race, ethnicity, and social class in recent leisure-recreation research. *Journal of Leisure Research, 20*(1), pp. 10-30.

Ibrahim, H. & Cordes, K. (1993). *Outdoor recreation.* Dubuque, IA: WCB Brown & Benchmark Publishers.

Interagency Guidelines Task Group for Accessible Outdoor Recreation. (1990). *Design guide for accessible outdoor recreation.* San Dimas, CA: USDA Forest Service, Technology & Development Center.

Jensen, C. (1985). *Outdoor recreation in America, 4th ed.* Minneapolis, MN: Burgess Publishing Company.

Jones, L. (1993). Ecotourism: Closing the gap between intent and action. In *The Buzzworm Magazine Guide to Ecotravel* (pp. 6-8). Boulder, CO: Buzzworm Books.

Kaufman, P. (1986). Early women claim park lands for adventure and aspiration. *Courier, 31*(10), pp. 16-18.

LaPage, W. & Ranney, S. (1988). America's wilderness: The heart and soul of culture. *Parks and Recreation, 23*(7), pp. 24-31, 66.

Maslow, A. (1962). *Toward a psychology of being.* Princeton, NJ: D. Van Nostrand.

Mertes, J. (1985). Trends in land use. *Parks and Recreation, 20*(5), pp. 46-57, 83.

Mitten, D. (1992). Empowering girls and women in the outdoors. *Journal of Physical Education, Recreation, and Dance, 63*(2), pp. 56

Neulinger, J. (1974). *The psychology of leisure.* Springfield, IL: C. C. Thomas.

Outdoor recreation for America. (1962). Washington, DC: U.S. Government Printing Office

President's Commission. (1987). *America outdoors: The legacy, the challenge.* Washington, DC: Island Press.

Sampson, N. (1986). Assessing the availability of private land for recreation. *Parks and Recreation, 21*(7), pp. 34-38, 59.

Statistical abstract of the United States: 1991. Washington, DC: U.S. Government Printing Office.

Statistical abstract of the United States: 1992. Washington, DC: U.S. Government Printing Office.

Wallace, G., Tierney, P., & Haas, G. (1990). The right link between wilderness and tourism. *Parks and Recreation, 25*(9), 63-66, pp. 111-112.

West, P. C. (1989). Urban region parks and Black minorities: Subculture, marginality, and interracial relations in park use in the Detroit metropolitan area. *Leisure Sciences, 11*(1), pp. 11-28.

Yerkes, R. & Miranda, W. (1982). Outdoor adventure courses for women: Implications for new programming. *Journal of Physical Education, Recreation, and Dance, 53*(4), pp. 82-85.

Zook, L. (1986). Outdoor adventure programs build character five ways. *Parks and Recreation, 21*(1), pp. 54-57.

CHAPTER NINE

The Professionalization of the Recreation and Park System

One of the characteristics of a social movement is its evolution toward professional status. Born of some unfulfilled social concern such as the need for adequate opportunities for the recreation expression, social movements generally pass through various stages. Initially, they are directed and administered by volunteers and interested lay persons, as was the case with the park and recreation movements at the beginning of the twentieth century. Ultimately, these movements enter an era of formal organization and professionally trained personnel. Those employed in the movement seek to establish their identity as professionals and develop programs of professionalization. Recreation and parks is in the stage of professionalization (Sessoms, 1990).

Professions differ from trades and other classifications of occupations in a variety of ways. Not every field of work becomes a profession, although there are professionals in nearly every area of service. The professional is thought of as one who is paid for his or her work and whose identity is tied to an occupation. A profession has several attributes which distinguish it from other fields of work.

Figure 9-1
The Trades, Professions, and Disciplines Triad

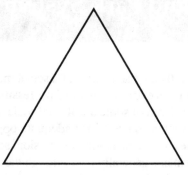

Professions
Solve problems;
form associations and societies;
offer programs of professional preparation

Trades
Are task-oriented;
form guilds and unions;
offer apprenticeships

Disciplines
Involve theory and research;
form academic and learned societies;
stress graduate study

Three basic types of occupations exist: trades, disciplines, and professions (see Figure 9-1). Each of these major groups has its unique concerns and characterizations which differentiate it from the other two. For example, the trade occupations focus on technique of performance. Tradespeople are not concerned about the theories behind their reason for service; they want to be good in the performance of their responsibilities. They offer a direct and immediate product or service and generally form guilds and unions. Machinists, carpenters, sheet-metal workers, truckers, and dry cleaners are tradespeople.

The disciplines are concerned with the furthering of the knowledge of their field of study through research and scholarly debate. They are more concerned about what their peers think about their study than they are about the public's assessment of their productivity and value. Advances in conceptual understanding and thinking about human behavior or the world in which we live tend to be their major interest. They form learned societies. Geologists, geographers, economists, sociologists, and historians are members of specific disciplines.

Professions tend to be a blend of the trades and disciplines. They tend to apply the techniques of specific trades and the theories of selected disciplines to some specific social problem or concern. This is readily apparent in the field of medicine, where the surgeon has to be skilled in the use of the scalpel while also being a student of anatomy and physiology. Professions also develop their own theories and methods to deal with the social concerns which brought them into existence. Those theories and practices become a part of the body of knowledge and practice which sets them apart. They also tend to form professional societies and associations and are always aligned with a specific field of work.

The relationship between a field of work and a profession is significant but somewhat confusing. Frequently, both appear to be one and the same. In fact, a field of work may embrace several kindred professions. The field of healthcare offers a good example. Within it are many professions such as medicine, nursing, and dentistry as well as such trades as laboratory and x-ray technology. Also within the healthcare field are various disciplines such as biochemistry, biophysics, and anatomy. All those who work in the healthcare field are health professionals (as opposed to volunteers and amateurs), yet only those who are licensed to practice medicine are members of the medical profession.

Parks and recreation is a field of work. It provides employment for a wide range of professionals from a variety of trades, disciplines, and professions. Foresters, geographers, economists, wildlife biologists, landscape architects, physical educators, and recreators work in the field of parks and recreation. But who are the recreation professionals? Does the type of employing unit such as a resort, local government, private hospital or travel agency define the profession or is it the training and expertise of the practitioner? Does a unique role in the field of parks and recreation exist that can only be filled by those who have been professionally prepared as recreation specialists? What constitutes that unique role and how does it differ from the other professions, trades, and disciplines who provide employees in the field of park and recreation services?

To get a better understanding of professionalization and the conditions necessary for the emergence of the park and recreation profession, the criteria of a profession must be examined. According to those (Shapiro, 1970) who study professions, those criteria are: (1) an alliance with some social concern, generally evolving because of some social condition which needs corrective action; (2) development of societies or associations; (3) establishment of a code of ethics and a sense of loyalty to the profession; (4) development a specialized body of knowledge and technique; (5) establishment of programs of professional education, training, and accreditation; and (6) institutionalized programs of certification and licensing.

The park and recreation movement, in its attempt to become a profession, has either met each of these criteria or has instituted programs to achieve them. It has allied itself with the social concern of providing opportunities and systems for the meaningful use of leisure and has been the only profession to directly articulate this concern. Of all of those employed within this field of work, only the recreation professional is uniquely concerned with the development and operation of the recreation and park system. The concerns of others interested in recreation services are rather specific: the study of leisure behavior, the design of recreation spaces, the maintenance of equipment and apparatus, the marketing of resources and services, the instructing of specific skills, and so on. Those promoting parks and recreation as a profession have established programs of professional preparation, organized professional societies, and instituted programs of certification and accreditation. Each of these actions and other distinguishing characteristics of the profession are discussed in this chapter.

Professional Recreation and Park Associations

The significance of recreation and park services in modern society is partially reflected in its advance as a profession. In addition to developing its own body of literature, research journals, and code of professional ethics, recreation and park professionals have established several organizations, associations or societies, dedicated to the advancement and improvement of recreation and parks as a profession.

These professional groups have given the movement and those preparing to enter it a chance to pool their common interests for their own benefit and that of society. Mutual interests, concerns, and experiences are shared through professional organizations. They provide a means for establishing and developing standards, for exchanging information and ideas, and for developing and influencing public action.

A variety of professional societies have identified themselves with parks and recreation throughout the years. Some have continued to serve the specific interests of a select clientele, whereas others have merged to form larger organizations which speak for a collective view (see Figure 9-2, page 286). The largest professional park and recreation organization is the *National Recreation and Park Association (NRPA)*. It came into existence in 1966 as the result of merger of five smaller organizations. They were:

The *American Institute of Park Executives (AIPE)* evolved from the New England Association of Park Superintendents, which was founded in 1898 and later known as the American Association of Park Superintendents. The American Institute of Park Executives members were drawn from executive positions in public parks throughout the United States and Canada. The Institute had a commissioners' section and a branch organization including the Midwest Institute of Park Executives, the California Society of American Institute of Park Executives, and the New England Park Association.

The *National Recreation Association (NRA)* was organized in 1906 as the Playground Association of America. As the first organization to address recreation specifically, this group was a major force in the development of the recreation movement for sixty years. The NRA membership included both professional and private citizens concerned with providing recreation opportunities for people of all ages. It was a service organization that implemented its programs by operating district, national, and international offices.

The *National Conference on State Parks (NCSP)* was founded in 1921 as a professional and service organization for those employed by federal and state natural resource agencies. Interested lay persons, especially conservationists, were also encouraged to be members. The purpose of the organization was to provide information to the public on the values and functions of state parks, historic sites, monuments, and recreation preserves. It encouraged the study of natural history and science, the preservation of wildlife in a natural setting, and the conservation of the natural environment.

The *American Association of Zoological Parks and Aquariums (AAZPA)* was established as an affiliate of the American Institute of Park Executives in 1924. Zoological gardens and aquariums were closely allied to the public park system, but their personnel require substantially different knowledge from that required of general park and recreation administrators. For this reason, the AAZPA was organized to provide a professional association for zoo and aquarium directors, curators, and other professionals concerned with the preservation of wildlife and its display for the general public.

The *American Recreation Society (ARS)* was established in 1938 as the Society of Recreation Workers of America. The primary objective was to unite, in one organization, all recreation professionals in the United States. To accommodate the special interest groups comprising the recreation movement, sections were created within the ARS so that those working in the armed forces, hospitals, industry, colleges and universities, public agencies, rural recreation services, and voluntary organizations could identify with their colleagues who also worked in those settings. The American Recreation Society was opened primarily to those employed in the field of parks and recreation and viewed itself as a professional rather than a service association.

Professionals Unite

During the first half of the twentieth century, these five organizations were the principal leaders in the development of recreation and parks as a profession. Each group had a different philosophy, direction, and scope which made cooperation difficult, although many of the same individuals often belonged to more than one group. As World War II drew to a close, however, various leaders in these organizations realized that the United States was on the threshold of a new leisure era that would require the combined effort of all. Unity within the profession seemed essential.

Professional and lay leaders concerned with resource management and recreation programming agreed that separate professional organizations were no longer practical and that some means should be found to unify them into a single body. The first discussions of unification came in 1948 when the Athletic

Figure 9-2
The Recreation and Parks Family Tree

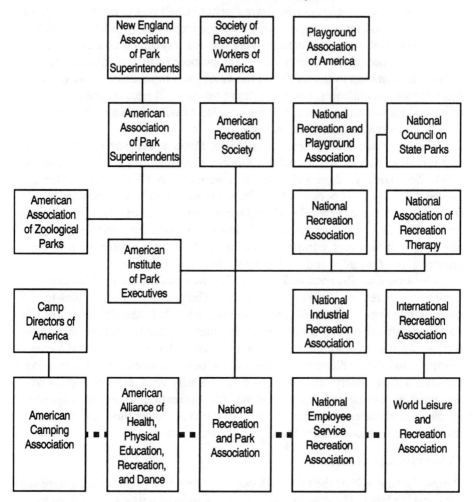

Institute financed a meeting between officials of the American Institute of Park Executives and the American Recreation Society. Although little was accomplished at this gathering, the merger seed was planted and sporadic talks continued throughout the 1950s.

In 1958, the American Recreation Society and the American Institute of Park Executives each appointed committees to further explore the possibility of unification. Across the nation, local park and recreation systems were merging into single units, and the federal government had created the Outdoor Recreation Resources Review Commission. The time seemed right for a meaningful dialogue. Talks continued for the next year, and in September of

1959, a Joint Committee of AIPE and ARS was established. Simultaneously with these deliberations, the American Recreation Society and the National Recreation Association conducted a series of exploratory talks. The members generally agreed that merger was a feasible and desirable idea.

As talks progressed, the executive director of the American Institute of Park Executives was directed by the AIPE Board in 1963 to enter negotiations with the National Recreation Association, the American Recreation Society and any other national park and recreation organizations to seek unification or federation. A forum was held for representatives of these three organizations at the National Recreation Congress later that month, where the report of the National Recreation Association—American Recreation Society Study Committee was presented.

In 1964 a merger plan was approved in principle at a joint meeting of the Boards of the American Recreation Society and the American Institute of Park Executives. Three months later, the National Recreation Association presented a counterproposal to merge all three organizations. The primary merger obstacle had been the makeup of the new organization's governing board; the issue was one of representation of lay and professional members. Both the American Recreation Society and the American Institute of Park Executives were comprised of professionals while the board of directors of the National Recreation Association was composed totally of lay leaders. Representatives of the National Recreation Association stated firmly that they would not enter any agreement unless the corporate board of the organization was comprised primarily of lay representatives. Eventually, the American Recreation Society and the American Institute of Park Executives Boards accepted the National Recreation Association's position: the majority of the newly formed National Recreation and Park Association (NRPA) Board of Trustees was to be lay persons. The merger into the National Recreation and Park Association became effective January 1966.

The first Congress of Recreation and Parks was held in Washington, DC, in October 1966. As a recognition of the significance of merger and the nation's concern for adequate recreation and park resources, its first national meeting was addressed by President Lyndon B. Johnson; the Secretary of Interior; Secretary of Agriculture; Secretary of Housing and Urban Development and the first National Park and Recreation Association president, Laurence Rockefeller. It was an auspicious beginning.

The Congress's business sessions were also productive. The National Therapeutic Recreation Society and the Society of Park and Recreation Educators were granted charters, thereby joining the American Park and Recreation Society and the American Association of Zoological Parks and Aquariums as the first four branches. The American Park and Recreation Society, the largest single branch of the NRPA, resulted from the merger of the American Institute of Park Executives and the American Recreation Society. The American Association of

Zoological Parks and Aquariums, an independent branch of the American Institute of Park Executives, was carried over into the new organization. Subsequently, the AAZPA withdrew from the NRPA and established itself as an independent professional body.

Four additional professional branches and three special interest sections have been established within NRPA since its first years of operation. They are the National Society of Park Resources, the Armed Forces Recreation Society, the Citizen and/or Board Members Branch, the National Recreation Student Branch, the National Aquatics Section, the Leisure and Aging Section, and the Commercial Recreation and Tourism Section. The philosophy of the National Recreation and Park Association is to promote professionalism through its branches. Each branch has its own officers, board of directors, and staff liaison with NRPA. The branch organizational structure allows identity with special areas of service such as education, government, and therapeutic recreation. Service to the profession is done primarily through branch activity, while the NRPA staff functions primarily to promote recreation and parks on a national level, thereby continuing the service tradition of the National Recreation Association. The section structure allows those who have a common interest in a specific service area or group to interact around that interest regardless of their branch or section affiliation.

The goals of the National Recreation and Park Association are (1) to promote awareness of, and support for, the values of recreation and parks in the lives of individuals; and (2) to provide services that contribute to the development of the National Recreation and Park Association members. It is financially supported through membership fees, public contributions, self-generated revenue, endowments, and grants. The NRPA national headquarters are in Arlington, VA; it operates five regional service centers. In 1991, approximately 25,000 people were members of NRPA.

To implement its goals, NRPA established six major program thrusts. They include: research and experimentation, information dissemination, education and professional development, awards and recognition, interagency liaison, and public relations.

1. *Research and Experimentation.* NRPA has conducted a wide range of surveys and studies on the status of parks and recreation, facility design and standards, personnel training, leisure counseling and consultation, salary studies, federal assistance programs, inner-city recreation issues, and model legislation. Its major research journal is the *Journal of Leisure Research.*

2. *Information and Public Awareness.* Probably no other function is as critical to NRPA's mission as its programs of public awareness. It has developed a variety of films, television spots, and popular publications

such as *Parks and Recreation* and *Friends of Parks and Recreation*. It operates the Joseph Lee Memorial Library Resource Center and has an extensive number of publications and video and audio cassettes for sale.

3. *Education and Personnel Services.* Throughout the United States, NRPA sponsors conventions, schools, seminars, workshops, and short courses for professionals in parks and recreation. In addition to the annual National Recreation and Parks Congress and district conventions, it publishes a national job bulletin, and has a consultant and technical assistance service.

4. *Awards.* Recognition awards are given annually to individuals and organizations throughout the country for their voluntary effort to promote better park and recreation facilities and services in their home communities. These are known as the Gold Medal Awards. Awards also are given to those volunteers, professionals, and political leaders who have made a unique contribution to the field.

5. *Interagency Liaison.* As the largest national professional and service organization in the park and recreation field, NRPA provides a structure for integrating many interests within the field including public, private, and commercial. NRPA is a spokesperson for park and recreation interests and professionals are frequently called upon to testify at congressional hearings on matters pertaining to the development of national policy and legislative action on parks and recreation.

6. *Public Relations.* Through publications, a speakers bureau, an awards program, and national visibility efforts, NRPA conducts a variety of public relations programs. For example, the President of the United States annually proclaims July as "National Recreation Month."

The National Recreation and Park Association is one of several national organizations representing the park and recreation profession. It is the only organization that is broadly based in its approach and membership and is not affiliated with a special interest or some other national movement. NRPA programs and priorities reflect the interest of the profession.

Additional Professional Organizations

An exhaustive list of professional organization activity concerned with recreation and parks would cover many pages. Consequently, just a few of them are described with respect to their purpose and function. They are offered alphabetically.

The Academy of Leisure Sciences. Formed in 1980, the Academy of Leisure Sciences is a honorary group with members being elected by the Academy. Members are recognized for their "exceptional scholarly and intellectual contribution to the growth and development of the understanding of leisure in contemporary society." The purpose of the Academy is "to promote the understanding of leisure through discussion, debate, and exchange of ideas." It is an interdisciplinary body with membership representation from the fields of business, the natural and social sciences, the humanities, and parks and recreation.

American Academy for Park and Recreation Administration. Also established in 1980, the Academy is comprised of distinguished practitioners and scholars committed to the advancement of park and recreation administration. It encourages the development and enhancement of "good" administration practices in the delivery of park, recreation, and leisure services. It publishes the *Journal of Park and Recreation Administration.*

American Association for Leisure and Recreation/American Alliance for Health, Physical Education, Recreation and Dance. The American Association for Leisure and Recreation (AALR) is one of the major divisions of the American Alliance for Health, Physical Education, Recreation and Dance (AAHPERD). The Alliance is a member organization of the National Education Association. It is dedicated to the improvement of health education, physical education, recreation education, and dance education throughout the United States. It sponsors district conferences and a national convention.

The membership of the Alliance is largely comprised of persons employed by educational institutions. The largest number of professionals affiliated with the Alliance are physical educators. Those who are primarily interested in recreation education and leisure studies are identified with the American Association for Leisure and Recreation. Prior to 1974, AALR was known as the Recreation Division of the Alliance. A number of other allied professional groups such as the National Girls and Women in Sports and Coalition for Outdoor Education are also affiliated with the Alliance.

The Alliance contributes significantly to the recreation aspects of the park and recreation movement through its publications and sponsorship efforts. It has been active in the establishment and promulgation of personnel and program standards and the support of legislation of interest to Alliance professionals. Efforts on behalf of accreditation and services to special populations are most noteworthy. A professional staff provides technical and consulting services to the membership. The publications include the *Journal of Physical Education, Recreation and Dance,* the *Research Quarterly, Leisure Today, Alliance Update,* and the *AALR Reporter*.

American Camping Association (ACA). This association was incorporated in 1910 and is made up of representatives of agencies and institutions interested in the development of organized camping in the United States. The ACA's membership consists of camp directors, members of camp staffs, educators, and others directly associated with the operation of camps or who are interested in the camping movement. It represents camping of all types: church, school, public, independent, and institutional camps. The expressed purpose is "to further the interests and welfare of children and adults through camping as an educative and recreation experience."

The American Camping Association serves as the voice of camping both nationally and locally. It assumes leadership in developing new camping areas and acts as a channel through which new trends in camping are disseminated to the membership and the public. Standards and operating codes for the improvement of camp practices are developed and camping is interpreted to related fields and to the general public. ACA consists of sections representing geographic areas of the country. ACA members receive advisory and consulting services through the national and sectional offices. The official publication of the Association is the *Camping Magazine.*

American Therapeutic Recreation Association (ATRA). Formed in 1984, ATRA has assumed a major leadership role in promoting therapeutic recreation services in clinical settings through its advocacy of certification and professional development for recreation therapists. ATRA members view therapeutic recreation as an "appropriate intervention strategy" to promote independent functioning through the development of a healthy leisure lifestyle. It has worked with the NTRS branch of NRPA in upgrading standards for therapeutic recreation practitioners.

National Employee Services and Recreation Association (NESRA). The National Employee Services and Recreation Association is dedicated to the development and improvement of employee recreation services. The membership is made up largely of companies, and their branches, that have employee recreation programs. NESRA is a clearinghouse through which information and ideas are exchanged on concerns related to the planning, organization and operation, of recreation programs serving employees and their families. It provides technical assistance and consulting services for its members, aids in the placement and training of recreation personnel, conducts surveys and research activities, and publishes guides, reports, and the *Employee Services Management* magazine.

Resort and Commercial Recreation Association (RCRA). Formed in 1982 to serve the emerging specialty of resort and commercial recreation, this membership organization promotes career opportunities in this area of service through its national meetings and job bulletins. It is a primary voice for those professionals administering and directing leisure services in resort communities and similar recreation developments. One of its major contributions has been the development of internship opportunities for students interested in seeking employment in a commercial recreation setting.

World Leisure and Recreation Association (WLRA). The World Leisure and Recreation Association promotes recreation and leisure interests throughout the world. It has worked cooperatively with various national organizations such as NRPA and the United Nations' UNESCO programs. It has promoted the professional preparation of leaders for recreation and leisure through its new program called the World Leisure and Recreation Association International Center for Excellence (WICE) in Leeuwarden, Netherlands. Begun in the early 1950s by Thomas E. Rivers as a special interest of the National Recreation Association, the World Leisure and Recreation Association, formerly the International Recreation Association, has become the voice of international recreation concerns. Its program efforts include the publishing of *World Leisure and Recreation* and the *WLRA Newsletter*, the conducting of various study tour groups, exhibitions, and symposia and world congresses on leisure and recreation. The WICE, an international course of study held each year in the Netherlands, is one of their more recent efforts.

Other Organizations

A variety of related professional societies and organizations makes an important contribution to the field of recreation and parks. Among them are:

The American Association of Fitness Directors in Business and Industry actively promotes fitness and exercise programs for company personnel as a means to improve employee productivity.

The American College Personnel Association includes professionals working with college unions, residence hall activity programs, and student personnel services.

The Athletic Institute is a nonprofit corporation whose purpose is to promote, encourage, improve, and help advance the field of sports and athletics, recreation, physical education, and health education.

The American Recreation Coalition is a group of organizations that have joined together for "the protection and enhancement of every citizen's right to pursue health and happiness through leisure-time activities." The coalition is largely comprised of single interest groups (e.g., the Kampgrounds of America, the United States Ski Association, the American Horse Council) which work to further the interest of their specific constituents by promoting the common interests of all.

The Coalition for Education in the Outdoors is a group of organizations that have come together to network and promote educational leadership in the outdoors. The group publishes a quarterly newsletter and hosts a biannual research conference.

The International Association of Amusement Parks and Attractions was formed in 1920 to give direction to the growth and development of amusement and entertainment centers throughout the world. It annually hosts a major trade show and seminar for the industry.

The International Federation of Park and Recreation Administrators seeks to promote and advance professional practice in park and recreation management. With support from various sponsoring agencies and delegates from over 35 nations, it annually convenes the IFPRA Congress.

The International Festival Association promotes the value and benefits of major festivals as attractions. It publishes *Festival Management and Event Tourism* and is closely tied to the field of travel and tourism.

The International Sociological Association has a research committee on leisure and publishes the *Leisure Newsletter* as well as conducts international meetings on research reporting.

The National Association of Social Workers has a group work section which strives to promote cooperation among education, recreation, and group workers to improve the quality of leadership and services, including the constructive use of leisure time.

The National Association of State Park Directors was formed in 1962 to "provide a forum for" the exchange of information on matters of state park operations and to encourage the development of professional leadership.

The National Intramural-Recreational Sports Association promotes campus recreation and sports participation.

The National Parks and Conservation Association is a nonprofit membership organization committed to "defend, promote and improve our country's National Park System" through educational and public informational efforts. Its awards program recognizes those who have made a major contribution to park systems at every level of government. *National Parks* is its official publication.

RECREATION INTEREST GROUPS

In addition to the professional fellowship and service organizations described, countless groups promote or represent a specific recreation activity or interest. From a list of over a thousand, the following examples are offered for illustration:

Academy of Model Aeronautics
Amateur Athletic Union of the United States
Amateur Badminton Association
Amateur Softball Association of America
American Baseball Congress
American Bowling Congress
American Canoe Association
American Contract Bridge League
American Federation of Arts
American Iris Society
American Lawn Bowling Association
American Library Association
American Power Boat Association
American Rose Society

American Shuffleboard Leagues
American Theater Wing
American Water Ski Association
American Youth Hostels
Hobby Guild of America
Izaak Walton League of America
Little League Baseball, Inc.
Model Yacht Racing Association of America
National Archery Association of the United States
National Association of Angling and Casting Clubs
National Association of Senior Citizens Softball
National Audubon Society
National Council of State Garden Clubs
National Federation of Music Clubs
National Field Archery Association
National Horseshoe Pitchers Association of America
National Shuffleboard Association
National Skeet Shooting Association
National Ski Association of America
National Softball Congress of America
National Wildlife Federation
The Nature Conservancy
North American Youth Sports Institute
Outboard Boating Club of America
Professional Golfers Association of America
Professional Lawn Tennis Association of the United States
United States Amateur Confederation of Roller Skating
United States Fencing Association
United States Handball Association
United States Karate Federation
United States Lawn Tennis Association
United States Ski Association
United States Table Tennis Association
United States Tennis Association
United States Volleyball Association

Professional Preparation Programs

The search for identity and the professionalization of parks and recreation has
also been reflected and influenced by programs of professional preparation of
recreation and park personnel. The need for professionally educated persons
to administer and operate park and recreation systems was recognized during

the formative years of the movement. As early as 1911, short courses and training manuals for instruction of playground workers were being prepared. Land-grant colleges were being encouraged to offer courses in park design and resource management through schools and departments of forestry and landscape architecture. By 1941, three national workshops on the nature and content of college-based recreation curricula had been conducted and the acceptance of parks and recreation as a legitimate academic major was insured.

According to the National Recreation and Park Association, over 260 institutions of higher learning reported having a recreation and parks major in 1990 (Bialeschki, 1992). See Figure 9-3. Of this number, ninety-six were accredited. No reporting of the actual number of students majoring in leisure studies was available, but certain trends were discernible including student interest, degree program enrollments, and graduation/placement data. Therapeutic

Figure 9-3
Number of Colleges and Universities Reporting
A Parks and Recreation Curricula 1930-1990

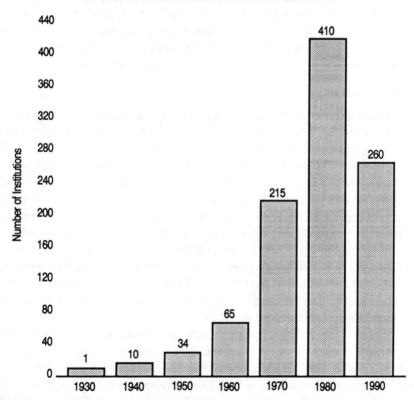

Source: Society of Park and Recreation Educators, National Recreation and Park Association, *1992 SPRE Curriculum Study.*

recreation was the most popular specialty at the baccalaureate level while administration continued to be the most frequently mentioned concentration for graduate study.

The growth of parks and recreation parallels the acceptance of recreation and parks as a career field. In 1960, prior to the expansion of the outdoor recreation interest, only 62 colleges and universities offered instruction in parks and recreation; the majority of these were domiciled in departments of Physical Education or Education (Sessoms, 1961). With the growth of the leisure industry and the expanded involvement of governmental agencies at all levels of recreation and park services, the number of positions in parks and recreation grew more rapidly than did the supply of professionally prepared graduates. In 1967, the National Recreation and Park Association (1969) conducted an analysis which projected the employment of over a million persons by park and recreation departments in 1985. As a result of these findings, both two-year and four-year institutions began developing curricula for the preparation of parks and recreation technicians and professionals. High school guidance counselors began recommending recreation and parks as a career. Shifts in curriculum content also occurred as an increasing number of programs were established in departments and colleges of natural resources and forestry, or established as independent departments of parks and recreation administration or departments of leisure studies and recreation administration.

The Job Market

In the 1980s, thousands of students were graduating each year from recreation and park curricula. These numbers, coupled with budget freezes and job cutbacks in communities and voluntary agencies, were limiting the potential employment opportunities of recreation personnel in many regions of the country. As Richard Kraus (1978) wrote, "The challenge today is no longer to encourage great numbers of new applicants to enter the recreation and park field. Instead, the profession hopes to strengthen the overall job market for recreation professionals by (a) identifying and creating new potential areas of employment for recreation graduates; (b) establishing new types of curricula which are more closely in touch with growing employment opportunities, changing job roles, and community expectations; and (c) improving the process of professional education and job placement, to ensure that qualified candidates find appropriate entry-level employment" (p. 291).

The field is responding to Kraus's challenge. Throughout the decade, opportunities in commercial recreation, travel and tourism and the private, nonprofit sector were exploding. *U.S. News and World Report* cited it as a "Blossoming Field," (Kraus, p. 349) while the U.S. Census reported that over 1.25 million were employed in parks and recreation. Of that number, 263,000 and 237,000 were in public recreation or therapeutic recreation positions, respectively

(Kraus, p. 350). The profession is growing and changing, including a greater presence of females at all levels of responsibility (Henderson & Bialeschki, 1990). It is also increasingly being characterized by competition for public financial support. If parks and recreation is to get a fair share of gifts and tax dollars, graduates must have management as well as programming skills.

Curriculum Focus

A variety of organizational patterns have characterized the development of recreation and park education. During the formative years of the professionalization of recreation and park service, recreation education and park education were separate and distinct. Those students moving toward a career in recreation services were equipped to be program leaders or activity specialists. Much of their education involved courses in the social sciences and physical activity. Park-oriented students were prepared to be resource managers and administrators of large land holdings, preserves, and municipal park systems. Their preparation involved course work in design, landscaping, architecture, horticulture, and the plant sciences.

During World II and the years immediately following, the focus on physical activity intensified. Whereas recreation had been seen primarily as a means to an end by the developers of the earlier professional programs of preparation, the new curricula developed from 1946-1955, considered recreation as an end in itself. The courses were largely activity-oriented and were administered by departments of physical education and/or education. But with the growth of outdoor recreation interest in the late 1950s, changes occurred. This was the time when local departments of parks and recreation merged. New programs of professional preparation were being established, frequently as separate departments of parks and recreation. Typically they were more concerned about management and administrative practices than they were with the preparation of activity leaders or park rangers. The technical training of professionals was left to community colleges and technical schools. Programs in schools of forestry and natural resources took on a more behavioral orientation while those curricula housed in departments of sociology, physical education, and education became more policy- and resource-oriented.

The third and more recent pattern has been the growth of therapeutic recreation and recreation management as the dominant course of study and interest. Therapeutic recreation has enjoyed the benefits of a health conscious society and the growth of the allied health professions. Universities that have less interest in recreation management have placed their recreation curricula in the Schools of Health and Education (such as New York University), while those more oriented toward travel and tourism have either been merged with Hospitality (Pennsylvania State University) or Business (University of Colorado). Accompanying the shift in focus has been the incorporation of more coursework in business, the health sciences, assessment and evaluation methodology, marketing, and an interest in leisure theory and leisure education.

Ideally, programs of professional preparation in parks and recreation at the baccalaureate level should attempt to: (1) provide students with a broad general education; (2) equip them with the skills and methodologies of the profession; and (3) provide them with practical experience through internships and supervised field practicums. Most educators consider recreation and parks to be a professional field of study that emphasizes the professional aspects of education rather than a program in the liberal arts. At the graduate level, most programs offer one or more specializations such as recreation and park administration, recreation resource management, and therapeutic recreation services (see Table 9-1). Most park and recreation educators agree that graduate study should be distinctly different from undergraduate study; the development of research and problem-solving skills at the graduate level characterizes that difference.

Table 9-1
**Gender and Nationality of Park and Recreation Doctoral Students
By Specialty Area 1989**

Specialty Area	Gender		Nationality	
	Male	Female	U.S.	Non-U.S.
Administration	31	14	33	12
Tourism	25	16	15	26
Leisure behavior	7	9	10	6
Therapeutic recreation	10	15	21	4
Outdoor/Natural resources	24	8	28	4
Total	97	62	107	52

Students enrolled in a major doctoral program, fall term 1989.

Source: *Journal of Park and Recreation Administration, 9*(1), 1991, p. 3.

The stabilizing of programs of professional preparation in recreation and parks reflects a certain maturity within the profession. It also reflects a shifting interest on the part of students in a changing pattern of college enrollments. Rather than attempting to prepare students for a wide range of positions within the park and recreation field, universities and colleges are now emphasizing the entry-level positions which have a definite professional orientation. Some of the job titles characterizing those positions that are filled by recreation and park graduates are recreation therapist, community center specialist, park ranger, program leader, program supervisor, events manager, host, tour director, recreation facility supervisor, and administrative assistant. Possibly the most significant force in stabilizing curricula content and in defining the entry-level position of the professional has been the enactment of programs of accreditation, certification, and registration.

Certification and Accreditation

Recreation and parks, like other fields seeking professional acceptance, is attempting to upgrade the quality of service through the type of education practitioners receive. This quality is assured by developing strong programs of certification and accreditation.

Certification is the act of legally certifying that one has met the minimum standards required for the practice of one's profession. At present, recreation and park certification programs are largely voluntary, although some states have enacted legislation of a permissive nature, which allows communities and institutions to include the certification of recreation personnel as a prerequisite for employment. In North Carolina it is now a legal requirement that one must be a certified therapeutic recreation specialist to use that title of "therapeutic recreation specialist." The National Recreation and Park Association (NRPA) and the National Council of Therapeutic Recreation Certification (NCTRC) have been the primary promoters and supervising agencies of certification. Both have developed certification examinations, each administering their first exam in 1990. Both organizations also require continuing professional education in the form of continuing education units (CEUs) for continued certification.

Most professionals advocate certification and licensing as acts of public protection. When certification is a requirement, the public is assured that employees have achieved a certain level of education, training, and/or experience. Certification says nothing, however, about the quality of the individual's experience or ability to perform. Opponents to certification argue that it is an act of exclusion because the field of parks and recreation may be closing out some individuals who could make a significant contribution to the profession simply on the basis of their failure to meet an educational or some other experience requirement. Furthermore, they argue that until the parks and recreation profession has defined which positions are professional positions, certification lacks validity.

Closely akin to certification is the act of registration. Following the lead of many state recreation societies, the National Recreation and Park Association approved a model registration plan in 1973 to differentiate between the professional and technician levels of responsibility. It became the basis for its National Certification effort which was implemented in 1981 by the NRPA Board of Trustees. The NCTRC certification program has its grounding in the work of the Council for Advancement of Hospital Recreation which was a registration agency. The move from registration to voluntary certification and the inclusion of the passing of a certification examination by both groups is a strong indication of a growing sense of professionalism. The next step is to enlist the support of city managers, civil service commissioners, hospital administrators, and other directors of personnel to make certification a requirement when one is employed in a professional recreation position.

The type of certification system used by a profession is directly related to its concept of a profession. When it accepts a bureaucratic model of action it tends to assume that each level of the hierarchy requires different levels of skill and training; it assumes a multi-certificate approach. There are advanced certificates, general certificates, associate certificates, and apprenticeship certificates. Education is a field in which the bureaucratic model has been accepted and implemented. When the nonbureaucratic or peer model is used, there tends to be only one level of certification—that of being a professional. Medicine and law use the peer model. Using the peer model is the direction recreation and therapeutic recreation have chosen to go with the Certified Leisure Professional (CLP) through NRPA and the Certified Therapeutic Recreation Specialist (C.T.R.S) through NCTRC. Both certify paraprofessionals as Certified Leisure Associates (CLA) and Certified Therapeutic Recreation Assistant (CTRA) through their respective programs.

Accreditation

Closely related to certification and registration is accreditation. Accreditation is a process by which colleges and universities are judged to have met the minimum requirements and standards for the preparation of students. Institutions and programs are accredited; individuals are certified or registered (Keller and Carter, 1989). Since 1963, a major effort on the part of professional recreation organizations to have parks and recreation accepted as a field needing an accreditation program has occurred. After several years of work to develop standards and procedures by an early committee and later the National Recreation and Park Association, a proposal for consideration was set forth in 1973 to the National Commission on Accreditation. The proposal was received but not approved. The park and recreation profession was encouraged by the Commission to continue its work in this area and to establish its own voluntary accreditation process. Accreditation for parks and recreation curricula became a reality in 1974 when the NRPA Board of Trustees, in cooperation with the Recreation Division of AAHPERD, established the National Council on Accreditation, later to be known as the Council on Accreditation. North Carolina State University was the first institution to be accredited, in 1977. Nine years later the Council on Postsecondary Accreditation granted the profession the right to accredit its programs

Accreditation and certification are interwoven processes. For certification to exist, recognition of training and education is necessary. This recognition is best achieved when applicants can demonstrate that they are graduates of accredited programs. When accreditation exists, graduates from these programs are automatically assumed to have obtained the basic preparation for the profession, and are therefore qualified to practice it. In both instances, the public is protected because minimum levels of quality are assured through experience and training. Accreditation like certification, however, has a restrictive effect; those opposing accreditation hold that time for experimentation is needed before a final model of professional preparation is accepted. Those advocating accreditation argue that as a result of it, educational planning will become more specific and more effective. Furthermore, advocates argue it will encourage the creation of independent academic departments of leisure services and/or recreation and parks rather than being a division within an existing department or school system such as physical education or forestry. Finally, they hold that accreditation will assist recreation and park curricula in securing additional fiscal resources and will aid recreation and parks in achieving recognition as a legitimate field of academic study.

At present, accreditation is concerned primarily with professional preparation at the baccalaureate level of training. No accreditation is done of two-year and graduate programs, although the two-year curricula have received guidance from the U.S. Office of Education, the Bureau of Education for the Handicapped, and the Society of Park and Recreation Educators (Kraus, p. 285).

Other Related Programs

Professionalization of parks and recreation has also been aided by the actions of various civil service systems and the demands of the profession for more programs of continuing education and professional development. In many states civil service systems and their counterparts determine the procedures to be used in the selection and employment of personnel for recreation and park systems. These systems generally include specific eligibility requirements such as residence requirements, examination scores, educational and experience requirements, and other personal and skill requirements consistent with the rules of affirmative action. Some personnel systems have included graduation from accredited curricula and/or certification or registration with the professional recreation agency as an eligibility requirement for specific position titles. In 1979 the National Recreation and Park Association urged the Office of Personnel Management (formerly the U.S. Civil Service Commission) to professionalize the entire recreation series which included both the GS188 recreation speciality job series and the nonprofessional GS023 outdoor recreation planner and GS025 park management series. Although these actions were not totally approved by the Office of Personnel Management, they further demonstrated the growing concern of recreators for identity and professionalization.

Professionals have also become aware of the need for programs for continuing education and professional development. In keeping with this, several universities and the National Recreation and Park Association have created a variety of "professional" schools such as the Revenue Resources Management School (NC State University and NRPA) and the Executive Development

School (Indiana University) to accommodate the demand. These efforts have been complemented by the programs of the National Park Service (the Rocky Mountain Training Institute and the Allbright Center), the U.S. Forest Service (Project Learning Tree) and the Great Lakes Park Training Institute. The value and importance of continuing education have been reinforced by tying it to certification.

Summary

The field of parks and recreation has undergone and is undergoing various professionalization efforts. Among the efforts are the establishment of professional associations and societies; the development of specific programs of professional preparation; the creation and implementation of programs of certification, registration, and accreditation; and the recognition on the part of "the profession" of its identity and the unique role played by those who call themselves "professionals."

In the formative years of parks and recreation, the professional was seen as one who developed and supervised activities such as nature hikes, tennis tournaments, and playground programs, or one who managed a physical resource such as a park. Today, the professional is more than an activity instructor or park ranger. The roles assumed by park and recreation professionals include manager, administrator, community organizer, therapist, educator, and policy formulator. These roles require a different set of skills and understanding than were required by those who served the park and recreation movement in the past. They do not negate the continuing need for program and activity personnel, but do suggest change in the way the public and the recreation profession defines the responsibility of the recreator. Parks and recreation is a profession in evolution.

Suggestions and Study Guides

1. Talk with a recreation and park professional about his or her professional organizations and views of professionalism. What does he or she see as the primary function of a professional organization? How do our present professional organizations measure against those expectations?

2. Do you feel recreators should be registered or licensed to practice their profession? Why? Can recreation and parks ever emerge as a profession without implementing some type of certification procedure?

3. Who is the recreation and park professional? Should all individuals employed by a recreation and park agency be professionals? Which positions are professional positions? What makes them so?

4. Design the ideal curriculum for the preparation of park and recreation professionals. What types of educational experiences and subject matter should be included in the curriculum? Compare your approach to that taken by the Council on Accreditation. If there are differences in approach, justify your position.

References

Bialeschki, D. (1992). The state of parks, recreation and leisure studies curricula. *Parks and Recreation, 27*(7), pp. 72-76, 95.

Crompton, J. (1991). A profile of students in recreation, park, and tourism doctoral programs at eight major U.S. universities. *Journal of Park and Recreation Administration, (9)*1 pp. 1-12.

Henderson, K. & Bialeschki, D. (1990). The feminization of the leisure service profession: Possible explanations and implications. *Journal of Park and Recreation Administration, 8*(3), pp. 1-12.

Keller, J. and Carter, M. (1989). Credentials for our growing profession. *Parks and Recreation, 24*(12), pp. 46-50, 64.

Kraus, R. (1978). *Recreation and leisure in modern society.* Santa Monica, CA: Goodyear Publishing Company.

National Recreation and Park Association. (1969). *Supply/demand study, professional and preprofessional recreation and park occupations.* Washington, DC: Author.

Sessoms, D. (1961). Recreation education in American colleges and universities today. *American Recreation Journal, 1*(7), pp. 28.

Sessoms, D. (1990). On becoming a profession: Requirements and strategies. *Journal of Park and Recreation Administration, 8*(4), pp. 33-42.

Shapiro, I. (1970). *A history of the professionalization of recreation administration.* Unpublished doctoral dissertation, University of North Carolina, Chapel Hill.

CHAPTER TEN

The Future

Speculating about the future is fun. What will tomorrow hold? Will there be another World War or Great Depression? Who will the Bulls play in the NBA finals? Will the next U.S. president be female? The list of speculative questions is endless.

Why seek to know the future? We can only live in the present and that present is ever changing. The direction of change is sometimes predictable and sometimes unpredictable. In many instances, however, the future is determined by present actions. In a sense, each individual creates his or her own future each day. It is necessary to plan for the future or have a vision for the future so each of us can create it and not just let it happen. Further it is useful to examine both the probable future as well as the preferable future to see what each individual may do to influence the kind of future that promotes a high quality of life.

A variety of techniques have been developed to forecast tomorrow's behaviors. For the most part, they tend to be satisfactory when dealing with time periods of fewer than five years; long-range forecasting has been less successful. One technique is to examine trends over a period of time to begin to extrapolate futures.

A popular example of this use of trends is the work of John Naisbitt and his colleagues in his bestsellers *Megatrends* (1982) and *Megatrends 2000* (1990). The trends identified represent social forecasting based on the trends information available about what is happening in society. Naisbitt suggests that without a structure or a frame of reference for thinking about the world, a vast amount of data will go right by people. For the 1990s, Naisbitt suggested, for example, that a renaissance in the arts will occur, global lifestyles will be mixed with national culturalism, a decade of women in leadership will emerge, and that a religious revival of the new millennium will occur.

Possibly the most frequently used method in parks and recreation for forecasting has been the plotting of trends of past behaviors and current actions based upon mathematical models and statistical data. This technique has been used in the recreation and park system for developing next year's operating budget, projecting program or visitor participation, or to plan capital construction projects.

Another technique is to rely upon the intuition and judgment of experts. Inherent in this process is the reading of dynamics affecting change and the ability of knowledgeable individuals to correctly assess their impact in specific areas of life functioning. For the most part, this technique has been used in developing long-range policies or conceptualizing the nature of a given program such as the scope and concept of future program needs. Whyte (1992) used the Delphi futures forecasting technique to solicit the opinions of 36 recreation administrators and scholars to explore the key trends and issues impacting local government recreation and park administration in the 1990s. They identified infrastructure deterioration, increased crime in communities and parks, declining park and recreation budgets, increased competition for tax resources, and massive public sector debt as the major trends in the 1990s.

A final approach is to write a variety of scenarios for the future, then carefully monitor each to see which scenario seems to be most accurate. A scenario is basically a well-thought-out story based on a careful "reading" of the forces which shape behavior and their interdependency upon each other. Scenario writing is couched in a holistic view of people and their environments. The value of scenario writing lies in the reader's ability to understand the scenario, its bases, and then to determine the implications for practice. An example of how one scenario might look is included below.

> In the socialist feminist view of the world in 2020, a modified governmental structure exists that is still largely controlled by patriarchy. However, the patriarchy is sensitive to aspects of race, class, and gender and how these intersect to create oppression. Women are not favored more than any other group; however, there is an acknowledgment that women have been oppressed in a society that has viewed "different" as deviant. The power of the

system rests in the power of the people to make laws for the common good. Women have benefited from all the social reforms that have taken place.

While women are not singled out specifically, their lives are less oppressed, and they have gained status and opportunity as a result of the socialist feminist perspective...Leisure is considered important for all because of its recuperative value. Many leisure opportunities exist with a focus on the improvement of physical, mental, and emotional health. Access to leisure is equal regardless of gender, race, or class. Leisure is affordable to all and provided for by the government. The government controls leisure policy with input from the people and leisure is considered necessary for the overall health of the nation (Henderson, Bialeschki, Shaw, & Freysinger, 1989, p. 150-151).

From this scenario, one might conclude we may be headed for a future society that values achievement rather than acquisitions with a work force where gender, race and ethnicity are not related to opportunity. The scenario suggests that all people will partake in the making of laws for the common good. In such a world "leisure is considered important for all because of its recuperative value." Many leisure opportunities will exist with a focus on the improvement of physical, mental, and emotional health.

Regardless of the technique or method used, the key to understanding the future is to understand the present. Understanding involves the identification of major dynamics that affect the daily lives of people and the assessment of their impact on the future. In other words, the past, present, and future are interrelated and interdependent. For example, consider the relationship of population to healthcare services. The "baby boom" of the 1940s and early 1950s, with a declining birthrate thereafter, has given the United States a maturing population with a median age of 33 in 1991 (*Statistical Abstract...*, 1991). This maturing population, coupled with present medical and healthcare technologies and approaches, will result in a doubling of the percentage of persons 65 or older in 2025, when one out of five persons will be 65 or older. Geriatrics rather than pediatrics may be the specialty in demand. The nursing home and daycare programs for older adults may be almost as prevalent as nursery schools and well-baby clinics.

The future is affected by both technological achievements and social evolution. To some extent, it is easier to anticipate the technological than the social. Who would have forecast in the late 1980s the social events that occurred in the falling of the Berlin wall and the demise of the former Soviet Union? It was certainly easier to predict the explosion of electronic mail use than the civil war and "ethnic cleansing" which took place in Bosnia in the early 1990s. Planners in the future must be more sensitive to social changes than they have been in the past. Technology does not have the answers to all problems; some require a political and social solution rather than a technological one.

Forces of Change

In a static society with no change, the future is like the present. In a dynamic society, the future is being created each day and requires people to modify their behaviors accordingly. What are the dynamics which cause change that will determine future behaviors? Among the major ones are (1) population patterns, (2) technological achievements, (3) the use and development of resources, (4) changes in the environmental health, (5) the occurrence of war or a major catastrophe, and (6) the development of new theories or changes in attitudes and beliefs (see Table 10-1).

Students of parks and recreation should be students of demography. A host of social changes are directly related to population patterns. The birth-rate, death rate, lengths of life, patterns of migration, marriage and divorce rates, and residential density all have an effect on the present and the future. These data are readily available through the Census Bureau. Changes in any one of the major population factors or changes in residential patterns can have a pronounced effect on all aspects of society such as the economy, political structure, and rates of utilizing natural resources.

Likewise, changes in technology affect the social and behavioral structures of society. Technologies that increase the mobility of the population or effect the hours of work have consequences. The high technologies that reduce the need for labor but increase the need for energy effect society differently than do those technologies that are labor intensive (i.e., require human labor, not the use of the machine). Among those technologies that need careful analysis are those relating to agricultural production, transportation, construction, communication, and bioengineering.

The discovery or development of new resources, or the depletion of existing resources, has an effect on the future. Through advancing technologies, people have been able to utilize earth's materials differently than they did in the past. The world's oceans have become potential resources for agro-development. Through irrigation, deserts have been made habitable; streams have been dammed and new water reservoirs created. With this technology, changes in lifestyles and living patterns have occurred. Some natural resources are being threatened by overuse which causes a search for alternative energy resources, less consumptive lifestyles, and the need to "reclaim, reuse, and recycle." Attitudes toward conservation are directly related to the presence and rate of use of natural and artificial resources.

Table 10-1
The Forces of Change and the Effect on Selected Social and Personal Patterns

Force	Effects
Population composition and rate of growth	Living arrangements
Technological advances	Work patterns
Rate of resource development and use	Governmental structures
Environmental health	Social systems
Catastrophes	Health and life expectancy
Discoveries and invention	Attitudes and beliefs

Like resources, the health of the environment determines present and future behaviors. The ability to control climates or change the environment through resource development and technology has affected social attitudes, the way time is organized and used, and living arrangements. Likewise, shifts in wind currents, the presence of acid rain, and the eroding effects of a changing tidal pattern have their consequences. Lakes die, beachfront property is washed away, and arid land becomes too expensive to farm without irrigation. The ability or inability to control the physical environment, especially its climatic aspects, shapes our future.

The ability or inability to cope with or prevent major catastrophes also shapes human destiny. Probably no single event can have as many social, economic, demographic, and environmental effects as does war. A nuclear war would change all relationships; a conventional war, depending upon its scope and scale, would alter the way people live. Likewise, a major economic catastrophe such as a world or national depression would alter our life behaviors. It is difficult to predict when a catastrophe will occur and its effects, but it is certain that catastrophic events will occur in the future and will serve as a source of change.

Even without catastrophes, shifts in population, technological advances, or discovery or depletion of natural resources, change could occur because people's wants and explanations of natural phenomena change. A shift in attitudes or values could result in changes in uses of resources, the meaning of cultural diversity in society, or in views on prolonging life. Political and social structures are based upon theories of order and explanations of existence. When these structures change, so does everything else. Likewise, changes in technology, population, and the environment can alter social values and theories of behavior. Once altered, new discoveries, new patterns of utilization, and shifts in behavior occur.

A Look at Our Near Futures

In recent years, a strong interest has developed in futures forecasting. Among the leaders are those who affiliate with the "Futurists," an international organization of social, behavioral, and physical scientists and theorists interested in the future. Rather than speaking on one future, they refer to alternative futures that have possibilities or probabilities. All futurists acknowledge the importance of dynamic change, but their individual forecasts differ depending upon the significance each assigns to each element of change within that dynamic. Using their approach, the future of leisure service delivery systems will first be discussed as a global society for the emerging twenty-first century and then present patterns related to dynamics of population, technology, personal and environmental health, and political and social attitudes will be addressed.

A Global Society

It is difficult to talk about the future by narrowing oneself to any one community, state, or nation. In today's "shrinking world," nothing happens in one place that does not have an effect on the people who live next door in the neighborhood as well as those individuals who may live 10,000 miles away. The hamburger you buy at a fast food restaurant in the United States may have come from cattle raised on land formerly in part of the world's rain forest. The athletic shoes you wear may have been made in a developing country, packaged in Oregon and sold by an English shoe firm. The recreation and pleasure that Americans undertake is reflected across the world.

Today people are connected globally almost instantly through the wonders of technological communications. In an instant electronic mail or faxes can be sent all over the world. Because of these connections now possible, we have the potential for understanding other people better. We have the potential for understanding individuals in a diverse world because communication is so relatively easy.

As a part of the leisure service delivery system, tourism has the potential as a great peace industry in the future as people meet face-to-face and establish strong, personal ties with one another. The tourism industry combined with the world parks system can make a contribution to living in harmony not only with each other but with the environment as well. Tourism makes possible the setting aside and preservation of large tracts of land as has been the case in Kenya to preserve the elephant and rhinoceros. The growth in student exchanges, cultural exchanges, sister cities, and international sporting events not only offers an appreciation of differences, but also shows the commonality of the goals and aspirations of a "human family." The collective outcomes of tourism experiences can help all humanity to appreciate the full meaning of a "global village" and the bonds that people everywhere have with one another

(D'Amore, 1988). The world is much smaller, but with that smallness also comes a concern that what is done anywhere will have potential ramifications to the global community.

Population

Several population changes in the United States merit attention. For example, since the late 1950s, the United States has experienced a declining rate of population growth. It has moved toward a steady state or maintenance society in which the replacement rate (i.e., birthrate) is approximately the same as the death rate. In the 1980s nearly all of our population growth was the result of immigration. Given the slow rate of growth and the large segment of the population known as the "Boomers," the median age of the U.S. population will continue to rise somewhat less in the 1990s than after 2000. The proportion of middle-aged Americans (aged 35-54) will sharply increase in the 1990s as will the proportion of Americans who are over 75 years old. This change has occurred at a time when the world's population growth rate continues to increase, especially among the emerging nations.

The diverse composition of the population will become more evident. A greater proportional growth among people of color will increase. It is estimated by 2035, one-fourth of our population will be either Hispanic or African American with the Hispanic group being the larger of the two. The labor force will be increasingly multicultural and multilingual (see Table 10-2).

The family has become a diverse institution as well, with many single-person households, single-parent families, and two-income families. The family is likely to grow in importance as a stabilizing factor with a slight decrease in divorce rates (i.e., but it will still remain at about a 50 percent rate) and in the growth of single-parent families (i.e., slightly below the 25 percent rate of today). At the same time, it may be difficult for the family to fulfill its traditional role without

Table 10-2
Population Composition of the United States: 1970, 1980, 1990, 2000, 2010

Year	Total Population (in millions)	White	Black	Hispanic*	Other
1970	203.8	178.7	22.6	-	2.5
1980	226.4	194.8	26.7	14.6	5.1
1990	248.7	208.7	30.4	22.4	9.5
2000[†]	274.8	224.6	35.5	30.6	14.7
2010[†]	298.1	237.4	40.4	39.3	20.2

* Hispanic included in figure for white population; no figure available for 1970.
† Projected population, using middle series projections.

Source: *1993 Statistical Abstract*, p. 14.

help from outside the family structure. The income inequality among families will increase with two-income households gaining and single-parent households falling behind. Under these conditions, family problems such as child and elder abuse may increase. Park and recreation professionals will need to increase their sensitivity to these issues and work cooperatively with other social service agencies.

Within the United States, a radical shift has occurred in the residential patterns in the last three decades, with the south and southwest experiencing an increased rate of growth while the northeast and midwest have had a population decline. Florida, Texas, and California have been the primary benefactors of this growth; their political and social influence at the national level has increased. Shifts in the population have affected federal policy concerning the role of government.

The implication of these population changes for the leisure service delivery system is significant. These data suggest an older population which, traditionally, has used its discretionary time and economic resources differently than have the younger populations. It will be interesting to see if the parks and recreation system, with its rich heritage of service to socially disadvantaged and youth groups, can adapt its program approaches and strategies to serve adults as well.

Technology

The technology of the coming decade will add to our access to information and knowledge. The high technology of the computer, the microprocessor, and the laser is leading to the information and communications age. For several years, futurists have written about life with the computer in the future. Today it is a reality. The development of the silicon chip paved the way for microprocessors and personal computers, but it is the fiber-optic cable that will revolutionize the way people interact in the future. The telephone will increasingly become the gateway to sophisticated and interactive communications services. Video, audio, and data transmission will increasingly be integrated into a single fiber-optic telephone system. When the computer, the television screen, the telephone, the CD-ROM, and the print duplicator are tied together in one system, they will provide people with communication and information potentials previously only imagined. Through the technology of electronics, the home will become a veritable communications center tied to information centers throughout the world. The computer and monitor screen will become even more of an entertainment medium and an instrument of instruction, interaction, and pleasure than it is today. They will become a tool for financial planning, budgeting, shopping, education, travel information, entertainment, and security. The list of possibilities is infinite. Because these electronic devices in the home will become so pervasive and user-friendly, they will not be considered "high tech" any longer (United Way Strategic Institute, 1990).

In addition, "mobile communications systems" such as portable phones, facsimile machines, beepers, and book-sized, portable laptop computers will make 24-hour communication possible outside the home for almost all people. Digital sketch pads, optical scanners, and voice recognition systems will gain increasing use as "keyboardless" data-entry devices. Virtually every individual in urban areas will have contact with computers in the home or work place by the year 2000 (United Way Strategic Institute, 1990). Information overload and the possible degradation of the quality of the information will become increasingly important issues.

Research is giving us more information about the world and especially about human behavior. It has provided a framework for better understanding so that more enlightened and informed changes can be made about what to do in the future. Every indicator suggests that this rapid pace of technological change will continue. The United States has lead in the development of global technology but this lead is likely to be challenged in the future. Global leadership in science and technology will likely determine economic leadership and how nations will interact in the 21st century (United Way Strategic Institute, 1990).

The technology of the present and future will have a pronounced effect upon living arrangements. For many forms of work, workers will be free from having to travel each day to a central office to perform their duties. They can stay at home and interact with their supervisors and other employees via electronic mail, fax, and computer systems. Word processors, central computers, portable computers, and similar machines have already altered our work habits and work patterns and will continue to do so. These devices have allowed the worker to be more in control of the workday, except now the worker is capable of (and expected to) doing more work. Many of the routine and clerical tasks will be displaced by the new technology. Due to robotics, fewer people will be needed to maintain assembly lines; service economies will expand. Flex-time and similar work schedules, which allow the employee to choose his or her own hours of work, will increase in popularity. Job sharing, a form of work in which two people share the same position, and part-time employment will also become more popular. These forms of work scheduling have the potential for providing more hours of leisure time and more opportunities for the recreative and leisure experiences but tend to leave the worker with less worker benefits and job security. The service industries that have employed part-time workers at low wages will provide the most available jobs. Unemployment, however, may be more of a reality because fewer people will be needed in some types of work. Further, the information technology will likely permeate the barrier between work and home having the potential for producing an indeterminate workday. In addition, concern will grow about the health effects of working at computer terminals, including stress, eye damage, and hand-muscle problems.

Technology will also influence recreation and leisure behaviors by allowing the participants to choose their time for instruction (using video instructional tapes), plan trips and vacations (using the computer travel/leisure information retrieval system), and compete with unseen opponents (playing computer games or interacting on a computer network). It may also afford greater opportunity for individuals to interact personally and more extensively with neighbors and family as people are freed from routine and tedious work. Technology has the potential for supporting and encouraging a holistic lifestyle, since the locus of control shifts from the agency or company to the individual and his or her use of the system.

Technology will also affect the tourism industry. The possibilities that exist today of guests being able to unlock their rooms with a credit card as well as order breakfast, receive messages, and keep track of expenditures all on TV are only the beginning. In the future, technology may allow individuals to enter a hotel with a sensing device that will automatically check them in and provide them with whatever services are needed using a simple programming device. These technologies will not eliminate hotel jobs but may free staff to spend more time serving their guests (*The Futurist*, 1989).

Paralleling the significance of breakthroughs in electronic technologies are the societal changes which may occur as a result of bioengineering gene research. Imagine a society where disabilities related to genetic structures are eliminated while the fetus is still in the womb or where new species of plants and animals, utilizing the same land area, provide more people with more food and better nutrition. Grasses which requires minimal watering or are virtually impervious to insect-carried diseases would be important to park and recreation agencies looking for a safe and durable ground cover for playgrounds and athletic fields. Consider how bioengineering can aid the restoration of damaged nerve tissue thereby eliminating paraplegic and quadriplegic conditions making architectural accessibility no longer an issue. These changes are within the realm of possibility through bioengineering and gene therapy; they probably will occur in your lifetime.

To a great extent, the future of parks and recreation systems will depend upon their abilities to utilize and become a part of the information system to reach citizens in their homes when they are at leisure. Technology may also reduce some of the operational costs of parks and recreation systems, particularly those involving the maintenance of facilities.

Personal and Environmental Health

Quality of life issues related to personal and environmental health are key areas of concern for the future. Although people are talking somewhat more about energy conservation particularly through such efforts as recycling, energy use continues to be up worldwide and oil prices are beginning to rise again. The

United States has 5 percent of the world's population, yet its people use over 30 percent of the world's petroleum. Governmental efforts to reduce oil use will be largely ineffective unless the price of gasoline is increased. As long as energy is "cheap," most people will probably see no particular advantage in economizing or modifying their travel behavior.

According to *The Futurist*, oil, coal, and natural gas will continue to be the major generators of heat and power during the remaining years of the twentieth century. Reliance upon nuclear energy will remain at about the same level, while exploration for new energy sources and the development of solar energy will accelerate, albeit slowly. Conservation practices will hold the key for the immediate future. Closely tied to the traditional technologies and the combustion engine are the problems of resource depletion, pollution, and environmental destruction. The most accessible oil has been retrieved from the earth. Offshore drilling, with its potential spills, is more expensive and potentially more environmentally damaging. Synthetic products, particularly petroleum-derived plastics, have given us convenient packaging and colorful containers which are almost indestructible waste products. Landfills can no longer handle the volume of garbage that is produced each day in the United States. This obvious pollution, when combined with chemical waste, nuclear waste, and oil spills, creates havoc for the environment and for the health of future generations.

The increasing cost of environmental cleanup and the rising price and lessened availability of oil will become increasingly important long-term factors to the U.S. economy (United Way Strategic Institute, 1990). The ozone depletion problem will persist and may prove unsolvable. Without substantial reductions in carbon dioxide emissions in the next 10-20 years, climatic changes from the greenhouse effect may significantly disrupt some regional economies. This global warming as it affects the weather patterns in the form of severe droughts and torrential rains may have major implications for the maintenance of parks and outdoor areas. Hotter summers may impact the use of recreation areas, especially outdoor facilities and daylight play, not to mention the additional costs of air-conditioning. Global environmental problems will have to be addressed at an international level.

Personal health and the healthcare systems will also be major concerns for Americans in the future. The link between personal behavior and disease will be prominent. The health of Americans in general has been improving, but the exceptions among the poor will be a growing concern. The quality of and access to healthcare services in the United States will continue to be questioned. The AIDS epidemic will be addressed along with issues surrounding long-term care.

With the shift of emphasis to health maintenance from mainly the treatment of disease and illness to prevention, greater attention will be given to those behaviors which maintain or improve health. Programs which emphasize fitness and wellness may even be given preferential consideration by insurance carriers. They are less expensive than programs of treatment and rehabilitation. Medical care costs could be reduced thereby creating funds to add to one's quality of life rather than merely prolonging it. Smoking, drug use, "couch potatoism," and junk food have little place in a society which values fitness and good health.

Attitudes

The United States is undergoing a transition again in its political and social attitudes just as it is undergoing enormous economic and industrial change. For nearly fifty years (1932-1980), with few exceptions, moderate and liberal groups controlled Congress. During that period, all levels of government, especially the federal government, accepted increasing amounts of responsibility for social programs and social services. Paralleling the growth of governmental responsibility was the growth of governmental regulations. To assure equal opportunity for all groups and the full implementation of governmental programs, governmental bureaucracies expanded as did the national debt. People with liberal attitudes supported a strong federal government, because they believed it was in the best position to assure equal opportunity including access to park and recreation programs and services. They also believed the government could help to break down the racial and gender barriers that prevented individuals from reaching their full potential. They were strong supporters of programs for people with disabilities and economic disadvantage.

Inspired by escalating gas prices, high interest rates, inflation, and increased levels of taxation, America's view of government began to change during the 1970s. By 1980, these forces had come together and we elected a noted conservative, Ronald Reagan, as President. A more conservative Congress was also elected. Federal cutbacks were immediate; recreation and park services, like most social services, were affected by those cutbacks, especially in terms of federal dollars for land acquisition and facility development. The shift to the political right continued throughout the 1980s. It resulted in fewer regulations and a shift of power from the federal to the state governments. Many Americans who were poor were forgotten when humanism was no longer the dominant philosophy.

It was assumed by many governmental leaders and even park and recreation professionals that the private sectors could make up the difference, that the free market approach would meet the public's needs. But history tells us that when it comes to the provision of a public good such as recreation services, the private sector approach has been found inadequate. Given this, America once again turned to those favoring social liberalism and elected Bill Clinton as President in 1992.

Scholars and futurists do not seem to agree on how Americans' attitudes toward work will change in the future. Schor (1991) in her acclaimed bestseller, *The Overworked American* argued that to reduce the propensity of Americans to work longer and longer, the work-and-spend cycle must be broken. She suggested this change can only occur by altering employers' incentives (e.g., employers reward and encourage employees to put in long hours and work "above and beyond" the call of duty), improving wages for the lowest-paid, creating gender equality, preempting the automatic spiraling of consumption, and through all this, establishing time's value independent of its price so that it can no longer be readily substituted for money. The plan Schor suggests seems overwhelming, at best. The irony of the work debate is that currently the United States and many European nations do not need all the workers that are employed (Sullivan, 1993).

Unfortunately, governments have not figured out how to take care of people if only 50 percent of them are working AND if most do not know how to use their leisure in ways other than to consume goods or look to others to entertain them. The work ethic is so deeply ingrained in Western culture that to break this cycle would create a monumental upheaval in our social world. These attitudes do not suggest that leisure is not important, rather that the notion of work is still predominant in so many people's lives. The implications for the leisure service delivery system are mind-boggling. Not only are government and the workers of America not ready for taking care of so many people with so much free time, neither is the leisure service delivery system. Park and recreation professionals, especially those in the public sector, struggle day to day to maintain a program with very little time or thought for long-range planning. Rather than take leadership for educating for a leisure society, most will probably continue "business as usual" until some major changes are thrust upon them.

When all of these dynamics are considered together, they suggest an interesting future for parks and recreation services. They suggest a society where economic growth will be slowed, where individuals again assume more responsibility for their future, where new technologies will allow for decentralized programming, and where work patterns or lack of full employment may force new opportunities for recreation and leisure expressions. They do not suggest a lessening of leisure concerns and interests, but a different approach to the provision of leisure services.

Below are some of the changes which seem to be occurring as America moves into the 21st century, a century of great change due to postindustrial values.

INDUSTRIAL VALUES	POSTINDUSTRIAL VALUES
self-denial ethic	self-fulfillment ethic
higher standard of living	better quality of life
traditional sex roles	blurring of sex roles
accepted definition of success	individualized definition of success
traditional family life	alternative families
faith in industry, institutions	self-reliance
live to work	work to live
hero worship	love of ideas
expansionism	pluralism
patriotism	less nationalistic
unparalleled growth	growing sense of limits
industrial growth	information/service growth
receptivity to technology	technology orientation

(Plummer, 1989, p. 10)

A Plan for Tomorrow

As part of their third nationwide outdoor recreation plan, the Heritage Conservation and Recreation Service (1979) included a chapter on "Future Directions." In the plan, they identified what they considered to be the more difficult problems, questions, and issues confronting public park and recreation systems during the coming decades. Their concerns were expressed in four questions that are still valid today:

1. What effect do the changes in population, social, and economic patterns have on the nation's public and private recreation delivery system?
2. What should the appropriate source of funding be for the development and maintenance of community park and recreation systems?
3. What is the appropriate level of response for all sectors including private, public, and commercial in providing recreation services?
4. What is the appropriate role for citizen participation in the decision-making process concerning the development, operation, and expansion of park and recreation systems?

Underlying all of these concerns is the ability of the system to respond and adapt to various social, political, and economic changes.

Answers to these broad questions can be found through more comprehensive planning that would change the decision-making process from being one of crisis reaction to one based upon a more diverse and appropriate set of objectives. These objectives must consider the interrelationship between housing, transportation, social and economic welfare, and the concerns for the parks and recreation system.

Needed Action

Every public service, profession, and social movements needs support to prosper in the future. The recreation and parks system has made rapid gains in the past, but these gains are small in comparison with the plethora of opportunities that lies ahead. The following needs are not listed in order of priority but do suggest a direction for future action if parks and recreation is to come of age in what may be a potential age of leisure.

A POLICY CENTER

The leisure service delivery system needs a high level, professionally distinguished, national policy commission whose task it would be to prepare, publish, and disseminate statements of matters concerning parks, recreation, and tourism. This commission would explore the recreation interests of the public, examine recreation and park developments, and identify leisure service problems before they become critical. It might result from the convening of a special National Recreation and Park Congress, a White House Conference on Leisure and Recreation, or a national study. It might be supported by professional organizations or a private philanthropy to be a responsibility of government. Preferably it should be separately endowed and should represent no single group or vested interest. The success of a national policy commission would depend largely upon the soundness and convincing quality of the policies it develops. Its recommended directions would shape the legislative and organizational patterns critical to the development and maintenance of quality leisure services.

A FEDERAL RECREATION SERVICE

The federal government needs to establish an independent recreation and park service to give overall direction to the planning and operation of park and recreation services at all levels of government. The Heritage Conservation and Recreation Services was an attempt at this type of needed service pertaining to outdoor recreation, although it was short-lived. A federal recreation service would serve as an information center, a repository of data on leisure and recreation behaviors, a compiler of resources and a measurer of demand, a source of technical assistance, and possibly, the manager of federal park and recreation services. Public recreation and park services at the community and state levels need a counterpart at the federal government level.

PARTNERSHIP DEVELOPMENT

As discussed throughout the text, the future of the leisure service delivery system is dependent upon the relationship and partnership of all its segments: public, private, and commercial agencies and businesses. The private and commercial sectors must be stimulated further to assist government in the provision of recreation services and government must create opportunities for that to happen. All are needed, and all have important roles to play. The strengthening of one should not be at the expense of either of the others.

Public, private, and commercial recreation agencies must work together if recreation opportunities for all people are to be achieved. The solution lies primarily in an increasingly clear definition and acceptance of the service role of each group. Neither the public nor private sectors can be expected to provide for the people what they can best provide for themselves. Concerns about duplication of services and "rights to operate" are less critical than the needs of the society and the disparities which occur when major population segments are forgotten or left out.

RESEARCH

The progress of recreation and park systems in the future will depend upon the quantity and quality of research undertaken. A well-defined approach is needed to carry out a continuing program of both applied and pure research. An agenda for research would be helpful in identifying where study is needed. The National Recreation and Park Association has begun to undertake such an endeavor but with the breadth of the field, it will be difficult to determine what research priorities ought to, or already, exist without involving other organizations and agencies. The need for an effective system of research dissemination and retrieval also is cited as a major concern of the recreation research community. The need has been partially addressed through Schole. Individuals who subscribe to the Schole network (NRPA) have access to all types of research that is currently "on line," but this is only the beginning.

An effective research system must involve and utilize resources of the academic community, private research firms, and research units of federal agencies. It also requires the support of foundations and private interest groups who are willing to underwrite the needed studies and investigations. Research is essential to the development of sound public policies and effective administrative practices. Studies are needed, for example, pertaining to the personal benefits (i.e., the effects of various forms of recreation expression on such aspects as the psychological and physiological well-being and behavior of participants) as well as the social benefits (i.e., community solidarity, economic impact) of recreation in communities.

ACKNOWLEDGING CULTURAL DIVERSITY

Many people have argued that recreation and parks is a right; that every citizen, regardless of race, creed, sex, economic condition, age, or physical disability, should have equal opportunity for the recreation experience. Parks and recreation professionals must be vigorous in their pursuit to eliminate those barriers which prevent each individual from enjoying that right. Much has been accomplished to open up the system to previously underserved groups in recent years, but the job is not finished. Inequalities exist between geographic areas, between neighborhoods, and between groups. The cost of remediation may be high, but the cost of discrimination is even greater.

Programs in park and recreation systems will change as the interests and social needs of a diverse population are considered. The growing disparity between the rich and the poor in the United States will likely create great social unrest in the future if not addressed. Parks and recreation have a role in addressing this problem as was underlined once again following the riots in Los Angeles in 1992. Lack of meaningful recreation programs and services was identified, along with the unemployment of youth, and a breakdown in social services and education, as a major contributor to the conditions underlying the social unrest which erupted. Various populations that have been traditionally underserved may not respond to our usual methods of recreation promotion and programming. Interorganizational networking, greater outreach, shifting hours of operation, and an emphasis on programs for target populations may be necessary (Whyte, 1992); see Table 10-3, page 322. In addition, the greater cultural diversity will require staff who are also diverse and possess the skills for working with particular populations.

The aging of America's population and changing ethnic composition will be a challenge to the leisure service delivery system. For many older people, retirement may not be possible or desirable. Different patterns in work and leisure may become commonplace as people work part-time or have periods of time off. Not only will these aging citizens be more adventurous and active but they will also want physically and intellectually stimulating activities. The focus on older people rather than youth is a definite philosophical change for the country and for the providers of leisure services.

The need to serve the growing Hispanic and Asian populations and the unmet needs of African-American citizens are equally significant. In many metropolitan areas, English will be the second language, not the native tongue, for children entering the first grade. The need to employ recreation and park professionals from these various ethnic groups, to develop neighborhood leadership who understand their cultural and social heritage, will require new patterns of recruitment of personnel and perhaps a structural modification of our current professional societies and organizations.

Table 10-3
Key Issues Confronting Public Park and Recreation Systems in the 1990s
(by Impact) as Perceived by Administrators and Academics

Total Ranking	Issue	Ranking by P&R Administrators	Ranking by P&R Academics
1	How to ensure adequate finances for capital development	1	2
1	What are the basic priorities to be protected when/if cuts occur	1	2
3	How to make parks safe from crime and drug use	4	1
4	How can parks and recreation strengthen its political position	1	5
5	How can parks and recreation compete successfully for funding	4	4
6	Should parks and recreation be managed more like a business	6	6
7	How to build on and use the wellness movement	12	7
8	How to make services more accessible to all people	13	9
9	How to increase tax support	7	12
10	How to build public trust and be accountable	7	12
10	How to foster coalitions and build networks with kindred groups	10	15
10	How to develop public recognition of the social/health effects of recreation	16	10

Source: Doctoral research of Digby N. B. Whyte, Indiana University. Reported in *Journal of Park and Recreation Administration, 10*(3), 1992, pp. 89-106.

RESOURCE PRESERVATION AND DEVELOPMENT

Recreation spaces are public commons. They are limited in number and the type of experiences they can accommodate. In the future, more attention must be focused upon the preservation and development of unique scenic areas, cultural heritage, and open spaces. The leisure experience is not limited to certain recreation area facilities or structured programs. Consequently, a systems approach to planning, development, and maintenance of all potential recreation and environmental resources is needed. The uniqueness of each element must be considered and used to its fullest extent.

Different kinds of recreational behaviors require particular types of settings; a balance between user-oriented areas and resource-oriented spaces will be needed. It is essential that parks and recreation make full use of "nontraditional" recreation areas for recreation expressions such as shopping centers, libraries, public gardens, private lands wildlife refuges, and open spaces such as cemeteries. These areas also afford the possibilities for leisure satisfactions and must be considered as complements to those areas and facilities managed by park and recreation agencies.

The provision of safe environment in which to recreate is an important issue in resource development. Crime has increased greatly in society and park and recreation programs are not exempt from this trend. In resource development for the future, planners must consider issues of safety through the design of areas and the consideration of security systems for areas and facilities. Parks are safer when they are filled with programs and people (Whyte, 1992), and this philosophy also has implications for the kind of programming that may be done. In addition, if people can be convinced that they have some "ownership" of outdoor areas and facilities, empowered citizen groups may organize themselves to address problems of vandalism or crime in local parks. Safety issues and issues of fear, unfortunately, unless addressed directly by leisure service providers, may be one of the major constraints to people's leisure in the coming years.

Finally, more thought must be given to outer space and to the world's oceans as recreation resources. Our play is no longer limited to terrestrial sites. Currently a plan exists to have a space hotel designed by 2020. In this concept, tourists could enjoy zero-gravity space walks and sports and even excursion tours to the moon. This hotel scheduled to be built in space by a Japanese firm, will be followed by a lunar hotel as the basis for an entire space-resort system (*The Futurist*, 1990).

EDUCATION FOR LEISURE

For generations, the public school system has prepared students for a life of work. Work has been the central interest of Western society since the industrial revolution. Both the skills and attitudes necessary to support a work-oriented value system and way of life have been taught. With the changing dynamics of work as the single most important activity, the educational system is being challenged to modify its approach and offerings. It must now prepare students for life in a postindustrial world. Education for leisure is a necessity. Instruction must not focus just on developing good workers, but people must be prepared for living and for finding meaningful existence in whatever they do.

Education for leisure is more than the teaching of physical education, music, and art or the providing of extracurricular activities for school children. It implies developing attitudes about life that free individuals to discover who they are and what is meaningful to them. It also suggests developing the skills necessary for those explorations and for an attitude that acknowledges a new interest can be developed at any point in time. Learning is a lifelong process; freedom is one of its by-products. As one becomes aware of alternatives and develops attitudes which encourage exploration and decision making, freedom is approached. What could be more challenging to the educational system than to truly free people, to enable each individual to find meaning in leisure?

Educational institutions also are providing new challenges to the leisure service delivery system as they find alternative ways for educating students. One such challenge lies in the implementation of the year-round school concept which is occurring in a number of schools throughout the United States. The system of having several short (i.e., 2-3 week) breaks from school rather than one long summer break has many implications for leisure service providers, especially local recreation and park departments and youth-serving agencies. Traditionally youth-programming has been done primarily during the summer and their agencies have used school facilities for many of their programs. Those facilities may no longer be available but alternatives such as camps, which have predominantly functioned during the summer, may be called upon to operate year around. Certainly the peak vacation season for many families has been the summer and those organizations that have relied primarily on seasonal employment of teens may also be affected.

RELATING WELLNESS AND HEALTHCARE

As stated previously, health issues have an impact on the way in which the parks and recreation system operates. The concept of wellness has become commonplace in discussions of the value of leisure for physical and mental health, stress management, and overall well-being. The benefits that recreation offers for health are critical for promoting the value of parks and recreation systems. In addition, with the reforms occurring in the healthcare system in the United States, the use of recreation and leisure as a treatment modality as in the case of therapeutic recreation, as well as the role that parks and recreation systems have in the area of community health, will need to be evaluated and promoted.

Related to health and wellness issues is the growing movement toward self-help. While Americans have tended to rely on the government for help, a realization now exists that government cannot do everything. People are doing what they can for themselves, forming neighborhood associations, community watches, drug action committees and the like. The number of self-help and support groups doubled in the United States between 1987 and 1990 and all indicators are that this pattern will continue.

The fitness movement as a further element of self-help has remained steady through the early 1990s and is likely to continue, although not necessarily grow, in the future. Fitness, too, is an example of people taking control of their lives. The reduction in fat intake and cutting down in smoking are other examples of self-help. The self-help is particularly evident in the number of private organizations to which people belong whether it is to address an environmental issue (e.g., Sierra Club), a recreation interest (e.g., Road Runners Club of America), or an addiction of some kind (Adult Children of Alcoholics). The emphasis on self-help has many implications for leisure services; park and recreation systems need to develop ways to help facilitate self-help. By providing information about opportunities and by providing facilities (not programs) for those who wish to direct their experiences, this may be accomplished.

LEADERSHIP RESPONSIBILITIES

The question of leadership is paramount in the consideration of the future of leisure services. The problem involves two kinds of leadership: (1) professional leadership that gives direction to techniques and program strategies, and (2) citizen involvement that gives the program validity and the movement political credibility. As a field of work, parks and recreation providers offer employment opportunities for individuals with a variety of backgrounds, skills, and professional orientations. Sociologists, economists, landscape architects, gardeners, maintenance workers, dance specialists, and technicians are all a part of the leisure delivery system. The parks and recreation professional who is uniquely prepared to give leadership to the overall operations of an agency or service system will continue to be needed.

The role of the park and recreation professional is distinct from the technician. Being a professional requires an understanding of interagency relationships, the need for long-range planning, and the significance of leisure and recreation in contemporary life. The technician is more concerned with the implementation of day-to-day activities and decisions and provides the professional with the data necessary for planning and action. In the future, park and recreation departments will increase their use of technicians, particularly since the number of part-time workers is likely to grow.

The role of women or the "feminization of leisure services" (Henderson & Bialeschki, 1990) is an issue that will likely influence the leadership of parks and recreation systems in the future. Currently more females than males are majoring in recreation and parks in universities and colleges. Women are taking on greater visibility in leadership in leisure services just as is occurring gradually in other professions. Issues will need to be addressed, however, concerning how work environments can be more hospitable to both males and females. Work environments will need to become more flexible for many women who still have primary childcare responsibilities in this society. In addition, issues that confront women in other professions such as sexual harassment, wage discrimination, the "glass ceiling," and related situations will need to be addressed so that the parks and recreation systems have the most highly qualified, competent females and males working in their organizations in the future.

Citizen involvement, particularly in the planning and policy aspects of recreation and park services, is essential. Indeed, all monumental changes in society have occurred because of citizen grassroots movements and this phenomenon offers the most potential for change in the future. As a public responsibility, parks and recreation services are affected by various political forces. The lay leadership is often in a better position to address those political forces than are most professionals. Likewise, citizen involvement in program planning assures programs of their own choice and content. With adult groups, being a part of the planning process is almost as important as the activity itself. Park and recreation professionals must nurture and develop citizen participation in the future.

BREADTH OF FINANCIAL SUPPORT

Public recreation and park services will need to strengthen and broaden the base of financial support. This change will occur through a combined effort of greater citizen support, the exploration of new funding sources, and improved long-range planning. Public park and recreation systems cannot afford to rely solely upon property tax revenues for operating budgets. Other revenue sources must be generated such as through increased fees and charges, but not at the cost of making programs inaccessible to people who have typically been underserved. Parks and recreation organizations also might do well to apply some of the proven market strategies developed in the commercial sector to the provision of program services. Among the techniques which may be used to expand park and recreation budgets and services are grants, trusts, endowments, gift catalogs (i.e., portfolios or catalogs that itemize the needs of an organization and solicit donations for those items), Friends of the Parks or "adopt-a-park" programs, co-sponsorships and corporate assistance, and volunteer services. Privatization, the assignment or contracting of certain functions to private and commercial organizations, may be another alternative way to expand services without increasing the tax rolls.

A broader base of public support and citizen involvement through a more diversified program approach is needed and should result in a greater potential for financial support. Getting citizen response in addressing solutions to critical problems may be the major challenge before professionals in the parks and recreation system. People who want high quality programs and organizations must make sure that quality is not sacrificed for quantity and funding possibilities. Increased taxation may be required.

Coalition building among the three leisure services sectors and among groups in the community is critical to the future of the field. "Turf wars" over who is responsible for what may are generally counterproductive. Public parks and recreation is only one of the many providers of recreation services but with its use of citizen boards and advisory services it is in the best position to coordinate planning and development.

As this chapter indicates, it is not possible to accurately predict the future, but many trends and issues are evident that can give park and recreation professionals information for making informed decisions about the near future but strategic planning is necessary. It is important to make plans for 3-5 years that can be revised each year so that the plans remain current with the specific situation and the rapidly changing global, national, state, and local situations. Citizen input is critical to this process as with all other aspects of recreation planning.

Political attitudes have an affect on public park and recreation services. If the public views recreation and parks as a necessity, they tend to support bond issues and the expenditure of tax dollars for recreation operations. They do not expect park and recreation professionals to be entrepreneurial; rather, they want their system to work for the betterment of the community. Interestingly, it seems this view is not dependent upon the economic condition of the country as exhibited during the Great Depression years when public recreation experienced one of its greatest moments of support. This scenario was also true during the war years and the war on poverty years. When recreation and parks have been viewed as a luxury or "nicety," public recreation has not always fared well. Given the economic condition of the national debt and the public's more recent attitude toward taxation, it is highly unlikely that local and state governments will restore the previous programs (e.g., Land and Water Conservation Fund—LWCF) which were largely funded by federal dollars.

Park and recreation professionals are seeking, and will continue to seek, new methods for funding park and recreation operations and developments. With a growing adult population, there will be greater pressure to offer self-supporting programs using fees and charges as the basic mechanism for recovering costs. The creation of land trusts to fund the acquisition of park land is an appropriate technique to replace or complement the federal funding programs such as LWCF. These trusts, created by both local and state governments, will draw support from philanthropists as well as special tax programs such as the fund generated through land transfer taxes. The scope and significance of these approaches will largely depend upon the values placed on park and recreation experiences.

PROFESSIONAL IDENTITY

Parks and recreation is a unique field of service. It is a part of the leisure service system, but it is not the leisure service system. It needs to establish and maintain cooperative relationships with the other sectors of the leisure service system but is the responsibility of those professionals within the parks and recreation system to define those responsibilities which are uniquely theirs. Professional identity will result from a clearly defined role set which is different from the roles assumed by other groups, individuals, and organizations. Our emerging body of knowledge obtained through research, as well as our programs of voluntary certification and accreditation, are assisting the profession in establishing its uniqueness. The activities of the National Recreation and Park Association and other professional associations can certainly aid that endeavor, but the burden of professionalism lies on those who identify themselves as professionals. A fragmentation of the movement into subspecialties or special interest groups will only retard the identification of parks and recreation as a unique profession.

What Is In Store?

Having identified some of the social forces shaping the present and future, and having discussed some of the needs confronting parks and recreation as a part of the leisure service delivery system, attention is now turned to summarizing some likely events and actions that will affect the park and recreation systems in the not-too-distant future.

1. The people of the United States will struggle to have more free time which can be used for leisure and recreation. While the attitudes of the public toward leisure and recreation will change as people feel less guilty when involved in a noneconomically productive activity, the reality of the economy may not allow for a great deal more freely chosen leisure and recreation. Enjoying themselves and pursuing activities for their own sake may become the only justifications needed for this sometimes scarce commodity.

2. The definition of recreation will be broadened. The recreation experience will not be defined and interpreted as narrowly as it has been in the past. It will be seen as more than sports, diversion, and entertainment. It will be accepted as any experience that provides pleasure and satisfaction, is freely entered into with no ulterior motives, and allows the individual to be at the center of control.

3. New residential patterns will develop, but the trend toward urbanization will continue. The need for environments where one can discover the leisure moment, be at ease with nature, and/or pursue a favorite form of recreation will increase as living spaces become more crowded. Interest in outdoor recreation and fitness will continue to expand although the forms of these recreation expressions may change.

4. Public concern for the acquisition, conservation, and protection of land and water areas will continue to be strong, but so will the pressures to develop and utilize land and other natural resources for residential, industrial, and tourism purposes. Conflicts between the conservationists and the developers will intensify. Compromises will likely be reached to develop patterns for using lands in ways that best conserve and protect them while not sacrificing other community and national needs. Those forces that threaten the environment such as poor management policies, overuse, soil erosion, industrial pollution, high density industrial and population use, and poor wildlife management must be better controlled.

5. Research will improve professionals' and citizens' understanding of the recreation experience and the proper administration of recreation and park systems. Research will move from the survey and inventory stages into investigations of what happens to people when they engage in various forms of activity. It will become directed toward people's recreation and leisure habits: the observing and assessing of the behavior aspects of these experiences and the impact of the recreation experience on individuals and the environment. From these findings will emerge the body of knowledge and the policies for the immediate and distant future.

6. Gains will be made in determining the optimum level of recreation services needed in a community and how that level might be achieved through a division of labor between public, private, and commercial agencies. Cooperation between and within all segments of the leisure service system will be recognized and sought. More attention will be given to determining which park and recreation services are indispensable, essential, or desirable based upon the needs and resources of the community and the attitudes of its people toward their recreation and leisure experiences.

7. The number of private and commercial recreation services will increase while the number of public park and recreation agencies will remain relatively stable. Greater cooperation will occur between the three sections as professionals in public agencies see the private and commercial services as a potential advocate and financial supporter of the parks and recreation system.

8. Experimentation will occur in the organization of community leisure service systems. In some communities, the park and recreation department, the library, the stadium authority, and the art centers may be merged into a single administrative unit, a department of public amenities or community services. In some instances, the economy may dictate the merger of these agencies; in other instances, the merger will result from a resolution of philosophical differences and an understanding of the universality of the concern for improving the quality of life through the development of more opportunities for a variety of leisure expressions.

9. As economic conditions improve, government at all levels but especially at the state and federal levels, will expand consulting, technical assistance, and information dissemination roles pertaining to parks and recreation. These consulting and service responsibilities may be assigned to a single state agency, and, hopefully, to one federal agency so the functioning of these services may be more uniform and consistent.

10. Recreation services for people with disabilities and other traditionally underserved groups (e.g., homeless, youth-at-risk, inner-city older adults) will continue to develop.

11. Parks and recreation will maintain its professional status as the unique body of knowledge is developed through research and as long as separate programs of professional preparation within universities continue.
12. The international aspects of recreation and park services will be furthered. The industrialized nations will assist the emerging nations in the organization and management of their resources so that all citizens of the world have more opportunities for the recreation experience.

These are only a few of the events which may be a part of the future of leisure services. At best the future is unpredictable, if predictability is equated with absolute certainty. The best that can be said of these forecasts is that they have their roots in the present and are logical extensions of today's patterns as we move into a new age of technology and understanding.

Leisure will be an important element in the world of postindustrialism, and recreation and parks will be a part of society's concern as we plan and develop systems to support the leisure potential. People are experiencing a change in the structure of their lives in relationship to uses of time, the value system which structures existence, and the technology which provides for survival. In the past these forces have offered more disposable free time, more disposable amounts of human energy, more disposable income, and an approach to life that stresses doing something satisfying and productive. Because of these changes, recreation behaviors have sometimes been rather frenzied and compulsively pursued. A new mode of leisure living is now possible (Gray & Greben, 1982).

The potential for leisure results from further advances in high technology and the emergence of a holistic view of life which has people in tune with nature's rhythms rather than those of the clock or the rules of the bureaucracy. Recreation and leisure expression can give people opportunities to express and empower themselves to be in control of their lives. The opportunities for leisure and recreation experiences must be freely chosen for the satisfaction derived from involvement. The potential for leisure is enormous and worthy of a system to protect and nurture it.

Suggestions and Study Guides

1. Try your hand at scenario writing. Decide what you think life in 2010 be like when home computers and CD-ROM technology will be as accessible as television is today.

2. What do you perceive the role of parks and recreation systems to be in the immediate future? How does that role differ from that of the immediate past? If there are differences in the role to be played, why?

3. What do you consider to be the major issues and challenges confronting the parks and recreation movement today? Justify your selection of issues and challenges. What do you think the park and recreation profession can do to meet these challenges and issues?

4. Given the current attitudes toward leisure and work, the present educational system, and the resistance to change, do you believe we will develop a leisure ethic? If so, how will that ethic develop, and what will its content and effect be? If not, why not?

References

D'Amore, L. J. (1988). Tourism: A vital force for peace. *The Futurist,* *22*(3), pp. 23-28.

The Futurist. (1989). High-tech hotels of the future. *The Futurist, 23*(4), p. 55.

The Futurist. (1990). Hotel for space tourists. *The Futurist, 24*(3), p. 52.

Gray, D. & Greben, S. (1982). Future perspectives II: The 1980s and beyond. *Parks & Recreation, 17*(5), pp. 52-56.

Henderson, K. A., Bialeschki, M. D., Shaw, S. M., & Freysinger, V. J. (1989). *A leisure of one's own.* State College, PA: Venture Publishing, Inc.

Henderson, K. A., & Bialeschki, M. D. (1990). The feminization of the leisure services profession: Possible explanations and implications. *Journal of Parks and Recreation Administration, 8*(3), pp. 1-12.

Heritage Conservation and Recreation Service. (1979). *The third nationwide outdoor recreation plan (The assessment).* Washington, DC: Government Printing Office.

Naisbitt, J. (1992). *Megatrends.* New York, NY: Warner Books.

Naisbitt, J. & Aburdene, P. (1990). *Megatrends 2000.* New York, NY: William Morrow Company, Inc.

Plummer, J. T. (1989). Changing values. *The Futurist, 23*(1), pp. 8-13.

Schor, J. B. (1991). *The overworked American.* New York, NY: Basic Books.

Statistical Abstract of the United States: 1991. (1991). Washington, DC: U.S. Government Printing Office.

Statistical Abstract of the United States: 1993. (1993). Washington, DC: U.S. Government Printing Office.

Sullivan, S. (1993, June 14). Life on the leisure track. *Newsweek,* p. 48.

United Way Strategic Institute. (1990). Nine forces reshaping America. *The Futurist, 24*(4), pp. 9-16

Whyte, D. N. D. (1992). Key trends and issues impacting local government recreation and park administration in the 1990s: A focus for strategic management and research. *Journal of Park and Recreation Administration, 10*(3), pp. 89-106.

GLOSSARY

Accreditation:
A process by which an organization is judged to have met the minimum requirements and standards set by an accrediting body.

Activity-Oriented Outdoor Recreation:
Activities such as softball, golf, tennis which normally take place in the out-of-doors but which are not dependent upon the natural environment for their satisfaction.

Activity:
A medium through which individuals satisfy their recreation desires and interests. Recreation activities tend to occur during one's discretionary time.

Administration:
The organization, direction, management, and control of all matters related to providing recreation and park services.

Advisory Committee:
A group whose function is to represent and interpret the constituency's desires, advise the park and recreation agency on matters of service, and advocate on behalf of parks and recreation.

American Alliance of Health, Physical Education, Recreation, and Dance (AAHPERD):
An national association consisting of the above related professions. The American Association of Leisure and Recreation (AALR) is the division of this parent organization that is most involved with leisure services.

Americans with Disabilities Act (ADA):
The legislation that guarantees the right to public and private recreation for individuals with disabilities.

Architectural Barriers:
Those impediments of a physical nature preventing access to buildings and facilities intended for human use.

Carrying Capacity:
The amount of use an area can stand before it becomes overused, thus diminishing the experience and the resource.

Certification:
The act of legally certifying that one has met the minimum standards required for the practice of one's profession.

Certified Leisure Profession (CLP):
An individual who has been certified by the National Recreation and Park Association to provide leisure services.

Certified Therapeutic Recreation Specialist (C.T.R.S.):
An individual who has been certified by the National Council for Therapeutic Recreation Certification to perform therapeutic recreation services.

Church Recreation:
A recreation program conducted for an/or by a particular religious denomination, its organization, individual churches, members, and their friends.

Commercial Recreation:
Recreation services and activities such as health clubs, hospitality services, bowling alleys, theaters, theme parks that are organized primarily for profit and provided by business people and entrepreneurs. It is also referred to as business or private, for-profit recreation.

Community Organization:
The process of organizing, mobilizing, and using the many resources of a community toward achieving some predetermined objective such as the provision of leisure services.

Community Recreation:
All recreation services and activities provided by public, private not-for-profit and membership agencies, and business and commercial organizations for persons who have a common geographical psychological, or institutional bond and common interests.

Community:
Comprised of people, a geographic territory, and a common purpose. The people are held together by psychological, sociological, and economic bonds and act together consciously or unconsciously for their concerns for their quality of life.

Employee Recreation Services:
Recreation services and programs provided for the members and their families within a business or organization.

Enabling Laws:
Acts of a "permissive" nature passed by a state legislature granting political subdivisions within the state the right to establish, maintain, and operate organized programs of recreation.

Entrepreneurship:
The opportunity to provide goods or services through risk taking and the creative development of innovative approaches and programs.

Environmental Barriers:
Obstacles, including architectural barriers, transportation, and attitudinal barriers, that prevent any individual from functioning to the maximum of his or her capacity or from fully utilizing the recreation and parks resources available to the public.

Environmental Education:
The provision of programs and services to address environmental issues such as pollution, uncontrolled development, and the destruction of natural resources.

Family Recreation:
Activities that may appeal to a varied age group and may be enjoyed in a family unit.

Forest Recreation:
Activities involving use of woodland and wilderness areas for recreation purposes; the forest itself is essential to the recreation experience.

Hospitality Industry:
That sector of the economy that allows people to find food and lodging as they travel for business or pleasure.

Infrastructure:
The highways, organizational structures, public works and services necessary for people to work or pursue leisure in an industrialized society.

Intergovernmental Cooperation:
Government units—municipalities, districts, states, etc.—working cooperatively to reach common objectives.

Leadership:
The process of leading and enabling individuals to experience recreation and leisure according to their individual or group goals.

Leisure:
An attitude or personal experience that includes a sense of freedom, and generally occurs during one's free time.

Leisure Service Delivery System (also known as *Leisure Services*):
Those agencies and organizations, regardless of their sponsorship (public, private not-for-profit and membership, or business/commercial) that provide individuals with opportunities to engage in recreation activities or leisure pursuits.

Leisure Service Industry:
The segment of the economy that addresses the free time and recreation activity interests of society.

Leisure Service Professionals:
Specialists working full-time in providing parks, recreation, and leisure services.

Maintenance:
The upkeep of recreation areas, facilities, equipment, and supplies in accordance with existing needs and standards for safety, sanitation, efficiency, and aesthetics.

Military Recreation:
Recreation services provided by the military for members, families and staff.

National Park Service:
The unit within the Department of Interior that provides outdoor recreation opportunities through the preservation of national parks and monuments, national historical areas and memorials, national seashores and lakeshores, parkways, riverways, and recreation areas.

National Recreation and Park Association (NRPA):
A professional association that addresses the broad interests of society concerning the provision of leisure services through public parks and recreation, military recreation, aging, therapeutic recreation, education, and student interests.

Natural Resource Management:
The management of land, water, and wildlife resources within a given area or unit.

NRPA/AALR Council on Accreditation:

The accrediting body that sets the standards and awards accreditation to colleges and universities that meet minimum standards for providing recreation, park, and leisure services coursework leading to the professional preparation of students.

Organized Camping:

A program and facilities established for the primary purpose of providing an outdoor living experience with recreation, social, and educational objectives. It is usually operated for a certain length of time and may vary considerably in its program emphasis.

Organized Recreation:

The provision of both supervised and unsupervised recreation programs, services, areas, and facilities by a recreation agency or agencies for a specific clientele or community at large.

Outdoor Recreation Experience:

Results from a complex set of interactions which include planning, anticipation, travel, outdoor recreation and recollection.

Outdoor Recreation:

Those activities of a recreational nature that normally take place in a natural environment and depend primarily upon the environment for satisfaction.

Park:

An area permanently dedicated to recreation use and generally characterized by its nature, historic, and landscape features. It is used for both passive and active forms of expression and may be designed to serve the residents of a neighborhood, community, state, region, or nation.

Participant:

A person not employed by the recreation agency who is taking part in a recreation activity or event promoted by the agency.

People with Disabilities:

Those individuals who have a temporary or permanent illness or disability that prevents them from functioning in typically defined "normal" ways in society.

Play Theory:

Explanations—grounded in behavior—as to why people participate in activities for their own sake. They give recreation professionals a direction for program planning and evaluation.

Private Not-for-Profit and Membership Agencies:
Those organizations that provide services for individuals similar to voluntary associations; much of the leadership of these agencies is provided by their membership.

Private Recreation:
A recreation program and/or services established under the auspices of an agency or organization which is supported by other than governmental funds such as the United Fund, private donations, and membership fees. Private agencies usually serve a particular constituency and often limit their services to a given area. Recreation services is often a technique or secondary function rather than the primary purpose of private agencies.

Programming:
The process of planning and providing direct recreation services to people.

Public Recreation:
Governmental provision of recreation and park opportunities and services available to all people. It is financed primarily by taxation and includes the establishment, operation, conduct, control and maintenance of program, services, areas, and facilities.

Quasi-Public:
Those organizations that are private and nonprofit in nature but have a public quality in that anyone can participate as long as they meet the agency's particular requirements such as personal characteristics or financial expectations (membership fee, etc.).

Recreation:
Those pleasurable activities or experiences in which one engages during free time and are motivated by the satisfaction derived from the experience. It knows no single form but may have one or more social, physical or psychological benefits.

Recreation and Park Services:
The structure or profession that provides opportunities for recreation and free time activities.

Recreation and Park System:
An organized structure of interrelated recreation activities, principles, and services that contribute to the coherent functioning of a comprehensive program.

Recreation and/or Park District:
A political structure whereby recreation services are provided as a separate governmental unit with the power to levy taxes for recreation and parks. It generally has a board or commission to oversee its operations.

Regulatory Laws:
Statutes enacted for the purpose of regulating, controlling, licensing, censoring, or supervising recreation activities in the best interest of the public's health, safety, and welfare.

Resource-Oriented Outdoor Recreation:
Those outdoor recreation activities that depend upon the use of natural resources for the activity and the satisfaction derived from it.

Service Laws:
Statutes that authorize agencies and departments to provide and operate specific services and facilities.

Special Project Laws:
Statutes that given local groups the right to act on a special matter that is of no interest or consequence to other communities in a state.

Special Recreation Services:
Those programs, activities and facilities provided for any group of individuals within a community who have typically not been included in the mainstream of recreation provision.

Therapeutic Recreation:
Those services that address the leisure and recreation interests of people with disabilities.

Tourism:
The experience people have when they leave their homes and travel to a destination to participate in recreation activities. Tourism is sometimes defined by distance traveled or time spent away from home.

Travel Industry:
Those services provided to enable people to leave home for business or pleasure interests.

United States Travel and Tourism Industry (USTTA):
The organization that provides leadership to the travel and tourism industry in the United States.

United Way:
> A community organization that exists with the primary purpose to coordinate fund-raising efforts for member groups.

Voluntary Youth-Serving Agencies:
> Those organizations that have as their primary focus youth and families within communities. Girl Scouts, Boy Scouts, 4-H, Campfire Boys and Girls, and YMCA/YWCAs are common examples.

Volunteer Organizations:
> Those agencies that rely primarily on volunteers for the provision of their services to their membership.

Volunteers:
> Individuals who give freely of their time, energy, and/or money to assist an agency to accomplish its goals.

Wilderness:
> A usually large, generally inaccessible area left in its natural state available for recreation experiences.

Work:
> Productive activity performed for its economic and/or social value.

SELECTED BIBLIOGRAPHY

General Works

Anderson, N. (1961). *Work and leisure.* New York, NY: David McKay, Co.

Andre, J. & James, D. (1991). *Rethinking college athletics.* Philadelphia, PA: Temple University Press.

Arian, E. (1989). *The unfulfilled promise: Public subsidy of the arts in America.* Philadelphia, PA: Temple University Press.

Austin, D. R. (1991). *Therapeutic recreation: Processes and techniques (2nd ed.).* Champaign, IL: Sagamore Publishing, Inc.

Avedon, E. M. & Sutton-Smith, B. (1971). *The study of games.* New York, NY: John Wiley & Sons.

Baker, W. J. (1988). *Sports in the western world.* Urbana, IL: University of Illinois Press.

Bammel, G. & Bammel, L. L. (1982). *Leisure and human behavior.* Dubuque, IA: Wm. C. Brown Publishing.

Bannon, J. J. & Busser, J. A. (1992). *Problem solving in recreation and parks (3rd ed.).* Champaign, IL: Sagamore Publishing, Inc.

Bell, D. (1959, 1988). *The end of ideology.* Cambridge, MA: Harvard University Press.

Brightbill, C. K. (1963). *The challenge of leisure.* Englewood Cliffs, NJ: Prentice-Hall, Inc.

Brightbill, C. K. (1966). *Education for leisure-centered living.* Harrisburg, PA: Stackpole Books.

Brockman, C. F. & Merriman, L. C., Jr. (1979). *Recreation use of wild lands.* New York, NY: McGraw-Hill.

Bullaro, J. & Edginton, C. (1986). *Commercial recreation service.* New York, NY: Macmillan.

Busser, J. A. (1990). *Programming for employee services and programs.* Champaign, IL: Sagamore Publishing, Inc.

Butsch, R. (Ed.). (1990). *For fun and profit: The transformation of leisure into consumption.* Philadelphia, PA: Temple University Press.

Caillois, R. (1961). *Man, play, and games.* New York, NY: The Free Press.

Carter, M. J., VanAndel, G. E., & Robb, G. M. (1985). *Therapeutic recreation.* St. Louis, MO: Times-Mirror Mosby.

Cheek, N. H., Jr. & Burch, W. R., Jr. (1976). *The social organization of leisure in human society.* New York, NY: Harper & Row.

Christiansen, M. I. (1977). *Park planning handbook.* New York, NY: John Wiley & Sons.

Christiansen, M. L. (1993). *Points about playgrounds.* Arlington, VA: National Recreation and Park Association.

Chubb, M. & Chubb, H. (1981). *One third of our time?* New York, NY: John Wiley & Sons.

Clawson, M. & Knetsch, J. L. (1966). *Economics of outdoor recreation.* Baltimore, MD: The Johns Hopkins Press.

Compton, D. M. (Ed.). (1989). *Issues in therapeutic recreation: A profession in transition.* Champaign, IL: Sagamore Publishing, Inc.

Cross, G. (1990). *A social history of leisure since 1600.* State College, PA: Venture Publishing, Inc.

Cross, G. (Ed.). (1988). *Worktime and industrialization: An international history.* Philadelphia, PA: Temple University Press.

Crossley, J. C. & Jamieson, L. M. (1988). *Introduction to commercial and entrepreneurial recreation.* Champaign, IL: Sagamore Publishing, Inc.

Csikzentmihalyi, M. (1975). *Beyond boredom and anxiety: The experience of play.* San Francisco, CA: Jossey-Bass, Inc.

Csikzentmihalyi, M. (1990). *Flow: The psychology of optimal experience.* New York, NY: Harper & Row.

Dattilo, J. & Murphy, W. D. (1991). *Leisure education program planning: A systematic approach.* State College, PA: Venture Publishing, Inc.

De Grazia, S. (1962). *Of time, work and leisure.* New York, NY: The Twentieth Century Fund.

Doell, C. E. & Fitzgerald, G. B. (1954). *A brief history of parks recreation in the United States*. Chicago, IL: The Athletic Institute.

Doell, C. E. & Twardzik, L. F. (1979). *Elements of park and recreation administration (4th ed.)*. Minneapolis, MN: Burgess International Group.

Douglass, R. W. (1993). *Forest recreation (4th ed.)*. Prospect Heights, IA: Waveland Press.

Driver, B. L., Brown, P. J., & Peterson, G. L. (1991). *Benefits of leisure*. State College, PA: Venture Publishing, Inc.

Dulles, F. R. (1965). *A history of recreation (America learns to play) (2nd ed.)*. New York, NY: Appleton-Century-Crofts.

Dumazedier, J. (1967). *Toward a society of leisure*. New York, NY: The Free Press.

Dumazedier, J. (1974). *Sociology of leisure*. Amsterdam: Elsevier.

Edginton, C. R., Compton, D. M., & Hanson, C. J. (1980). *Recreation and leisure programming*. Philadelphia, PA: W. B. Saunders.

Ellis, J. J. (1973). *Why people play*. Englewood Cliffs, NJ: Prentice Hall.

Ellis, T. & Norton, R. (1988). *Commercial recreation*. St. Louis, MO: Times-Mirror Mosby.

Farrell, P. & Lundegren, H. M. (1991). *The process of recreation programming theory and technique (3rd ed.)*. State College, PA: Venture Publishing, Inc.

Findlay, J. (1986). *People of chance: Gambling in American society from Jamestown to Las Vegas*. New York, NY: Oxford University Press.

Fine, G. A. (Ed.). (1985). *Meaningful play, playful meaning*. Champaign, IL: Human Kinetics Publishers.

Ford, P. & Blanchard, J. (1993). *Leadership and administration of outdoor pursuits (2nd ed.)*. State College, PA: Venture Publishing, Inc.

Godbey, G. (1989). *The future of leisure services: Thriving on change*. State College, PA: Venture Publishing, Inc.

Godbey, G. (1994). *Leisure in your life: An exploration. (4th ed.)*. State College, PA: Venture Publishing, Inc.

Goodale, T. L. & Witt, P. A. (Eds.) (1991). *Recreation and leisure: Issues in an era of change (3rd ed.).* State College, PA: Venture Publishing, Inc.

Goodale, T. & Godbey, G. (1988). *The evolution of leisure: Historical and philosophical perspectives.* State College, PA: Venture Publishing, Inc.

Graefe, A. & Parker, S. (Eds.). (1987). *Recreation and leisure: An introductory handbook.* State College, PA: Venture Publishing, Inc.

Gunn, C. (1988). *Tourism planning (2nd ed.).* New York, NY: Taylor & Francis.

Harris, L. (1987). *Inside America.* New York, NY: Random House, Vintage.

Henderson, K. A. (1991). *Dimensions of choice: A qualitative approach to recreation, parks and leisure research.* State College, PA: Venture Publishing, Inc.

Henderson, K. A., Bialeschki, M. D., Shaw, S. M., & Freysinger, V. J. (1989). *A leisure of one's own: A feminist perspective on women's leisure.* State College, PA: Venture Publishing, Inc.

Hjelte, G. & Shivers, J. S. (1978). *Public administration of recreational services (2nd ed.).* Philadelphia, PA: Lea & Febiger.

Howard, D. R. & Crompton, J. L. (1980). *Financing, managing, and marketing recreation and park resources.* Dubuque, IA: Wm. C. Brown.

Huizinga, J. (1955). *Homo ludens: A study of the play element in culture.* Boston, MA: The Beacon Press.

Hultsman, J., Cottrell, R. L., & Hultsman, W. (1987). *Planning parks for people.* State College, PA: Venture Publishing, Inc.

Hunnicutt, B. (1988). *Work without end: Abandoning shorter hours for the right to work.* Philadelphia, PA: Temple University Press.

Ibrahim, H. (1991). *Leisure and society: A comparative approach.* Dubuque, IA: Wm. C. Brown.

Ibrahim, H. & Cordes, K. A. (1993). *Outdoor recreation.* Dubuque, IA: Wm. C. Brown.

Inge, M. T. (1989). *Handbook of American popular culture.* Westport, CT: Greenwood Publishing.

Iso-Ahola, S. E. (Ed.). (1980). *Social psychological perspectives on leisure and recreation.* Springfield, IL: Charles C. Thomas.

Jackson, E. L. & Burton, T. L. (1989). *Understanding leisure and recreation: Mapping the past, charting the future.* State College, PA: Venture Publishing, Inc.

Jensen, C. R. (1985). *Outdoor recreation in America (4th ed.).* Minneapolis, MN: Burgess International Group..

Jubenville, A., Twight, B., & Becker, R. H. (1987). *Outdoor recreation management: Theory and application (revised and enlarged).* State College, PA: Venture Publishing, Inc.

Kaiser, R. A. (1986). *Liability & law in recreation, parks, & sports.* Champaign, IL: Sagamore Publishing, Inc.

Kaplan, M. (1960). *Leisure in America.* New York, NY: John Wiley & Sons.

Kasson, J. (1978). *Amusing the millions: Coney Island at the turn of the century.* New York, NY: Hill & Wang, Inc.

Kelly, J. (1985). *Recreation business.* New York, NY: John Wiley & Sons.

Kelly, J. (1987). *Freedom to be: A new sociology of leisure.* New York, NY: Macmillan .

Kelly, J. R. (1990). *Leisure (2nd ed.).* Champaign, IL: Sagamore Publishing, Inc.

Kelly, J. R. & Godbey, G. (1992). *The sociology of leisure.* State College, PA: Venture Publishing, Inc.

Kerr, W. (1962). *The decline of pleasure.* New York, NY: Simon & Schuster.

Knapp, R. F. & Hartsoe, C. E. (1979). *Play for America: The history of the National Recreation Association: 1906-1965.* Arlington, VA: National Recreation and Park Association.

Knudson, D. M. (1980). *Outdoor recreation.* New York, NY: Macmillan.

Kraus, R. G. (1990). *Recreation and leisure in modern society (3rd ed.).* Glenview, IL: Scott Foresman and Co.

Kraus, R. G. (1994). *Leisure in a changing America: Multicultural perspectives.* New York, NY: Macmillan.

Kraus, R. G. & Curtis, J. E. (1990). *Creative administration in recreation, parks and leisure services (3rd ed.).* St. Louis, MO: Times-Mirror Mosby.

LaGasse, A. B. & Cook, W. L. (1965). *History of parks and recreation.* Wheeling, WV: American Institute of Park Executives.

Larrabee, E. & Meyersohn, R. (Eds.). (1958). *Mass leisure.* New York, NY: The Free Press.

Levy, J. (1978). *Play behavior: A person-environment interaction model.* New York, NY: John Wiley & Sons.

Linder, S. (1969). *The harried leisure class.* New York, NY: Columbia University Press.

MacLean, J. R., Peterson, J. A., & Martin, W. D. (1985). *Recreation and leisure: The changing scene (4th ed.).* New York, NY: John Wiley & Sons.

Malkin, M. J. & Howe, C. Z. (Eds.). (1993). *Research in therapeutic recreation: Concepts and methods.* State College, PA: Venture Publishing, Inc.

McIntosh, R. W. & Goeldner, C. R. (1990). *Tourism principles, practices, philosophies (6th ed.).* New York, NY: John Wiley & Sons.

Medved, J. (1992). *Hollywood vs America: Popular culture and the war on traditional values.* New York, NY: Harper Collins.

Messner, M. & Sabo, D. (1990). *Sport, men and the gender order: Critical feminist perspectives.* Champaign, IL: Human Kinetics Publishers.

Millar, S. (1961). *The psychology of play.* Baltimore, MD: Penguin Books.

Murphy, J. F. (1981). *Concepts of leisure (2nd ed.).* Englewood Cliffs, NJ: Prentice Hall.

Murphy, J. F., Niepoth, E. W., Jamieson, L., & Williams, J. (1991). *Leisure systems: Critical concepts and applications.* Champaign, IL: Sagamore Publishing, Inc.

Nash, J. B. (1960). *Philosophy of recreation and leisure.* Dubuque, IA: Wm. C. Brown.

Nelson, M. (1991). *Are we winning yet? How women are changing sports and sports are changing women.* New York, NY: Random House, Inc.

Neulinger, J. (1978). *The psychology of leisure: Research approaches to the study of leisure.* Springfield, IL: Charles C. Thomas.

Neulinger, J. (1981). *To leisure: An introduction.* Boston, MA: Allyn & Bacon.

O'Sullivan, E. L. (1991). *Marketing for parks, recreation, and leisure.* State College, PA: Venture Publishing, Inc.

Opie, I. & Opie, P. (1969). *Children's games in street and playground.* London, U.K.: Oxford University Press.

Oxendine, J. (1988). *American Indian sports heritage.* Champaign, IL: Human Kinetics Publishers.

Parker, S. (1971). *The future of work and leisure.* New York, NY: Praeger Publishers.

Peterson, C. A. & Gunn, S. L. (1984). *Therapeutic recreation program design: Principles and procedures.* Champaign, IL: Sagamore Publishing, Inc.

Pieper, J. (1963). *Leisure: The basis of culture.* New York, NY: Pantheon Books.

President's Commission. (1987). *America outdoors: The legacy, the challenge.* Washington, DC: Island Press.

Rodney, L. S. & Toalson, R. F. (1981). *Administration of recreation, parks and leisure services (2nd ed.).* New York, NY: John Wiley & Sons.

Rossman, J. R. (1989). *Recreation programming: Designing leisure experiences.* Champaign, IL: Sagamore Publishing, Inc.

Rybczynski, W. (1991). *Waiting for the weekend.* New York, NY: Viking Penguin.

Sapora, A. V. & Mitchell, E. D. (1961). *The theory of play and recreation (3rd ed.).* New York, NY: The Roland Press.

Schor, J. (1991). *The overworked American: The unexpected decline of leisure.* New York, NY: Basic Books.

Sessoms, H. D. (1993). *Eight decades of leadership development. A history of programs of professional preparation in parks & recreation 1909-1989.* Arlington, VA: National Recreation and Park Association.

Shivers, J. S. (1981). *Leisure and recreation concepts: A critical analysis.* Boston, MA: Allyn & Bacon.

Shivers, J. S. & Fait, H. F. (1980). *Recreational service for the aging.* Philadelphia, PA: Lea & Febiger.

Smigel, E. D. (1963). *Work and leisure.* New Haven, CT: College and University Press.

Van Doren, C. S., Priddle, G. B., & Lewis, J. E. (Eds.). (1979). *Land and leisure: Concepts and methods in outdoor recreation (2nd ed.).* Chicago, IL: Maaroufa Press.

Veal, A. J. (1987). *Leisure and the future.* London, U.K.: Allen & Unwin, Inc.

Walsh, R. G. (1986). *Recreation economic decisions: Comparing benefits and costs.* State College, PA: Venture Publishing, Inc.

Weiskopf, D. C. (1982). *Recreation and leisure (2nd ed.).* Boston, MA: Allyn & Bacon.

Winslow, R. M. & Halberg, K. L. (1992). *The management of therapeutic recreation services.* Arlington, VA: National Recreation and Park Association.

Basic Journals

Camping Magazine. Published by the American Camping Association, Martinsville, IN.

Church Recreation. Published by Southern Baptist Convention, Nashville, TN.

Employee Services Management. Published monthly by the National Employee Services and Recreation Association, Chicago, IL.

Journal of Park and Recreation Administration. Published quarterly by the American Academy of Park and Recreation Administrators, Champaign, IL.

Leisurability. Published by Leisurability Publications, Inc., Ottawa, ON, Canada.

Loisir et Societé. An international journal published twice a year by the Committee on Leisure Research of the International Association of Sociology, Trois Rivières, PQ, Canada.

Leisure Sciences. Published by Taylor and Francis, New York, NY.

Park Maintenance. Published by the Madison Publishing Division, Appleton, WI.

Parks and Recreation. Published by the National Recreation and Park Association, Arlington, VA.

Parks and Recreation Resources. Published by Mahoph Publication, Inc., Okemos, MI.

Schole: A Journal of Leisure Studies and Recreation Education. Published annually by the National Recreation and Park Association, Arlington, VA.

The Journal of Leisure Research. Published by the National Recreation and Park Association, Arlington, VA.

The Journal of Physical Education, Recreation, and Dance. Published by the American Alliance for Health, Physical Education, Recreation, and Dance, Reston, VA.

The Research Quarterly. Published by the American Alliance for Health, Physical Education, Recreation and Dance, Reston, VA.

Therapeutic Recreation Journal. Published quarterly by the National Therapeutic Recreation Society (NRPA), Arlington, VA.

Trends. Published by the National Recreation and Park Association as a part of its Park Practice Program, Arlington, VA.

WLRA Journal. Published by the World Leisure and Recreation Association, Shabot Lake, ON, Canada.

The professional journals of sociology, psychology, economics, forestry, and ecology frequently contain articles on recreation and parks. These and the publications of the U.S. Government Printing Office provide an excellent supplement and complement to the above-mentioned journals.

INDEX

A

B

OTHER BOOKS FROM VENTURE PUBLISHING

OTHER BOOKS FROM VENTURE PUBLISHING

Leisure in Your Life: An Exploration, Fourth Edition
    by Geoffrey Godbey
A Leisure of One's Own: A Feminist Perspective on Women's Leisure
    by Karla Henderson, M. Deborah Bialeschki, Susan M. Shaw and Valeria J. Freysinger
Leisure Services in Canada: An Introduction
    by Mark S. Searle and Russell E. Brayley
Marketing for Parks, Recreation, and Leisure
    by Ellen L. O'Sullivan
Outdoor Recreation Management: Theory and Application, Third Edition
    by Alan Jubenville and Ben Twight
Planning Parks for People
    by John Hultsman, Richard L. Cottrell and Wendy Zales Hultsman
Private and Commercial Recreation
    edited by Arlin Epperson
The Process of Recreation Programming Theory and Technique, Third Edition
    by Patricia Farrell and Herberta M. Lundegren
Quality Management: Applications for Therapeutic Recreation
    edited by Bob Riley
Recreation and Leisure: Issues in an Era of Change, Third Edition
    edited by Thomas Goodale and Peter A. Witt
Recreation Economic Decisions: Comparing Benefits and Costs
    by Richard G. Walsh
Recreation Programming and Activities for Older Adults
    by Jerold E. Elliott and Judith A. Sorg-Elliott
Research in Therapeutic Recreation: Concepts and Methods
    edited by Marjorie J. Malkin and Christine Z. Howe
Risk Management in Therapeutic Recreation: A Component of Quality Assurance
    by Judith Voelkl
A Social History of Leisure Since 1600
    by Gary Cross
The Sociology of Leisure
    by John R. Kelly and Geoffrey Godbey
A Study Guide for National Certification in Therapeutic Recreation
    by Gerald O'Morrow and Ron Reynolds
Therapeutic Recreation: Cases and Exercises
    by Barbara C. Wilhite and M. Jean Keller
Therapeutic Recreation Protocol for Treatment of Substance Addictions
    by Rozanne W. Faulkner
A Training Manual for Americans With Disabilities Act Compliance in Parks and Recreation Settings
    by Carol Stensrud
Understanding Leisure and Recreation: Mapping the Past, Charting the Future
    edited by Edgar L. Jackson and Thomas L. Burton

Venture Publishing, Inc.
1999 Cato Avenue
State College, PA 16801
phone (814) 234-4561
FAX (814) 234-1651